Comments on "Hear My Story"

"Dean Borgman is the Godfather of troubled youth ministry. He's been a student of at-risk youth his whole life, and I pay close attention to whatever he learns. This book reflects Dean's heart and passion for hurting kids—and it's contagious! It also encapsulates a lifetime of Dean's learning. If you have a heart for troubled kids, *Hear My Story* is a must."

> Scott Larson
> President of Straight Ahead Ministries and author of *At Risk: Bringing Hope to Hurting Teenagers*

"This is a must-read work on troubled youth. Dean Borgman has developed a very comprehensive work that will be helpful for every youth worker, pastor, counselor, or health care professional who works with young people. He presents a remarkable, well-integrated, holistic approach with reflection questions thoughtfully inserted throughout the text. The stories are powerful illustrations of youth's search for meaning in a fragmented culture. Dean reminds us of the need for a truly incarnational approach to reaching and helping youth. Don't miss this one!"

> Raymond F. Pendleton
> Professor of Pastoral Care and Counseling and Director of the Clinical Counseling Program, Gordon-Conwell Theological Seminary

"*Hear My Story: Understanding the Cries of Troubled Youth* is a journey into the world of young people and the stories that shape it. *Hear My Story* challenges and equips the reader to enter the world of young people by listening to the stories they tell and understanding the experiences that have shaped their lives. Stories are not an end in themselves, according to Borgman, and thus he invites the reader to consider how the Story, the good news of the gospel, intersects with and is able to redeem young people's stories in order that their stories become part of the Story. *Hear My Story* is an enticing adventure into the world of young people that will enable the reader to better understand the challenges and opportunities for ministry."

> Darwin K. Glassford
> Associate Professor of Bible and Christian Education and Assistant Academic Dean, Montreat College

"This is an indispensable resource for those who work with the almost overwhelming challenges of deeply troubled youth. It is full of clear thinking, spiritual wisdom, and much needed hope and help for those working with adolescents who are living on the edge."

> Christian Smith
> Professor of Sociology and Director of the National Study of Youth and Religion, University of North Carolina at Chapel Hill

"In this book, Dr. Borgman has not only captured the sound of the gut-wrenching cries echoing from the broken hearts of today's youth, but he has also supplied us with a Biblical, clinical, and practical theological tool with which to address those cries.

"This book doesn't just teach us about theology, it teaches us how to 'do' theology by giving a clear voice to the hardly heard and often misunderstood youth of today, and then teaching us how to answer back with all of our educational and theological faculties, and as individuals.

"Every youth worker needs this book on their shelves and in their hands because this tool will give them an insight into troubled youth that is both heartfelt and well reasoned. It has both the guts and the brains to be useful to the practitioner and the student who seek to touch the lives of the least, the lost, and the left behind."

> Rev. Chris Hill
> National Youth Evangelist, Chris Hill Evangelistic Association

"Look under almost any stone in Youth Ministry and you will find that Dean Borgman has already been there. This is a refreshing, remarkable book that looks beneath the programmatic planning to the issues affecting the lives of troubled teens. Dean focuses on the hard-to-reach kids, those who fall through the cracks all too easily because they are a worry, an inconvenience, and a conundrum. His insatiable curiosity about kids along with his tender Christ-centered heart are evident in this hopeful, informative book. This is a book I will use in my classes. It invites the heart and mind to delve into the dark world of troubled kids and emerge with HOPE!

"The references are phenomenal!"

> William P. Quigley
> Instructor of Youth Ministry, Malone College

"I have known Dean Borgman for years—he skied with me one day in 1970 and that night I met Jesus Christ. But professionally I have admired and followed him generally from afar. I am one of those who walks in the shadow of Dean's life and work, for he is one of the most significant prophetic voices for authentic and critical Christian care of youth in the world. From Nairobi to Copenhagen, Boston to Pasadena, Dean has maintained a consistent call to those who say they love kids—we must know and love those we seek to reach. I see this book as Dean's magnum opus—a brilliant work that brings together the best of current scholarship, sound theology, and radical understanding of the wildly changing urbanized culture in which we all live. This will be required reading for all my students for many years to come.

"I loved the book!"

> Chapman R. Clark
> Associate Professor of Youth, Family, and Culture and Director of the Student Leadership Project and Youth and Family Ministry Programs, Fuller Theological Seminary

HEAR MY STORY

Understanding the Cries of Troubled Youth

Dean Borgman

HENDRICKSON PUBLISHERS

Hendrickson Publishers, Inc.
P. O. Box 3473
Peabody, Massachusetts 01961-3473

ISBN 1-56563-489-6

Printed in the United States of America

Second Printing — June 2004

Library of Congress Cataloging-in-Publication Data

Borgman, Dean, 1928–
    Hear my story : understanding the cries of troubled youth / Dean Borgman.
        p. cm.
    Includes bibliographical references and index.
    ISBN 1-56563-489-6 (pbk. : alk. paper)
    1. Church work with youth. I. Title.
    BV4447.B672 2003
    259'.2—dc21
                                    2003010843

To my old buddies in wild youth work: Jack Carpenter, Reid Carpenter, and Bill Milliken, who walk their talk and have gone on to renown.

To my students whose questions, suggestions, and encouragement have helped make this book.

To my four children, John, Debbie, Matt, and Christie, who taught me to be real . . . and still love me.

And especially to my wife, Gail, for her incredible love, support, and professional advice.

Table of Contents

Part 4: Addictions, Healing, and Reconciliation

Preface

Do you care about kids? Do you want to understand their struggles? Would you like the world to do a better job nurturing youth? Are you involved or want to be involved in the lives of troubled young people? If you answer yes to any of these questions, read on.

This is a book for those who care deeply about the masses of youth, the transience, the vulnerability, the pain, and the powerlessness of youth. You may care about young people generally, about a particular subculture, or about small groups or gangs. But it's mostly because you care about young people as individuals that you would come to such a book. Such caring desires to do something about both corporate and personal cries, or silence, of young people.

This book explores the potential and power of young people, but its particular concern is for troubled youth: those in danger of hurting others or themselves unless effective intervention occurs.

It is written for heroic practitioners in the classroom, on the streets, and working in helping organizations or institutions. Parents may find certain chapters helpful in understanding difficult children or wayward teens. I would be honored to have parts of it critiqued by young people.

My special hope is that this book might encourage a more integrative study among college and graduate students. Too often our research in the behavioral sciences is divorced from biblical and theological endeavor, our academic lives, and our practical experience. The integration of all of these areas is what I see as doing theology. In the midst of all kinds of craziness and learning so many complex theories, we stop to ask: What in the world is God doing? What is God's perspective on these human beings and social systems? and What would Jesus do in this scene? Whatever your discipline,

I hope you can read this book with Bible, anthropology, sociology, psychology, and theology texts at hand.

There is more urban, rural, and global emphasis here than is found in most books of this sort. If we are to find holistic answers to our problems, we must look beyond our own corner to get a larger picture. Those of us concerned about youth need to know the problems are shared by people around the world—and we need to share and learn from one another.

The stories in this book are dramatic and painful. Often the wounds are from childhood abuse or neglect. It is rather easy to comprehend the terrible cycle of abuse from generation to generation, and abused kids easily become serious troublemakers. Children from good homes, by contrast, are often lured by peers and encouraged by media into risky behaviors. Sometimes, there doesn't seem to be a reason why a young person does a horrific act against herself or someone else.

You may not get far into this book before asking, "Why are there so many depressing stories here?" It is because most of us don't realize just how much suffering is going on out there, because each story is different, because hurting young people need to be given voice, and because many of these stories represent particular kinds of hurt and confusion. You don't want a doctor who has treated only a couple of cases like yours. We must hear and hear again before we begin to comprehend.

You and I don't claim or expect neat answers or easy solutions for troubled people; we do seek patterns and a moral and theological framework for wise and compassionate responses. I will attempt to be biblical, to assume the preciousness of life, the importance of growth and wholeness, and the necessity of redemption. I seek to draw inspiration from the compassion and skill found in Jesus as he noticed and touched those in need. This study hopes to fuse biblical principles with your experiences, those of others you know, what you see on television and read, and your sociological and psychological studies.

The approach will attempt fidelity to social science, for to understand how young people are changing we must consult sociology and psychology and seek insights as to how social systems are shaping our children. Such knowledge provides insights into emotions driving young people to noble acts or destructive patterns.

Most of all, I hope this book will serve those who share in youthful struggles. If it doesn't address those on mean streets, in residential treatment centers, and in group homes or prisons, it has missed its mark. If this book doesn't sound right to hurting or angry teenagers, I have also failed.

This book should generate discussion among young people in difficult places. Tough love demands talking honestly about the way things are and what makes us do the things we do. In the most difficult context, I want to be able to say, "I wrote this book, and it's far from perfect, but I stand by its hard message of tough love and true hope."

Adult society is too quick to label troubled kids, to sensationalize suffering (as television news often does), and to blame the victims. I try to avoid such adult tendencies, but admit this book's negative emphasis and recognize that preoccupation with negatives can paralyze positive efforts. We don't read much about young people—the large majority— who are doing fine. Even heroic young leaders do not make the news as much as the few causing mayhem. I apologize, then, for another emphasis on troubled youth. Since we adults have made it so difficult for kids, we must take time to understand our problem. Therefore, this book is also about troubled adult society and troubled adults.

So painful and heavy is this material that I suggest it be read in pieces. It may be good to read sections that interest you most or that you are currently studying, and then allow your experience and reflections to influence what's been read before you come back to the book.

Considering troubled youth requires, first of all, a willingness to experience the pain of all kinds of individuals. At the same time we are dealing with issues within ourselves that call for acknowledgement and healing. Finally, we must look at the social systems that influence us all.

Each one of us is called upon to mentor the young. We cannot deny, as some celebrities have tried to do, that we are role models for young people who see us. Since that is the case, we will endeavor together to understand the complexity of risks facing young people.

Finally, this book asks to be read with mind, emotions, and spirit. If the issues raised here are to be faced holistically, we need all our intellectual, emotive, and spiritual resources.

We seek help for our endeavor from the prayer attributed to St. Francis:

Lord, make me an instrument of your peace
Where there is hatred . . . let me sow love.
Where there is injury . . . pardon.
Where there is discord . . . unity.
Where there is doubt . . . faith.
Where there is error . . . truth.
Where there is despair . . . hope.
Where there is sadness . . . joy.
Where there is darkness . . . light.

O Divine Master, grant that I may not so much seek
To be consoled as to console.
To be understood as to understand.
To be loved as to love.

For
It is in giving that we receive.
It is in pardoning that we are pardoned.
It is in dying that we are born to eternal life.

Introduction: How This Book Is Organized

I hope this book becomes a useful reference volume on the shelves of treatment centers, youth oganizations, schools, and churches. Hopefully, people who want to work in difficult situations with young people at high risk will study it to clarify their understanding and evaluate their motives. It is especially intended for students of human behavior who wish to integrate their experience, study of behavioral sciences and theology.

To understand some of what goes on with troubled youth, to try to get to the bottom of it and put it all together, is an awesome task. As my family, students, others in the field and I have asked God's help for its writing, may you also seek divine grace and wisdom in its reading.

Each section of chapters looks at troubled youth in different ways. Each of these parts concludes with a chapter of particular theological reflection.

Part 1 deals with the scope of youthful troubles and our style of response; it prepares us for the challenge of responding to troubled young people. Chapter 1 suggests that since the context of young lives is so complex and confusing, we need certainty about a Way. Their postmodern context makes our use of stories especially important. Chapter 2 previews global and personal dimensions of the book. Chapter 3 concludes this first section with a biblical reflection on the way Jesus approached troubled people.

Part 2 emphasizes the importance of growth and socialization. It further prepares us for our consideration of specific crises in the lives of youth. Chapter 4 considers the importance of growth and how society has warped God's intended growth process in many ways. Chapter 5 drives us into our subject with stories of violent death in the urban, the working class, and the more affluent suburbs. We pause in chapter 6 to reflect on a theology of suffering.

Part 3 is the heart of the book, the longest and most difficult section. Chapter 7 considers trauma and resiliency in situations such as children in war; while chapter 8 looks at disorders behind the suburban shootings of the 1990s; chapter 9 looks at disadvantaged environments, the context for urban gangs, crime, and drugs; chapter 10 acknowledges child abuse when young children kill other children; and chapter 11 considers various types and factors in suicide. Chapter 12 takes a challenging look into the nature and a theology of violence.

Part 4 examines other risks young people face—sometimes as relief from violence, often inter-related to violent acts. Addictions like smoking, drinking and drugs are discussed in chapter 13, and sexual deviations in chapter 14. Chapter 15 moves toward healing and personal wholeness, and chapter 16 moves to the larger issues of justice and peace.

Along with the text of these chapters you will find:

- questions for personal reflection or group discussion

- an exercise providing a chance for you to respond to a given case

- suggested resources besides the concluding bibliography

Hopefully this book will prepare you for, and enrich your ministry and deepen your thinking as you integrate personal experience with the behavioral sciences and God's Word. Hopefully, it may also reveal places in your own life which need healing and encourage your personal growth.

Part 1

Context and Scope of Trouble

1 The Postmodern Challenge . . . and Stories

*In those days there was no king [authority] . . . all
the people did what was right in their own eyes.*
—*Judg 21:25* NRSV

**Young people are growing up in a new, shifting, and compli-
cated world.** In response to modernism's objective, scientific
certainty, postmodernism describes the world in terms of
subjectivism, relativism, and uncertainty. Generations since
the 1960s no longer find security trusting in science and education. They no longer believe in the essential goodness of
humankind and the inevitability of human progress. To many,
the world looks more chaotic than orderly, cynicism seems
more appropriate than faith or patriotism, and deconstruction of traditional structures brings ironic satisfaction. Faith
and truth, however anyone wants to hold them, are not so
much argued as tolerated.

Postmodernity has brought serious searching but few
moral parameters. People say they are spiritual but are suspicious of religious truth. Some of the appealing features in the
movies *Contact* and *The Matrix* and in the television series
The X-Files are that they point through paradox to meaning,
promising postmodern youth a truth that is somewhere out
there and can be discovered.

About truth, God once told the people, "Nor is it too far
away. It is not in heaven, that you should say, 'Who will go up
to heaven for us, and get it for us that we may hear it.' . . . No,

the [truth] word is very near to you" (Deut 30:12, 14 NRSV).
Some scientists and engineers who believe in the exploration
of space, on which billions of dollars are being spent, hope
to find intelligent life in the universe. Science fiction is certainly filled with such quests. If such beings are malicious,
we hope to defend against them. If they represent a saving
reality, we hope to learn from them.

Modernism rejected the first and final causes that the ancient Greeks posited. Scientific positivism was interested in
efficient causes empirically observed. But without a source
(the first cause) and an end or purpose (final cause), life becomes one-dimensional and meaningless. Postmodernism may
seem like a bumpy and circuitous path, often ironically funny,
searching out some lost truth.

The anger and despair of some postmodern youth may
come from holding a sense of high expectations while being
deprived of meaning and stripped of hope. In the midst of
social flux and complexity, there is an undefined longing for
certainty and moral guidelines. Young people sense that science cannot explain everything, yet they are turned off by religion's occasional rigidity and condemning stance. Many
youth are looking for moral guidelines—and adults who will
have the courage to set limits.

In reaction to prevalent worldviews, some young people
are dissatisfied with deconstruction, irony, and pastiche.[1]
They are looking for some source of beauty, truth, and meaning. There is a quest for justice and peace. That quest may
sense that justice without any moral base evaporates and that
peace without final hope is a mirage.

The loss of objective certainty often causes post-
moderns to seek support in relationships. They have been
conditioned from birth to be attracted to images and to learn
through stories. Generally they are active learners who want
to discover things for themselves. If they are respected and

---

[1] Deconstruction suggests the instability of traditional structures
and the need for each individual to determine meaning. Pastiche refers to
imitating or copying what others have done in the manner of a collage or
striking mix, as in rap and pop music. Irony is often used by cynics who
have given up on truth.

taken seriously, they are open to truth. If their stories are heard, they may be able to find God's truth through God's story.

Young people often long for mentors who possess moral assurance, who will accept and respect them, and who can point them toward purpose and significance.

This book respects the many paths young people are traveling. When their choices lead to destructive ends, we seek to understand objectively and theologically. In the midst of complexity and ambiguity, we try to offer grace, truth, and hope.

In dealing with sensitive and controversial issues our challenge is to hear people's stories while standing firm in God's truth. We commit ourselves to walking many ways with them while pointing toward the Way.

🦦 Imagine yourself as a leader of a small group of teenagers. One of the teenagers is very postmodern whether she realizes it or not. She is tolerant of all positions to an extreme and very relativistic in her ideas about truth. Another is very scientifically minded, wants proof for everything and trusts evolution as fact and as an adequate explanation of origins. Another is dabbling in Eastern religions and sees these as a necessary complement for Christian teaching. Another likes and needs the group but is rather uninterested in discussion of issues. Another is seeking spiritual truth, but doubts any one religion has an exclusive hold on truth. You also know that two of these young people are using drugs and another is struggling with depression.

How might you use stories to lead these young minds toward truth? How might you get them to tell stories of highlights in their own lives? What movies interest them and how could stories from these movies be brought into your discussions? Could stories from your own life be appropriately shared? How might these discussions lead to biblical stories and especially stories of Jesus? The telling of stories can build strong relationships and point to the Way? What resources might help you in this process? (See Resources at end of this chapter.)

Note: You may find a poetic, dramatic, or musical way to consider the word "way" or "path" (Hebrew derek) in the Psalms and Proverbs. A character study on how biblical persons found wisdom or the way might be especially helpful. The idea of "wisdom" as a means of truth might also come through the biblical teaching on wisdom, e.g., Psalm 51:6, 90:12, 104:24, 111:10 and especially Deuteronomy 29:29. Finally, be aware of the Bible's emphasis on stories.

Stories for Healing and Growth

We have set for ourselves an ambitious task. To accomplish our goals of analysis and application we will rely on stories—for through stories we come to care, and through analysis we can appropriately respond. Reflective questions at the end of each chapter seek points of contact between the stories of young people and you, their helpers. Finally, we humbly seek convergence between youthful stories and the great story of their Creator, Healer, and Enabler.

I hope you love stories as I do. Stories can be means of healing and growth. An old Jewish tale concludes that God loves stories and that's why the Creator made us as people who love and crave stories. Stories help us make sense out of life, which suggests that existence seeks union and significance. Even in the saddest dramas redemption usually struggles to overcome tragedy. God's design is for all people to find ultimate union and significance in the Creator.

Children grow up on stories; in traditional societies they've done so throughout history. In urban cultures, stories come to children from their families, communities, schools, and increasingly through the media and their peers.

Fortunate young people are also molded by stories from their faith communities. The stories we hear in childhood—about the world and ourselves—gradually shape our emerging story. Great storytellers influence not only individuals but also cultures.

Every person has a story to tell, and personal stories are parts of a culture's story. We must make sense of our stories—to ourselves, to others, and to our Creator. When we don't, and our lives seem to have no meaning, we stumble in our journey. Our stories tell us who we are, where we are going, and what difference it makes. Each individual digression can bring confusion or may even produce a menace to the human community. The human chronicle needs each individual story. God has made our stories part of the divine story.

Many stories in this book are accounts of being tripped and trapped. Behind each story is a person on life's path, struggling to find a way that leads, whether one realizes it or not, to the way of life. Not only is each path unique; what also varies are our perspectives on the ways other people choose. Respecting all kinds of choices and each person's story, it is easy to give up on truth. There are so many paths and views. We get lost culturally and personally. We need to know that behind life's mysteries and complexities there is a way to truth.

The Way

Is there a way through this life's maze? Young people question deeply and differently. Contemporary life assumes only ways: your way and mine, this way and that; no real answer, no sure way. The Way we speak of is life's moral framework: a way to make sense of it all. Speaking of the Way assumes reasons for such things as gravity, growth, justice, and peace. The Way is the foundation allowing life to make sense, and it involves choices, positive results and negative consequences. A speaker and writer, E. Stanley Jones, wrote a book called *The Way,* in which he says:

In regard to all phases of life in the universe there is "the way" and "not-the-way." In chemistry H_2O produces water. You may fight the formula and try to twist it into something else, but in the end you will surrender to it, accept it, obey it, or you will not produce water. . . . Aviators tell us that every moment they must obey the laws [of aerodynamics] upon which flying depends—or else! There can be no moral holidays in the air.[2]

Whether we are hang-gliding or driving a car, we need to respect the laws of nature. Nature is arranged in a special way, according to fundamental principles. Human culture and relationships are also guided by basic principles in moral and spiritual realms. Although there is great variety in cultures and many differences among individuals, there is still need of a consolidating principle summed up in a single word: respect. Respect is the principle behind all human rules. The Ten Commandments are more than Ten Suggestions. And the commandments boil down to respecting God, self, and others.

Babies grow into productive adults with proper nurture from family and society. Obedience to the way things are brings positive results; disregard produces negative consequences. Each person's way needs guiding principles derived from a higher Way. As human beings we continually choose between the positive and the negative, ways that lead to health and growth or paths that lead to irresponsibility and destruction. This book assumes there are ways life works—and ways it won't work.

We will be realistic about the ambiguity and mystery, about the gap between principles and any given case. Even after a great deal of listening, we may have only questions. But those questions will be informed by an assurance about the way things are supposed to work and a confidence that those who seek will find. We want, then, to be realistic about right ways and the many shortcuts and detours that take us away from better paths.

Physicists have been surprised to see a randomness and unpredictability in the subatomic world. Their observations

---

[2] E. Stanley Jones, *The Way* (New York: Abingdon, 1946), 2.

have led to chaos theories. Bright young people have picked up on this and said, "Yeah, that's what life really is—just chaos." But as these scientists step back and look at the atomic and molecular worlds, the working of organs, people, and the universe, they find a basic order—albeit with unexplained twists and turns.

Christians believe Order lies in and beyond this universe. Step back from the transience of life to the transcendent realm of the divine, and you will find the Logos— the ultimate principle creating and making sense of it all. Christians are under a mandate to share this key to reality, the meaning of life, with all those who seek. It does not mean that we have an adequate explanation about children who kill, why someone commits suicide, or that we know what to say to a dead child's parents. It does mean that we can turn hurting people toward effective and ultimate healing.

How great the responsibility for those who enter youth cultures to share keys of understanding with those who experience life as chaos. Among the ways leading to death, there is a way to life and hope. When young people cry out in pain, we cannot respond with a shaking of our heads, detachment, and silence.

The physical, biological and social sciences all have words for order and disorder. So does theology. We will attempt to bring together insights from the behavioral sciences and theology. Proper order and balance lead to *shalom,* or holistic well-being. This book gives particular attention to disorder, to extremes, violence, and despair. Specific stories behind all of these will occupy our minds. If we are to hear and respond to the stories of hurting young people, we need a holistic understanding of human pain and violence, a holistic approach to forgiveness and healing. We must believe it can all make sense.

To many young people the world is ugly and unfair (they have starker language for this). Someone must tell them how beautiful the world is, how beauty, truth, and goodness (morality) go together. As for the pain and viciousness, it doesn't have to be like this.

Paths and Choices

Many stories are about losing and finding the way. Reflection on the Way, and our many ways, gives stories significance and excitement.

Along life's path we've all taken big trips and side trips. Trips involve choices that turn out for good or bad, and these choices have special importance in adolescence.

As a high school teacher years ago, I was intrigued by the fascination students found in Robert Frost's "The Road Not Taken." The poem, you remember, is a short story of the poet's experience as a hiker choosing between two paths, equally attractive. He finally takes the "one less traveled." Our reading in class often led to discussions about freedom and fate, the mystery of the future, the power of choice— decisions that make "all the difference."[3] They were, of course, probing the possibilities and parameters of their own lives.

Young people are in the process of acquiring a new sense of identity and self-consciousness. They discover their newly acquired strength for the journey and its dangers— often with feelings of invincibility. Without experience, they often make impulsive decisions. The challenge and excitement of choices and exploration, of risks and accomplishments, make their lives exhilarating. Along with those of us who are older, they often sadly discover the truth of the biblical proverb: "There is a way that seems right to a person, but its end is the way of death" (Prov 14:12 NRSV). Still, there is the hope voiced in another proverb: "A person's heart must plan his way, and the Lord direct his steps" (Prov 16:9 author's paraphrase).

Though they may not always acknowledge it, young people need love and support if they are to succeed. Whether they understand it or not, their lives are stories demanding significance.

---

[3] Robert Frost, "The Road Not Taken," *The Oxford Book of American Verse* (New York: Oxford University Press, 1950), 556–57.

Stories in Youth Work

Every person is a story in progress—but to be a story without significance is unbearable. Ultimately all our stories are begun and are completed in God. We reflect the Creator's spirit, intelligence, and passion. This Creator has communicated to us in the form of person and story. We are creatures of the great storyteller; deep within us is a sense that our stories strive toward love and significance.

Human stories are so poignant and powerful, it is easy to forget the main story. That's how we fall into despair, cynicism, or apathy. In all the stories related in this book we will try to remember the overarching theme of transcendent importance. The great story is a narrative of relational love, grace, and hope. Everyone approaches the great story from his or her personal story; it can be no other way. And if one can, through the hurt and fear or pride and doubts, hear the story, one can find affirmation of one's story no matter how plain or tortuous it may be.

The great story is a narrative of divine initiative, creation, and redemption. Relationship, ultimate love and rejection, painful consequences, forgiveness, and final reconciliation are themes of this story. Think of almost any story and it probably draws on these themes. This great story describes ultimate reality to those who hear: why we were made and for what. Without the great story's sense of design and destiny, people perish. The great story is a vision of the Way.

We not only love stories; we are stories. We are all stories shaped by significant social systems: family, community, schools, media, peers, and perhaps church. Human beings are born wonderfully unique, with a DNA and gene system distinct to each person. But we are amazingly malleable at birth and throughout childhood we are shaped by family and society in unique ways. The story of our shaping includes joys and sorrows, benefits and hurts.

The development and playing out of life stories calls for coaches, acting directors, or mentors. The nurturing of children and mentoring of youth might be diagrammed across a

great spectrum from good to bad. For those who have known
only bad directors, the story is almost bound to go off track
at some point. Stories often get back on track when good directors will allow the story to unravel until it reaches a safe
setting, a stable plot, and a supportive cast of characters.

For these reasons I like to describe youth ministry as including the following steps:

- attracting young people to a safe place

- providing young people with caring mentors

- enabling young people to hear someone else's story

- empowering young people to tell their own stories and
  be affirmed

- sharing the story of God's love

We might conclude a definition of youth ministry in terms of
empowering young people to become storytellers able to
help others and serve the human community.

Not only have contemporary societies made adolescents "a tribe apart" (a term coined by author Patricia
Hersch),[4] but also our cultures don't seem sincerely interested in the stories of hurt and resiliency that come from
young people who are marginalized and vulnerable.

For too long the adult world has ignored the voices of the
young. Robert Coles and Jonathan Kozol are among the exceptions who have carefully listened to and told stories of youth.[5]
The human family, as dysfunctional as it can be, cannot ignore
stories that demand telling . . . stories of oppressed minorities
or ethnic groups, of persecuted faiths, of battered women,
abused children, and enraged young people.

---

[4] Patricia Hersch, *A Tribe Apart: A Journey into the Heart of American Adolescence* (New York: Ballantine Books, 1998).

[5] Robert Coles, Children of Crisis (series; Boston: Houghton Miff-
lin), *The Moral Life of Children* (1986), *The Political Life of Children*
(1986), *The Spiritual Life of Children* (1990); Jonathan Kozol, *Amazing
Grace: The Lives of Children and the Conscience of a Nation* (New York:
Harper Perennial Library, 1996), and *Ordinary Resurrections: Children in
the Years of Hope* (New York: Crown, 2000).

Understanding the Stories

All of us need attention. Our efforts seek affirmation, our needs crave attention, our hurts seek healing, and our hopes prosper with encouragement. Jesus was a master in the way he attended to individuals. He noticed, he asked questions and listened, and he often touched as if to affirm his listening care. The ministry of Jesus was need-based, and by example and instruction he taught his followers to be compassionate shepherds.

Teenagers especially need attention. If they are not offered good attention from friends and adults, they will take bad attention from anyone; bad attention seems much better than no attention. Hearing the stories of young people involves caring, taking time, waiting for them to feel confident and for teachable moments, encouraging them to share and to develop their stories.

In one dramatic way after another, adult society has shoved young people into silent margins; there they must tell their stories—if not in words, in silent, self-destructive acts or bold outbursts of violence. This is the simplest explanation of self-injury or self-immolation, of gangsta rap, school shootings, and perhaps bullying and rape.

The complexity and horror of bizarre, violent outbursts can lead to oversimplification of causes or blaming the victim. Social science begs careful analysis of complicated and interrelated factors. The absence of moral order and theological principles, however, can lead to excusing the perpetrator. Neither extreme is productive. When human groups or individuals participate in vicious ethnic cleansing, wanton terrorism, or random, deadly shootings, stories cry to be heard. Social and historical perspectives need attention at individual and communal levels.

Whether a killing is accidental, impulsive, or planned, it is proof that something went terribly wrong, and thus, systemic factors must be investigated. As human beings, we can leap into murder or war, but we can only crawl toward reconciliation and peace. This book will attempt to point out how immediate and forceful vengeance, though easier, is usually less productive in the long run than careful and patient prevention and treatment of social ills.

Hearing stories is a necessary prerequisite to prevention and reconciliation. Unless we hear the stories of those whose struggle for significance has taken destructive shortcuts, adult strategies are bound to fail. Too often adults seek an easy solution; one that misses the unmet needs of youth.

The principles we seek here must work in the secular as well as Christian or religious worlds. Christians, Jews, Muslims, followers of other faiths, and agnostics can live together in pluralistic societies. If justice and peace are to be achieved in mixed societies, there must be respect for the common moral base in various scriptures and traditions. The Golden Rule is still a basis for crucial consensus in today's world.

Redeeming the Negative, Seeking the Positive

This book is a painful look at all kinds of troubled and suffering youth's experience. It does not, however, intend its readers to become paralyzed by negativity. We can learn important lessons from pain and failure. Even childhood abuse can be turned, after years of healing, to profit. Listen to the way Wayne Muller begins his book on childhood suffering:

> When we are hurt as children, we can quickly learn to see ourselves as broken, handicapped, or defective in some essential way. . . . At times the enormity of our childhood sorrow can fill us with a sense of hopelessness, disappointment, and despair. . . .
>
> Yet, at the same time I have also noted that adults who were hurt as children inevitably exhibit a peculiar strength, a profound inner wisdom, and a remarkable creativity and insight.[6]

---

[6]Wayne Muller, *Legacy of the Heart: The Spiritual Advantages of a Painful Childhood* (New York: Fireside Books, Simon & Schuster, 1992), xiii.

According to J. Curtis McMillen, "The social work profession has long been concerned with how people's lives are altered by adverse experiences. . . . During the past twenty years, many social workers have preferred models that emphasize human potential in the face of adversity."[7] Our study will move toward positive conclusions, but it must first hear the pain of real stories.

Along with hearing painful stories, we will hear stories about children whose actions changed their lives or other people's. Among them are children in Columbia who used the country's new constitution to bring political change, and the North American youth, inspired by the courageous example of a Pakistani boy, who publicized the issue of abusive child labor. American readers need a broader, global perspective. Solutions to our problems will not come from America, or the Western world, alone.

This book does not offer quick and easy answers or simple solutions to the complex issues surrounding troubled youth. This book seeks to consider global crises among youth with attention to social science and biblical principles in the tradition of historic Christianity. It proposes that science and faith speak to the need and hopes of individuals and human groups.

There are important issues, however, where faith and science seem to fail us and call for an additional guide. Where science has not yet arrived at empirically proven explanations and where Scripture does not provide clear answers, we must still decide and act. In many such cases prayer and common sense must be used. We must neither force weak arguments and opinions nor become paralyzed waiting further clarification. Not enough has been written or said about the need to go beyond science and Scripture in the shaping of public policy and group behavior, although we should never disregard true science and should not wander from sound biblical teaching. Common sense draws on social science, faith, and experience

---

[7]J. Curtis McMillen, "Better for It: How People Benefit from Adversity," *Social Work* 44, no. 5 (September 1999): 455–67.

when it suggests limiting gun excess or reducing media's sensationalism.

In the midst of controversial issues, we must serve our children and youth. Our basic assumption is that young people and human groups search for a significant place in the scheme of things. That quest is expressed in the story every person and each society has to tell. Behind terrible news is a common tragedy: that no one was there to listen and make sense of a story while it was going wrong. This book asks for caring hearts to hear the cries of young people, patient ears in hearing their stories, and an open mind to consider issues and responses.

Questions for Reflection and Discussion

1. What do you want to get from this book?

2. What will the study of painful stories cost you?

3. How do you understand and react to postmodern trends—seeing truth as relative, deconstructing traditional patterns, and the abundant use of irony?

4. Do you think people are more attracted to stories than plain logic? Why or why not?

5. Do you see a special need for stories these days? Explain.

6. Can you accept the paradox and mystery in both many ways and one Way? Explain.

7. You are not called to fully understand a person's problems, nor will you fully understand God's solution. Can you find confidence even so?

8. Are you ready to integrate social science and biblical principles? Do you see how you will bring your experience to both?

9. Do you respect troubled young people? Explain.

Questions, cont'd.

10. Do you believe you have a lot to learn from troubled young people? Explain.

11. What will be most difficult for you about this book?

12. What will you do with questions or problems you find?

Internet Resources

www.centerforyouth.org ⚑ This is the website for the Center for Youth, and it contains the *Encyclopedia of Youth Studies*. In it you will find information and provocative discussions on a broad range of issues.

www.cpyu.org ⚑ Walt Mueller's Center for Parent and Youth Understanding will give you good movies reviews and information on pop music, etc.

www.hci-online.com ⚑ Here you will find a large collection of excerpts from Health Communications' books, *Chicken Soup for the Soul* and *Chicken Soup for the Teenage Soul*.

www.ileadyouth.com ⚑ This site will provide you with stories and many more resources including ways to use movies in youth discussions.

www.youth.co.za/theedge/movies ⚑ This South African site offers further movie reviews.

www.youthministrytools.com ⚑ You will have to decide whether the approaches of these resources are your style. This is a general resource providing stories and other helps in youth work.

2 Scope and Cost of Response

Some sit in darkness and gloom . . . when they are diminished and brought low through oppression, trouble and sorrow . . . but (the Lord) raises up the needy out of distress. . . . Let those who are wise give heed to these things, and consider the steadfast love of the Lord. — Psalm 107:10a, 39, 41, 43, NRSV

The context of each story in this book includes the social systems of family, community and church, schools, media, and peers as they interact with larger social systems within and beyond that loop. Family systems interact with community (sometimes church) and media, for instance, as well as with larger economic and political systems. Families, communities, and schools affect peer groups. Youthful cohorts, or generational groups,[1] are especially influenced by media and other peer groups as they work out their dynamics. Individuals interact with all these interlocking systems at the same time. It is our task to discover the profound effects that various systems might have upon a troubled individual, while at the same time try to understand the psychological aspects of his story.

It has been evident for several decades that we must understand and respect subcultures if we are to relate to all kinds of young people. Research in the late 1980s and 1990s

---

[1] Cohort is used here to signify all youth of the same age. We might be speaking generally of all teenagers in the world or about those designated "Millenials" or "Hip Hop Generation" in the U.S. Peer group usually includes all the young people a teenager knows; cliques are restricted to friendship groups.

has shown us that cliques and subcultures take shape even before middle school.

The Adlers have done an extensive review of the sociological literature on preadolescent peer groups and carried on an eight-year investigation in their Colorado city. Their introduction includes two rather chilling stories of power brokering among fifth-grade boys and fourth-grade girls.[2] The kind of betrayal, rejection, and isolation they describe can produce lasting emotional damage.

In the elementary schools studied, there were hierarchies of four strata. First is the highest or popular clique along with a second-tier fringe group of "wannabes." Beyond them is a large middle group of assorted subcultural styles. At the bottom of the social ladder are social isolates (losers or loners) who occasionally find a playmate but often play alone.[3] One of the Adlers' informants was a fifth-grade boy, Taylor.

> The cool group is at the top. At one school it amounted to about 35 percent of the kids. Then you've got the cool followers [wannabes], the ones that follow the cool kids around, who amounted to 10 percent in that school. The medium group was the biggest, around 45 percent. They're all divided up into little groups, but there's a lot of them. Then the rest are in the outcast group, maybe 10 percent there too.[4]

Giannetti and Sagarese point to seating patterns in the cafeteria as an illustration of grade school and high school cliques. "Make no mistake," they say, "your child's self-image is affected by where he fits in both inside and outside the cafeteria. . . . Don't forget the caste system has a definite pecking order."[5] The authors further explain:

> As peers divide up, children form into cliques. . . . Cliques deal in social power. Formed around a leader or two, the pack lets it be known that *not* everybody is welcome. Certain

---

[2] Patricia A. Adler and Peter Adler, *Peer Power: Preadolescent Culture and Identity* (New Brunswick, N.J.: Rutgers University Press, 1998), 1–4.

[3] Ibid., 75.

[4] Ibid., 76.

[5] Charlene C. Giannetti and Margaret Sagarese, *Cliques: Eight Steps to Help Your Child Survive the Social Jungle* (New York: Broadway, 2001), 24.

children are dubbed "worthy" while others are judged "not to be good enough." Excluding becomes a primary activity. . . . The way cliques operate in middle school creates a great deal of stress. Unsuspecting young adolescents become targets for the more powerful and popular clique members to ridicule, and free-roaming bullies who don't fit anywhere add to the climate. Belittling others solidifies power.[6]

Wherever teenagers and preteens get together—on urban streets, in suburban schools and malls, or among child soldiers—cliques and power will be present. To understand a school shooting we must consider the dynamics of family, community, media, school life, cliques—and more.

A Global Challenge

Six billion human beings were living on planet earth at the beginning of the twenty-first century. Of these, those 10–24 numbered 1.7 million—more than a quarter of the world's population and they were the largest group ever poised to enter adulthood.[7]

Almost thirty million of them in the U.S. will increase to about thirty-five million by 2010.[8]

If you want to figure out how many children and teenagers are in various countries, take fifty percent of South Africa's almost forty-five million or India's almost one billion, or figure sixty-five percent of Kenya's thirty million, Mexico's almost one hundred million and Nigeria's one hundred fifteen million. That's millions of kids! How many of them are homeless or growing up in abject poverty? How many of them are being programmed to take drugs, commit crimes, and sell themselves for sex? How many of them are being recruited for guerilla warfare, forced into child labor, or sold as virtual slaves? And what about those smothered by ma-

---

[6] Ibid., 14.

[7] "The World's Youth 2000," Population Reference Bureau, U.S. International Statistics and Trends (www.prb.org).

[8] U.S. Census Bureau, Population Reports, and U.S. Labor Bureau Statistics.

terial gifts from absent parents? Pampered kids may also drift in a void.

We must think of our subject as a global issue. Describing the world's children, Bryant L. Myers writes:

> Many of the world's children are dying. Every day almost 40,000 children under the age of five die. If we examine child mortality rates around the world, children are in danger in Africa, Brazil, the Andean countries of South America, the Middle East, South Asia, Cambodia and Indonesia. Looking at children whose lives are at risk from another perspective, half of the world's 36 million refugees and displaced persons are children.[9]

In the 1990s there were about forty wars going on at any one time. Glimpses (which is about all the attention most people can take of such widespread human suffering) of these wars as covered by the news media show fighters who are mostly young—even children.

At times it seemed as if demons of divisiveness and violence were unleashed after the collapse of authoritarian colonialism and state communism. Submerged animosities continue to spring out as Christians strike down fellow Christians and those of other religions. Christians are also enduring the most widespread persecution of all history. Racial, ethnic, class, nationalistic, and religious prejudices have produced bloody feeding frenzies that astound and trouble us until we find fitful peace and relief in numbness or denial.[10]

Women and babies often suffer most in these conflagrations. Mothers lament the senseless death of their children in many corners of the earth.[11]

---

[9] Bryant L. Myers, "State of the World's Children: Critical Challenge to Christian Mission," *International Bulletin of Missionary Research* 18, no. 3 (July 1994): 99, quoting *The State of the World's Children: 1991* (Oxford: Oxford University Press, 1991) and *World Refugee Survey: 1991* (Washington, D.C.: U.S. Committee for Refugees, 1991).

[10] See Samuel P. Huntington (1996) *The Clash of Civilizations,* Simon & Schuster; James A. Haught (1995) *Holy Hatred: Religious Conflicts in the 90's,* Prometheus Books.

[11] See the "Declaration on the Protection of Women and Children in Emergencies and Armed Conflict," UN High Commissioner of Human Rights (www1.umn.edu/humanrts/instree/e3dpwcea.htm); "The World

They ask a reason for this madness and beg some sort of relief from escalating violence. The children who observe or participate in this violence are often left with post-traumatic stress. They, along with youth around the world who watch, are also being conditioned to use violent behaviors in the war's aftermath.

Children are killing children, children are having children, children are growing old before they have a chance to mature. Homeless kids spend days sniffing from a can of glue hidden up the sleeve of tattered sweaters. Such brain-destroying escape provides momentary relief from gnawing hunger, pain, and hopelessness.

The inner poverty of rich kids, suffering from a poverty of soul rather than poverty of circumstance, denies them healthy growth and a sense of significance. Possessing material advantages, they may try to escape their hurt and rage in a mixture of alcohol, drugs, and sex. Feeling desperate and invincible, they can end up killing themselves and their closest friends in reckless driving accidents.

Rapidly increasing global rates of risky sexual activities, new epidemics of teen smoking, drinking, and drug abuse, and outbreaks of violence demand our attention. Despite a tradition of conformity and exceptionally strict gun laws, Japan was shaken by juvenile violence occurring in the latter part of the 1990s. This violence has been particularly traced to dysfunctional and withdrawn youth known as *hikikomori*. This term describes both youth who withdraw (into their rooms) and those who lash out.[12]

At its highest rate in twenty-three years, this youthful violence includes murders in a bus hijacking, the stalking and rape of a young woman, and random murders of elderly. According to the executive director of the Hakuhodo Insti-

---

of Refugee Women: Of 50 million uprooted around the world, between 75–80% of them are women and children." (www.ivillage.co.uk "refugee women); "Safeguarding the Health of Women and Children," International Federation of Red Cross and Red Crescent Societies (www.ifrc.org/what/ health/mch/index.asp).

[12] Search "hikikomori" at www.time.com/time and see www.wdog.com/ rider/writings/hikikomori.htm.

tute of Life and Living, Hidehiko Sekizawa: "It's particularly Japanese. These kids are . . . too passive. [The outburst of violence are] a kind of passive aggression." Adolescent psychiatrist Hidehiko Kuromoto describes these youth as having a lack of self-esteem and "an inability to separate the real world from the world of their imagination."[13]

Studies by the Japanese Ministry of Education have concluded that "Japanese kids are lacking a moral education"[14] and that "Japanese children receive less parental instruction and discipline than children in Korea, Britain, Germany, and the United States."[15]

A similar conclusion is being reached in the other countries mentioned as evidenced in the movement toward character education.[16]

Defining Troubled Youth

Who arc troubled youth? We use that term as something beyond "youth at risk." The latter term is broader. "Youth at risk" includes those who are in situations or have manifested early behaviors that may only point in the direction of trouble or suggest minor difficulties. We arbitrarily define "troubled youth" as young people in imminent danger of inflicting serious injury on themselves or others. We are talking especially about suicidal and homicidal behaviors among teenagers.

Those who have worked with young people for a long time and studied the research suggest that twenty percent of U.S. teenagers to be especially mature and self-realized at one end, and a striking twenty percent in difficult, high-risk situations at the other. Were we to chart the thirty million American teenagers—and this is a always a questionable exercise

---

[13] Sharon Moshavi, "Wave of Violence by Teenagers Leads to Japan Hand-wringing," *Boston Globe*, 21 May 2000, A20.

[14] Ibid., A20.

[15] Ibid., A20.

[16] Martha Groves, "Core Values Teaching Soars in Response to School Violence," *Boston Globe*, 10 April 2001, A14.

and a superficial analysis—the spectrum would look something like this:

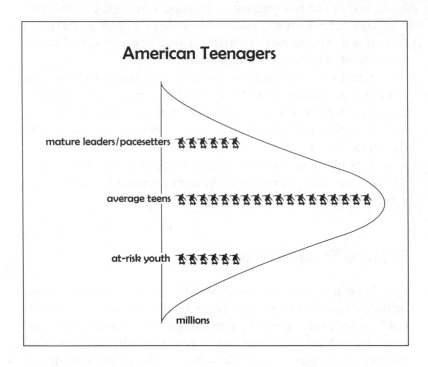

Many global societies have a similar configuration. Estimates from the U.K. are close to those from the U.S., while Canadian researchers Bibby and Posterski estimated a lesser ten percent of their population to be what society sometimes labels "high-risk youth": "Approximately one in ten young people are severely down on themselves, and see themselves as failures. They enter their teenage years as damaged goods; yet all have important and necessary stories to tell."[17]

In 1989 the Carnegie Council on Adolescent Development issued a clear warning that U.S. youth at risk constituted even greater than twenty percent. This report, *Turning*

---

[17] Reginald W. Bibby and Donald C. Posterski, *Teen Trends: A Nation in Motion* (Toronto: Stoddard, 1992): 313.

Points: Preparing American Youth for the Twenty-first Century, was followed in 1992 by a second report, *Fateful Choices* which concluded:

> By age 15, about a quarter of all young adolescents are engaged in behaviors that are harmful or dangerous to themselves and others. Of 28 million adolescents between the ages of ten and eighteen, approximately 7 million young people—one in four adolescents—who are extremely vulnerable to multiple high risk behaviors and school failure. Another 7 million may be at moderate risk.[18]

Offenders may also come from those we considered top leaders; like adults, they may commit suicide,[19] jealous murder, or thoughtless infanticide,[20] often without warning and without reason. In some countries warlords seize children and youth and force them to become killers.[21] In many war zones, the percentages we've given may be temporarily askew. In America, social critics see video games and other media as effective as military training in producing a killer mentality.[22]

Many young people can be influenced to act differently based on the situation—such as when a crowd of average students is suddenly persuaded to invade a girls' dormitory and rape student friends.[23] A gang-rape fad swept U.S. campuses

---

[18] Fred M. Hechinger, *Fateful Choices*, Carnegie Council on Adolescent Development, Carnegie Corporation of New York, 1992, 21-22.

[19] Sonia Nazario, "Schools Struggle to Teach Lessons in Life and Death," Second article in series, "Suicidal Tendencies: When Kids See Death as an Answer," *Los Angeles Times*, 10 March 1997, A1, See LA Times Online Archives. This article shows that even gifted kids may be among the 1 in 12 who attempt suicide and the 24% who seriously consider taking their lives, according to CDC.

[20] Jerry Hager, "New Jersey Teens Sentenced for Killing Newborn Son," *USA Today*, 10 July 1998, 3A. Accounts of several maternal killings of newborns surfaced in the late 1990s.

[21] Reuters, "African Armies Reported to Enlist 120,000 Children: UN, Amnesty Groups Say Some Soldiers Are as Young as 7," *Boston Globe*, 20 April 1999, A2.

[22] David Grossman, "Trained to Kill: A Military Expert on the Psychology of Killing Explains How Today's Media Condition Kids to Pull the Trigger," *Christianity Today*, 10 August 1998, 31.

[23] Nairobi's *Daily Nation* ran several accounts of such rapes during the 1990s.

in the late 1980s.[24] In response to group rapes in Africa and America, educators pondered: How could nice students take part in such brutality? When the incident is over, these young people may return to the positive mainstream.

Further along our spectrum, however, are those losing hope of mainstream success. At the end of our continuum are those who have been called "super-predators,"[25] those obsessed with causing trouble to themselves or others— resorting to violence and killing without apparent remorse.

How many of these are troubled according to our working definition (see pp. 23, 97)? We can't say for sure. We may estimate that five percent, a total of 1.5 million, U.S. young people totter on the verge of destructive behavior to self or others. Such a percentage would be realistic in many other cultures as well. They are runaways on city streets, delinquents, severely addicted, and mentally ill. These troubled young people represent not only an incredible amount of pain but also a challenging need for intervention. Despite the many people trying to help troubled youth around the world, many young people are still falling through the cracks.

Ministering to Youth

Around the world young people have also brought about revolutionary changes. Many times, when adults had given up in places such as China, Palestine, or South Africa, children and young people faced down the authorities with stern looks or stones and stirred the imagination of the adult world. They have shown they can be leaders—and want leadership from adult mentors and guides.

---

[24] Peggy Reeves Sanday, *Fraternity Gang Rape: Sex, Brotherhood, Privilege on Campus* (New York and London: New York University Press, 1990).

[25] John J. Dilulio Jr., "The Coming of the Super-Predators," *The Weekly Standard,* 27 November 1995, 23. David J. Krakicek, "Super-predators: The Making of a Mess," *Youth Today* 8 (April 1999): 1. Here Krakicek attacks academic criminologists John J. Dilulio Jr. (who populaized the term "super-predator") and James Fox (who used the phrase "the young and the ruthless") for creating stereotypes and an atmosphere of castigation.

Even in confusion and violence, most young people are doing remarkably well. There are indications that parents are spending more quality time with children, and many youth are emerging as leaders with a high desire to serve and make things better.[26] They operate best in supportive relationships and work well in small groups. They respond to those positive role models who are close enough to care. Furthermore, there is increasing evidence that the most effective antidote for destructive behaviors is a combination of therapeutic healing and empowerment though training methods such as service learning (which trains young people to serve others).[27] There is a new moral tone among many young people. Theirs is a realistic idealism.

Newsweek magazine, which has taken a special interest in teenagers, has acknowledged this idealism. Several of their periodic articles have noted an optimism not seen among kids in decades. Most commentators on this rising generation (born after 1981) observe how they grew up in a time of relative peace and the longest economic expansion in US history. Teenagers themselves speak of their being a new generation, tired of being confined by negativity and mired in a lack of moral values. Some separate themselves from the negative excess of so-called Gen Xers and admit they may go over the edge with optimism.

Acknowledging this new spirit, *Newsweek* described teens of the new millenium in these words:

> No one teen incorporates all the attitudes and characteristics that the teachers who teach them, and parents who raise

---

[26] Neil Howe and William Strauss, *Millennials Rising: The Next Generation* (New York: Vintage, 2000), 31–33, 43–44. These authors make an important observation when they write, "Over the next decade, the (American) Millennial Generation will entirely recast the image of youth from downbeat and alienated to upbeat and engaged" (4), but they miss much of the reality of the *Hear My Story* documents. Bakari Kitwana (2002) makes the same point about young Blacks of "The Hip Hop Generation" (the title of his book).

[27] Briefly, service learning is a method of teaching that enriches learning by engaging students in meaningful service to their schools and their communities. For further definition and links see National Service-Learning Clearinghouse (www.servicelearning.org).

them, the researchers who study them and the kids who are them name as the identifying marks of this generation. In large part that is because "today's teens may have less in common with each other than those in generations past," says psychologist William Damon of Stanford University. "Some are absolutely on track: they're bright-eyed, genuine and ambitious. But a significant number are drifting or worse."

Innumerable teens, then, will not recognize themselves in the portraits that follow. Yes, of course there are teens for whom adults are a strong presence, and teens who seldom volunteer. There are teens who are emotional wrecks, or even mentally ill. There are teens to whom "Instant Message" means Mom's telling them right away who phoned when they are out. And there are teens who belong to no clique— or "tribe." But according to (this) *Newsweek* Poll as well as sociologists who have studied tens of thousands of kids born between 1981 and 1987, those teens are the exceptions . . . a portrait of the millennial generation is emerging.[28]

In order to deal with such complexity, we must live with teenagers more than ever before, learn from them, and enter into learning and serving contracts with them if the world is to be served and changed by this new generation.

We will get nowhere if we approach this generation by putting denigrating labels on them. Such labels add to the hurt they already feel. Of course, we must delineate various kinds of hurting and understand the psychological and sociological factors leading to violence. To come alongside and help involves genuine respect for each young person as unique—and to understand all that has brought them to a particular place.

In a play by socially concerned playwright, Kia Corthron ("Boom, Boom") two gang girls are talking in jail. Cat, in urban slang, spits out a comparison of adult and juvenile violence:

> News never say three times as many murders are committed by late forties as by under-eighteens. . . . News never mention for every one violence committed by a under-eighteen, three

---

[28] Sharon Begley, Pat Wingert, Scott and Hope White, Ana Figueroa, Devin Gordon, Susannah Meadows and Michael Cronin, "A World of Their Own" (cover story) *Newsweek,* 8 May 2000, 54, 55.

violence committed by adults to under-eighteens. . . . If we are violent, where we learn it?[29]

To help others also takes an admission that we share commonalties with the worst offenders we meet or hear about. Beyond the inner, sinister tendencies that lurk in the dark sides of all of us, we must comprehend the power of systemic evil that can hurt a child and warp human growth and behavior. Only after we contemplate our disposition to perversion and violence and have admitted society's dysfunction, can we deal effectively with the behavior of troubled youth.

Ministering to youth demands that we listen to their stories. Effective listening requires knowledge of ourselves, our world, and young people. For Christians, such understanding must be grounded in the truth of Jesus Christ and God's Word, the divine explanation. Of course, knowledge without love is useless. So we always get back to the foundation of effective youth ministry, which is found in healthy and caring relationships. All we do must flow out of the way we lovingly relate to ourselves, to Christ, and young people. Love without knowledge is frustrating and self-defeating; thus we seek to combine knowledge and love.

Jesus' key question is always, Do you want to be whole [or healthy]? This is not an easy question to ask someone who is hurting or angry; it may feel outrageous to those for whom failure has become a comfort zone. We might ask, Do you want to find what you're looking for? Is finding real significance worth your efforts? Do you want to find real meaning to your life?

Christ's second set of questions is equally challenging: Are you willing [now that you are being healed] to follow me, learn, grow, and serve others? Are you willing to die to self to live with me among others? Helping others is dangerous work, especially for those who have not helped and been helped themselves.

---

[29] Vanessa Jones, "Fighting for the issues . . . Outspoken playwright Kia Corthron takes on girl gangs," *The Boston Globe* 9 March 2003: N1,8.

🏃 Many youth workers seem frustrated about their strategy; there just doesn't seem to be enough time to cultivate the relationships needed and desired. It might help to consider Jesus' strategy. First of all, his radical approach tended to cut "normal social ties" to get out among people. When you consider his time with people, you see Jesus concentrating on his chosen leaders and on troubled people . . . people with striking needs. That may suggest your need to spend extra time encouraging the potential in your leaders and a special time with a troubled kid or two that God seems to bring your way. If this is done faithfully, you will find you don't need quite so much time with those in the middle of our graph. Will you be able to follow such guidelines without stereotyping, labeling, or putting any young person "in a box"?

Helping others is not a simple thing, as the story of Joseph and his brothers can show. How God created heaven and earth takes two chapters in Genesis; bringing healing to a dysfunctional family covers Genesis 42–50! You might also study the healing of the blind man by Jesus in John 9. Such a study is the subject of our next chapter.

If we want to follow Jesus in his concern for troubled youth, we must be prepared to have our social systems and lifestyles challenged. True discipleship in such ministry involves reflection about our dreams, fears, and defense mechanisms. We need to be willing to leave our comfort zones and face the danger of threatening persons and situations. It also demands study and hard work.

Troubled youth feel the pain of dysfunctional systems. We will be challenged by these hurting people not only in our neighborhoods and institutions but also in our own weaknesses. They are sensitive and brilliant in picking up on our little hypocrisies and blind spots. As we admit our sins and weaknesses, we will be better able to serve.

The global situations and all communities need adults who care about young people. Such servants must prepare themselves professionally. Furthermore, they must seek the motivation of God's Spirit rather than that of any self-centered or politically inspired agenda. Youth ministers around the world are finding ways of coming together in professional networks, gaining further training, reading instructive research and books, and upgrading their ministries. They are becoming more able to hear the real stories of young people and appreciate their search for significance. Active listening is a skill that needs to be learned and practiced along with, and perhaps beyond, all other youth work and teaching skills.

Among those seeking to bring peace to troubled youth, there must be theologians: those who study violence, suffering, healing, and unity from God's perspective. It is a difficult study, but for the sake of many hurting young people and burned-out leaders it is worth the effort.

Questions for Reflection and Discussion

1. How difficult was it for you to read this chapter? Was it a helpful overview or a sensationalistic distraction? Explain.

2. Considering the verse that begins this chapter, how do you see God's perspective on all those who suffer and struggle in today's world?

3. Do you sense a calling or part of your calling to serve troubled youth? How do you see this calling: as a specialized part of a larger ministry to youth or something to which you are primarily called? Describe further this calling.

4. What is your definition of troubled youth? Do you object to such a description?

5. How can we identify and yet not label young people bent on violence to self or others?

Questions, cont'd.

6. How do some youth ministries and some churches avoid dealing with extremely troubled youth?

7. How would Jesus reach the most dangerous young person in your town?

8. Is there any way we can minister to youthful leaders, the average crowd, and those with extremely negative attitudes and behaviors at the same time?

Book Resources

Bo Boshers, et al. *Reaching Kids Most Youth Ministries Miss.* Loveland, Colo.: Group Publishing, 2000.

Kenneth Hitchner and Anne Tifft-Hitchner. *Counseling Today's Secondary Students: Practical Strategies, Techniques & Materials for the School Counselor.* Paramus, N.J.: Prentice Hall, 1996. 🐧 Not only for school counselors, this book might well be in a church library for use in all those who encounter the problems of young people and who create curriculum for teenagers.

Scott Larson. *At Risk: Bringing Hope to Hurting Teenagers.* Loveland, Colo.: Group Publishing, 1999.

Keith Olson. *Counseling Teenagers: The Complete Christian Guide to Understanding and Helping Adolescents.* Loveland, Colo.: Group Publishing, 1984. 🐧 This licensed therapist discusses teenagers and their families and Christian approaches to counseling before dealing with special issues: defense mechanisms, depression, suicide, identity problems, sexuality issues, delinquent behavior, experiences with loss, and spiritual problems.

John Reaves and James B. Austin. *How to Find Help for a Troubled Kid: A Parent's Guide to Programs and Services for Adolescents.* New York: Henry Holt, 1990. 🐧 Not just for parents, this sourcebook covers the kinds of resources available (alternative schools, self-help groups, group homes and shelters, residential treatment centers, alcohol and drug treatment, the criminal justice system, counseling and referral, and more).

Rich Van Pelt. *Intensive Care: Helping Teenagers in Crisis.* Grand Rapids, Mich.: Youth Specialities/Zondervan, 1988. ⚟ This book discusses suicide, sexual abuse, death, troubles with the law, disrupted families, eating disorders, substance abuse, and sexuality.

Internet Resources

www.health.org ⚟ This site for the National Clearinghouse for Alcohol and Drug Information provides a helpful list of issues surrounding youthful use of alcohol and illegal drugs.

www.kidspeace.org and www.teencentral.net ⚟ These sites are for teenagers, especially younger teens, themselves. Here are stories and resources along with the opportunity to respond or ask for help.

http://misslink.org/help.html ⚟ Teen Challenge and Assemblies of God has immediate biblical help for teenagers in distress and for those who serve them.

www.reclaiming.com ⚟ This is the site for the Reclaiming Youth Network, Larry Brendtro's program, resources, and network.

www.straightahead.org ⚟ This is the site for Straight Ahead Ministries, which contains many resources for hurting youth, their parents, and those who work with them.

3 Facing Troubled People with Jesus

*And there came a leper to him . . . And Jesus,
moved with compassion, put forth his hand,
and touched him. — Mark 1:40a, 41a, KJV*

Into scenes of child slavery and sex trade, war and terrorism, homicide and suicide we want to bring the presence of the Healer. We want to ask, What would Jesus do? but how are we to do this? First, people must come before principles and relationships before labels. Finding Jesus in stories of troubled people means returning to the encouragement and principles of Holy Scripture. Most Christians begin their theology with a biblical foundation. What does the Bible have to do with troubled youth? And how does Jesus fit into the situations we have described?

It is in story form that we first know God, and the Bible is a great narrative packed with many stories. When we gather to celebrate a reunion or the death of a loved one, pictures are important aids for our imagination. The Bible is like a great photograph album; it helps us imagine God, and people like ourselves, all in relationships. Where the relationships are positive, justice and peace are evident. Where relationships are twisted and broken, chaos and suffering follow.

All human narratives are stories of relationships. When the Creator decides to create humankind, God establishes and risks relational gain and pain. God suffers the loss of relationships from those he would bless. The narrative of our rebellion and God's suffering is the story of biblical redemption. Divine vulnerability is a key notion of this theology of troubled youth. God risks shaky relationships and the pain of all our trouble.

This pain begins early in the Old Testament. There is something wrong with the primeval relationship among Adam, Eve, and the Creator (Gen 3). As they seek to be something more than "the image of God" ("You shall be as God or gods"), they lose their theocentric orientation, and become egocentric and out of balance with nature and one another. Cain wants what his brother has and uses his own means to achieve that goal. Lamech continues the violence (Gen 4). At times God seems ready to give up (Gen 6:5–7). God continues his attempt of partnership with humankind and wants to be a friend of Abraham, but it isn't easy. God seeks reconciliation between crafty Jacob and greedy Esau. Relationships between God and humankind, and human relations as well, are complex and difficult. Some relationships degenerate into madness. All of these stories are worthy of imagination and reflection.[1]

King Saul is described as a troubled man. Uncontrollable jealousy and rage prompt him to throw a spear at a young musician trying to calm his troubled spirit. Young David, the musician, is probably a teenager. At a very young age, David had defeated Israel's enemy, won Saul's admiration, and become a close companion to Saul's son. But Saul, an admired hero and king, was slipping into madness, and killing David became his obsession (1 Sam 18:6–10).

Saul is not the only troubled person in the Bible; the Scriptures describe people in the process of destroying themselves or others. They are often described as having an evil spirit or being empowered by demons. This chapter will examine Jesus as he engages one such person, whose story is found in Mark 5 (as well as Matt 8:28–34 and Luke 8:26–39).

---

[1] See Paul Borgman, *Genesis: The Story We Haven't Heard* (Downers Grove, Ill.: InterVarsity Press, 2001). This insightful commentary will open up a new appreciation of biblical stories and lay a foundation for a fuller appreciation of God's redemptive plan.

Jesus, the Wounded and Compassionate Healer

In *The Wounded Healer,* Henri Nouwen asks, "Who can
save a child from a burning house without taking the risk of
being hurt by the flames? Who can listen to a story of loneli-
ness and despair without taking the risk of experiencing
similar pains in his own heart and even losing his precious
peace of mind? In short: 'Who can take away suffering without entering into it?' "[2]

At the end of the chapter comes an answer:

> Christian leadership asks for personal concern, a deep faith
> in the value and meaning of life, and a strong hope which
> breaks through the boundaries of death. . . . This service
> requires the willingness to enter into a situation, with all the
> human vulnerabilities a man has to share with his fellow man.
> . . . Indeed the paradox of Christian leadership is that the way
> out is the way in, that only by entering into communion with
> human suffering can relief be found.[3]

Such a vulnerable healer is found in the person of Jesus.
Our hopes of being servant leaders and wounded healers
point to his life and approach. Ultimately our ministry and
counseling are most effective when they are christocentric.
The finest model of humanity is found in the person of Jesus.
In him God wrapped up all wisdom, compassion, and beauty.
To look into the face of someone who suffers is to see the
face of Jesus, and to bring holistic healing is to do so in the
name and style of Jesus Christ.

Prophecies of this Healer note his entering into our suffering: "He is despised and rejected . . . a Man of sorrows and
acquainted with grief, . . . He was oppressed and He was af-
flicted. . . . Surely He has borne our griefs and carried our
sorrows. . . . He was wounded for our transgressions, He was
bruised for our iniquities" (Isa 53:3, 7, 4–5 NKJV).

The New Testament reflects theologically on this historical reality giving us pastoral insights: "We do not have a

---

[2] Henri J. M. Nouwen, *The Wounded Healer* (Garden City, N.Y.:
Doubleday, Image Books, 1979), 72.

[3] Ibid., 77.

high priest who is unable to sympathize with our weaknesses, but we have one who in every respect has been tested as we are, yet without sin" (Heb 4:15 NRSV). "Although he was a Son, he learned obedience through what he suffered" (Heb 5:8 NRSV). Little is known and little said about the way Jesus learned. He must have learned about suffering from those who were hurting, as well as from his sufferings. Contemporaries were amazed at the attention he gave lepers, prostitutes, and all who were infirm. His dying hours were spent with two criminals, one of whom was the last—and only one noted—to have encouraged him.

Christ's rich experiences with suffering give power to his teaching. In Luke 15 Jesus defends his ministry to the lost and troubled. The Pharisees and scribes are embarrassed and angry because they so often see Jesus surrounded by tax collectors and sinners. A trilogy of stories about a lost coin, a lost sheep, and a lost son defends his relationships and ours with the lost and troubled.

Of special encouragement to those who care for troubled youth is the story of the prodigal son (Luke 15:11-32), which teaches that God especially loves and is concerned about those who are lost. Along with that primary lesson, there are insights into the adolescent search for identity and fulfillment.

Erik H. Erikson in his study of human development calls its task in adolescence the identity crisis. This working out of one's identity is called individuation. Failure to clarify one's identity is what Erikson calls role confusion. James Marcia develops Erikson's idea and describes stages in the process of identity formation.[4] These stages move from foreclosure to identity diffusion, to prolonged moratorium, to the resolution of a clear identity.

Foreclosure describes a rather blind acceptance of parental opinions. Some young people may copy the identity and values of an authority figure or system (perhaps of a religion or cult). *Identity diffusion* describes the way young

---

[4]James E. Marcia, "Identity in Adolescence" in Joseph Adelson, ed. *Handbook of Adolescent Psychology* (New York: John Wiley and Sons, 1980), chapter 5, 159-87.

people in rebellion accept values and opinions of those around them without critical evaluation and with no clear boundaries. A prolonged *moratorium* may postpone the conclusion of individuation through some kind of interim experience such as travel or study (or in prison, a group home, foreign service, or the military).

In the parable of the prodigal, the young son takes a moratorium, a time out or getting away. With temporary wealth and false friends, he loses all sense of himself. His pursuit of pleasure and status may psychologically be described as a state of diffusion. The climax and turning point of the story takes place when the rebellious son hits bottom and takes responsibility for his situation ("But when he came to himself . . ." [Luke 15:17]). In contrast, the older brother never comes to himself (the psychological term is foreclosure), instead imitating the values of his father and society. The elder son never finds his place in a dynamic and changing family and human community. Rigid and stubborn, he lacks a forgiving spirit.

The father in the story stands out as a caring mentor for both sons—giving them freedom to fail, to reject, and to hurt him deeply. Despite the parental pain and longing for a mature relationship and healthy family, the father remains constant in love and commitment to his sons' growth.[5] All young people need such mentors.

This is how Jesus, the wounded Healer, taught. Although God's healing takes place under many auspices in the world, we here focus on the example and teaching of Jesus Christ.

The Wild Man of Gadara

We must face our feelings of inadequacy, fear of threatening symptoms, or shame of failure. Those working with wild young people must sometimes think, I know Jesus had

---

[5] It was Sam Adams of Oxford Youth Works in England, in a fine paper she presented, who first got me thinking about this. See also the wonderful reflection on this story in Henri J. M. Nouwen's *The Return of the Prodigal Son: A Story of Homecoming* (New York: Doubleday, Image Books, 1992).

nice things to say about troubled people, but I wonder what he would do in this scene with such a wild kid? Did Jesus ever experience fear in a terrifying situation? We may argue about this, but it is clear Jesus was at least tempted to be frightened, overwhelmed, and even to lust, or there would be no point in saying, "He was tempted in all ways as we are." There was one time Jesus must have sensed human fear.

🏃 Have you played out in your mind what you would do in various emergencies that can take place with young people? Maybe an epileptic seizure, an overdose, someone crazed with alcohol, or a psychotic event. Imagine yourself leading a meeting, driving a van, or directing an activity at a camp when someone becomes delusional and acts in a bizarre manner. How would you handle it?

First, stay calm and act in a confident manner. Your prayer is that the Spirit of Jesus will be with your group, with you, and with the distressed person. Have someone take over your responsibility as you take charge of the person. Do so firmly, respecting the person while making sure of his safety as you lead him to the proper kind of help at an emergency room or a secure location while you make the necessary phone call(s). Stay with the person as long as is appropriate. Be realistic and assuring during the following day(s). Someone who has experienced such an incident is often frightened and sometimes shameful. Both he and the group will need instruction and encouragement to deal realistically and supportively with what has happened.

In general, one looks for physical causes of distress first, then emotional, and finally spiritual. You are therefore advised to look for psychiatric expertise first and then, in rare cases, a spiritual exorcist. You are there for first aid; then, you should immediately seek proper referral.

Caught in a terrifying storm on the Sea of Galilee, Jesus and his disciples reach the territory of Gadara (or Gerasa) at night. The storm has driven them to a desolate cemetery. As they drag themselves out of the boat, they are attacked, so it seems, by a crazy man. Naked, with tangled and matted hair, probably bloody and stinking, he is a disgusting and frightful sight. "This man had an evil spirit in him and lived among the tombs. Nobody could keep him tied with chains any more; many times his feet and his hands had been tied, but every time he broke the chains and smashed the irons on his feet. He was too strong for anyone to control him. Day and night he wandered among the tombs and through the hills, screaming and cutting himself with stones" (Mark 5:2–5 TEV).

Imagine having a madman (two men, according to Matthew [8:28]) spring out at you just as you stumble, tired and vulnerable, onto a strange beach. We could well understand their jumping back into the boat and taking off. The disciples probably would have done so if Jesus had not been there. Cemeteries and pig farms were sites to be strictly avoided because they made Jews unclean and unworthy of worship. That Jesus did so much of his work in places of disrepute and with unacceptable people is a lesson we cannot afford to miss.[6]

This story raises questions we may not be able to answer. Did this man have a mental illness compounded by or explained in terms of demons? Did any biblical characters suffer from schizophrenia or multiple-personality syndrome? Can people today be controlled by demons and misdiagnosed as being mentally ill? Did Jesus have compassion on the demons when he granted their request? And why would the demons want to inhabit swine who were about to drown? This is not an easy story.

What we do know is that Jesus was confronted by a frightening situation. Jesus stood his ground and faced this very troubled person. Brought to his knees, the man shouted out in rage. Jesus calmly asked him a question. Soon this wild, naked man was sitting calmly and fully clothed. He had

---

[6] Some details here have been incorporated from storytellers like Clarence Jordan and youth leader Tim Melton.

been healed by this stranger. Maybe he had been bathed by Jesus in what would appear to be almost a baptismal cleansing. Perhaps the disciples, humbled to generosity, gave the man clothes to cover his nakedness.

Instead of praising Jesus for an excellent deed and for ridding the area of a dramatic nuisance, the townsfolk asked him to leave the country. We have to conclude it was because he ruined a business and revealed a power the people could neither understand nor control. This story offers many lessons to those who minister to troubled youth.

Evil Spirits and Mental Illness

Why do we see Jesus not as a therapist healing emotional illness but as a healer casting out demons? Why does much of the church so seldom deal in exorcisms? Are demons a reality or just an ancient description of mental illness? If demons are real, what is the boundary between mental illness and demon possession?

One suggestion is that the biblical authors wrote from a prescientific worldview that didn't understand mental illness and attributed such maladies to evil spirits. Those biblically described as demon-possessed were paranoid schizophrenics or suffering from a bipolar illness. An opposite extreme rejects modern psychiatry and sees most disturbed people today as possessed by spirits. This view contends that our unbelief and lack of faith label distressed people as mentally ill and prescribe medications to deaden their symptoms. We may not reach agreement on the relationship of mental illness to demon possession, but it will help if we begin by considering the use of the word "demon" in biblical times. T. H. Gaster offers this explanation:

> In considering the question of demonology in the Bible, it must be borne in mind at the outset that the modern definition of a demon as a devil, or malign spirit, is the result only of a long development. As used by ancient writers, the word often means something far different [many bearing] quite distinctive names and of quite different character.

In the original sense, a demon may be defined broadly as an anonymous god—i.e., as a personification of one or another of those vaguer, less identifiable powers and influences believed to operate alongside the major deities and to condition particular circumstances and experiences. . . . Such demons [in ancient literature] can be beneficent as well as harmful; indeed, where they are the latter, Homer often characterizes them expressly as noxious or bad.[7]

Gaster sees demoniacal possession in the Old Testament as an externalization of psychological experience. Powerful feelings or abilities were seen as coming upon a person rather than from within him. He believes our use of such terms as "stricken by disease," "awestruck," or "love-struck" are unconscious throwbacks to the ancient language of demonism.[8]

Another author, P. L. Hammer, interprets the thirteen uses of the term "demoniac" in the New Testament as "a form of mental sickness. Demoniacs were a class of persons healed by Jesus. They are to be distinguished from the physically ill although the condition sometimes influenced such physical ailments as dumbness and blindness."[9]

What is important to recognize is that we can't impose medieval or modern concepts and categories upon the biblical writers. They wrote from within an ancient worldview. It is necessary for us to consider their cultural understanding of human nature and life situations.

From Mark we learn of several stories about demons (Mark 1:23-27 NRSV):

> Just then there was in their synagogue a man with an unclean spirit, and he cried out, "What have you to do with us, Jesus of Nazarus? Have you come to destroy us?" . . . But Jesus rebuked him, saying, "Be silent, and come out of him!" And the unclean spirit, convulsing him and crying out with a loud voice, came out of him. They were all amazed, and they kept on asking one another, "What is this? A new teaching—with authority! He commands even the unclean spirits, and they obey him."

---

[7] T. H. Gaster, "Demon, Demonology," in *The Interpreter's Dictionary of the Bible* (New York: Abingdon Press, 1962), Volume 1, p. 817.
[8] Ibid., 1:818.
[9] P. L. Hammer, "Demoniac," *IDB* 1:824.

And a second instance (Mark 1:32, 34 NRSV):

> That evening, at sundown, they brought to him all who were
> sick or possessed with demons. . . . And he cured many who
> were sick with various diseases, and cast out many demons;
> and he would not permit the demons to speak, because they
> knew him.

Finally, in the story we are considering (Mark 5:6–13 TEV),
[The wild man] was some distance away when he saw Jesus;
so he ran, fell on his knees before him, and screamed in a
loud voice, "Jesus, Son of the Most High God! What do you
want with me? For God's sake, I beg you, don't punish me!"
He said this because Jesus was saying, "Evil spirit, come out
of this man!" So Jesus asked him, "What is your name?" The
man answered, "My name is 'Mob'—there are so many of us!"
They kept begging Jesus not to send the evil spirits out of
that region. . . . Jesus let them go, and the evil spirits went
out of the man and entered into the pigs.

Contemporary readers can interpret biblical stories
about demons in three different ways. With which interpretation are you most comfortable?

1. These are stories about physical and mental illness, the
    latter referred to in terms of evil spirits. Jesus heals ills of
    body and soul. Today healing comes through medicine
    and therapies.

2. Evil spirit or demons were and are a reality. If the church
    had the Spirit and power of Jesus Christ, it could heal all
    manner of disease and do away with a lot of counseling
    and medication.

3. Although the Bible does not speak of mental illness,
    there are today diseases of the mind and demonic posses-
    sion. They may overlap: a person may have an emotional
    illness and a demon. But the emotional and spiritual need
    to be treated in different ways.

Few people believe that schizophrenia and multiple
personality or dissociative disorders are figments of imagination on the part of professional therapists. Although there
may be discussions about the categories, certain patterns of

mental illness are clear. It seems logical that similar forms of mental illness exist today in traditional societies and were present in biblical times. We see familiar characteristics of emotional illness in biblical stories. Scripture and contemporary traditional societies describe emotional problems and bizarre behavior in terms of demonic possession.

The question remains: Whatever their relationship to naturally explicable mental illness, do evil spirits ever influence or even possess human beings? Immediately we are forced to define evil spirits or demons in a way that honors biblical teaching while appreciating the difference in worldviews. G. E. Ladd, a biblical theologian, goes further than Gaster and Hammer; he accepts the reality of a personal devil and evil spirits:

> In the Synoptics, the most characteristic evidence of the power of Satan is the ability of demons to take possession of the center of people's personalities. Clearly, demons are represented as evil supernatural spirits. . . .
>
> Demon possession manifested itself in various ways. Sometimes it was associated with other afflictions of a physical nature: with dumbness (Matt 9:32), with blindness and dumbness (Matt 12:22), and with epilepsy (Matt 17:15, 18). There is only one place where demon possession is identified with mental illness. Obviously, the Gadarene demoniac who dwelt in the tombs and was possessed of superhuman strength was insane. The record says that after his healing the man was found clothed and *in his right mind* (Mark 5:15, emphasis mine). While this suggests that the man may have been insane, we need not conclude that his illness was a case of simple insanity. Rather the derangement was due to the center of his personality falling under the influence of foreign powers.[10]

Ladd suggests an opinion as to the relationship between mental illness and demon possession. Speaking as a biblical theologian rather than a psychologist, he explains his position further:

---

[10] G. E. Ladd, *A Theology of the New Testament* (rev. ed.; Grand Rapids, Mich.: Eerdmans, 1993), 49.

It is not accurate, however, simply to explain away demon possession by saying it is an ancient interpretation for what we now know to be various forms of insanity. Frequently in the Synoptics demon possession is distinguished from other diseases. Jesus healed both the sick and those possessed by demons. However, demon exorcism was one of the most characteristic of Jesus' acts of power. There were, to be sure, those who practiced magic arts and incantations, and claimed to exorcise demons. However, belief in demons and their exorcism in the ancient world at large was intertwined with magic of a crude sort. By contrast, the amazing factor in Jesus' ministry was the power of his mere word: "What is this? A new teaching! With authority he commands the unclean spirits, and they obey him" (Mk. 1:27).[11]

My experience among troubled people and their healers in many cultures and the biblical narratives force me to accept the reality of demonic influence and possession. In many parts of the world, people know there are demons at work. Still, the nature of these spirits and the relationship between mental illness are mysteries to me. The lack of a full understanding, however, need not hinder a healing ministry.

One of two videos in my collection portrays the wonderful array of therapies used in treating the multiple-personality disorder of a woman who had a history of terrible abuse during her childhood. A second video describes an exorcism by a well-trained Roman Catholic priest. The similarities in these two extraordinary cases are striking, yet there are telling differences. If I were confronted by a person in dissociative[12] crisis or someone possessed by a demon, I know what I would immediately do. In both cases I would do my best to calm and assure the person in Christ's name (implicitly or explicitly) and then look for appropriate experts, psychiatrists first and then an exorcist.

One of the basic rules of therapeutic intake is to consider physical causes of disorder before attributing the malady to emotional factors. It would be terrible to treat a person's

---

[11] Ibid.

[12] A technical term used for persons who lose their identity and touch with reality. They may consider themselves to be someone else or to be in some other reality.

emotional imbalances session after session when a brain tumor or a chemical imbalance causes the problem. The general rule in responding to serious mental illness is to consider it holistically with attention given first to physical factors, then emotional, and finally spiritual. Exorcism is recommended only when all possible physical and mental factors are ruled out as primary causes of suffering. Whatever your ministry with troubled youth, consider first physical factors, then emotional issues, before reaching conclusions about demonic possession.

The overarching intention of the demonic spirits or powers, as I see it in simple terms, is to keep men and women from becoming all God intended them to be. Humans enjoyed such a condition in the garden, and the deceiver did all possible to rob God of his glory and centrality in human endeavor. Having wrested human beings from the Creator's direction, evil spirits are now intent on keeping us from Jesus Christ, who alone can liberate and restore. Demons seem to interfere differently in Stockholm and in the Congo.

Considerations of troubled youth demand a careful balance of many things. We hold together compassion and comprehensive understanding, theology, social science and experience, faith and practice. We humbly admit all we don't know while acting confidently according to what we have learned.

Lessons from the Wild Man's Healing

What lessons can we find in this story of the demoniac? We admire—and feel our need for—the compassion, courage, and faith of Jesus. (He would later explain that his healing power came only from the Father.) Our world has desperate need for those who care enough and can stand their ground against killing and craziness.

Only words between Jesus and the evil spirits are recorded in this narrative, but conversation between Jesus and the man must also have taken place. In some way or other

Jesus found the man's story and assured him of a significant place in the world and in the kingdom.

The story does not end as we might expect; in fact, we may find our greatest difficulty in its conclusion. With a new-found freedom from raging spirits, the man craved further time and mentoring from Jesus: "Please take me with you! I'm not ready to be left alone with those who are rejecting you and me." Jesus said: "Go home to your friends, and tell them how much the Lord has done for you and what mercy he has shown you." Sometimes rules, such as nurturing young faith, have to be broken. Sometimes we don't get what we're sure we need, but God's mercy is enough. Jesus knew how to deal with a world that was not ideal. Christ shows implicit trust in the resilience of the human spirit and the power of God's grace.

Jesus also places a person's value over that of a business, in this case a swine industry that was contrary to the Mosaic law. When we use people for profit, we sin and society begins to go astray. (Some religions forget corporate sin and deal only with individual sin, while others, absorbed with social sin, are uncomfortable dealing with individual sin.) This incident may expose the corporate sin of avaricious institutions. Though the rich may prosper from greedy exploitation, a society will pay for its rejection of divine priorities and misuse of human potential.

I've heard sermons and read commentaries on this passage with little concentration on the demoniac. Certainly it is a story about Jesus, but further comments on this story emphasize how dangerous or distressed the man was, how unfair the townspeople were, how fearful the disciples must have been. Even the swine sometimes get more attention than does the man. With his quaint and vivid imagination, the wonderful storyteller Clarence Jordan saw this madman as the prodigal son.[13] Such imaginative storytelling at least

---

[13] Clarence Jordan, Christian pacifist and civil rights advocate, was the founder of Koinonia Farms in Georgia. See his *Parables of Liberation* (Scottdale, Pa.: Herald Press, 1976). This writer heard many of his stories firsthand in the 1960s.

sees the man as a person with a special story to tell. Whoever he was, we know this man was once a babe at his mother's breast, a toddler, and a playmate. Perhaps he knew romance and some early success in work. But things had fallen apart, gradually or suddenly. Now he lived among the graves, isolated and dangerous.

When the townsfolk came out to see what happened, they found a man transformed by Jesus. They saw the naked, raging madman not as an angel or a superspiritual saint but as a normal human being. The man's story was validated. He became what his mother and father had hoped for, someone who could make a partner happy, who could seek gainful employment . . . a real person. That's what Jesus does—and it is our goal as well: to aid in the restoration of true humanity, the wholeness of a human spirit, and full participation in life.

Once the disciples asked Jesus, What caused this man to be born blind? Who sinned, this man or his parents? (John 9:2). In the dark cemetery, as they were standing damp and scared, the disciples may have been asking similar questions: How does a person get into this condition? What kind of sin does he commit, or how did his parents fail so badly? Jesus holds people accountable, but he never blames the victim. He sees more deeply and broadly into the human condition. Jesus understands and accepts the mystery of suffering.

When Jesus surprisingly allowed the demons to enter a herd of swine, he may have been dealing with the systemic ills of that society. Jordan's combination of two biblical stories, that of the demoniac and the prodigal, pictures a Jew falling so low as to feed swine, then further into lunacy and demon possession. Such an interpretation concludes the story with Jesus allowing the son to go home to his father.

We will never know the connection of this man to the pig business, but his ills may have had systemic as well as personal causes. If we treat symptoms without causes, we may compound the problem. Or it may have been that Jesus allowed the pigs to rush to their destruction in order to show this one man his troubles were finally over, as William

Barclay suggests.[14] The etiology (cause or origin) of human trouble is personal and systemic. Both need to be recognized and rectified.

Dealing with Our Fears

> People went out to see what had happened, and when they came to Jesus, they found the man who used to have the mob of demons in him. He was sitting there, clothed and in his right mind; and they were all afraid. (Mark 5:14b-15 TEV)

When people find Jesus, or us who follow him, they ought to see evidences of healing—justice and peace. But justice can be frightening. Those who cannot understand radical healing and peace may become afraid. Uncontrollable change causes fear; ignorance or sinfulness is afraid in the presence of God or godliness. Fear may be the deepest human negative emotion, and the ultimate fear is rejection—the essence of hell. In everyday life, we are often afraid to take a stand or confront because someone may be upset and we may be rejected.

It is important for healers to deal with their fear. A consideration of fear from a biblical perspective involves profound personal and theological reflection. From Genesis to Revelation, biblical characters wrestle with fear. Rejection of God ultimately involves isolation and fear. It is a beginning of madness and a primary source of trouble. Healers and sufferers must deal with their fear of the malady and the unsettling consequences of healing.

Systemic and Individual Sin and Responsibility

If a theme of Mark's Gospel involves conflict between two kingdoms and a binding of the strong man, how fitting this story is! If, in Mark 3:22-27, we take the strong man to

---

[14] William Barclay, *The Gospel of Mark* (Philadelphia: Westminster, 1975), 120.

be Beelzebub, then we as Christians are meant to plunder the enemy's kingdom. Our ministry to troubled youth is a way of defeating demons and binding the evil one.[15]

From this perspective we see the wild man both oppressed by society *and* tormented by inner conflict. Mark's story of the man with evil spirits begins with a description of a social outcast. Those in control of the swine business and the countryside could exploit such marginal persons, but they could not control this man's final madness. The story's conclusion contrasts their fear with the outcast's peace and empowerment.

A child grows up as part of, and is shaped by, various social systems. It is God's plan that these systems lead children to maturity and fullness of life. Disorder in these systems can produce disorder in the life of the emerging adult. Young people in distress suffer from their own irresponsibility and poor choices, but they also suffer because systems have failed them. Many grow up in abusive or unreliable families. Schools may label them and make them feel worthless day by day. Bullies often degrade them in front of their peers. The media does more than inform; it may, especially in the most vulnerable, stir up feelings of inferiority, unbridled greed, irresponsible passion, and senseless violence. Employment may seem hopeless; government, an enemy. To troubled youth, religion often appears as one more negative and critical social system. Even if you don't live with high-risk youth or walk side by side with them every day, you can watch movies like *Hurricane Streets, A Hero Ain't Nothin' But a Sandwich, Fresh, Gummo, War, The Outsiders,* or *American History X* and feel the inevitability of trouble.

Young people in many different parts of the world suffer from atrocities and terrible events. Many have withdrawn; others have become violent; some have broken

---

[15] Ched Meyers, *Binding the Strong Man: A Political Reading of Mark's Story of Jesus* (Maryknoll, N.Y.: Orbis, 1992). This remarkable but too little known book interprets Mark's Gospel in a way especially relevant to all oppressed segments of today's world.

down. After experiencing violence or rape, one can suffer symptoms described as post-traumatic stress syndrome (PTSS). The experience of horror in children and adults can lead to what psychologists call post-traumatic stress disorder (PTSD). Children whose lives have been threatened or who have witnessed traumatic events may become subject to deep feelings of fear, horror, or helplessness. They may have flashbacks or nightmares and physical reactions long after the trauma. Those who care must understand these varied responses and the need for different kinds of love and healing.

What has happened to our world that we treat children so cruelly? Systems meant to support the growing child are infected by oppressive racism, greed, class privilege, cultural divisions, and bureaucratic bungling. Even the secular press describes atrocities in terms such as "unleashed furies or demons." Various theologies and church traditions may understand the powers and the demonic in somewhat different ways.[16] Whatever our view, we cannot allow the biblical emphasis on systemic evil to be lost in our theology and teaching.

Our world situation is far from hopeless. As society moves further and further from supporting children's growth in the way God intended, many are intervening in the lives of troubled youth—and more of us must do so. We must also confront the various demons that give spiritual force to destructive behavior. Walter Wink describes the reality of such principalities and powers: "In the biblical view [principalities and powers] are both visible *and* invisible, earthly *and* heavenly, spiritual *and* institutional. . . . The Powers are the simultaneity of an outer, visible structure and an inner, spiritual reality. The Powers, properly speaking, are not just the spirituality of institutions, but their outer manifestations as well."[17]

---

[16] Thomas H. McAlpine, *Facing the Powers: What Are the Options?* (Monrovia, Calif.: MARC, 1991). Various interpretations of the demonic, principalities, and powers are summarized from a missiological perspective.

[17] Walter Wink, *Engaging the Powers: Discernment and Resistance in a World of Domination* (Minneapolis: Fortress, 1992), 3.

As we feel the power of racism and poverty, inadequate education, unemployment, exploitation, and oppression, we are dealing with social systems and institutions influenced to one degree or another by evil principalities and powers defeated only and ultimately by the lordship of Jesus Christ. Meanwhile, Wink urges powerful prayer as well as strategic action. He calls us to:

> An existential struggle against the "impossible," against an antihuman collective atmosphere, against images of worth and value that stunt and wither full human life.
>
> Prayer, in short, is the field-hospital in which the diseased spirituality that we have contracted from the Powers can most directly be diagnosed and treated.
>
> Intercession is spiritual defiance of what is, in the name of what God has promised. Intercession visualizes an alternative future to the one apparently fated by the momentum of current contradictory forces.[18]

In the name of the Creator, who was willing to live in a defiled world and confront all opposition to what is right, who had compassion on all who were hurting and confronted all who oppressed the weak, we seek to reach out to troubled youth.

Remembering our weakness, we begin with prayer, we commit to care, we address all systems and situations that hinder their growth and welfare, and we stop to listen to their stories. We call on Christ to bind all that troubles them, whether these negative influences are systemic, relational, or internal. Our goal is *shalom,* their peace and welfare.

---

[18] Ibid., 298.

Questions for Reflection and Discussion

1. How do you think you would respond if you were confronted by a wild person at night?

2. What would you have been thinking, feeling, and doing if you had been with Jesus that evening?

3. do you think was wrong with the man?

4. How do you think Jesus healed him?

5. What analogy do you see between the craziness of that man and wild behavior of troubled people today?

6. How do you define mental illness, antisocial behavior, and demonic power?

7. Should you want to learn more about the demonic, where would you turn?

8. How important are social systems to the growth of children and to the behavior of teenagers?

9. To what extent do you see the demonic in systems that oppress and hurt people?

10. What lessons would you draw from the story of the man with evil spirits for your ministry to troubled youth?

11. Can such ministry be accomplished effectively without prayer? What kind of prayer is needed?

Book Resources

See Resources from previous chapter.

William Barclay. *The Gospel of Mark,* Revised Edition. Philadelphia: Westminster Press, 1975. ⚡ Pages 117–26 provide commentary with interesting background on Jesus' healing of the mad man.

Rodney J. Hunter, ed. *Dictionary of Pastoral Care and Counseling.* Nashville, Tenn.: Abingdon Press, 1990. ⚡ This is a helpful desk encyclopedia of 1,346 pages.

Internet Resources

www.aacap.org/web/aacap/publications/factsfam 🐧 American Academy of Child and Adolescent Psychiatry: Facts for Families. A good list of issues explained (in English, Spanish, French, and German)

www.centerforyouth.org 🐧 We again mention this basic site.

www.mentalhealth.com 🐧 Canadian psychiatrist Phillip W. Long, MD, has created this helpful site with descriptions of many ills and popular links, American and European, for particular disorders.

www.nimh.nih.gov 🐧 This site is provided by the National Institute of Mental Health. Choose For the Public, For Practitioners, or For Researchers for articles on mental health in children and adolescents. Also see www.nlm.nih.gov/medlineplus/childmentalhealth.html.

Part 2

Growing Up Healthy and Unhealthy

4 Growth and Socialization

*The boy Samuel continued to grow both in stature
and in favor with the LORD and with the people.*
—*1 Sam 2:26 NRSV*

It is important to think about healthy growth with a loving and hopeful heart. Without such understanding and anticipation, we will deal inadequately with those having problems in growing up. Any consideration of troubled youth should be framed within expectations of healthy growth. Growth is the object in ministering to young people. Understanding what leads children to make choices to kill or take their lives demands knowledge about the nature of growth. Healthy growth leads to good fruit while stunted or damaged growth may lead to rage and destruction.

Growth: God's Intention

God's original intention for creation was its growth (Gen 1-2, especially 1:27-28). Biblical instructions and metaphors impress us with God's desire for and nurturing of his creatures' growth. Furthermore, God desires partnership with human beings in fostering growth of all kinds. Because God is not static, we can expect growth throughout eternity. Scripture's emphasis on growth also includes many woes upon those who stunt the growth of God's creatures.

In the story of Samuel, the Bible emphasizes his physical, social, and spiritual growth (1 Sam 1:22-24; 2:18, 21b, 26; 3:1-10, 19). Luke 2:52 highlights the importance of growth in reference to the boy Jesus, adding the dimension of intellectual growth. Growth to maturity is a law of nature and a declared goal of God's will—and this was necessarily true even for his Son (Heb 5:8).

Because we often take growth for granted, it is helpful to stop and imagine the absence of growth in any living creature. What a tragedy we would watch if a baby could not grow! Hindering God's intended growth in a child is therefore a terrible evil. The divine intention for all human beings is that they become, through families and society, all the Creator intended them to be.

The theological idea of the fall sees human behavior and social systems as dysfunctional through separation from God. When egocentricity replaces theocentricity, moral rules are broken and hostilities rise. Similarly, to the degree that social systems and nations are anthropocentric rather than theocentric, they operate from self-interest and end up in conflicts with other systems or countries.

God did not make growing up easy; it may have been a challenge even before the fall. Individual and systemic sin make the process more complicated. Youth leaders are especially conscious of this. They see, first hand, personal failures but also realize how dysfunctional families and unhelpful systems confuse a young person's life and hinder growth. Effective youth workers are forced to be advocates as well as counselors as they deal with difficult interactions between young people and their families, schools, communities, and in some ways the whole world. Imagine God's anger toward unhelpful social systems that frustrate children's growth!

The Chief Shepherd has entrusted the rearing of children to lesser shepherds—parents, teachers, media producers, advertisers, employers, and politicians—and divine rebuke describes the way human shepherds can neglect those under their care:

> You take care of yourselves, but never tend the sheep. . . . You have not taken care of the weak ones, healed the ones that are sick, bandaged the ones that are hurt, brought back the ones that wandered off, or looked for the ones that were

lost. Instead you treated them cruelly . . . the sheep had no shepherd. (Ezek 34:2b–5a TEV)

God's intention for the care of vulnerable people is expressed positively in promises of recovery and redemption. The failure of human leaders and systems focuses our attention on our source of help.

I, the Sovereign LORD, tell you that I myself will look for my sheep and take care of them in the same way as a shepherd takes care of his sheep that were scattered and are brought back together again. (Ezek 34:11–12 TEV)

This chapter includes the implied challenge for us to become good shepherds of youth. In light of the shepherds' failures, God promised another shepherd (Ezek 34:23). Christ claimed to be that shepherd (John 10:1–21). Believing in God's shepherding initiative and accepting the model of our Lord Jesus Christ does not remove human responsibility. Human shepherds and the sheep are held accountable to civil society and to the Creator.

> 🦅 How could you use a Bible picture book, or some other children's book, to get a young boy or girl to talk about his or her feelings? It is important to name feelings, then to own feelings, and finally to talk about response to feelings. How can such use of stories strengthen the relationship between you and them? What does this have to do with growth?

We must understand that God will hold politicians, business leaders, advertisers, media moguls, educators, and parents responsible for the welfare of children. Youth leaders who would do God's will and follow Christ are especially called to be faithful, human shepherds in their care of the young (reflect on John 10:11–15; 20:21; 21:15–17). Crucial to the purpose of this book is a deep sense that God cares for the sheep and puts solemn responsibility not only on every individual but also on shepherds at every level of the human community. It is important, then, to study carefully the nurture of human beings. Too many studies of human growth and development miss important social dimensions and responsibilities.

The Nature of Human Growth

Traditional philosophy understands human growth in terms of four causes. The *material cause* is the infant or child you hold in your arms. It is a living being whose meaning would be lost should it never grow. The material cause speaks of the potential for growth.

The *formal cause* is the model or blueprint for growth. It is the actuality of the potential; the idea of full human adulthood towards which growth is directed. The formal cause is the result of growth, the maturity of a person.

The *efficient cause* is the engine for growth. It includes all inner drives and external influences that effect the growth of a child. Efficient causes move the child or young person toward the formal cause of maturity.

The final cause is the *meaning of growth*. As the purpose of proper diet and exercise is health, the purpose of human growth is to become a significant human being. It involves taking one's adult place in the human community, receiving and contributing to family, friends, and society.

Beyond these four causes Christians understand a First Cause. The Unmoved Mover, the Creator, initiates, guides, redeems, and concludes the whole process of growth and change. Even more, belief in God gives transcendent meaning to life and growth. This adds to our appreciation of all the above causes. With such faith we understand that God takes the stuff of this earth, breathes into it the breath of divine life, and we become living souls (material cause). Believing ourselves to be made the divine image, we have much greater appreciation of our formal cause—what it means to be truly human. To the limitations and dysfunction of human life, God adds grace as a dynamic efficient cause. Now we come to understand our destiny in fuller and final terms: the fullness of life on earth and an eternal significance. This enables us to live not only for ourselves and others, but for the glory of the Eternal One.

Significance: One's Story Is Important

As soon as a person achieves a sense of selfhood in youth, it becomes important to see one's self, and be seen by others, as having significance. Growth is important, first of all, so we can *understand* significance. Growth further develops the *capacity* to contribute and make a difference. Then we grow in the *practice* of making a difference, contributing to self, family, and the larger society.

Rocks, trees, pets, and human beings are significant in different ways. Humans are not meant primarily to be climbed upon or to "dog" a master. We exist to mean something to others and ourselves. The goal of growth, then, is to find a place of significance in the human scene. By *significance* we mean that one's story makes sense and is important to others. A significant life is not filled with meaningless happenings; it fulfills its potential in terms of its situation and resources.

The developmentalists have much to teach us. Yet, in reading Sigmund Freud, Erik Erikson, Jean Piaget, Lawrence Kohlberg, Carol Gilligan, and John Fowler—from their works and as summarized by others—it seems something is missing. My students sometimes find their description of stages less important than other factors in their young people's lives. Without current cultural and sociological information, developmental psychology is not as insightful and helpful as it might be. We cannot dismiss the principles taught by these renowned psychologists—their definitions and explanations provide a necessary foundation for effective practice—but we need to supplement their findings with interdisciplinary insights, common sense, and wisdom from above.

With Erikson, Gilligan, and others in mind,[1] we want to understand a person's story as a struggle against adverse situations toward a significant contribution to self and others. We further hope each person will find identity and significance in God through Jesus Christ.

Most people face life with a combination of inner resources: physical, mental, emotional, social, and spiritual. Samuel and Jesus were given distinct resources in different centuries, and both used them well. They achieved their purpose in life. Other biblical characters, such as King Saul, were well supplied with resources but never realized their purpose.

Believers in Jesus Christ have guidelines for discovering their distinct significance. Those principles and instructions are found especially in the person of Christ and in the Bible. When we work in secular settings with those who may not be people of faith, we still direct them to common sense principles (with general social acceptance) as guidelines for their lives. They may not accept the lordship of Christ in their lives, but they still have choices to make between destructive and more positive directions in life. Like Jesus, we have a responsibility to help people regardless of their faith commitment.

It is important, then, to take what the developmentalists have taught us and see each human individual striving to be all that he or she can be.[2] Nature (God) has made us to grow toward significant achievement within a given situation. It is outrageous for a human being not to find significance. Those with no stories of significance are filled with rage or depression.

Security and a sense of belonging, however, must come before significance. Families give a child the love in

---

[1] See Dean Borgman, *When Kumbaya Is Not Enough* (Peabody, Mass.: Hendrickson, 1997), 89-104. This section includes a summary of developmental theory. A fuller description is found in Doula Nicolson and Harry Ayers, *Adolescent Problems: A Practical Guide for Parents and Teachers* (London: David Fulton Publishers, 1997), 4-19.

[2] We will deal with the main ideas of the developmentalists later in this chapter.

order that he or she can develop skills and perform. We shall look at examples of children who, without security or a sense of belonging and love, end up killing at a very young age. Although we do not wish to oversimplify, we seek a deeper appreciation of the human drama played out by every human being.

🏂 Imagine a young person you have difficulty working with. Feelings of antipathy are mutual. Yet the two of you are in continual contact in a classroom or youth group. With prayer, determination, and support from a wise supervisor, you hope a partnership with this person will develop. She may have absolutely no interest in the project at first. How might persistence and the miraculous bring about new discoveries, a new relationship, and a new sense of significance?

Young people who commit suicide or homicide have somehow been stunted in their growth and frustrated in any real sense of purpose. A combination of circumstance and disposition has left them in depression or rage. To understand what drives them to such extremes we must understand healthy growth patterns and what has gone awry.

Although vigorous arguments about the age limits and therefore definition of youth continue, we take adolescence (or youth, the preferred term in much of the world) to be the transitional age between childhood and adulthood, the latter defined as mature and nondependent functioning within a given culture. Such a working definition of youth is flexible across cultures. The transition we call youth varies greatly, but it is always there.

This transition to adulthood and maturity includes puberty, a time of drastic change in a child's body and mental framework to new adult potential. This new power leads to the proverbial sense of invincibility. Youthful disregard of consequences is rightfully feared by most parents.

Children, dependent on family or some other social structure, must determine who they are, whether in individualistic societies such as Western Europe and North America or in cultures in which individuals are, to a greater degree, subordinated to and see themselves as part of a larger group. Even in Asia and Africa, globalization and media bring new desires for individual expression.

In traditional societies rites of passage help children move to adulthood. Not only have urban societies prolonged, segregated, and marginalized youth; they have left them to devise their own, often dangerous, rites of passage such as high-risk experiments, binge drinking, and losing one's virginity. Traditional rites of passage announced to the community that these youth were ready to become significant adults. For most youth today, such markers have vanished.[3]

Church and society must provide young people with positive social rites and markers, with positive experiences, instructions, and celebrations, or youth will devise dangerous rites of their own.

In today's societies, a dangerous distinction has grown between the way youth and adult cultures define significance. There are important differences among what various groups of young people and adults find important. It almost seems as if we pay popular culture to add to the confusion, for it reflects *and* suggests damaging extremes to young people. The point is this: a sense of present and coming significance cannot wait; delayed significance will not do.[4] Significance is a human requirement for adolescents and adults. As youth culture changes, there must be a constantly changing and healthy interpretation of significance for young people.

The telling of stories reveals significance. Human beings need significant stories, individual and corporate. Finding significance begins in the family, but it cannot be achieved without help from all society.

---

[3] David Elkind, *All Grown Up and No Place to Go: Teenagers in Crisis* (Reading, Mass.: Addison-Wesley, 1998), 111–34.

[4] Again, I am not talking about a definition that can be learned by parents or schoolchildren but a process of determining destiny and meaning for cultures and individuals.

Socialization: Shepherding Children to Maturity

The second creation account (Gen 2:4–25) notes "It is not good for man to be alone" (Gen 2:18, author's paraphrase). The next sentence is startling: "*So* out of the ground the Lord God formed every animal." (Gen 2:19, NRSV). When God sees that humanity alone with animals is still not enough, male-female partnership and, by implication, human community in partnership with God completes the picture.

Which comes first: a human being or social groups? Students often have difficulty with this question, because Western logic leans toward seeing individuals preceding a group. But, a child cannot become fully human without a group.

It takes many social systems to socialize an infant. I often ask students to imagine a newborn child. It is important to contemplate its helplessness and vulnerability. Many animals are instinctively self-sufficient from birth, but human infants rely on learned behavior to grow up. This is a critical difference between animals and humans. We have few instincts (sucking and grasping) and must learn our basic behaviors: how to eat solid food, how to walk, how to talk—in fact, how to be human.

God made human infants as creatures needing nurture and shepherding to reach maturity.[5] This process is called socialization. The Creator knew it would take great effort from family, school, the community, media, peers, and others to teach the growing child. The process leading to mature human life depends very much on all these shepherds.

---

[5] To the contrary, Judith Rich Harris, *The Nurture Assumption* (New York: Free Press, 1998) writes that "in the formation of an adult, genes matter and peers matter, but parents don't matter" (xii). Harris is not denying the importance of socialization but affirming the importance of inherited characteristics. As to her devaluing of parental significance, her writings have been critiqued by many experts. Research and experience show that parents do matter—especially in the younger ages. The impact of divorce, for instance, is shown to matter throughout children's lives.

What if a child *never* receives human instruction or socialization? This is an important question for those who care about youthful growth and welfare to study.

Children Lacking Socialization

In the summer of 1724, in the hay fields near Hameln, Germany, a worker noticed "a naked, brownish, black-haired creature, who was running up and down, and was about the size of a boy twelve years old."[6] This creature was enticed into town, where the street kids made fun of him and named him Peter. For his protection, the town's burgomaster placed this strange creature first in a local hospital and then in the poorhouse. Later Peter was sent to Hanover and London for study. Expert opinion was that Peter's "nature lacks humanness and there is no hope that he will ever learn anything."[7]

Without socialization, without contributions from mentors and social systems at the opportune time, a child can't become human. Obviously, distorted socialization can also produce dire consequences.

Peter's story does not stand alone in the annals of social science. Before him were the wolf boy from Hesse (1344), a Lithuanian bear boy (1661), an Irish sheep boy (1672), a girl from Cranenburg (1717) and another from Champagne (1731).[8] All were called feral children: children raised primarily alone or by animals and with behaviors like those of animals.

The first case of feral children I learned about, and for me the most dramatic, is the story of two girls in India who apparently had been abandoned as infants and dragged by wolves into a cavern under a giant anthill. There these girls were tended by a she-wolf, who fed them and cleaned up their messes. When these wild girls learned to go outside, the natives of the area became terrified of "the ghosts," as the girls were called.

---

[6] Douglas Keith Candland, *Feral Children and Clever Animals: Reflections on Human Nature* (Oxford and New York: Oxford University Press, 1993), 9.

[7] Ibid., 11.

[8] Ibid., 13.

Reverend Singh and his wife ran an orphanage in this region. Singh, who had a keen interest in anthropology and the animals of the forest, would also go on missionary ventures into the jungle. The natives begged him to get rid of the ghosts. The girls were thus discovered and captured in October 1920. Brought back to the orphanage, the girls were found to be covered with sores needing critical treatment. Kamala was eight, and Amala, eighteen months. They could not walk; instead they crawled, ate, and snarled like animals: "From the very beginning their aloofness was noticeable. They would crouch together in a corner of the room and sit there for hours on end facing the corner, as if meditating on some great problem. . . . They wanted to be all by themselves, and they shunned human society altogether."9

About a year after they came to the orphanage, both girls became very ill from round-worms. The younger, Amala, did not survive. When Kamala found she could not waken Amala, she cried two tears and sat in the corner for a week.

Reverend Singh considered the girls to be creatures who needed taming, and, with love and trust, could develop human capacities. Mrs. Singh did develop a caring relationship with Kamala over the course of a year, and Kamala showed real affection for her. She also learned some words and colors from Mrs. Singh and came to eat from a plate and drink from a glass. Kamala would go to the bathroom if either Mrs. or Reverend Singh were present, but if they were not, she would urinate at will and never became toilet-trained. A visiting bishop observed the following after Kamala had been in the orphanage for five years:

> When I saw Kamala she could speak, quite clearly and distinctly, about thirty words . . . but she never used her words in a spontaneous way. . . . If she were left alone, she would retire to the darkest corner, crouch down, and remain with her face to the wall absolutely listless and with a perfectly blank expression on her face. . . . I saw her again two years later, and except that she had learned a good many more words, I did not notice any mental change.

9 Ibid., 60.

What interested me the most was to find . . . that while the
wolves had not been able to teach anything especially human
to their little human cubs, so that there was no sense of
humor, nor of sorrow (except in the case when Kamala wept
at Amala's death), very little curiosity, and no interest except
in raw meat, neither had [the wolves] taught them anything
bad. . . . Human vices seem to have been as little inherited (or
learned from the wolves) as human virtues.[10]

This last paragraph is especially important. It seems that
it is extremely difficult for feral children socialized into animal cultures to be completely socialized into human life and
intimacy. The wolves were not able to help these children become human; they could teach them neither positive nor
negative human traits.

> 🏃 How do you understand the relationship between a
> child's failure to bond with caregivers and attachment
> disorders? (This is sometimes found in children adopted
> at an older age.) What would you do with a child who
> exhibits symptoms of attachment disorder? First, they
> need your long-term high investment and consistency.
> You shouldn't take their disregard or disrespect
> personally. Second, realize that this disorder is
> controversial and very difficult to diagnose and treat,
> even by professionals. Symptoms overlap with other
> conditions such as hyperactivity and attention deficit.
> Get to the best specialist and judge the diagnosis against
> your gut feeling. From your area and from the Internet
> find a support group and network. Resources are out
> there. Trust yourself and appreciate the arduous work,
> love, and commitment you are bringing to this
> relationship. At the same time realize your own limits;
> don't take on too much or go beyond your strength and
> abilities. It is much better to get help than to break
> down.

---

[10] Ibid., 67.

The feral children did not learn how to talk and think normally. Certain windows of opportunity for when a child can learn skills and attitudes were lost forever in these cases. All died at young ages. They remained in what theologians call the age of innocence—with sinful natures like us all, but without comprehension of human vices, virtues, and responsibility.

These stories highlight the fact that animals live mostly by instinctive behaviors; human beings by learned behaviors. A duck becomes a duck no matter who raises it. But we become human beings only when reared by humans.

In 1937 Konrad Lorenz trained newborn ducks and geese to regard him as their mother and follow him. This is called *imprinting,* the instinct for some animals to follow the first movement they see after birth and regard the first caregiver as mother. We have seen television shows of geese learning to migrate as they follow a mother figure in an ultralight aircraft. Still, the duck is a duck and will feed and act like a duck. Human *bonding* is a more complex process.

Experts debate the nature and importance of bonding between mother and child before and just after birth. No one dismisses the importance, however, of human bonding in general. While we lack definitive data regarding the significance of immediate bonding with a mother, we know that a child must develop trust in a care-giver. As delightful as it was for me to watch my children bond with their mother immediately after their births, had they been in an incubator for weeks, bonding could still have taken place. Had both parents been killed in an accident, bonding through the loving care of adoptive adults could later occur.[11]

Opportunities for teaching physical, cognitive, emotional and social skills fill the first months and years of life,

[11] You can trace some of this discussion in M. Lamb, "Early mother-neonate contact and the mother-child relationship," in *Journal of Child Psychology,* 24(3) (1983): 487–94. and D. E. Eyer, *Mother-Infant Bonding: A Scientific Fiction* (New Haven, Conn.: Yale University Press, 1994); and Mary Dozier, et al. (2001) "Attachment for Infants in Foster Care: The Role of Caregiver State of Mind" in *Child Development,* Sept–Oct, v. 72, i5, pl 1467 (11).

with early months and the first three years being crucial. It is important that children learn to trust, to master and sense accomplishment in performing basic tasks, to identify and express their feelings, and to learn empathy.

Highly respected pediatrician and author Eli Newberger[12] distilled the wisdom of his study and experience into Five Things Kids Need:[13]

1. At least one adult in their lives who is crazy about them (parents are best, but studies show another caring adult will do; this highlights importance of mentoring programs).

2. Children, boys especially, need words to identify and express what they feel (use of picture books of baby faces and good stories of feelings are helpful).

3. Kids need inductive discipline; deductive discipline follows merely from authority of parent but inductive flows from relationships and explains the use of rules that protect.

4. Boys and girls need protection against violence (not only the 13,000 murders a child sees on television from ages six to thirteen) but the many diverse threats in the world around them.

5. Children and young people need the opportunity to give back, from chores to service projects of all kinds.

The extended consideration of feral children is meant to deepen our comprehension of socialization. Children who experience extreme neglect and abuse parallel the experience of children reared without adult care. Taken as a whole, these stories return our thoughts to a newborn baby, helpless, vulnerable, and needing to be taught everything there is to be learned about being a human being.

---

[12] Eli H. Newberger, *The Men They Will Become: The Nature and Nurture of Male Character* (Cambridge, Mass.: Perseus Publishing, 1999).

[13] Eli H. Newberger, speech at the Essex County Youth Conference, Endicott College, Beverly, Mass., 5 June 2001.

Nature demands nurture. Parents, families, neighbor-hoods, teachers, coaches, storytellers (television), drama-tists (movie producers), musicians, employers, business leaders, politicians, and friends all take part in helping a baby reach human maturity. If we would better understand why Kurt Cobain killed himself or Eric Harris shot his Col-umbine classmates, we need to take a closer look at the so-cialization process.

Socialization in Traditional and Urban Cultures

When I teach in Africa or in other traditional cultures, I often say that I am pretending to be a little child in front of the class. Then I ask a student to place around me those from among their people who would be responsible for my grow-ing up. Mother is usually closest; next, perhaps older sib-lings, an aunt, grandmother, father, and so on. Each adult has a clear role, along with the rest of the village, in rearing a child.

In a second exercise, I become a child in the nearest large city and ask students again to show how I am brought up. In urban families, there are fewer mentors; usually a nanny and television have replaced extended family mem-bers as critical nurturers. In urban societies, families, child care, community, schools, and perhaps the church cooperate to socialize the young. Yet all these social systems are under stress and in some sort of disarray.

Rapid change and complex choices are hallmarks of urban societies. Coming to the aid of family and schools—or taking their place—are the media and friendship groups. Ad-olescents must have peer groups, be they gangs, cliques, or a straggling twosome. That is where adolescents' identities are worked out. Increasingly they not only live in an electronic age but also are nurtured and instructed by television and computer. Family, community, school, media, and friends are the five critical social systems that rear contemporary chil-dren. Burning these images into our minds and hearts will help us understand the struggles of troubled youth.

Those who care for troubled youth desire a special un-derstanding of human growth. When we lose our wonder of human birth and life, we are not fit to minister. Since Jesus was concerned for the children of his day ("Let the little children come to me," Matt 19:14 NRSV), wouldn't he also be concerned about what kids go through today?

Urban, postmodern society has fragmented human life. Families, schools, and businesses often feel like separate compartments, isolated from the whole human enterprise. Teachers become critical of parents, who in turn feel misunderstood by the school and let down by the rest of society. Dysfunction and a lack of unity and communication, infect all aspects of modern life.

In the mid-1990s Robert Putnam found that more Americans were bowling than ever before, but that between 1980 and 1993 bowling in organized leagues had plummeted.[14] That was cited as a whimsical fact reflecting significant declines in voter turnout, membership in civic organizations, attendance at parent-teacher associations (PTA), and churchgoing. Since de Toqueville, noting the proliferation of nineteeth-century associations, observed that democracy in America is strong because of social networking, we've realized that democracy needs social contact and communities. "Social capital," as Putnam used the phrase, refers to the benefits a person reaps from formal and informal communal relationships. His argument is that since World War II, and especially from the 1960s, four factors have eroded the social adhesion of American families and communities.

1. Urban sprawl, increased mobility, and time spent commuting.

2. Movement of women into the workforce, more divorces, fewer marriages, and fewer children in each family.

3. Technological transformation of leisure by television and the VCR. This factor is most important and receives most approbation in Putnam's critique; he hopes that the Internet and renewed social creativity will revive American communal life.

---

[14] Robert D. Putnam, "Bowling Alone: America's Declining Social Capital," *Journal of Democracy* 6, no. 1 (January 1995): 65–78.

4. Generational differences: children reared with less attention, by more media, and in a more isolated culture will accelerate tendencies toward individualism and isolation.[15]

Such sociological analysis highlights the challenge for sound socialization of the young. For many parents and adults, life seems at best like a juggling act with incredible pressures. At worst people give in to pressures and follow the flow. Still, the human spirit rises to meet these challenges and produce healthy offspring and citizens. Today's challenge is the bringing of our social systems together for the sake of children.

Questions for Reflection and Discussion

1. How does the material in this chapter match your understanding of biblical principles of healthy growth?

2. How might Putnam's critique and suggestions be applied to all those who "shepherd" children and young people today?

3. What suggestions would you have for a single parent of two or three kids and to busy parents who must both work and put their children in childcare and preschool?

4. List several principles that you can apply to your ministry or family.

5. How can you more effectively shepherd the children in your family or ministry?

6. How can you help children and teenagers see the significance of their stories?

---

[15] Ibid.; see also Robert D. Putnam, *The Collapse and Revival of American Community* (New York: Simon & Schuster, 2000).

Book Resources

Rev. Chris McNair. *Young Lions: Christian Rites of Passage for African-American Young Men.* Nashville, Tenn.: Abingdon Press, 2001. 🐾 Many have realized how appropriate a rite of passage program is for urban young men. Many children growing up without "social markers" could profit greatly from adaptations of this program.

Doula Nicolson and Harry Ayers. *Adolescent Problems: A Practical Guide for Parents and Teachers.* London: David Fulton Publishers, 1997 (available in the U.S.). 🐾 This handbook has an excellent introduction on adolescence and adolescent development. It describes six theoretical approaches to adolescent counseling and then gives professional advice in dealing with behavioral difficulties, emotional difficulties, learning problems, relationship problems and sexual relationships.

Internet Resources

www.abingdonpress.com 🐾 Abingdon Press will provide you with much more than *Young Lions* (above). Request a catalogue from the following publishing companies or enter their search window for children and teenagers.

www.attach-bond.com 🐾 This site provides basic information about attachment disorder with help for parents.

www.cokesbury.com 🐾 Here you will find more books and resources from the United Methodist Church. Search for children and teenagers.

www.cookministries.com 🐾 At top of page "Click-N-Go" find "Choose a dept." and scroll down to children's ministries and youth ministries.

www.grouppublishing.com/cat_child.asp

www.grouppublishing.com/cat_youth.asp 🐾 These sites will give you books and resources from Group Publishing.

www.leaderresources.org 🐾 This site is Episcopalian in background; look especially at their fine program, "Journey to Adulthood," which includes Rite-13 (sixth–eighth grades),

J2A (eighth–tenth grades), and YAC (tenth–twelfth grades). J2A includes 6 critical skills for teenage growth and relationships in community.

www.search-institute.com ✚ This provides a positive, re-searched approach to promoting healthy kids in healthy communities. Become familiar with their asset-based pro-gram for youthful growth.

www.syix.com/adsg/index.htm ✚ This Christian website supports parents of Unattached Children.

www.youthspecialties.com ✚ Here you will find links, re-sources, and training events from Youth Specialties. Se-lect site tours from home page to reach: For Rookies, For Volunteers, For Students.

5 Fostering Healthy Development

The situations surrounding the births of my four children were interestingly different: from a jungle clinic to a modern African hospital, to an almost-too-late arrival at the delivery room, and finally the birth of my youngest, who was delivered by a fine missionary doctor. He brought her, with the briefest cleaning and attention, to her mother's breast. Laying one hand on the baby's head and the other on my shoulder, the doctor prayed a beautiful blessing. Watching the bonding between mother and suckling child over the next few hours gave me a new appreciation of a mother's privilege.

The roles of mothers and fathers are defined by culture. As society changes, so do those roles. We should learn as much as we can from other cultures and apply what is best and most applicable to our situation. That is why the Bible is not an operations manual but a book of exalted principles. God has left us with the challenge to work out these divine principles in diverse cultural situations. Each generation and people in every situation have a responsibility to work out Scripture's principles and examples of justice and healing.

The Challenge of Mothering

There is much we do not know about prenatal life and development. What has been found indicates that a fetus responds to pleasure, withdraws from pain, and possesses a rudimentary memory.[1] Experiments have found that the bonding of mother and child begin in the womb. At birth, babies prefer female voices, especially that of the mother. As God forms the child (Ps 139:13–16a), the fetus begins to recognize the mother's voice and to absorb much more, much of which we don't yet fully understand. We do know enough to say that pathological parenting can begin in the womb—fetal alcohol syndrome and crack addiction are only two examples.

Mothers give children a basic sense of the acceptance they need. There is an unconditional aspect of mothers' love, but it should also have appropriate boundaries. When a mother's affection comes from a person who has a life of her own and clear standards, that affection continues through life to give inspiration, guidance, and security. Good mothers know how to embrace and how to let go.

In *Raising Cain,* Dan Kindlon and Michael Thompson describe a mother's relationship to her son during a trip to the park. She settles down on a bench to read and watch, while the son observes his new surroundings. The two-year-old is quickly off discovering rocks and sticks and whatever catches his attention but soon comes back to give Mom a hug and climb on her back. It is not long before he sets off on another investigation a bit further and then returns again. Next time he goes a bit too far for mother's comfort; she calls to him and meets him halfway.

> This is the fundamental pattern of the relationship between a boy and his mother. He is the explorer; she is his "home base." Emotionally, as well as physically, throughout his childhood, as a boy explores, he carries the safety and familiarity of his mother with him. As he grows, a boy must be able to

---

[1] Some researchers would take this much further, but their work is still an inference of the data.

leave his mother without losing her completely and return to her without losing himself. A mother's loving task is parallel: she must try to understand and respond to what her son needs at different stages of his life. When a relationship has this balance, we describe it as *synchronous.* Mothering comes down to this delicate balance of closeness and distance.[2]

If, instead of keeping a healthy balance, the mother in the park becomes absorbed in her book and her toddler wanders off, we call that neglect. If she continually hits him, that is abuse. If she cannot leave him alone to discover and hovers over him as if he needs a constant partner, it is called *enmeshment.* Linda Nielsen describes enmeshment as

> a relationship in which two people are overly involved in each other's lives. . . . When a parent and child are enmeshed, they behave as though they share the same feelings, same perspectives, same thoughts, and same needs. . . . Mothers are far more likely than fathers to be enmeshed with one of their children. . . . Enmeshed children focus too little on their own ego development and too much on a parent. As a result, by the time they reach adolescence, these enmeshed children have not developed social maturity, self-reliance, close friendships, and self-confidence of most people their age.[3]

Enmeshment also involves the failure of boundaries between parent and child. Nielsen defines boundaries as "unwritten, yet clearly understood set of expectations that protects each person's identity, feelings, and opinions from being overly entangled with another person's. For example, a mother is violating her son's ego boundary when she convinces him to despise someone who has treated him well for years, but whom she hates for reasons of her own."[4]

It takes involvement and wisdom to help teenagers form their identities, clarify their values systems, and under-

---

[2] Dan Kidlon and Michael Thompson, *Raising Cain: Protecting the Emotional Life of Boys* (New York: Ballantine, 1999), 116.

[3] Linda Nielsen, *Adolescence: A Contemporary View* (rev. ed.; Orlando, Fla.: Harcourt Brace, 1996), 127 and the research she cites.

[4] Ibid., 127.

stand and respect their boundaries. When an adolescent fails in his life tasks, he may experience a rage he does not understand. Negative defense mechanisms and antisocial behavior may take the place of healthy productivity.

It is not easy to find a balance. Boys need a strong emotional bond with their moms; from this they receive the intimacy they need. But boys also need to learn how to take hard knocks. The soccer mom who rushes out on the field to inspect her son's injury is seen as smothering the boy. But if he comes to her on the sideline and needs comfort, it should be given.

It is a tough challenge to be a good mom these days. Mary Pipher speaks of the dilemma that many mothers of teenagers experience:

> Mothers are likely to have the most difficult time with adolescent girls. Daughters provoke arguments as a way of connecting and distancing at the same time. They want their mothers to recognize their smallest changes and are angry when their mothers don't validate their every move. They struggle with their love for their mothers and their desire to be different from their mothers. They trust their mothers to put up with their anger and to stand by them when they are unreasonable. This is an enormous compliment, but one that's hard for most mothers to accept because it's couched in such hostile terms.[5]

Many urban cultures push mothers to work double shifts. From a full-time job in the workplace, they return to their second job as home manager, cook, cleaner, taxi driver, cheerleader, coach, or patient fan at their children's games, tutor—when it's time for homework—and much more. It is too much, and the strain shows. Still, most mothers are doing the best they can. Single and dual parents must decide whether the work separating them from their children is a craving for higher lifestyle or a necessity. During the 1990s American parents began to make sacrifices to give them more quality time with their children.

---

[5] Mary Pipher, *Reviving Ophelia* (New York: Ballantine, 1994), 286.

The Need for Fathers

The story is told of a famous man, busy in public life, who took his son fishing one day. So special was the occasion for the boy, he entered these words in his diary. "Went fishing with father today—the most wonderful day of my life." Years later, after the father had died, his diary was found, and on that very day his entry read: "Went fishing with my son today—day wasted."

Carl Sandburg was walking with his dad on a Christmas morning before daybreak. As they walked hand in hand, Carl looked up at the clear, star-canopied sky and then remarked to his father: "You know, some of those stars are millions of miles away." With an indifferent shrug, his father quipped, "We won't bodder about dat now." The memory never left Sandburg, and years later he wrote, "For several blocks neither of us said a word and I felt, while still holding his hand, that there were millions of empty miles between us."[6]

Striving for love and significance, a boy will turn to his father. Even when a father is missing or abusive, a boy still looks for some ready and trustworthy father figure. Kindlon and Thompson speak powerfully to this basic need:

> There is little that can move a man to tears. . . . When a grown man cries in therapy, it is almost always about his father. . . . The word *love* rarely comes up in the stories men tell, but that is what these stories are all about. Fathers and sons are players in a tale of unrequited love—a story told in yearning, anger, sadness, and shame.
>
> An emotional gulf separates most sons from their fathers, and it is uniquely damaging to a boy because of the central role a father figure plays in a boy's developing view of himself.[7]

---

[6] Carl Sandburg's autobiography, *Always the Young Stranger,* quoted by Kindlon and Thompson, *Raising Cain,* 95.

[7] Kindlon and Thompson, *Raising Cain,* 94-95.

🛼 A child in your class or club displays a style and behavior that seems like father hunger. You find out that, in fact, the father is absent or totally uninvolved. What might you do?

Pre-teen boys who lack friends or are acting in anti-social ways are often greatly helped by having a big brother—someone who will spend an hour with them once a week, and who will remember birthdays and special times with a card or small present. Boys and girls profit from clubs, sports, and extra-curricular activities of any kind that provide not only a positive group, but a caring adult who will give them a little extra attention. Appropriate father figures are very important.

Essence published a series of articles in a special issue on fathers in the African-American community (November 1998, 128–200). That series shows the critical need of fathers for girls as well as boys. Diane Weathers writes of her father, who was in the merchant marine and who would gamble until broke and then ship out. As Weathers read his journal, she found that "My mother (the only woman he ever married) and I were minor anecdotes in his life story. Nothing personal; his interests were elsewhere."[8]

Diane's father left them when she was a toddler; she never saw him again until she tracked him down when she was in college. Soon after they were estranged again because of "his meanness," and they never reconciled. She remembers he told her immediately that she was probably better off without him, and she came to realize he was right: "The father who is never there for you is not the father you need," . . . still there was the longing. Her obsession, as she calls it, for a missing father became the "central drama in my life . . . the overriding theme, of course, rejection."[9] In her teens she found

---

[8] Diane Weathers, "Daddy Hunger," *Essence,* November 1998, 130.
[9] Ibid.

herself awkward around boys, and later, in more intimate relationships with men, she felt consumed by fear of rejection.

> I was clueless when it came to men. I couldn't distinguish one
> who was deeply devoted to me from one who was only pass-
> ing through. I felt more comfortable with types who are at
> best ambivalent, and at worst indifferent, emotionally or physi-
> cally remote, . . . Such men, I realized only after reading my
> father's manuscript, could have been dead ringers for my
> absent father.[10]

Girls who grow up without their fathers, writes Jonetta
Rose Barras, "tend to have sex earlier than girls who grow up
with both parents. Sometimes sex isn't enough. Fatherless girls
develop an obsession with having a baby."[11] She continues,

> By the time I was eight years old, I had already lost three
> fathers—Bill, John, and Noel. Each one abandoned me. Each
> one wounded me—emotionally and psychologically. . . . A girl
> abandoned by the first man in her life forever entertains pow-
> erful feelings of being unworthy or incapable of receiving any
> man's love.[12] For thirty-six years I had stoically struggled to
> reconcile myself with the loss of my fathers and forged an
> identity in the face of their absence. I had searched the faces
> of men looking for my father.
>
> I know the symptoms of the syndrome . . . We think every man
> wears our father's face . . . I go from house to house, from bed
> to bed, from wrong man to wrong man—sometimes the right
> man for the wrong reason. I am impatient and intolerant. Abso-
> lutely confused. I proclaim victory where there has been
> none and declare defeat far too prematurely. This is wisdom
> sculpted from hindsight, disappointment, fear, and resolve.[13]

David Blankenhorn studied research about teen pregnancy, crime, drug abuse, and sexual abuse and identified
these problems with missing fathers. A central statistic of his
book is that forty percent of American children do not live

---

[10] Ibid..
[11] Jonetta Rose Barras, *Whatever Happened to Daddy's Little Girl:
The Impact of Fatherlessness on Black Women* (New York: One World of
the Ballantine Publishing Group, 2000), p. 70.
[12] Ibid. 1, 3-4.
[13] Ibid. 89.

with their biological fathers.[14] Nor is this crisis restricted to the U.S.; for I have heard similar complaints in South Africa and around the world.

I don't mean to raise a dogmatic cry because sometimes there are no fathers. Clearly it is good to have a father, but when no father is present we must find and encourage father figures. Years ago Jawanza Kunjufu stressed the importance of fathers and father figures for children in the African-American community.[15] Crises of violence in the 1990s focused the attention of many experts on the plight of fatherless children among all groups. One of these experts, Michael Gurian, urges a "masculine nurturing system" of fathers and father figures:

> In order to build a new design of adolescent development for our males, we must retrieve and refine one of the primary nurturing structures in male adolescence: the masculine (or male) nurturing system. By this phrase we mean a nurturing system, male-driven, in which discipline, morality teaching, and emotional sustenance are provided *by* males *for* males. We mean elder men, with women alongside, helping high-density male groups—as in classroom or sports fields or community programs. We mean older boys nurturing younger boys in male peer groups. . . .
>
> We do not mean that women are unimportant in the clan. They are and will always be essential. We mean simply that there is a lot women can't do, especially when it comes to adolescent boys.[16]

"Fathers are not male mothers," William Pollack further explains.[17] Fathers have unique styles of loving, disciplining,

---

[14] David Blankenhorn, *Fatherless America* (New York: Harper Perennial, 1996), 336.

[15] Jawanza Kunjufu, *Countering the Conspiracy to Destroy Black Boys* (Chicago: African American Images, 1985), and *Developing Positive Self-Images and Discipline in Black Children* (Chicago: African-American Images, 1984).

[16] Michael Gurian, *A Fine Young Man: What Parents, Mentors, and Educators Can Do to Shape Adolescent Boys into Exceptional Men* (New York: Penguin Putnam, 1999), 298.

[17] William Pollack, *Real Boys: Rescuing Our Sons from the Myths of Boyhood* (New York: Random House, 1998), 113.

teaching, and guiding. The interactions between father and son while hunting, fishing, camping, in athletics, or in the home are special and cannot be replaced by female role models, as important as those may be.

In response to the fathering crisis there is good news. Father and mothers are beginning to realize the high priority of parenting, and both are adjusting to new ways of parenting in changing times. *Life* describes the changing role of fathers:

> Fathers have always come in all sizes, shapes, colors and accents, . . . Now we have stay-at-home dads. Single dads. Reconciling dads. Recovering dads. Of course there are still kiss-the-wife-goodbye, off-to-work dads—25 million of them—but even they're different.[18]

According to James Levine, director of the national Fatherhood Project based in New York City, men's notions of what it means to be successful as a father have changed over the past twenty years. There used to be a focus on being a good provider. Increasingly fathers realize that being a father involves both being a provider and being involved with the kids. A new emphasis on father involvement is working out in actual behavior, dads are spending more time with the kids these days than in the past. We all know moms still do more, but the gap has narrowed. Furthermore, Levine contends, most studies and books have examined mothers juggling work and home responsibilities. Levin and his colleagues believe fathers need the same help.[19]

Considering the wonder of fathers from a child's perspective, Roger Rosenblatt wrote about "the unreachable, unfathomable greatness" of fathers in a *Time* essay: "It is the fate of fathers to be enormous, and the responsibility as well. One must be careful not to abuse one's stature, not to be harsh, not to bully, not to crush."[20]

---

[18] "The Good Father," *Life* Cover Story, June, 1999, 54.

[19] James A. Levine and Todd L. Pittinsky, *Working Fathers: New Strategies for Balancing Work and Family* (New York: Harvest Books of Harcourt Brace, 1998. See additional book and website in Resources at chapter's end.

[20] Roger Rosenblatt, "The Greatest Dad in the World," *Time,* 21 June 1999, 90.

Parents need one another and help from outside the home.[21] As much as possible let us support, instruct, and build support around all families. Instruction will include information about parenting styles and communication. Studies show, and most of us realize, that extremely permissive or autocratic parenting is a predictor of adolescent abandon or rebellion. Whether a family's style is more democratic or authoritarian, it will work as long as it is not extreme, is consistent, and is open to discussion.

Families who can't talk about feelings and don't demonstrate concern for each member's growth and well-being are troubled or at least crippled families who will pass their limitations on to children. Human growth, especially in contemporary societies, demands that we develop internal parents by adulthood. We will now consider the way in which we all become our own parents.

From Parents to Self

Parents fulfill a child's basic need for love and attention, discipline and instruction, along with basic skills in relationships and communication. But there is more. God has made us seemingly insatiable in our need for love and affirmation so that our restless souls seek love and affirmation in God above all else. At a human level none of us has ever received all the love and encouragement we needed from either parent. Those unmet needs should drive us spiritually to God, and, on a human level, to become parents for ourselves.

During infancy a child is a "desiring appendage" of the mother. Gradually the child becomes aware of "I want" and "I don't want." After offering their infants unconditional love, parents must add an increasing number of cautions and prohibitions. The child learns what no means. Have you ever smiled at a three-year-old telling her younger brother, "NO!" in an authoritative tone? The three- and four-year-old girl or

---

[21] Johann Christoph Arnold, *Endangered: Your Child in a Hostile World* (Farmington, Pa.: Plough Publishing House, 2000).

boy can also cradle the younger sibling in loving embrace. Already she or he has learned not only to be a child (receiving, adapting, or even rebelling) but also to be a little parent (nurturing and disciplining). Maturity involves the holistic functioning of parent, child, and adult within each of us.

Absent or faulty parenting and abuse from siblings can leave human beings with no ability to parent themselves. Drugs, sex, and addictions or behaviors that act out the anger of inner deprivation may result. Listening to teenagers or older clients complain how others are treating them often leave counselors wondering, Why are you hurting *yourself* like that? and Why can't you affirm and love the child in you more effectively?

When we can't nurture ourselves, we expect other people, or things like sex, alcohol and drugs, to do so for us. When we are exceptionally critical of ourselves, the criticism of others has an extra sting. People who have not received love and guidance may not be able to love and guide themselves. They may look in all the wrong places for happiness and guidance. For example, not having experienced fatherly love, young women who grew up without fathers neither know how to love themselves nor to receive love appropriately. Dr. Gwendolyn Goldsby Grant, a psychologist, sex counselor, and author of *The Best Kind of Loving: A Black Woman's Guide to Finding Intimacy,* says, "You might as well call daddy hunger 'skin hunger.' That absence causes a real need to have someone to be close to. There was a woman I interviewed for my book who said, 'I needed a hug, Dr. Grant, and I got pregnant.' Half these little girls going around having sex really just needed a hug."[22]

This not only helps us to understand the epidemic of teen pregnancy but also shows how much we need to hug ourselves and thereby soak up and appreciate hugs from others—instead of reckless sex. The still broader picture is that human beings need loving and supportive families so they can grow up. Really growing up involves loving and support-

---

[22] Gwendolyn Goldsby Grant, "Daddy Hunger," *Essence,* November 1998, 132.

ing ourselves so that we can do the same for others. Understanding this and implementing proper training can break
the cycle of fatherless and motherless kids becoming inadequate parents. Extraordinary effort given this generation will
reap great benefits and save inestimable pain in future families and societies.

Family and Community Support

Francis Ianni produced one of the most comprehensive
studies of adolescence in the 1980s. This Columbia Teachers'
College professor and his students listened to three hundred
urban, suburban, and rural adolescents and those to whom
they were closest for more than 1,500 hours over a period of
ten years. They focused on two questions: "What are the
codes of rules which structure and organize the transition
from child to adult status in the social contexts of actual communities, and how do the adolescents in these communities
internalize and learn to use or abuse these rules?"[23]

Through their research Ianni and his coworkers discovered that "the dilemma of adolescence is not simply how to
develop a self-concept: it is a question of where to look for
the personal guidelines which will allow a teenager to satis-
factorily relate the sense of self with the social structure he
must negotiate."[24]

Ianni and his associates concluded that where the major
social systems around children and adolescents convey a
congruent message, young people are not at risk. But where
the messages and values of families, schools, community,
peers, and media are at odds, young people are at high risk.
As we noted in the previous chapter, parents, teachers, community leaders, and the producers of media are shepherds
who stand accountable in rearing our children and for the
health of the next generation.

---

[23] Francis A. J. Ianni, *The Search for Structure: A Report on American Youth Today* (New York: Free Press, 1989).

[24] Ibid., 261.

Ianni strongly encourages community youth charters, a shared set of expectations and common goals written out for all to see. He also stresses the importance of adult guides and mentors in the lives of young people. William Damon carried Ianni's conclusions further in his writing[25] and with his Center on Adolescence at Stanford University, through which he works with parent groups, school districts, and youth organizations in promoting the moral development of young people. Search Institute, through vast research and involvement, is helping many communities build up the forty assets they've found to be vital in growing healthy kids.[26]

Building a Life Pattern

I remember Manny and Maria (not their real names, sixteen and fifteen years of age), an attractive Puerto Rican couple on the Lower East Side Manhattan. They and their friends had broken the "decent code" of their parents to hang out on the streets. There we had become friends. They planned on finding jobs, getting married, and settling down in an apartment. But none of this happened; Manny found the drug scene instead of employment and Maria got pregnant. Maria's mother threw her out, and I discovered she was staying with some girlfriends and guys who were drug pushers. The guys often pushed the girls into prostitution. As I talked to Maria, the baby slept on the other side of the bed. Before leaving I reached over to stroke the baby, who jumped off the mattress. Spontaneously this baby reacted out of mistrust.

Besides needing to learn how to move their bodies, focus in on objects, distinguish people and gestures, eat and

---

[25] William Damon, *The Youth Charter: How Communities Can Work Together to Raise the Standards For All Our Children* (New York: Free Press, 1997).

[26] Peter L. Benson, *All Kids Are Our Kids: What Communities Must Do to Raise Caring and Responsible Children and Adolescents* (San Francisco: Jossey-Bass, 1997).

so much more, babies must also learn to trust; that is what Erik Erikson called the first task of human beings.

> The first demonstration of social trust in the baby is the ease of his feeding, the depth of his sleep, the relaxation of his bowels. The experience of a mutual regulation of his increasingly receptive capacities with the maternal techniques of provision gradually helps him to balance the discomfort caused by the immaturity of homeostasis [the ability of an organism to adjust to environmental changes] with which he was born.

> The infant's first social achievement, then, is his willingness to let the mother out of sight without undue anxiety or rage, because she has become an inner certainty as well as an outer predictability. Such consistency, continuity, and sameness of experience provide a rudimentary sense of ego identity.[27]

Picture a nurturing mom or dad with three kids in the toddler, pre-toddler, and post-toddler stages. Watch them at home or in a park attending to the needs and constant demands of each one. It is a nonstop love scene with each child being nurtured, challenged, and affirmed in rapid-fire succession. Babies and toddlers, girls and boys grow in different ways. It is difficult for adolescents to comprehend the responsibilities of parenting. Even older folks who have been through it once or twice get tired watching it all.

Imagine how a mother on drugs, or a desperately poor and depressed mother, may abuse an infant or provide inconsistent care. Other people may also hurt the child. The baby hears angry noises. In such an atmosphere the baby begins to learn fear instead of love. Erikson explains this first developmental stage as a crisis: basic mistrust versus basic trust. He also likens family faith and trust to that found institutionally in religion: "All religions have in common the periodical childlike surrender to a Provider."[28]

Developmental psychology sees each stage of human development as dependent on the accomplishments of the

---

[27] Erik H. Erikson, *Childhood and Society* (2d ed.; New York: Norton, 1963), 247.
[28] Ibid., 250.

previous period. Failure to learn trust will hinder a child throughout life unless the child relearns that lesson. Erikson describes the alternatives in further stages of child development as autonomy versus shame and doubt, initiative versus guilt, and industry versus inferiority. Without trust, autonomy cannot come, and without autonomy, a child struggles unsuccessfully with initiative and industry. In the process of seeking autonomy, the child needs to know his or her name, hear stories, and celebrate rituals through which his or her story comes to have significance. A child's story moves either toward autonomy, initiative, and industry or to mistrust, shame, guilt, and inferiority.

Gradually the child approaches puberty and adolescence. According to Erikson, success in these stages are needed to develop a strong self-concept:

> The child's danger, at this stage, lies in a sense of inadequacy and inferiority. If he despairs of his tools and skills or of his status among his tool partners, he may be discouraged from identification with them and with a section of the tool [industrialized] world.

> [There is a] danger threatening individual and society where the school child begins to feel that the color of his skin, the background of his parents, or the fashion of his clothes rather than his wish and his will to learn will decide his worth as an apprentice, and thus his sense of *identity.*[29]

This background brings us to Erikson's view of adolescence. He describes the life task and crisis of adolescence as identity versus role confusion. The transition between childhood and adulthood became so important for Erikson that he wrote a book about it.[30]

In adolescence a person awakes to new self-consciousness.[31] A teenager may feel herself on a world stage with every audience member scrutinizing the most trivial imperfection.

---

[29] Ibid., 260.

[30] Erik H. Erikson, *Identity: Youth and Crisis* (New York: Norton, 1968).

[31] Two excellent descriptions of adolescence are found in James E. Marcia's "Identity in Adolescence," in Joseph Adelson, ed. *Handbook of Adolescent Psychology* (New York: John Wiley & Sons, 1980), 159–87

Striving to leave the protective custody and pervasive control of parents, the young person tries to define herself, develop good relationships, and find a rewarding life. If earlier developmental stages thwart such necessary growth or situations prohibit personal expression or fulfillment, tremendous pain and rage may ensue. Any kind of acting-out behavior may be expected. To these stories, acted out, cried out, or unexpressed, this book is dedicated.

There is a remedy for deeply ingrained, negative life patterns. This becomes evident when one visits Boys' Town in Nebraska, Dale House in Colorado Springs, or many other helping centers. It is amazing to see troubled young people catching up on developmental stages through re-parenting. This process involves a "going back" to grow up again in a structured environment where there is love and discipline. In a few months tough kids can move through years of twisted development if they find adequate attention and understanding, love and discipline.

Laying a Foundation for Ministry

It is important to apply and integrate all this theory into our practice of youth ministry. What follows is an attempt to state our understanding of healthy human growth as a foundation for ministry to troubled youth. This summary also provides clues as to how Christians can work with secular colleagues and young people as well as those in a faith community.

We assume genuine concern for young people and a willingness to grow personally among those ministering to troubled youth. Our effectiveness depends upon an understanding of how human development affects behavior. We look for understanding, for clear concepts and principles from secular persons as well as to Christians. We want to help young people whether or not they possess a faith commitment.

(Marcia builds on Erikson's theory); and in David Elkind, *All Grown Up and No Place To Go* (Reading, Mass.: Addison-Wesley, 1998).

We assume growth to be the universal task and need of all children and young people. Although secular persons see human growth as natural and self-evident and moving toward socially approved roles and behavior, Christians understand growth to be God's will, moving to the full image of perfect humanity as found in Jesus Christ.

These assumptions about growth hopefully produce two universal ethical criteria: Whatever hinders human growth is wrong. Whatever fosters human growth is good. Such principles should work in religious and secular settings and across cultures.

Healthy growth takes into account the true needs of an individual and the reality of the social order. Activity that overlooks or denies real human needs within or destroys the communal ideal is unhealthy. Consider these factors:

- A life in tune with self and society is healthy and whole.

- A life in tune with self, society, and God is healthy, whole, and holy.

- A life that attempts to please God without regard for self and others ends up self-serving and insular.

- If social structures become pathological, individuals and groups within the dominant culture must attempt to remain healthy according to natural or divine law.

- The difference between a sociopath and a revolutionary may be a hard judgment call. Still, we must struggle to find agreement in distinguishing terrorists and revolutionaries.

The two basic desires or drives of human beings are union and significance. We all need to love and be loved, to be affirmed as worthwhile, and to help others realize their personal worth (see William Glasser's *Reality Therapy*). We believe all human beings are made to seek justice (fairness) and peace.

Human growth takes each individual through progressive stages, each with its own developmental tasks. Healthy growth allows individuals to realize greater union and significance at each successive stage of their lives. If growth is thwarted in any stage, an individual enters the next developmental stage without adequate ability to handle further growth. Therapy, whether personal counseling, group work, or structured activities, is a second chance for growth—a kind of re-parenting.

Unhealthy growth forces an individual to protect an inadequate soul with defense mechanisms. Everyone needs defense mechanisms, but when these shut out truth or people or hinder growth and effective living, they may include negative factors.

- The inadequate soul is afraid of union or intimacy and fears exposure of inadequacy or lack of significance.

- An inadequate person defends himself or herself by aggressive or withdrawing patterns of behavior.

- Escapist patterns include the abuse of sex, alcohol, and drugs, the Internet, food, music, and work.

Dysfunction, disease, and sin occur not only in individuals but also in systems. Systemic sin is found and affects individuals from families to communities, institutions to nations. The Bible emphasizes corporate sin and need for repentance fully as much as individual sin and need of redemption.

The only perfect model of health is our Lord Jesus Christ, who reflects the harmony and perfection of the blessed Trinity. All the rest of us suffer some lack of wholeness and struggle with various consequences of our sinfulness and the sinfulness of others.

The perfect model of communal health is the kingdom of God. God's loving intention is for us to be healed of our hurts, to be freed from our impediments, and to grow together toward maturity. Natural creation processes and supernatural redemptive grace find their intersection in Jesus Christ. Christ is the model and active mediator of growth and healing processes. The Blessed Spirit is the supreme Healer, Comforter, and Enabler. The triune God brings redemption to human lives and communities. The significance of individual and corporate stories are important to our God and Creator.

If this theology of growth and healing is not an adequate beginning, it should at least provide some suggestions

for thinking theologically about young people and our ministry with them. If we are to minister to young people with
wisdom, we need a clear sense of how young people are
meant to grow, what is healthy and what is injurious, and
how Christ interacts with natural processes. Such determination and commitment to growth may well keep some young
people from terminal violence and may encourage young
leaders to become significant servants of others.

Questions for Reflection and Discussion

1. Has this chapter given you an understanding of
   developmental theory and growth to serve as a
   foundation for your ministry with troubled youth?
   Do you now have a better appreciation of growth,
   dysfunction, and healing? Explain.

2. How do you respond to this chapter's emphasis on
   mothering and fathering?

3. How does the material in this chapter match your
   understanding of biblical principles of healthy
   human behavior?

4. List several principles that will be immediately
   helpful to you in your ministry or family.

5. What questions do you have about the material
   from this chapter?

6. Are there points you do not understand or that
   were skipped? What are they?

7. Do you disagree with some of the views given
   here or see some dangers in what has been suggested? Explain.

8. How would you prefer to see such things
   approached or principles stated?

Questions, cont'd.

9. Do you see how thinking about normal human development in supportive social systems can help us understand antisocial behaviors arising from stunted development in abusive systems?

10. Think of one young person to whom something here applies and explain how this might be of help.

11. Identify one principle of human development from this chapter you can use in your own life and personal growth.

Book Resources

Johann Christoph Arnold. *Endangered: Your Child in a Hostile World.* Farmington, Pa.: Plough Publishing House, 2000. Cited in a footnote, this book offers wonderful encouragement and advice to parents from a social critic, family counselor, father of eight, and member of the Bruderhof community.

Nina Barrett. *I Wish Someone Had Told Me: A Realistic Guide to Early Motherhood.* Chicago: Academy Chicago Publishers, 1997. ♠ Based on interviews with sixty new mothers, this book is sobering, funny, and realistic.

Ken R. Canfield. *The 7 Secrets of Effective Fathers.* Wheaton, Ill.: Tyndale House, 1995. ♠ Based on profiles from 5 years of research of 500 U.S. fathers, this book offers practical techniques for overcoming barriers to effective communication with sons and daughters.

James C. Dobson. *Bringing Up Boys: Practical Advice and Encouragement for Those Shaping the Next Generation of Men.* Wheaton, Ill.: Tyndale House, 2001. ♠ In line with many of those who would assert the uniqueness of masculinity, Dobson argues a biblical and conservative approach to raising boys with encouragement and practical advice for parents.

James Levine. *Getting Men Involved: Strategies for Early Childhood Programs.* New York: Families & Word Institute, 1994. ♚ This is a handbook for those who would involve fathers in early childhood programs.

James Levine. *New Expectations: Community Strategies for Responsible Fatherhood.* New York: Families & Work Institute, 1995. ♚ This is a review of research, consultation, and a guide to over 300 programs on getting men more involved in rearing children.

Mary Pipher. *Reviving Ophelia: Saving the Selves of Adolescent Girls.* New York: Ballantine Books, 1994. ♚ An eye-opener to the crisis of girls coming to adolescence in an aversive culture, this book is a must for the mothers and fathers, teachers and youth leaders of adolescent girls.

Leonard Pitts Jr. *Becoming Dad: Black Men and the Journey to Fatherhood.* Atlanta, Ga.: Longstreet Press, 1999. ♚ The author resents the stereoptype of black men as absent and negligent. Based on interviews with African-American fathers, this book explores the painful experience of black men in America and goes on to encourage and instruct in strong, positive parenting.

Internet Resources

http://family.org ♚ This is the site for Focus on the Family. Type father, mother, daughter, or son into Search window. There is much more here as well from a conservative Christian perspective.

www.fatherhoodproject.org ♚ The Fatherhood Project helps working fathers to become more effectively involved with children.

www.motherstuff.com ♚ Motherstuff provides encouragement and general information on many aspects of prenatal, birth, and childhood issues. It also has a broad list of links on specific issues.

www.wahm.com ♚ Work at Home Moms helps mothers to find employment at home.

6 Hearing and Responding to Stories

When I did speak of some distressing stroke that my youth suffered, my story being done, she gave me for my pains a world of sighs. — Othello[1]

We define "troubled youth," for the purpose of this text, as young people who may, without timely intervention, significantly injure themselves or someone else. This book deals particularly but not exclusively with the problems of homicide and suicide. We want to find Jesus Christ in the stories of those who have taken their own or someone else's life, because we believe Jesus wants to be in these stories. Two books address these issues: the anonymous diary of a teenage suicide, *Go Ask Alice,* and Sam Anson's *Best Intentions: The Education and Killing of Edmund Perry.*

Doubt and Conflict

Alice

According to her diary, fifteen-year-old Alice had a pretty good family, good school, nice friends—and some not so nice. She lived a comfortable and rather typical suburban

---

[1] William Shakespeare, *Othello,* Act 1, Scene 3, *Great Books of the Western World,* Chicago: Encyclopedia Britannica Inc. Vol. 27, 1952, 210. I've used these words of Othello out of context, but they still convey a sense of the power of stories.

life. Slightly overweight and tormented with doubts and nightmares, her self-doubts grew after she dabbled in drugs and sex. Sometimes she wished she could erase her mistakes, but nothing seemed extraordinarily wrong with her or her life. Toward the end things seemed to be going better, until suddenly she was gone.

Alice tried what might be called an adolescent solution for her adolescent problems. Students reading this book often get so close to Alice they find themselves crying. It's hard to figure out why she committed suicide. Much of her story was told, but something was left out. To find that missing ingredient, one would have to go ask Alice, and it's too late for that.

We seek to imagine what difference Jesus might have made in Alice's life. She worried about her experiences with drugs and sex. Although she had a deep crush on Roger, she lost her virginity to Bill while high on acid at a party. Then she worried if Roger could ever forgive her.

> How could he ever forgive me? How could he ever understand? Would he? If I were only a Catholic maybe I could do some kind of terrible penance to pay for my transgressions. I was brought up to believe that God would forgive people's sins, but how can I forgive myself? How could Roger forgive me?
>
> Oh, terrors, horrors, endless torment.[2]

Because of who he is and the way he is, Jesus is the real answer to such questions and pain. Christ left his disciples to do even greater works than he had done (John 20:21b). How could they do that? They were meant to be as Christ all over the world. And now we find ourselves in the place of the disciples—caring for kids like Alice.

Alice did her share of talking, and she did a great deal of writing—diaries and letters that come close to what was going on in her. But in all of this, she never told her story. If someone had helped her to do so, the story would have surprised Alice as much as anyone. Though no one ever did help

---

[2] Anonymous, *Go Ask Alice* (New York: Avon, 1967), 45.

Alice tell her deepest story, there are others who can be reached if we don't let them pass by. Because getting their stories can be so difficult, it's easy to let them pass by.

> 🗼 Alice is in your class, or youth group, or neighborhood. How might you account for her sometimes wild behavior? How might you intervene?
>
> Could this be a matter of one adult who shows care for her consistently over several years? How much listening would you have to do? She finally confides in you her worst hurt, your next steps might combine talks with her closest teacher, guidance counselor, and parents. You would first have to win their respect.

We ought to know about the youth workers, counselors, clinics, and hospitals who are dealing effectively with many Alices. Their stories ought to encourage us to be more observant and respond carefully to those who seem depressed or lost.

Edmund

Edmund Perry was a Phillips Exeter honor student who was shot and killed in Harlem in the mid-1980s by an off-duty cop who said the boy had mugged him. When the news came out that a white cop had killed a black kid headed for success at Stanford University, it caused an uproar. How could you believe a policeman? The book reads like a murder mystery as the author tries to find the real story and the real Edmund.

Edmund was a young man struggling for an identity—caught between two conflicting cultures. Each of his worlds robbed something from the other. The street kid robbed something from the preppy, and the preppy seemed to have done in the street kid. Edmund was determined to be on top of both worlds at the same time.

Robert Sam Anson, whose son was a classmate of Edmund's, had marched with Martin Luther King Jr. Anson went to Harlem and Phillips Exeter searching out those who had been closest to Edmund. Their reflections at last produced a story that made sense, tragic as it was. The author found his final clues from a wise man of Harlem, friend to Sam Anson and Edmund. The insights he gave were deep:

> I wasn't surprised when [Edmund] told me he wanted to go away to California to college. The psychosis of the lies he was spinning about himself was getting him in deeper and deeper. He wanted to get away from Harlem, away from Exeter, away from everything, just as far as he could possibly get. He talked about "getting over" on people, about running a game on them, and in a way he was very successful in his pretensions. But the game was beginning to catch up with him. . . .

> The last time I talked with him, I guess it was a couple of months before his death, you could sense a real spiritual exhaustion in his voice. "It sure is rough, dealing with all those white people." All this black/white stuff was really grinding him down, and he knew it wasn't going to go away. Yeah, he was going to Exeter, and yeah, he was going to Stanford, but he was never going to be a member of the club. He was always going to be Edmund Perry, the smart black. Even if he wanted to be anything different, Harlem wasn't gonna let him. That boy [felt himself to be] in a box, and he was going to have to deal with that box all the rest of his life.

> I remember thinking to myself [the night the news came of Perry's death], Eddie didn't get killed. He committed suicide. That's what it was, you know. Suicide.[3]

The key adolescent issues for Alice and Edmund and many young strugglers are identity, relationships, and significance, along with inner factors such as chemical imbalance. Jesus dealt with these issues more deeply than anyone. Christ's manner of helping people work out their identities and significance is wonderfully effective. His style transcends

---

[3] Robert Sam Anson, *Best Intentions: The Education and Killing of Edmund Perry* (New York: Vintage, 1988), 206-7.

all cultural obstacles. How would Jesus have approached Edmund, and where might their conversation have led?

> The bottom line [this wise friend from Harlem concluded] is that Eddie didn't have anyone to talk to about his weaknesses and vulnerabilities. So he had to deal with things like drugs on his own. And the way he did it was to justify his amorality in terms of what whites had done to blacks over the course of hundreds of years.[4]

Edmund did a lot of talking, but he never told his essential story. Somehow we must get to such stories before it is too late. Only when we get inside the lives and world of troubled storytellers will we hear what needs to be heard. Troubled people must be seen as people rather than mere problems. When someone's essential story is heard, down to the basic issues in the drama, there is hope for real change. We should be grateful for the churches and youth groups who have done more than just get to know young people like Edmund—who have sought to understand their struggle for an acceptable personal identity.

Common Themes in Different Settings

Small Town Reckless Rampage
Pursue this loss of clear identity, positive relationships, and hopeful significance in youthful lives. Picture a scene of a hostile, belligerent group of five high school boys. They will soon receive national attention for a reckless spree and brutal killing.[5] They skip school and they retreat to their special hangout. They sit on crumbling concrete steps that lead down into a narrow, dark, railroad underpass. In the background are the boarded-up windows of abandoned brick factories symbolizing the economic decline of the town and the area. There they spend their time smoking cigarettes, drinking beer, bragging, laughing, and cursing.

---

[4] Ibid., 206.
[5] Charles M. Sennott and Jeff Kramer, "Seeking Escape, Athol Youths Took Road to Trouble," *Boston Globe,* 12 June 1994: A1, 10–11.

No one bothers them; no one seems to care. No parents come to chat. Schoolteachers and coaches see no reason to stop by. No friends are worried about what they are up to; they are a group to themselves. The church? No youth worker ever spent time with any of them. Only in this small group can they tell their stories. Labeled losers, they try to understand life and develop a worldview. Their dreams and plans will be constructed within the confines of this clique.

They do not come from happy families; most don't have fathers at home. They are not doing well in school, and all have been in trouble with the law. Their camaraderie is based on their unhappiness in Athol, Massachusetts. Like characters in the movies *All the Right Moves* and *October Sky*, they only want to get out.

> 🎿 What if you lived in Athol? In fact, you see those guys hanging out. Like everyone else you would most likely pass them by. It would take hours and weeks and maybe months to get to know them and be accepted on any basis. It might take years before they, and especially their leader, Floyd, would really open up. In fact, their "salvation" might not come through words and discussion, though there would be plenty of that. You would probably take them on several trips, to camp, deep-sea fishing, and get them into a GED program or alternative school. You would spend a lot of time finding the right jobs for them. It would take a tremendous amount of time; it would cost a lot to reach these boys. Would it be worth it? Take a minute to figure out how much these boys cost the town and state when it's all over. It is costing thousands of dollars each month to keep them in prison. And then there is the cost of a life.

Planning their getaway, Floyd La Fountain Jr., sixteen and leader of the group, vows: "We're not coming back to

Athol alive." Among troubled youth today there is often a preoccupation with death. So on June 1, 1994, they steal a blue
Chevrolet Caprice from a parking lot downtown and head
north on back roads. They stay overnight with friends, first
in Maine and then in Vermont, where they also break into
several homes and steal a shotgun and two rifles. Speeding
south on I-95 with radio blaring, the boys sing along with
Guns and Roses and other heavy-metal groups. From the
driver's seat, Fountain boasts, "If we get stopped, we're takin'
out a cop."

Mark Dickinson, fifteen, and Edward Kitchen, sixteen,
begin to have doubts about the venture and are ditched in
Virginia, where police notify their parents and put them on a
bus back to Boston.

La Fountain, Kyle Moran, sixteen, and Michael Dupuis,
fifteen, are now headed for Tampa, where La Fountain has
worked with Peter Foster, who is sixty-eight. This older
friend has promised La Fountain that his friends can find
work in Tampa and not have to return to Athol. Arriving in
Tampa, they find the restaurant for which Foster and La
Fountain had painted a sign. They are given free sandwiches
and then call Foster, who invites them to stay in an empty
apartment next door.

Instead of appreciating what they've been given, the
boys plot to kill Foster and steal several hundred dollars and
his Cadillac. On the way home the next day, however, they
break into a nearby house and are surprised to encounter
the owner. Manuel Herta is a retired bus driver and a beloved figure in the Hispanic neighborhood. Some construc-
tion workers see the boys breaking in and notify the police,
but by the time they arrive, Herta has been shot in the head
and lies dying in a pool of blood. The boys, hearing the
cops, try to hide upstairs in the attic, where they are
apprehended.

Peter Foster, their would-be benefactor, feels lucky to
be alive. Three young men traded in the confinement of
what they felt to be a small, dead town for the confinement
of prison and possible execution.

Urban Death and the Boston Miracle

While the three boys from Athol were stealing and killing, the *Boston Globe* reported on a continuous and terrible loss of lives.[6] The Reverend Eugene Rivers is a street activist in Boston and has seen it all. He has attended too many funerals, and his house has been shot into on two separate occasions. He walks the streets confronting pushers and encouraging young men and women. He condemns "a too-commercialized culture where sex and degradation fuel a tide of black-on-black crime—taking on a life of its own."[7]

When Rivers puts himself inside the head of the young man believed to have most recently shot at his home, he imagines the young man explaining why he pointed the gun at Rivers' house and pulled the trigger: "I shoot because I hate myself. I've internalized the worst feelings about myself."

Rivers also blames a loss of faith on the crisis of black-on-black killing. "The liberals who get weak in the knees when anyone starts talking about God won't like hearing it, but secular, therapeutic institutions like government, foundations, public schools, the whole panoply of non-faith-centered self-help outfits are not going to speak to the depth of psychic and moral decay." How are we to confront the racism, disadvantage, and the low value of human life with which too many young people are growing up? We cannot listen to the stories of troubled youth without dealing with systems that confound them.

In the late 1980s, 1990, and 1991, Boston had an extremely high rate of violent teen deaths. The mayhem reached a climax when a gang assaulted a funeral service at the Morningside Baptist Church. No Mafia or gangs had ever desecrated a house of worship. From this tragic event emerged the powerful Ten Point Coalition of black activist pastors.

---

[6] Kevin Cullen and Efrain Hernandez Jr. "Five Killings and Mounting Frustration: Double Standard Seen in Boston Police Response," *Boston Globe*, 11 June 1994, B1, 4.

[7] Paul Langner "Minister to Help Man who Shot at his Home," *Boston Globe*, 15 April 1995, B 18.

Neighborhoods and municipal leaders were also awakened to the crisis. Operation Night Life allowed police and parole officers to enter homes to check on parolees during evening hours. Antigang groups, street workers, and neighborhood leaders collaborated in action that produced the Boston Miracle: no violent teenage deaths for more than two years. The whole nation took notice.

Suburban Death and Denial

Do middle-class, suburban kids use cars in the way that urban youth use guns? Is there a common dissatisfaction and anger, a similar disregard for life and excessive risk taking? Here is how a local paper described an accident that took the lives of two young men within a week of their graduation.

> A 17-year-old Wenham (Massachusetts) youth is scheduled to be arraigned today following a tragic car crash Saturday afternoon that killed two of his classmates from Hamilton and Essex and left a third in critical condition. All four youths had graduated from Hamilton-Wenham Regional High School just days before. One had received two all-star athletic awards; another had recently become an Eagle Scout—all college bound.
>
> Police estimate that William Hall was driving 60 or 70 miles per hour in a 25-mile-per-hour zone when he came to an S-curve on the street where he lives. His Volkswagen Jetta sheared a telephone pole in half, spun and hit another.
>
> A half-empty bottle of rum and drug paraphernalia were found in the driver's knapsack. Only six weeks before Hall had been arrested for possession of alcohol as a minor. In addition, Heath and Hall were involved in another automobile accident last year in which Heath had broken his back!
>
> Another friend of these boys, and member of the same class of 1994, was killed in a similar accident last June before his senior year. Boynton and Heath represent the eighth and ninth alcohol-related deaths of the past few years in this one small high school. . . .
>
> Police chiefs of all three towns, the school administration and guidance counselors have anticipated such a tragedy and worked hard to avert it.

The school's principal said, "These were good kids making bad decisions." He and others worried about excessive drinking and driving leading to avoidable tragedies. On May 4 he had delivered a stern warning to parents of the class of 1994: "I said that as a faculty, we were afraid for what we knew about this class. We still have parents who wink at it, who would rather see kids drinking beer in their house than driving around somewhere. The result is a mixed message."

The high school's assistant principal was also working hard to stem alcoholic and drug excesses that year. He saw in the weekend tragedy further proof that parents and school must work together to curb excessive drinking. "I felt that we've been trying to keep these kids alive for the past year because we knew they engaged in high-risk behavior."[8]

The accident, however, left the small town deeply divided. Parents willing to sponsor parties where their children and friends could drink felt condemned and defensive. They interpreted some remarks as smacking of an I-told-you-so attitude. School administration and police, who had tried to curb drinking and drug excesses, were charged with arrogant and insensitive intrusion.

Several teens admitted they drink and drive. "It could have happened to absolutely any one of us," said one youth who refused to give his name. "It's [incrimination of the driver] totally uncalled for," another student commented. A third student said the weekend tragedy would not stop his peers from continuing to party: "If they want to drink, they're going to drink—yes, even after this."[9] At the same time many young people in these towns found something positive to live for with support from Young Life,[10] church youth leaders, and school personnel.

The first task of youth leaders after such a tragedy is to comfort the bereaved. But then they must contribute leader-

---

[8]John Madden, "Two Teens Die in Crash: Wenham Youth Faces Charges," *Beverly Times,* 13 June 1994, A1, 12.

[9]Michelle Boorstein, "Adults, Teens View Crash Differently," *Beverly Times,* 13 June 1994), A12.

[10]Young Life is a national parachurch organization whose leaders relate to kids on their turf and share with them stories and hope in Jesus Christ.

ship and instruction. Some youth workers see their task as only empathizing with the feelings and attitudes of kids, but we must confront destructive behaviors.

Thrown-Away Kids

Most countries have homeless youth or street kids. For people who notice, these youth can be seen begging, doing menial jobs, rummaging for food, hanging out, or sniffing a can of glue hidden under long, loose sleeves. At night many are forced into prostitution. Within a day or so, most children or young people coming into a city homeless shelter are involved with crime, sex, and drugs. To survive, they often form families with older or more experienced youth who take care of the younger and newcomers. Organizations in most cities serve this population, but it takes more than such efforts to solve this problem.

It is estimated that 1.1 million young people leave home in the U.S. each year. Of these, a third are said to return home, usually within a week. Most of the rest could never return; they have been thrown out a final time or the abuse is too serious. The distinction is sometimes made between runaway and thrown-away kids. Though a few runaways strike out on their own through defiance or search for excitement (like the biblical prodigal son), the majority of runaways are thrown away by neglectful and abusive social systems.

In the late 1980s a few of Hollywood's thousands of homeless kids formed a group called the Trolls. Sonia Nozario wrote, "Living in THE HOLE: Troubled Teen-agers Create a Fragile Family Beneath a Busy City Street."[11] A character called Pops (John Soaring Eagle) connected with these kids. He was forty-seven, skinny, bearded, and claimed to have served twenty-two years for murder, although this claim was never substantiated. Pops took kids into his shelter, a cavern left by the California transportation department when it constructed a section of the Hollywood Freeway beneath

---

[11] Sonia Nozario is a freelance writer who submitted this article first to the *Los Angeles Times.* It was then used by the *Wall Street Journal* and carried by the *Beverly Times,* 21 February 1992, A5, where I found it.

Hollywood Boulevard. His ex-con, drinking, and robbing buddies were gradually pushed out as more kids came in. Temporary partitions were put up along with wall hangings; dilapidated couches surrounded a fire pit. There were no bathroom facilities, so the kids used the bushes and scrounged showers at the Y when they could.

Pops gave the group strict rules and organization. Among these rules: "Everything that Pops says goes" and "LSD, marijuana, and alcohol are allowed, but no shooting up." Trolls were asked to give Pops approximately ten percent of what they robbed or made through prostitution, although none were pushed to prostitute.

> To the girl Trolls, Pops is more than a father, less than a lover. "I'm Pops' princess," says Jamie, 18, as she paints her lips with a black eye liner and fluffs her lime-green Mohawk hair style. Around her neck is a dog collar, and a spider earring is clamped on her nose.

> Three years ago, when Jamie first joined the Trolls, she followed the custom of sleeping in Pops' bed, "for protection," she says. "He just hugged me like a father would hug his child. Eventually, he got me my own bed."

It's clear the kids received attention, a listening ear, protection, and a sense of belonging from the Trolls. Opinions of social agencies differ on Pops's role. Some saw him as providing some help; others viewed Pops as a sick adult figure. Pops did provide the group with stability, and when he left, the Trolls lapsed into some bizarre activities and fell apart.

The lesson? "They can pour their hearts out to me," Pops said. A director of one Hollywood runaway shelter commented: "He's the first adult many of them have seen who takes an interest." Whatever our opinion, it's clear such kids need someone to care, pay attention, hear their stories, and protect their lives. If they don't find positive role models, they may settle for some less desirable.

In Hollywood, Options House, Covenant House, Los Angeles Youth Network (LAYN), and My Friends Place do care and serve such young people. In Colorado Springs it's Dale House, in Toronto, Yonge Street Mission and others. In all these organizations there are strong positive role models. We should all know who is there to help homeless kids in our cities.

Repentance and Response

In these several examples of troubled youth, there are common themes. Everywhere, stories—with disclosure of animosities and fears—are not being told. Young people, their parents, and the media play around the truth. Those who share the blame for such terrible losses try to retreat from reality behind wise-guy remarks, defensive postures, music, and stylish stories. There are times when a community, as well as a young person, needs to repent and become honest about itself.

Whether we are talking about small towns that seem dead and close-minded, sophisticated suburbs, or challenging urban neighborhoods, it is difficult to gain cooperation among courageous clergy, community leaders, educators, and youth leaders. Resentment against kids and attitudes changes only gradually. But all these groups must work together if we are going to deal effectively with the issue. By now we are beginning to see how the issues of troubled youth, troubled families, troubled communities, and troubled societies are all a part of our complex challenge.

The simple responses to wanton violence without remorse are more arrests, tougher sentences, and larger prisons. But young aggressors are often caught up in complicated cycles of violence and abuse—living out their lives under unbelievable pressures. Neither those who would declare them innocent because of social circumstances nor those who only want to see them punished hold any hope of escape from the violence.

Young criminals need punishment and much more. They need radical personal readjustment and a new social environment. Many of their lives could move in different directions if there were a sense of life's meaning and dignity. Then they could experience true remorse, find self-confidence, acquire social skills, and accept adult responsibilities. This chapter is a call to people willing to intervene and prevent suicides and shootings. At some critical point they can be that essential listening ear and helping hand.

These stories of young lives make us want to understand more about human behavior and the dynamics of social systems bringing about such deadly consequences. Our study must avoid morbid curiosity and sensationalism; rather, it must be motivated by a desire to care and to become involved.

Jesus expressed his compassion for people in terms of spiritual and social needs. The challenge of this book demands such a model of concern and response:

> Then Jesus went about all the cities and villages, teaching . . . and proclaiming the good news of the kingdom, and curing every disease and every sickness. When he saw the crowds, he had compassion for them, because they were harassed and helpless, like sheep without a shepherd. Then he said to his disciples, "The harvest is plentiful, but the laborers are few; therefore ask the Lord of the harvest to send out laborers into his harvest." (Matt 9:35–38 NRSV)

The compassion Jesus showed to outcasts is well known. Less attention has been paid to his anger, which was focused primarily toward systems betraying their God-given trusts to serve people. We see this anger in Jesus' harsh condemnations (Matthew 23) and in his strong action against those defiling the temple (Matthew 21:12). But along with his anger, Christ cared about social institutions and displayed concern for those they affected. He condemned unjust systems but died to redeem them. His compassion for a great municipal system of his day is clear:

> Jerusalem, Jerusalem, the city that kills the prophets and stones those who are sent to it! How often have I desired to gather your children together as a hen gathers her brood under her wings, and you were not willing! See, your house is left to you, desolate. For I tell you, you will not see me again until you say, "Blessed is the one who comes in the name of the Lord." (Matt 23:37–39 NRSV)

Christ's anger is similar to that of Isaiah's. When state systems, communities, or families neglect or abuse those entrusted to their care, God is angry. Christ confronts such evil with indignation and is then willing to die for that system (Col 2:15; John 11:51). In his suffering for individual *and* corporate sins, our Lord cries out, "Father, forgive them, for they know not what they do." When the violent acts of kids reflect parental abuse, we are justifiably angry, but we retain an underlying love for dysfunctional parents and faltering family systems. We need the same attitude toward abusive police, judges, media, and government systems.

In Jesus we see balanced concern for corporate structures and individuals. The need for a Christ and the attractiveness of Jesus created great crowds. Notice how individuals with deep needs do not get lost in those crowds; the heart of Jesus constantly goes out to specific persons. For example, among the masses following Jesus were a certain woman, a certain ruler, a certain child, a certain blind man, leper, or prostitute. These people were noticed with special attention and care.

We will be forced to categorize various issues of troubled youth, but compassion for each unique person must never be lost. We must focus not just on troubled youth but also on the issues and potential of each young woman or man. Listen to kids silently pleading: "I am not just a problem. I am a young man or woman." We not only listen to past stories of hurt; with young people we imagine future stories of hope.

Questions for Reflection and Discussion

1. How do these stories make you feel? Do you take exception to the way some of this has been written or to some of the opinions expressed here?

2. To what extent can you identify with these young people and feel what it is like to be in their world?

3. In reading and mulling over this chapter, what questions or personal opinions come to your mind? What hinders discussion about these matters in our society?

4. How might Jesus heal each of the young persons described, and how might he confront social systems and offend the communities where these young people grow up?

Questions, cont'd.

5. How are we to balance ethical, social science, criminal justice, and spiritual issues in considering troubled youth?
6. What happens when we turn all our emphasis to individuals and forget the systems? Is there also a problem with dealing with systems apart from individuals? How will you and your church or organization keep this balance?
7. Can you empathize with someone's past hurts, and are you able to encourage their future hopes?

Book Resources

Bo Boshers, Scott Larson, et al. *Reaching Kids Most Youth Ministries Miss.* Loveland, Colo.: Group Publishing, 2000. ⚜ This book provides short chapters on a range of topics.

Larry Brendtro, Martin Brokenleg, and Steve Van Bochrn. *Reclaiming Youth at Risk: Our Hope for the Future.* Bloomington, Ind.: National Education Press, 1990. ⚜ This book has deep insights drawing from experts and Native American wisdom, and provides alternative approaches to discipline and dealing with troubled youth.

Mariam Neff. *Helping Teens in Crisis.* Wheaton, Ill.: Tyndale House, 1993. ⚜ With a foreword by Josh McDowell, this book has clear, simple, and spiritual advice from a high school counselor.

Internet Resources

www.girlsandboystown.org/store/departments.asp; 1-800-448-3000 ⚜ Girls and Boys Town presents excellent resources for teenagers in trouble and for parents.

7 Theology of Suffering

Why did you bring me forth from the womb? I loath my life. —Job 10:18a, 1a NRSV

Why do you hide your face, and count me as your enemy? —Job 13:24 NRSV

How much longer will you forget me, LORD? Forever? How much longer will you hide yourself from me? How long must I endure trouble? —Ps 13:1-2a TEV

My God, my God, why have you forsaken me? —Ps 22:1 NRSV

The secret things belong to the LORD our God, but the revealed things belong to us and to our children forever. —Deut 29:29 NRSV

A theology of suffering means reflecting on this world's suffer-ings—as much as we are able—from God's perspective. We feel the anguish of the world. We raise the biblical questions Why . . . ? How much longer? Why have you forsaken us? We realize we can't understand, that the secret things belong to the Lord our God. But for the sake of those who suffer and ask, we search for what has and is being revealed to us.

To some readers, this book has already brought an-guish and suffering. Theologian Karl Barth suggested start-ing each day with the Bible and a newspaper, yet if we follow current events we suffer vicariously. We may need to limit the amount of painful input, but to the degree we enter into the world's hurt, we must deal with the problem of suffering. Those who deal directly and daily with pain and loss suffer at even deeper levels. As we see and experience suffering, our need to see it through the eyes of Christ increases. Those who suffer need to do so with Christ. This seems easy to say, but what does it mean and how can it be realized? Martin Luther King Jr. once reminded us how his slave ancestors took the age-old question mark of the prophet ("Is there no balm in Gilead?") and bent it into an exclamation mark, singing, "There is a balm in Gilead . . . to heal the wounded heart!"

As we have said, our consideration of youthful struggles must begin theologically. What is God's perspective on troubled youth? How does God respond to suffering? Where is God when evil overtakes good people? How can we respond to suffering we don't understand? This chapter does not promise to answer all questions; it does consider approaches for dealing with those in deep pain. We will honestly probe the mystery of suffering.

Hearing the Cries

The Suffering of Children

"I'll start, chaplain," Thomas blurted. He was 24. There was still a boyish cast to his face, but something in his eyes denied innocence. His eyes spoke of dark alleys and long nights. "Where was God when I was raped. . . . Where was he? I was just a kid! I needed help. How could he let things like that happen? Where was he when I was being abused— raped again and again! Where in the hell was he? What was he doing?"

"That's a tough question. But it is real," I said aloud to the group. The words "tough" and "real" echoed in my head, and from within a critical voice taunted me, "Sometimes you are so profound."[1]

How would you have responded to this young man's cry? How would you face these prisoners when such a chal-

---

[1] Horace Duke, *Where Is God When Bad Things Happen?* (St. Meinrad, Ind.: Abbey Press, 1991), 9–10.

lenge is raised? There is no way out; nothing but sheer courage and compassionate realism will do. But do you simply
quote Scripture and pray with them? Do you leave as
quickly as possible? Do you give your best answer? Do you
shut up or turn it back to them? You're sitting there with
tough guys, vulnerable enough to demand some answers.
Can you hurt with them, depend on a higher response
from the Holy Spirit, then bring them and your questions
to Christ?

Horace Duke was the leader of that group; he faced the
challenge that day. As a prison chaplain, trying to respond to
the questioner and his small group of prisoners, he was
gripped by a nagging fear that he sounded phony. The opening chapter of his book describes that scene from a prison
spiritual-life therapy session.

The author continues, asking us to picture a nine-year-
old girl in bed hearing once again her father's (or stepfather's
or older brother's) approach. She cries out to the two
persons in all the universe who should care and protect:
"Mommy, don't let Daddy come in here!" "Dear God, don't
let it happen again!" Not once or twice but dozens and
scores and uncountable times over the years this terrible intrusion continues. Who can imagine the damage done, the
trust destroyed, the personhood crushed? Screams of "Why,
God?" and "Where were you, God?" rise from dark beds all
over the world. These cries challenge nice beliefs and shake
theological foundations. The people who cry out ask us to
get inside their skin and their pain—and inside their view of
God and the world.

A Teenager's Suffering

From prison and bedrooms we move to a hospital. On
July 30, 1967, seventeen-year-old Joni dove into shallow waters of the Chesapeake Bay and was paralyzed. Some people
seem to adjust from sudden accidents and affliction more
readily than others. The way Joni tells the story, hers was
a life too active and social to live as a quadriplegic. Joni
also seems very American . . . since in general Americans
don't deal well with pain, especially with pain that persists

and problems that can't be solved. In the agony of therapy, having lost mobility and health, happiness and hope—as well as many friends—Joni raised her cry:

> No one else is being punished like this. Why did God do this to me? . . .
>
> In bed for a year, completely dependent on orderlies and nurses . . .
>
> How much more can I take? I'm at the end of my rope! . . .
>
> The bedsores, stitches, bone surgery . . . and I'm still surrounded by canvas, catheter tube, and urine bags. . . . I'm trapped in this gloomy hospital where we sit like zombies waiting to die. . . . I'm trapped! Stryker frame, straps, and Crutchfield tongs . . . and God doesn't care. . . . He doesn't even care.[2]

Those of us who are healthy and mobile have no idea what life is like realizing—at seventeen—the loss of college life, career, romantic life, sex, and freedom. The terrible and constant physical pain and the loss of personal dignity and freedom, is something we cannot imagine. In the greater metropolitan area of the U.S. there are hundreds of young men in wheelchairs because they were wounded in shootings. Besides constant pain, one is trapped, bored, and suffering indignities of many sorts. Yet through this suffering Joni and many others have become unique counselors and inspirations to other disabled sufferers.[3]

Simone Weil[4] distinguishes between pain and affliction. One can suffer physical, psychological, or social pain, but affliction involves all three dimensions over a prolonged time. Joni endured this kind of affliction, compounded suffering that wouldn't go away.

---

[2] Joni Eareckson, *Joni* (Grand Rapids, Mich.: Zondervan, 1976), 79-80.

[3] You will find how Joni dealt with the theological issue of suffering not only in *Joni* but in a later book: Joni Eareckson Tada, *When God Weeps* (Grand Rapids, Mich.: Zondervan, 2000).

[4] Simone Weil, "The Love of God in Affliction," in *Waiting for God* (New York: Putnam, 1951), 117-18.

🦅 Gradually all of us must help ourselves deal with our pain and sorrow. A young seminarian sat in my office feeling disconsolate. I told him I heard him crying inside. "How do you comfort yourself?" I asked. He didn't know. He could easily comfort a crying child, he admitted. But he had no clue how to bring solace to the child within himself. Few of us do this well. We don't understand the multiple parts of our souls, and we don't think our inner self needs our comfort. The mere notion of this may sound too psychological, "New Age," or soft. Yet we need to tend our souls and hear our own cries before we can fully comfort others. In light of the truths of Lev 19:18 and 2 Cor 1:4, how well can you comfort your inner child? Of course our suffering sometimes goes beyond our capacity to console. At such times we cry out to God on account of the suffering that is more than we can bear—and hope for friends more faithful than Job's.

An Infant's Suffering

As an ethicist, Stanley Hauerwas struggles with the idea of suffering. He watched a baby in a neonatal ward taken off life support before an adequate diagnosis was made. It was the mother's wish, and the medical staff justified the decision according to quality-of-life logic. The baby might have to deal with severe physical problems, with ugliness, and with a mother who didn't really want him. Such consideration raises questions, among them: Is suffering an inevitable and necessary part of life and growth? This is a key question in our inquiry. Hauerwas continues: "What is suffering? What is its relationship to pain? How are suffering and death related? I suspect that such questions may be unanswerable as they are important, but I am going to try to make some headway on them."[5]

---

[5] Stanley Hauerwas, *Suffering Presence* (Notre Dame, Ind.: University of Notre Dame Press, 1976), 24.

We are forced to further questions: When and how should pain and suffering be escaped, anesthetized, or terminated? When and how must pain and suffering be accepted? The sudden death of a loved one is a unique loss. No death is easy or painless, but the lingering death of a child drains the life energy of anxious parents.

Parental Suffering

There is a particular poignancy in the pain of parents looking on suffering for which they can do nothing. Rabbi Harold S. Kushner's firstborn, Aaron, was bright and cheerful, but at eight months he stopped gaining weight and began losing his hair. Doctors failed to diagnose the boy's illness. When Aaron was three, the Kushners moved to the Boston area. The day their daughter was born, a specialist finally diagnosed their son as having the rare disease of progeria, or rapid aging. Aaron would never grow beyond three feet tall and would die soon after becoming a teenager. "How does one handle news like that?" Kushner asks, "What mostly I felt was a deep, aching sense of unfairness."[6]

The feelings experienced in such exquisite parental suffering are universal. The particular way we process such grief depends upon our culture, our personality, and our belief system. Here is how Kushner describes his religious faith and view of suffering at the time:

> Like most people my wife and I had grown up with an image of God as an all-wise, all-powerful parent figure who would treat us as our earthly parents did, or even better. If we were obedient and deserving, He would reward us. If we got out of line, He would discipline us, reluctantly but firmly. He would protect us from being hurt or from hurting ourselves, and would see to it that we got what we deserved in life. Like most people, I was aware of the human tragedies that darkened the landscape . . . car crashes . . . crippling diseases, retardation. . . . But that awareness never drove me to wonder about God's justice, or to question

---

[6] Harold S. Kushner, *When Bad Things Happen to Good People* (New York: Avon, 1981), 2.

His fairness. I assumed that He knew more about the world than I did.[7]

The assumption that the suffering we read or hear about will not happen to us or ours tends to be universal. But in their home was a suffering that could not be explained. Kushner relied on his worldview and his view of God to make sense out of his and his wife's pain and healing.

> It didn't make sense. I had been a good person. I had tried to do what was right in the sight of God. More than that I was living a more religiously committed life than most people I knew. . . . I believed that I was following God's ways and doing His work. How could this be happening to my family? If God existed, if He was minimally fair, let alone loving and forgiving, how could He do this to me?

> And even if I could persuade myself that I deserved this punishment for some sin of neglect or pride that I was not aware of, on what grounds did Aaron have to suffer? He was an innocent child, a happy, outgoing three-year-old. Why should he have to suffer physical and psychological pain every day of his life? Why should he have to be stared at, pointed at, wherever he went? Why should he be condemned to grow into adolescence, see other boys and girls beginning to date, and realize that he would never know marriage and fatherhood? It simply didn't make sense.[8]

True to predictions, two days after his fourteenth birthday, Aaron died. Even godly people cry out in pain. The pain of this young life and its premature death forced the rabbi to grapple with explanations of suffering in a bestseller that have helped many.

In my dark night, when everything collapsed and all seemed lost, friends backed off for a variety of reasons and with different motivations. The few who were there for me could not possibly understand. Those first few days, I stumbled through the motions of my work and could only pray, "Oh, God!" Gradually I was able to pick up a Bible and was drawn to the Psalms—first to Ps 57:1b, which I paraphrased,

---

[7] Ibid., 3.
[8] Ibid., 2.

"I will hide myself in the shelter of Your wings until this storm is past." The dark tunnel, the comforting Presence, and finally the guiding Light were, for me, unique in all history. I came away with precious scars God has used in special ways. Our wounds are all different; they cannot be compared. Though we ask for the wounds to heal, scars are left for the blessing of others—and ourselves.

Probing the Mystery of Suffering

Many people have given answers to sufferers. Some rely on a superficial interpretation of Rom 8:28: "All things work together for good . . ." Others remind sufferers to turn from sorrows they can't control to the God who controls all life's exigencies. Others may declare that the question is not Where is God when bad things happen? but Where are people? All assured answers to terrible suffering may contain wisdom but miss the core issue and immediate needs of the sufferer.

As a rabbi, Kushner had listened to countless stories of pain and suffered with people in their tragedies. Often these people explicitly or implicitly blamed their suffering on their sins. This is the simplistic religious answer; it was what Job heard from his friends as they tried to argue him into a confession that would make sense of their world. Kushner further quotes several Scriptures that teach "no harm happens to the righteous, but the wicked are filled with trouble" (Prov 12:21 NRSV). This is conventional wisdom on the matter, as Kushner points out: "By believing *that,* we keep the world orderly and understandable. We give people the best possible reason for being good and for avoiding sin. And by believing that, we can maintain an image of God as all-loving, all-powerful and totally in control."[9]

I don't find ultimate hope in this book. The rabbi's conclusion is found in the rather negative and cynical[10] wisdom of Eccles 9:11, 12a (NRSV):

---

[9] Ibid., 9.
[10] Compared with the more positive, traditional wisdom of Proverbs.

I saw that under the sun the race is not to the swift, nor the battle to the strong, nor bread to the wise, nor riches to the intelligent, nor favor to the skillful; but time and chance happen to them all. For no one can anticipate the time of disaster.

Still, the deep suffering of the Kushners provides insight. Those like Kushner and Job, who cannot accept the simple notion that suffering is a punishment for sins, are left with the dilemma of an all-powerful and loving God juxtaposed to innocent and (from divine perspective) preventable suffering. There are many intermediary causes of suffering, but the problem is God's ultimate responsibility as Creator. We may not accept Kushner's conclusion that God is not in control, that God is bound by the laws of his creation, and that there are no miracles to deliver the godly from evil. But Kushner forces us to reconsider our view of God and evil.

Certainly the Bible teaches that God punishes people for their sins (Lev 26:18; Isa 13:11; Luke 11:49-50; 1 Pet 4:17). Scripture also portrays God as chastising and disciplining us, who as children, athletes, and soldiers accept discipline (Ps 119:71; Prov 3:12; Heb 12:5-11). Healthy guilt may accompany punishment, and discipline calls for courage and persistence. Finally, some suffering, not from the Lord (we may infer), may be used for our growth and benefit (2 Pet 1:6-7). Accidents, illness, and injury from others fit into this category.

God's Place in Suffering

This consideration of suffering has put us is in the middle of the theological problem of evil. How can God be omnipotent, omniscient, and good when there is so much terrible suffering being endured by those God has promised to protect? How can a good God allow such bad things to happen in our lives? Predestinationists believe God must know and therefore ordain all that happens to us—good or evil—and does so for God's ultimate glory. Another popular and more liberal position is referred to as process theology; it sees God and humans struggling together amidst forces of good and evil—releasing God from control over, and responsibility for, evil.

A middle position denies that God fully controls all things (as the predestinationists believe), but it does not attribute imperfection or lack of knowledge to God (as held by process theologians). God knows all things but does not control all things. Late medieval theologians referred to this as the middle knowledge of God. Clark Pinnock, a contemporary theologian, describes this idea as the "openness of God."[11] Many scholars have criticized Pinnock, Greg Boyd,[12] and others for sacrificing or limiting the Almighty to provide us with acceptable human answers, but such theologians still must struggle with difficult mysteries to which none of us has adequate answers.[13] John Sanders describes this way of understanding sovereign God who allows things he does not determine.[14]

> If God is completely unconditioned by anything external to himself, then God does not take any risks. According to the no-risk understanding, no event ever happens without God's specifically selecting it to happen. . . . [15]

> According to the risk model of providence, God has established certain boundaries within which creatures operate. But God in his sovereignty decides not to control each and every event, and some things go contrary to what God intends and may not turn out completely as God desires. Hence, God takes risks in creating this sort of model.[16]

Although this is highly offensive to many kinds of conservative theology, the position more literally accepts bibli-

---

[11] Clark Pinnock, *The Openness of God* (Downers Grove, Ill.: Inter-Varsity, 1994).

[12] Greg Boyd, *God of the Possible: A Biblical View to the Openness of God* (Grand Rapids, Mich.: Baker, 2000).

[13] See also the excellent discussions of this issue in Clark Pinnock, Richard Rice, John Sanders, William Hasker, and David Basinger, *The Openness of God: A Biblical Challenge to the Traditional Understanding of God* (Downers Grove, Ill.: InterVarsity, 1994).

[14] John Sanders, *The God Who Risks: A Theology of Providence* (Downers Grove, Ill.: InterVarsity, 1998). Note title and see his Introduction, pp. 10–14.

[15] Ibid., 10b.

[16] Ibid., 10b–11a.

cal texts describing God as frustrated or changing his mind.[17] Our purpose is not to argue one position or another but to open the discussion about suffering in God's world.[18] Many great leaders and saints have experienced what must be described as the mystery of suffering. Grieving the loss of his beloved wife, C. S. Lewis questioned:

> Meanwhile, where is God? This is one of the most disquieting symptoms. When you are happy, so happy that you have no sense of needing Him, if you turn to Him then with praise, you will be welcomed with open arms. But go to Him when your need is desperate, when all other help is vain and what do you find? A door slammed in your face, and a sound of bolting and double bolting on the inside. After that, silence. You may as well turn away.[19]

Many people know these mighty sounds of silence in one way or other, and some need to utter their frustration and anger toward God. In the depths of my pain, I didn't feel the door slammed in my face. Instead I experienced an awesome silence and a sense that I must walk on through the dark alone, at least for a time. I remember crying out with a realization that my pain was real and wouldn't go away, that my cries were heard, and that somewhere there was a comforting Presence.

Some sufferers realize, at least after the fact, that the single set of footprints on the stormiest section of the beach were those of the Lord's carrying the hurt one on strong shoulders. But others, like Lewis, experience a walking alone through the storm with the Lord somewhere up in the mountains praying (see Mark 6:45-48a)—the footprints are theirs alone! Meanwhile, where is God?

The Suffering God

I am convinced there is no human solution or answer to the mystery of suffering. Theological mysteries can be

---

[17] Ibid.; see Sanders's "Old Testament Materials . . ." and "New Testament Materials . . ." Ch 3, 4, pp. 39-89.

[18] The answer may lie somewhere between—or above—open and closed theism.

[19] C. S. Lewis, *A Grief Observed* (New York: Bantam, 1963, 1976), 4-5.

answered only by further theological mysteries. We speak of the mysteries of the incarnation, the passion, and the *eschaton* (final and eternal resolution). Especially among young people, the crux of spiritual relief comes not from religion generally or from the institutional church but in a new view and relationship to Jesus Christ and loving people.

Reflecting theologically on suffering brings solace from the fact that God has not chosen to remove our suffering but to enter it. The mystery of the incarnation is that in Christ, we see a suffering God:

> For unto us a child is born . . . The mighty God. . . . Behold a virgin shall conceive and bear a son, and shall call his name Immanuel [which means God with us]. . . .
>
> Behold, my servant [says Yaweh] . . . He is despised and rejected of men; a man of sorrows, and acquainted with grief. . . . (Isa 9:6; 7:14; 52:13; 53:3 KJV)

I often tell the story of Ivan and Alyosha from Dostoyevsky's *The Brothers Karamazov.* After years of separation, Ivan, the agnostic, and Alyosha, the Christian monk, are together during their father's terminal illness. Ivan explains to his believing brother his general belief in God but rejection of God's ways in the world, especially as in the case of suffering. Narrowing his discussion to the suffering of Russian children, he tells the story of a five-year-old girl terribly abused by "respectable" but sadistic parents. One night her cries so bothered them that they filled the infant's mouth with her excrement and shut her away in an outside privy.

Ivan urges Alyosha to imagine this poor, innocent child beating her tiny fists against the cold outhouse floor, weeping "her meek unresentful tears to dear, kind God to protect her."[20]

And don't tell me that God will someday punish the parents, Ivan adds. That only brings more suffering into the scheme of things. Tell me, Alyosha, Ivan says, if you were the almighty and all-knowing God, would you consent to the fab-

---

[20] Fyodor Dostoyevsky, *The Brothers Karamazov* (Chicago: Encyclopedia Britannica, 1952), 127.

ric of your universe being woven with the threads of this one tiny creature's unavenged tears?

In the pause that follows, Alyosha shakes his head no, with tears glistening in his eyes.

> "No, I wouldn't consent," said Alyosha softly . . . "[But you asked] just now, is there a being in the whole world who would have the right to forgive and could forgive? But there is a Being and he can forgive everything, all and for all, because [He entered into our suffering and] gave His innocent blood for all and everything. . . ."

> "Ah! The One without sin and His blood! . . . I've been wondering all the time how it was you did not bring Him in before, for usually all arguments on your side put Him in the foreground."[21]

The violated God must be central in all our consideration of suffering. Are we comforted by a suffering God? Can God be said to suffer? To deal with such questions, we enter the tension between authentic biblical and systematic theology. We must acknowledge our need to speak of God metaphorically. In doing so we neither take metaphors too literally nor dismiss them as containing little truth. We acknowledge that Greek philosophers—followed by medieval theologians—denied any notion of passivity or passion in their concepts of God. We accept a biblical God who admits to feelings, grief, and frustrations.[22] Where such realities do not fit with our systematic notions, we admit to the mystery of it all.

The idea of God's suffering is strong in Terence Fretheim's biblical theology. In *The Suffering God,* he accepts the divine reality of a God who suffers because of his people (because they have rejected his love, Isa 7), a God who suffers with people who are suffering (Isa 8), and a God who suffers for the people (to bring them out of darkness and destruction to light and well-being, Isa 9).[23] The God who enters into our suffering does so in the form of a child called

---

[21] Ibid., 124–27.

[22] E.g., Hosea 11:8b–9.

[23] Terence E. Fretheim, *The Suffering God: An Old Testament Perspective* (Philadelphia: Fortress, 1984).

"God with us" ("Immanuel," Isa 7:14). This "child . . . born for us, the son given to us" is named "the Mighty God, the Everlasting Father" (Isa 9:6). Indeed, God did not send the Son into the world to condemn the world but that the world might be saved through him (i.e., through his sufferings, John 3:17).

Alyosha knew that One. It was clear to him that Christ alone fully understands. Christ alone experienced our suffering, and only Christ can fully comfort. It is to Christ, who experienced full human and divine suffering, that we look for healing and restored wholeness. Because he suffered and was tempted in all the ways we hurt and question, Christ is the mysterious link between a good God and terrible evil.

> For God sent not his Son into the world to condemn the world; but that the world through him might be saved. (John 3:17 KJV)

> Although he was a son, he learned obedience through what he suffered. (Heb 5:8a NRSV)

> [We have a high priest who is able] to sympathize with our weaknesses . . . who in every respect has been tested as we are. (Heb 4:15 NRSV)

> For our sake God made him to be sin. (2 Cor 5:21a NRSV)

I marveled at my first reading of Elie Weisel's *Night.* He confessed that his faith in God disappeared as he watched the smoke from the crematoria where babies were burned evaporate into the cloudless sky that day.

Later in this short, powerful book, I winced as I read how SS guards would punish even small violations by hanging offenders at the entrance of their crude dining hall. So dehumanized had they become, Weisel admitted, they could pass the body of a comrade and eat their daily meal.

But one day no one could pass, for hanging with an offender was a small child, hanged just because he was a helper of the man. That afternoon the barbarity of the sight forced the crowd to hold back. The man was dead, but the child's body so light, it still quivered in the noose. There was an awful silence until someone shouted out, "Where is God now?" After a long pause another voice responded: "There he is, hanging on the gallows!" Rarely had I been so deeply touched: this powerful story from an agnostic Jew had taken me to the heart of the Scriptures and the crux of Christian theology.

Bringing Suffering and Darkness to the Cross

The cross is the crux of our theology of suffering. The atonement, moreover, is just one part of the mystery of the incarnation; both mysteries are intertwined. A news reporter, disillusioned with the church, came to our seminary. To shock us out of complacency, he told the story of a recent rape and killing of a child. He was with the officers when they returned from the scene of the dreadful crime. He watched them pace the room in restless frustration. A couple of them stroked the pistols at their side until one of them blurted out: "F___ it all; I just want to shoot the bastard." The reporter asked us why the church is never present in situations like this.

The church is especially needed, we realize, since the church knows of mysteries that speak to the deepest frustrations of the human heart. There is only one place where the killer and little girl, sadistic parents and their abused child, Nazi guards and Jewish victims, can all meet.

The ultimate means of reconciliation, whether people and religions of good will recognize it or not, is the cross. God's response to human suffering is to be found in the mystery of the incarnation. We suffer, innocently or not, because we have left God. Still, God comes to us and enters our suffering. God enters the arena of human sin so that human beings may find redemption. According to Phil 2 (NRSV), the cross is part of the whole descent of the Son into our world. Paul there describes the incarnation as Christ emptying himself (of divine attributes of the "form of God"), being "born in human likeness . . . in human form," and becoming "obedient to the point of death . . . even death on a cross."

This death involved entering into our darkness, into the power and suffering of sin, and into hell (2 Cor 5:21; Matt 27:46b). This descent and death on the cross led to what

Jesus spoke of as "being three days and nights in the heart of the earth" (Matt 12:40 NRSV). It involved what Paul describes as defeating principalities and powers (Col 2:15) and reconciling all things to himself (Col 1:20; 2 Cor 5:19). The writer of the first epistle of Peter describes Christ as descending to the abode of spirits in prison. After descent into our deepest darkness, all is ascent—from the grave to life and from earth to heaven (John 20:17; Acts 1:9; Phil 2:9–11). This is the hope to which this book points.

Not only are we told that Christ suffered, but also we are reminded that Jesus wept. There must have been many reasons Jesus broke down after Lazarus's burial. Was one of them his realization that his timely arrival might have spared the sadness? What we do know is that Jesus felt all human emotions and sadness.

His tears over Jerusalem highlight the fact that Jesus loves systems as well as individuals. He understood why he had become so popular and knew the reasons for his rejection. This city and the Jewish people were the main focus of his life. Jesus is lamenting that the people have to suffer because they failed to listen to God.

The deepest sorrow of Jesus' life came in the garden before the trial and crucifixion. He wept for himself as he trembled before separation from God, but these were universal tears symbolizing compassion for the whole of human history and suffering. The cup (Matt 26:39) that Jesus prayed to avoid also symbolizes the price of redemptive suffering. As Jesus called James and John to share that cup (Matt 20:22–23), so Christ calls us to suffer with him for all who suffer (Col 1:24; 1 Cor 1:7).

Pastoring Those Who Suffer

Whatever your theological position on evil and suffering, you need a pastoral theology that works. Effective, theologically-minded pastors—be they Calvinists or Arminians, Catholics or Orthodox—have amazingly similar styles when it comes to dealing with people in extreme grief. Skilled and compassionate chaplains and comforters know there is much that cannot be explained, that God is compassionate and comforting, and that deep pain usually demands our silent presence. Each instance of suffering is unique in its particularity. That's what Job's accusers failed to understand.

> 🕊 How do you respond to someone's suffering to which you have no adequate explanation, and more important no words of comfort that make sense? Another question points you in a wise direction. What do you know of the ministry of silence? Job's friends ministered to him a lot more effectively the first week than the second (Job 2:13). Beyond a soft, "I'm sorry," the look in your eyes and your quiet, confident, and sensitive presence (knowing how close to get and when to leave) is usually the best way to deal with overwhelming grief.

Job's friends did several things that were right. They recognized his suffering, they came to his terrible suffering and wept, they tore their clothes and cast dust over their heads (a great sign of empathy in that culture). Finally they sat in silence for a whole week (Job 2:11–13)! Having done so much that was right and laudable, they proceeded to prove themselves so unhelpful that God had to intervene.

Philip Yancey describes three visitors who came to a young friend's bedside. She and her husband had been crushed by news of her lymphatic cancer. She began to suffer the ravages and indignities of terrible cobalt treatments. First, a solemn deacon dogmatically declared her a sinner who needed to repent: "Surely something in your life must displease God. Somewhere, you must have stepped out of God's will. These things don't just happen. God uses circumstances to warn us and to punish us. What is He telling you?"[24]

---

[24] Philip Yancey, *Where Is God When It Hurts* (Grand Rapids, Mich.: Zondervan, 1977, 1990), 5.

Next came a "plump, scatterbrained widow who had adopted the role of professional cheerleader to the sick. She brought flowers, sang hymns, and . . . read happy psalms about brooks running and mountains clapping their hands. Whenever Claudia tried to talk about her illness or prognosis, the woman quickly changed the subject."[25]

A third visitor was a devotee of faith-healing, money-raising televangelists. She insisted that God could heal Claudia if she had faith. "Sickness is never God's will! Haven't you read the Bible? . . . Remember, Claudia, faith can remove mountains and that includes Hodgkin's disease. Simply name your promise in faith, and then claim the victory."[26]

These three responses to suffering are all too common. Each represents poor theology and pathetic pastoral care.

As we deal with troubled youth and their families, we need to understand different experiences and beliefs about suffering. You may be with a mother screaming over the body of her son, or parents numb from the rape and strangling of their child. You may know a family abandoned by an unfaithful father. You may work with children traumatized by unspeakable agonies. Or you may know a young man about to avenge his brother's murder, or a teenager contemplating suicide. In all these cases, compassion and confidence are needed—compassion for someone who hurts more or differently than you can possibly know. You also need to convey confidence that life can and will go on.

My wife, Gail, and I were teaching a counseling course in Africa. A student in the class had traveled up country over a long weekend, and returning, had come upon an overturned bus. Approaching the tragic scene, he found a mother, crushed under the vehicle and evidently dying, still clutching her infant. Looking at her with compassion, he took the child and simply said, "It's all right, Mama." Then she was gone. That was good pastoral presence supported by African theology—a direct and simple faith that God is in

---

25 Ibid.
26 Ibid.

control, that God will take care of us in any bad situation, that we need simply believe and respond.

You will be thrust into similar pastoral crises—suddenly, unexpectedly, and in various and surprising ways. You will be called upon to be there: sensitively, usually quietly, with confidence, trusting in Christ your Lord and empowered by the Holy Spirit. You will respect the extreme differences of circumstances and responses, of questions and beliefs. You will accept as much pain as you are capable of handling. You will be confident. It is crucial that you believe in the resiliency of the human spirit, the healing power of nature and time, and especially the power of God's grace. In all this, you will need to accept the deep mystery of it all.

We cannot always distinguish physical, emotional, and spiritual suffering or how each focus of pain interacts within ourselves.[27] The mystery of suffering includes the mystery of its existence, the mysterious way in which it happens to us, and the mystery of healing. This mystery also demands further theological reflection. Let us consider further these challenges of healing and believing.

The Healing of Suffering

There is no easy or simple answer here because there is no single process of grief and healing. Denial, shock and numbness, questioning and bargaining, anger or sometimes a deep hurt and melancholy, depression, and finally, acceptance are usually seen as elements in the healing process. Some people deal with deep loss with quiet and private resolve to hurt, cry, remember, grieve, obey, strive, and heal. As we respect the various circumstances and immediate responses to suffering, so must we appreciate the different ways in which people heal.

A family may watch their mother die of cancer; the illness entails a long period of mourning. When she dies,

---

[27] Western medicine is beginning to learn from Eastern healing techniques in this regard.

there seems to be more relief than grief. Still the loss is important to them over the years that follow. A man loses a
precious spouse and within a few months is in love with another woman. We cannot deny his genuine grief or predict
how he will mourn for years to come. Some people seem to
move through the anguish of suffering or tragic death
in months; for others, the anguish is apparent for years,
maybe a lifetime.

Rejection can be more painful than death. To see the
body of a loved one lowered into the ground is terrible, but it
can be worse to know the body of your beloved is living and
in someone else's arms. In such cases, there's no funeral, no
closure, no formal social support. Adult society knows how
to sympathize when adults and children lose a loved one. But
we often miss an adolescent's extreme pain when young love
fails. People may think, "This is just puppy love; perhaps it's
even better this way." For young people the devastation of rejection and love lost may seem to be the end of all things.
And to sense parental relief that a relationship has ended
deepens youthful despair. Such adolescent pain can lead to
suicide. Few adults understand the tragic drama of adolescent hurts. Few can listen to it all non-judgmentally or without premature advice. Those who do understand youthful
suffering and despair can be wonderful aids in the healing
process.

You may find it helpful to compare emotional healing
with physical wounds. A friend of mine once became so
angry at his motorcycle, he revved it up full throttle. His bike
took off across the parking lot, hit a truck, and tore his leg
apart. We visited him in the hospital and looked into a
wound open to the bone. "It must drain and heal from the inside out," we were told. In a similar way, deep emotional
wounds cannot be closed too quickly. Some physical wounds
become infected and need to be lanced; emotional wounds
that fester must over time find catharsis from bitterness and
self-pity.

Emotional suffering leaves scars on the soul. Our wounds
need to be healed, but we do not want to lose the benefits of
the scars. Scars preserve some preciousness of what has been

lost and allow us to become wounded healers. Untreated wounds fester, but scars preserve memories and offer hope to other sufferers. Discussing this with a friend, she turned over her arms and said, "These are my scars." The marks were commemorations of early hurts; those marks gave hope and confidence to her as a wounded healer. In every significant loss a gift was given, which can be unwrapped over time and during recovery. Pain is a gift that protects and instructs.

Something in human nature wants to do away with pain and get over suffering. There is light at the end of the tunnel, we say. And sometimes we think that light is from an oncoming train charging dangerously toward us. Sometimes the tunnel is so long and has so many bends that no light seems possible. We need patience in going through such tunnels with people and wisdom to know when and how to encourage their acceptance and recovery.

Popular culture can shed light on various aspects of youth culture and is to be praised when it empathizes with youthful suffering and points to healing and reconciliation. But part of our darkness today is virtual, electronic darkness. Our critique of much found in mass media today is threefold:

- It manipulates children's and young people's fears and morbid curiosity.

- It loses redemptive benefits by glorifying violence as an end in itself and equating lust with love.

- It glorifies those who act without moral conscience.

Such gratuitous violence and sex are found in movies, television, video games, music, commercials, and on the Internet. Some of the most vulnerable of our society are dying under the influence of such dark voices, and many more are desensitized by its effects. Recognizing such evil does not trap us into blaming all or most of our ills on the media. There are many powers of darkness in our world. Child abuse and domestic violence in families, materialism, greed, racism and sexism in society, sensationalism in newscasts and docudramas, corruption and compromise in high places—these are powers that create havoc and suffering.

Popular culture is not primarily to blame for social decline, nor is it without redemptive features. Some drama has
confronted the evil of our times and suggested possibilities
of redemption more effectively than have Christian voices.
The world and pop culture have demonstrated their willingness to confront and name the demons and spiritual powers
of darkness behind human suffering in film dramas like *The
Omen* and *The Exorcist.* Such movies take us into the heart of
evil. Movies like *Superman* (1978) and *The Matrix* (1999) go
further. Their Christ figures enter the darkness of evil and
offer hope. They confront the powers behind suffering and
give them a name.

It is sad when popular culture replaces the church's prophetic and redemptive responsibilities. The mystery of the
incarnation involves Christ's entering all of human culture:

- to reclaim the material creation and demonstrate full
  human potential

- to proclaim the coming of God's kingdom

- to die for us as the Lamb of God

- to descend into the pit of darkness defeating all evil powers and releasing the captives

Youth ministers and seminarians sometimes ask me
what the Apostles' Creed means by "Christ descended into
hell." I'm not sure, but we must discover and proclaim a
Christ who names the darkest evil and confronts the powers
behind suffering. The church must not lag behind popular
culture's attempt to do so. St. Paul made a statement that has
never been rivaled and continues to astonish: "God made
[Christ] who had no sin to be sin for us, so that in him we
might become the righteousness of God" (2 Cor 5:21 NIV).

To contemplate the darkest sins and deepest suffering
laid on Christ—to think of Christ on the cross becoming an
oppressor, a rapist, a sadistic parent, or camp guard—is to
understand why Jesus prayed, "Let this cup pass from me."
To see him suffering as those most terribly abused at the
same time that he accepts the punishment for the vilest of
sins is to appreciate his suffering cry: "My God, my God, why

have you forsaken me?" This is the cross where "he was wounded for our transgressions and bruised for our iniquities." To this cross we take a suffering world.

It is only in the shadow of the cross that agonizing human questions about suffering can find not simple answers but some kind of divine response and human resolve. Suffering will ever remain a mystery to the human mind. If it cannot be answered, it can at least be endured. Where is the cross in this situation? How can this sufferer and I approach the cross? What will Jesus say as he looks down upon us?

Even closer than the connection between the incarnation and the cross is the way Christ's death, resurrection, ascension, and Pentecost blend in what Jesus referred to as his glorification (John 7:39; 12:23; 13:31). On the cross Jesus died for our hurt. Christ's resurrection heals our hurts, his ascension fills all our losses and voids, and the gift of his Spirit enables our scars to serve in the healing of the world. Some Christians emphasize the cross apart from the resurrection. It is essential to keep Christ's facing all evil and death together with his conquering all darkness, his taking the church up into heaven, and his future and glorious return. Our theology must move from creation to eschatology (re-creation), or we will be left floundering in a pit of despondency and burnout. The mystery of the incarnation includes the whole of Christ's descent into suffering, his ascension into glory, and his coming again. This is the great story we call the gospel or good news.

Our challenge is to hear the stories of those most troubled, to allow them to hear stories from their peers, and in that context share the greatest, deepest, most comprehensive of all stories. It is the story of God's redemption, and it is the basis for all human stories, including those of popular culture.

These are great truths, but still not enough to resolve all problems of suffering. Triumphalistic theology loses its power by attempting to comfort sufferers with overly simple answers and dogmatic demands for blind faith when we have been called to groan under the burden of unresolved issues.

We know that the whole creation has been groaning in labor pains until now; and not only the creation, but we ourselves, who have the first fruits of the Spirit, groan inwardly while we wait for adoption, the redemption of our bodies. (Rom 8:22–23 NRSV)

For all our theological reflection on suffering and Christ's victory and despite our understanding of and belief in the healing process, we still groan and wait. We try with Paul to "consider that the sufferings of this present time are not worth comparing with the glory about to be revealed to us" (Rom 8:18 NRSV). Praise God for the wisdom, strength, and faith of oppressed slaves who sang, "He may not come when we want him to come, but he comes on time!" With them and all other sufferers we wait the final healing and reconciliation of all things when "God will wipe away all tears."

The only survivor of a shipwreck found himself washed up on a small, uninhabited island. Surprised to be alive, he nonetheless grieved the loss of everything he held dear. Daily he prayed to God for rescue. But scanning the horizon for signs of help, he saw nothing and felt helpless and alone. Somehow he managed to build a little hut for shelter. This at least could store what he gathered and protect him against storms. One day as he searched for food and sustenance, he noticed his hut on fire and returned to find it burning to the ground. Stunned by grief and anger, he cried out to God, "How could you do this to me?" and gave up on prayer. All was now really lost and hopeless. The next day, however, the man was awakened by the sound of an approaching ship. It had come to rescue him.

"How did you know I was here?" he asked.

"Yesterday, we saw your smoke signal," his rescuers replied.

As sorrow does its work in our lives, we may be able to comfort others (2 Cor 1:3–4). And when we have come through suffering, our souls can find with St. Francis the desire to be instruments of peace and healing: "Grant, O Lord, that we may not so much seek to be consoled as to console; to be understood as to understand; to be loved as to love. For it is in giving that we receive; it is in pardoning that we are pardoned; and it is in dying that we are born to eternal life."[28]

Questions for Reflection and Discussion

1. What problems or special successes have you had in helping others in times of suffering?

2. What did you learn from helping others in times of suffering?

3. What was the deepest experience of suffering in your life?

4. What did you most need at that time? What helped pull you through?

5. What was most helpful and least helpful to you about this chapter?

6. What questions do you have from reading this chapter? How would you like to discuss them in a group?

7. What arc some things you can use from this chapter in your ministry with others?

8. Where might you go for a further study of suffering or the healing process? Consider using some of the books referred to as a starting point.

Book Resources

Helen Fitzgerald. *The Grieving Teen: A Guide for Teenagers and their Friends.* New York: Simon & Schuster, 2000. 🏃 A renowned counselor writes about and for teenagers in grief.

Marilyn E. Gootman, ed. *When a Friend Dies: A Book for Teens about Grieving and Healing.* Minneapolis, Minn.: Free Spirit Publishing, 1994. 🏃 A quick and helpful read for teenagers who have lost a friend.

---

[28] *The Book of Common Prayer* (New York: The Church Hymnal Society, 1979), 833. We say only that this prayer is attributed to St. Francis.

C. S. Lewis. *A Grief Observed.* London: N. W. Clerk, 1961, and later in the U.S. by Seabury Press and Bantam. 🕊 A confirmed bachelor finally met a woman he loved, Joy Davidman. Four wonderfully happy years later, she died. In his inconsololable grief, the famous writer began a journal with God. This journal describes his struggle to regain life.

John D. Morgan, ed. *The Dying and the Bereaved Teenager.* The Charles Press, 1998. 🕊 This book provides guidelines for dealing with death, suicide, and major transitions in school and family settings.

Gerald L. Sittser. *A Grace Disguised: How the Soul Grows Through Loss.* Grand Rapids, Mich.: Zondervan Publishing House, 1998. 🕊 This book has been of great help to many desperately grieving persons. When an accident took his wife, child, and mother, this author felt forced to make some kind of sense of it and to find an extraordinary comfort.

Sheldon Vanauken. *A Severe Mercy.* San Francisco: Harper, 1987. 🕊 This is another book for the mature who suffer deep loss. Vanauken shares insights out of a profound journey toward faith, from a deep love relationship which suffers jealousy when love for God enters the relationship, and from the termination of a rich marriage by untimely death. This book will help those who have suffered unfathomable losses.

Internet Resources

www.compassionbooks.com 🕊 Here are some 400 books and resources to help children, teenagers, and adults deal with serious illness, death, grief, and bereavement.

www.teencentral.net 🕊 This site is developed by KidsPeace, dedicated to helping older children and teenagers deal with crisis in their lives. At TeenCentral young people can ask advice or seek comfort from other teens using an anonymous codename. There are great benefits and limitation to peer counseling, of course.

Part 3

The Problem of Violence

8 Children and Trauma

Let the little children come to me, and do not stop them; for it is to such as these that the kingdom of heaven belongs. — Matt 19:14 NRSV

Most troubled teenagers have experienced trauma somewhere in their lives. Still, many traumatized children somehow do well in life. We need to know more about trauma and resiliency. Childhood trauma is occurring around us in urban, rural and suburban settings. Most studies of and response to childhood trauma have taken place in war zones. So, because we should know about this global suffering, and because we have much to learn from it, this chapter focuses primarily on children of war.

The consequences of war and terrorism are so terrible they cry out for explanation. What happens to children caught in sudden terror and violence drives us to consider the nature of warfare: Does it merely illustrate human political and cultural evils?

In apocalyptic style, Daniel describes spiritual beings behind military conflicts in his time (Dan 10). Paul, in his letter to the Ephesians (6:11–12), speaks of rulers, authorities, and forces of evil in heavenly places. These, he says, are not of flesh and blood. The Bible refers to spiritual warfare behind all the calamities of this life, and a variety of authors have picked up on that idea in our day. Spiritual wisdom suggests that we neglect neither spiritual nor social dynamics of military violence. What we are about to consider leads us to an appreciation of the demonic in social systems gone astray and begs a holistic response from social science and religious faith.

Children and Violence

In December 1998, according to Amnesty International, there were at least 300,000 children fighting wars around the world. A global survey by the Coalition to Stop the Use of Child Soldiers established a similar figure in June 2001. UNICEF reports two million children killed and six million injured by war in the last decade of the twentieth century.[1]

Historically the main casualties of war were soldiers, but broader battlefields and bombings brought civilian casualties up to fifty percent in World War II. More recently civilians make up ninety percent of war's injuries and fatalities world-wide;[2] women and children account for most of these. Today's wars force children to become soldiers, and children are deliberately targeted by snipers, as in the former Yugoslavia, in attempts to break the enemy's spirit.

The High Commissioner for the United Nations for Human Rights, Mary Robinson, describes war's changing codes: "civilians are no longer just victims of war—today they are regarded as instruments of war. Starving, terrorizing, murdering, raping civilians—all are seen as legitimate. Sex is no defense nor is age. . . . That is a strange, terrible state of affairs in the year after we commemorated the 50th anniversary of the Universal Declaration of Human Rights."[3]

Child Soldiers

Some newspaper readers fail to notice the youthful faces of Russian, Serbian, Albanian, or African soldiers. Around the world many of these young fighters are children and teen-

---

[1] United Nations Children's Fund, "State of the World's Children 2000, Undeclared War, Conflict and Violence: No Haven for a Child," 1, cited by Kurt Shillinger, "A World of War Sears a Generation of Youth," *Boston Globe,* 16 April 2000, A33.

[2] Op. cit. Shillinger, A33.

[3] Mary Robinson, online, 17 September 1999, www.unhchr.ch.

agers. "Colombia rebels are said to force teenagers into their ranks," announces one article. Another headline declares, "African armies . . . enlist 120,000 children," with a subheading: "UN, Amnesty groups say some soldiers are as young as 7."[4]

The U.K. Coalition to Stop the Use of Child Soldiers collaborates with the U.N. Children's Fund and Amnesty International. In 1999 this organization urged African governments to refrain from enlisting minors under eighteen into armed forces. Although boys are primarily recruited, rebel groups seek girls to be wives or consorts of young soldiers. A news release from UNICEF continues: "Some children volunteer to join the armed forces but tens of thousands of children are forced to join, up, sometimes at gunpoint. . . . Government-sponsored militias pose particular problems, as they are not adequately trained or monitored, but the worst abuses have been committed by armed opposition groups."[5]

The Child Soldiers Report of the CSUCS explains, "Often children are recruited because of their very qualities as children: They can be cheap, expendable, and easier to condition into fearless killing and unthinking obedience."[6]

In Rwanda some war orphans found refuge with army units, but more often children are exploited in combat situations. "When not engaged in combat, children are often used to man checkpoints. Adults tend to stand further back so that if bullets start flying, the children will be the first victims."[7]

Terrible atrocities have been committed by child soldiers. Reports from Liberia described drugged child soldiers coming into a village with candy—and then shooting the little ones who gathered. Olara Otunnu is UN Secretary General Kofi Annan's representative for children in armed conflict. He adds, "As the fighting parties run out of adults and as the adults become disillusioned the longer a conflict

---

[4] "African Armies enlist 120,000 children," Reuters news wire story from London, *Boston Globe,* 20 April 1999, A2.

[5] Ibid.

[6] Mike Collett-White (Reuters), "300,000 Called Child Soldiers: Some Aged 7 Said Pressed into Wars in Africa, Asia," *Boston Globe,* 13 June 2001, A14.

[7] Ibid., A2.

lasts, they turn more and more to recruiting children, by force or coercion."[8]

Guy S. Goodwin-Gill and Illene Cohn have written a book about child soldiers,[9] and other writings have reported the effect war has on young children.[10] Important questions drive these studies:

- How does the trauma of witnessing war's violence affect children in the short and long term?

- How does socializing children in the aggressive context of war affect their perpetuation of violence in the future?

- What can we learn about human resiliency and peaceful resocializing of children that might make for a more peaceful world future?

Children in War Zones

Five-year-old Jeton Hasani was extremely close to his grandmother. He would sit on her lap at night and watch cartoons while she knitted. One night the peacefulness of their lives was interrupted, first by NATO bombings and then by Serbian mortars directed against their town, Metrovica. Jeton's grandmother was struck running for shelter. The blast also shut off their electricity. In the dim glow of his father's lighter, Jeton listened to his bloodied grandmother gasp for breath and watched her die.

After the fifty-seven-year-old matriarch's burial, Jeton would not leave his mother. They were in the garden the next morning when the Serb paramilitary ordered them out of town. Piled on their tractor, they made it to a no-man's land on the Macedonian border. In a refugee camp, they

---

[8] Ibid.

[9] Guy S. Goodwin-Gill and Ilene Cohn, *Child Soldiers: A Study on Behalf of the Henry Dunant Institute, Geneva* (New York: Oxford University Press, 1994).

[10] Roberta J. Apfel and Bennett Simon, eds., *Minefields in Their Hearts: The Mental Health of Children in War and Communal Violence* (New Haven, Conn.: Yale University Press, 1996), and Keith Elliot Greenberg and Bruce Glassman, eds., *Bosnia: Civil War in Europe* (Children in Crisis) (Woodbridge, Conn.: Blackbirch Marketing, 1997), and similar publications to be cited.

were located in tent D-284. That night, "inside the tent, Jeton sat in his mother's lap, clinging to her and staring out at a descending darkness." They watched the continuous stream of refugees adding to the camp's misery: a mother crying over her dying twins; children crying incessantly, "I want to go home!" Military and relief workers tried to bolster children's spirits and begin the healing with games, sports, and jokes.

Nearby Johona seems to be responding and adjusting differently. "See the five-year-old girl over there laughing on a swing?" someone asks. Her name is Johona Alieu, and she was found a few days ago wandering alone through no-man's land. No one knows about her parents. Three older women from her village have taken her in. "I have three grandmothers," the giggling girl explains. A math teacher, twenty-eight, who has fled Pristina, says, "Children are so resilient. Look at them." But there is also deep hurt under the surface.

> You can't see the damage in Jeton's eyes or in the shy smile he gives a stranger. But it is there, his parents say. He doesn't sleep. He is easily frightened. He won't leave his mother's side.

> "He is at an age where he will never forget," says Fatmire Hasani, 30, his aunt. "We're afraid this image [especially of the grandmother's death] will never disappear. He wakes up at night . . . very afraid and never lets his mother leave him."[11]

In April of 1999, when President Bill Clinton visited Kosovo, he was introduced to a large audience by a fourteen-year-old boy: "You promised to bring us back to our homes, and you did. We love you, President Clinton," the boy said. For some of the president's speech there was wild applause. But he went on to reflect on Kosovo's suffering and the aftermath of war: "The time for fighting has passed. Kosovo is for you to shape now. . . . No one can make you forgive those who have inflicted such pain on you, but that is what you must try to do." At these words there was no applause, only silence. Afterwards adults told reporters, "We [Albanian

---

[11] This and other quotations in this story are from Charles M. Sennott, "For Kosovo's Children of War, the Wounds Run Deep," *Boston Globe*, 18 April 1999, A1, 31.

Kosovars] can never live with them [the Serbs]. Look at what they have done to our children. Some are still traumatized." This is the challenge.

Even children ask and conclude, as did one Albanian girl: "How can they kill children? I am always angry and mad and unhappy. I can never forgive the enemy."[12] Serbian kids have said the same things, as have Palestinian and Jewish girls and boys, Catholics and Protestants in Northern Ireland, Hutus and Tutsis in Rwanda. And yet, could it be that these children may in the future lead their elders toward the reconciliation that adults see as neither possible nor desirable? Creative programs for Jewish and Arab young people in the Middle East and special integrated schools of Catholic and Protestant students in Northern Ireland offer hope.

To witness the devastation of war upon children and to listen intently to innocent victims tell about their loss of limbs or family is to resolve that we must end the killing. The consequences of war for children are so devastating the world must accept a new moral imperative to reconcile human differences—whether caused by ethnic memories and desire for revenge, religious and cultural clashes of values, greed, or lust for power. Making peace must become the highest priority of a civilized world. We will need the leadership and creativity of children, and they must see in us genuine models of peace and authenticity.[13]

Domestic and Neighborhood Trauma

Childhood trauma is by no means limited to war zones. Describing studies on childhood trauma in Texas, *U.S. News and World Report* prefaced Shannon Brownlee's article with a picture of two very small boys standing attentively while medics treat a victim shot outside their housing project. The article begins by describing three little girls at Houston's Texas Children's Hospital. You would not imagine from their

---

[12] Alan and Susan Raymond, "Children in War," documentary shown on HBO.

[13] See Hans Küng's *Global Responsibility: In Search of a New World Ethic* (London: SCM, 1991) and *Yes to a Global Ethic* (London: SCM, 1996).

appearance that two days ago two armed men raided their apartment, tied them up, and shot their older sister in the head. The youngest, age three, was specifically threatened with a gun. Now as they sit quietly and calmly—and despite the time lapse—their little hearts are still racing at more than one hundred beats a minute. Their blood pressure also remains high. More ominously, the experts tell us, the biological chemicals of fear change the structure of their brains.

One of these experts is Bruce Perry, child psychiatrist at Children's Hospital and Baylor College of Medicine. "People look at kids who seem so normal," he notes, "and say, 'All they need is a little love.' Actually the results are far longer lasting."[14]

> A single traumatic experience can alter an adult's brain: A horrifying battle, for instance, may induce the flashbacks, depression, and [the] hair-trigger response of post-traumatic stress disorder. And researchers are finding that abuse and neglect early in life can have even more devastating consequences, tangling both the chemistry and architecture of children's brains and leaving them at risk for drug abuse, teen pregnancy and psychiatric problems later in life.[15]

Understanding Childhood Trauma

Early studies of trauma looked at adults such as war veterans, but Perry is one of those particularly interested in the effect of trauma on children. "The event will play itself out in the mind of a child again and again."[16] Storytelling, drawings, and play help children to do this. "The more outside the range of the normal experience and the more life-threatening the experience, the more difficult it will be for the normal mental mechanisms to work efficiently to process and master that

---

[14] Shannon Brownlee, "The Biology of Soul Murder: Fear Can Harm a Child's Brain. Living with Fear Puts Children at High Risk for Problems Later in Life," *U.S. News & World Report,* 11 November 1996, 71.

[15] Ibid., 72.

[16] Bruce Perry, "The Effects of Traumatic Events on Children: Materials for Caregivers," Civitas Initiative, Baylor College of Medicine, 1994, 2.

experience."[17] When acute post-traumatic stress responses last beyond six months, a "child or adult is then considered to be suffering from post-traumatic stress disorder."[18]

Post-traumatic stress syndrome (PTSS) describes the various symptoms that follow a person after serious trauma. Post-traumatic stress disorder (PTSD) is the term used for the pattern of symptoms affecting such an individual:

- reexperiencing of the traumatic event, flashbacks

- the emotional numbness that usually follows: a gradual withering of previous interests, personal involvement, and the ability to feel and be intimate

- a variety of symptoms such as hyperalertness, failure of concentration and memory, and sleeplessness

Most of us know this, but what has not generally been known is the long-term effect such trauma has on children. Psychiatrist Martin Teicher at McLean Hospital, in Belmont, Massachusetts has added to Perry's research, finding fewer nerve cell connections in the brain's left hemispheres of children who had been abused.

G. Straker (1987) urged the addition of a new category in trauma effects diagnosis: Continuous Traumatic Stress Syndrome. This research, combined with the studies of Dawes and Tredoux (1989), make it increasingly clear that ongoing violence affects children more than a single terrible event.

Among the many studies of childhood trauma, not enough attention has been given its moral and spiritual aspects. Gita Sereny is an insightful European journalist who after World War II worked with children, mostly from ages four to twelve, who had been traumatized by experiences in the camps or as forced laborers. She makes some interesting points about the differences in results and what they had in common.

> Some were silent to the point of being catatonic. Others were hyperactive, talking not only all day but through the night in their sleep. Some wanted to be held, others trembled

---

[17] Ibid.
[18] Ibid.

at the least touch and pulled away. But one thing almost all of them had in common on arrival, and for many weeks afterwards, was an absolute rejection of anything that smacked of moral concepts. The words "good" and "bad" had no meaning for them; their faces went stiff, their eyes blank at any attempt to explain the necessity of a few rules for their safety.

There was a minimum of imposed discipline, but at the slightest indication by an adult of disapproval or impatience, many of them exploded, forcing us to watch them acting (for acting it was) wilder, "badder," more knowing in every way than they essentially were.[19]

The UN report *Children and War: A Call for Protection* speaks to the breakdown of moral sensibility as it quotes a child soldier and then comments:

"I've killed more people than I can remember. We are given drugs in the daytime to make us brave to fight. In the evening we are given alcohol to make us forget what we did. But the memories keep coming back—I can't forget."

Forced to lay aside the innocence of childhood, they are immersed in a sea of adult hatreds to learn to kill or be killed for causes they don't fully understand in a world increasingly hostile to their experience.[20]

Dr. Neil Boothby also observed the moral effects of war on the six- to sixteen-year-old Mozambican boys served at the Lhanguere Reception Center:

I have come to learn that [the child soldier's] re-entry into a society is as much a moral struggle as a psychological one: a long, often anguished quest into one's own soul to discover the very moral sensibility that was obliterated through having committed what, in nearly every culture, is the gravest sin of all.[21]

Wartime trauma in children clearly includes the shock and pain of atrocities seen, of torture and injuries experienced, as well as results from violence they themselves may have

---

[19] Gita Sereny, *Cries Unheard* (first American edition) (New York: Henry Holt & Co., 1999), 104–5.

[20] Quoted in Phyllis Kilbourn, ed., *Healing the Children of War,* (Monrovia, Calif.: MARC, 1995), 19.

[21] Ibid.

committed. War's trauma includes for children tremendous losses—of childhood, play and school, home and community, family and friends, safety and security, innocence, beliefs and moral development.[22]

These children exist in what Lars Gustafsson (1986) has called a "triangle of chaos." There is the trauma and confusion within themselves, the disruption and pain of torn families, and the "chaos within the community and family." Phyllis Kilbourn notes how psychosomatic symptoms, regressive reactions, and aggressiveness fill the limited space around the triangle of chaos in the circle of a child's life: "The triangle of chaos limits the space available for creating incoming information about violence, losses, and exploitation. The triangle of chaos blocks the children's abilities to communicate their true feelings and it conceals what is really going on inside the children."[23]

Treatment of Traumatized Children

Kilbourn came to appreciate the power of the triangle of chaos while working with children of the civil war in Liberia. There she developed a program described as a STOP sign model.

> Caregivers helping such children must also try to stop the devastating process of chaos—strengthening the mitigating factors—through planned interventions. A basic strategy, symbolized by the "STOP" sign, is used. . . . Each letter of "STOP" represents an important action for helping children overcome by the psychological traumas they have experienced in war.
>
> S = Structure . . . decide which structures we can reestablish for the children, or perhaps we will need to create some new ones until the restoration of the former ones.
>
> T = Talking and Time . . . Talking . . . is the starting point in the children's healing process. The children need someone who is ready to listen to them. In war, parents and other adults often are so preoccupied by their own fears and sorrows that they reject or neglect the children's stories.

---

[22] Ibid., 11–30.
[23] Ibid., 140.

O = Organized Play. Play is important for a child's normal development. Children regard playing activity as real, and it is their way of gaining life experiences. . . . When children are surrounded by adults experiencing fear and grief, they do not feel that they dare play and enjoy themselves. Play . . . also . . . brings children into touch with their feelings and to the children these feelings seem too dangerous to handle. So the children keep quiet. Interpreting children's actual playing behavior is one of the tools used in psychotherapy for children. Role playing and artwork provide meaningful ways for children to express the horrors of their experiences . . . and release emotional tensions. Play also restores and preserves cultural traditions, thus helping children to regain a sense and feeling of normalcy.

P = Parental Support. The influence of parental support is considered the most important factor for all children whether in war or in peace. . . . Therefore we must be careful to ensure that all our efforts to help children traumatized by war include the parents or other significant caregivers. . . . We must provide children with a sense of belonging.[24]

Asad Isazadeh, a remarkable physician living in Baku, Azerbaijan, leaves his home every weekend and travels three hours to work among Azerbaijan's one million refugees in camps. His mission is preventing violence among children and youth who have been traumatized by war. He tries to explain the emotional scars these kids have suffered:

The older children remember the horrors of war. They are kids who may have seen the heads of parents severed in front of them, or friends drown next to them as they tried to swim across a river.

Under normal circumstances such trauma gradually disappears, but these refugees don't live under normal circumstances. In the camps, a youth can get into a fight over a small matter and often it becomes a fight to the death.[25]

This cycle of violence has been interrupted by the intervention of volunteers like Isazadeh and organizations such as

---

[24] Ibid., 145–46.
[25] Ruth Daniloff, "Tending to Children's Inner Wounds from War," *Boston Globe,* 23 January 2000, G2.

the Norwegian Refugee Council called BUTA (an ancient Zorastrian symbol for fire and, according to myth, the symbol of transformation). Correspondent Ruth Daniloff describes the mission of BUTA as "transforming traumatized children into responsible citizens, through art, sports, music, and storytelling."

Isazadeh further explains: "Ordinary psychotherapy doesn't work. Most of the people here are from rural areas. The parents tell us their children aren't insane so they don't need psychological help. We have to treat them without treating them as patients."[26] Isazadeh has also organized a children's democratic government in the refugee camp. He's gotten them to elect deputies, a judge, five ministers, and a newspaper writer. There's a lot of argument, but their decisions are wise. Therapy merges with effective education for the future.

The doctor realizes that "saving the children is a monumental task, and maybe impossible. But to fail is to lose an entire generation. I could not save our land [he says referring to his stint as a soldier fighting against Armenia] so all I can do is try to help save the people."[27]

🦋 As a young couple you and your spouse decide to take in four desperately needy children from a ravaged war zone, the ages are 1 to 3. You have one 2-year-old child and decide to have no more of your own. One of you will stay at home, and the other has a well-paying job. Consider the difficulties involved in such a venture. With whom might you want to discuss this matter and upon what resources could you draw? What are some alternative ways to help the millions of desperate children in this world?

---

[26] Ibid.
[27] Ibid.

Resiliency and God's Grace

Twin beliefs must accompany those who minister to those traumatized by deep suffering: faith in (1) the amazing resilience of the human spirit and in (2) the power of the God's grace ("where sin increases, grace abounds all the more," Rom 5:20b NRSV, with change in verb tense). Paul's explanation of salvation—contrasting Christ to Adam—also summarizes the story of the Bible. Book after book of Scripture describes human failure, greed, chaos, and violence. Judges is a dramatic example, with its continuing cycles of human rebellion, evil consequences, cries for help, divine grace, and deliverance.

The Bible also records the strength of the human spirit. Job is smashed down to the point of total loss; still his spirit is not crushed. Joseph, with only a youthful dream to sustain him, experiences shame and adversity for thirteen years. Yet he manages not only to endure but also to distinguish himself as a house servant and as a prisoner. The divine spirit in all humankind (see Gen 2:7) is not weak but surprisingly resilient.

By resilience we mean the ability, after being stretched or bent, to return to an original shape. It describes the ability to recover from serious injury or misfortune. Resilience requires a set of characteristics that promote successful healing, adaptation, and growth in the face of high risk and harm.

Children are amazingly resilient. In the face of terrible trauma, however, their resilience needs effective support. UNICEF tells of an African girl ten years of age who was forced to witness her mother being raped and then murdered. For two years the girl became a concubine for the rebel soldiers. Finally she managed to escape and make her way to a hospital:

> A nurse realized there was something particularly wrong with the girl. In addition to having contracted a sexually transmitted infection, she was very withdrawn and sad. Encouraged by the nurse's soft and caring treatment, the girl told her story. She repeated it later to a social worker and was moved to a foster home, where she developed a close relationship with her foster mother. At the girl's wish, a

traditional cleansing ceremony was held to rid her of all the
bad things that had befallen her.[28]

If we would heal, we must discover cleansing ceremonies
and healing rituals. The inner resilience of children can be reinforced in many ways. When we are sensitive, creative, and
open to the Spirit, we will also find opportunities for grace
to intervene. It is crucial to understand resilience and grace.

In 1954 Drs. Emmy Werner and Ruth Smith began their
famous study tracking 698 infants born in 1955. They were
able to follow 505 of them over a thirty-year period. About
one third of these children were designated by the researchers as being at high risk on the basis of four or more risk
factors at birth and/or in their early years. What these researchers found, as have several other longitudinal studies, is
that a third of the children from high-risk situations overcame adverse circumstances. They dealt successfully with
stress that leads others into crime or bouts of mental illness.
The resilient ones overcame the odds.

> Two-thirds of these children [who encountered four or more
> such risk factors by age 2] did indeed develop serious learn-
> ing or behavior problems by age 10 or had delinquency
> record, mental health problems, or pregnancies by the age
> they were 18 years old. Clearly the odds were against them.
>
> Yet one of three of these high-risk children grew into compe-
> tent young adults who loved well, worked well and played
> well, and expected well. . . . They succeeded in school, man-
> aged home and social life well and set realistic educational
> and vocational goals and expectations for themselves. . . . By
> the end of their second decade of life they had developed
> into competent, confident and caring people.[29]

What are the characteristics of resilient youth? Traits
mentioned are usually insight, autonomy, relationships, responsibility, initiative, humor, and morality. These might be

---

[28] Graça Machel, UNICEF, "Impact of Armed Conflict on Children."
Online: www.un.org/rights/introduc.htm, "Promoting Psychological Recovery and Social Integration," 5.

[29] Emmy E. Werner and Ruth S. Smith, *Overcoming the Odds: High
Risk Children from Birth to Adulthood* (Ithaca, N.Y., and London: Cor-
nell University Press, 1992), 192.

restated as social skills, problem-solving skills, optimism, and a strong sense of purpose.

The question remains as to why some people are more resilient than others. That still seems to be a mystery. Most researchers admit the importance of inherited qualities or constitutional differences, but there is no way we can be sure about resiliency's internal factors. Werner and other researchers suggest the following external factors bringing positive results:

- strong family nurture

- ability to find other sources of help and support

- an important person outside the family circle

- being well liked by friends and peers

- ability to make school a sanctuary or home away from what may be a chaotic family situation

- participation in extracurricular activities

- help from a church group, youth leader or minister

Resiliency begins with a person's determination to survive and optimism about doing well, and healing entails telling one's painful story. Recovery from trauma gathers support first of all from those closest at hand and then in larger social circles. It often has a specifically spiritual basis.[30] Resiliency is reinforced by achievement.

Heroic Resiliency in Children

Justice and Peace in Colombia

Many adults don't realize the great potential for leadership in children and youth. They haven't heard the dramatic stories of children in Colombia, South America. Not knowing that the longest conflict in the Americas has been waged in

---

[30] James Garbarino, *Lost Boys: Why Our Sons Turn Violent and How We Can Save Them* (New York: Free Press, 1999). This psychologist has studied trauma and resiliency in boys for thirty years and concluded that "the ultimate resiliency lies in the spiritual life" (159).

Colombia (from 1948 to the present; more than half a century, first as a civil war and then violence between drug lords and the government),[31] they fail to understand what children have accomplished there.

Children were terribly harmed and increasingly involved in Colombia's violence, as victims and also as forced soldiers. Finally children began to do something about their plight, and what they accomplished merited their being nominated for a Nobel Peace award in 1998.

Sara Cameron, consultant and freelance writer, came back from Colombia with astounding stories. The country's Children's Movement for Peace began to emerge in the 1990s in regions where violence was most fierce. The town of Aguachica, in eastern Colombia, held a referendum on violence that was destroying the town. A thirteen-year-old boy, Juan Elias Uribe, asked the mayor if children could vote. Excited about the positive affirmation he received, Juan toured the town, playing peace songs on his guitar and urging children to vote. They did so, but most people saw this as merely a quaint and childish symbol. It represented, however, something much more substantive.

Near the town of Apartadó, guerrillas and paramilitaries were resorting to terrible atrocities, and children were both victims and witnesses. Farliz Calle, fifteen, lived in the midst of this with her two sisters, brother, and parents, both of whom were plantation workers. Apartadó was about to receive a visit from a famous researcher and children's advocate, Graça Machel, expert of the Secretary-General of the United Nations and now married to Nelson Mandela. Apartado's mayor, Gloria Cuartas, asked the area's children to prepare a presentation for Ms. Machel and helped the children use a Week of Reflection to decide what they would present. Support for this preparation came from the Roman Catholic Church, the Red Cross, and UNICEF as well as the town. From five thousand children who assembled from schools in fifteen townships, a core committee of twenty students was

---

[31] Barry Turner, *The World Today: Essential Facts in an Ever-Changing World* (New York: St. Martin's, 2000), 196.

formed. They helped arrange the stories, poems, letters, pictures, and sculptures created by the children. They also com-
posed a touching Declaration of the Children of Apartadó.

> We ask the warring factions for peace in our homes and for
> them not to make orphans of children, to allow us to play
> freely in the streets and for no harm to come to our small
> brothers and sisters. We said that while it is not in the power
> of children to stop the killing and assassination, we must
> always denounce it. We wrote that neither the guerrillas or
> the paramilitaries held the solution to our problems and they
> had no role to play in the future of Apartadó. On the contrary,
> we—the young people—need to be a part of those solutions
> so that our own children will not suffer as we have done.[32]

The presentation was a great success, but most adults
did not expect it to accomplish much. Farliz, however, was
part of a group of students who found out about their rights
under the new constitution (1991) and formed a local government of children. They chose Farliz to be the first child
mayor of Apartadó. Nearly two hundred children came to
meetings three times a week. Farliz began a habit of rising before dawn—working on children's matters, along with her
schoolwork and home chores, until late at night. She and her
friends were realistic:

> We were very disorganized in the beginning. We knew there
> were limits to what children could do—for example, we
> could not stop the violence ourselves, we could not stop pov-
> erty, hunger, or unemployment.

> I never speak out against any particular group. If I did then I
> know I could become a target. Once a journalist tried to trick
> me into saying things that were dangerous, just to get a story.
> He would have sacrificed me for that. All the children in
> Apartadó know they must be careful about what they say.
> This is not difficult. When you live with fear, silence is natu-
> ral. We describe the violence but we do not know who is re-
> sponsible for these terrible events. We simply do not know.

> Peace cannot happen immediately, we know that. The young
> people in Colombia, those who are 15 and older, are the ones

---

[32] Sara Cameron with UNICEF Columbia, "The Children's Movement
for Peace in Columbia" (1999), 3 (by permission of the author).

who are really going to make the difference . . . the children
who are 7 years old and younger are the ones who will
enjoy it.[33]

Violence, killings, and kidnappings continue in Colombia, but a new spirit of peace and possibilities is also spreading. And the children are leading the way to hope in a just and peaceful Colombia.

Crusading Against Abuses in Child Labor

When he was only four, Iqbal Masih's family borrowed money from a wealthy carpet maker to pay for their oldest son's wedding. Iqbal was given to the carpet factory's owner to serve as security until the loan was repaid. He joined other child weavers who, twelve hours and day and six days a week, made tiny knots for expensive carpets.

By the time he was ten, Iqbal realized that high interest rates on the family debt made his redemption impossible. At the age of twelve, and helped by a human rights organization, he freed himself from slavery and got into school. In time Iqbal Masih was able to help more than three thousand child laborers escape from servitude. For this he was brought to Boston, where he received a Reebok Human Rights Award.

Back in Pakistan, Iqbal was murdered while riding his bike. Most independent investigators believe he was killed by the carpet mafia, but the official line is that it was an accidental shooting.

Craig Kielburger, twelve, was being home schooled in Canada. As a pastime he loved to read the comics in the *Toronto Star.* One day it was the headlines that caught his attention: "Boy, 12, murdered for speaking out against child labor."[34] Craig read on to find out the boy was Iqbal Masih. Craig discovered that worldwide, 250 million child workers work half or full time in sometimes hazardous conditions. With his friends he began organizing an organization called Free the Children.

---

[33] Ibid., 3–4.

[34] Free the Children. Online: www.freethechildren.org/info/whatisftc1b.htm, "History: How Did Free the Children Begin?"

This group of children wrote petitions and letters to people of prominence. In that first year, Craig was asked to speak in Toronto to an audience of two thousand at the Ontario Federation of Labor Convention. His time was limited to three minutes, but Craig spoke for fifteen minutes and received a standing ovation. Union members were so touched that they donated $150,000 for a rehabilitation center for freed child slaves in Alwar, India.

Craig has traveled to many countries, had speaking engagements in schools and hearings, appeared on CNN and *60 Minutes,* received prestigious awards, written *Free the Children.*[35] He is proof that a person doesn't need experience and education before speaking out.

The story of Iqbal also touched an American girl, fifteen-year-old Elizabeth Bloomer of Braintree, Massachusetts. Inspired by the young Pakistani, Elizabeth created a local chapter of a national organization, Operation Day's Work, in its crusade against child labor abuses worldwide. In March 2001 she joined other speakers addressing the General Assembly of the United Nations. "I didn't intend to be a spokesperson," she says. "There are a lot of kids who are spokespersons too. . . . I've realized the power kids have to make a difference." Elizabeth is dedicated to telling the story of Iqbal Masih and has helped her chapter raise more than $100,000 to build a Pakistani school to memorialize him.[36]

🖋 You and a couple of friends decide to set up a feeding station in an urban slum of a poor, developing nation. The number of children you are feeding keeps growing and news of what you are doing draws money from donors. Discuss why this might not be the best way to deal with the issues of street kids and hunger.

---

[35] Craig Kielburger with Kevin Major, *Free the Children: A Young Man Fights Against Child Labor and Proves That Children Can Change the World* (New York: HarperCollins, 1998).

[36] Sandy Coleman, "Child's Death Stirs Another's Crusade," *Boston Globe,* 2 March 2001, B1, 7.

Storytelling for Hope and Action

Christiane Amanpour saw herself as an international news correspondent who could take anything, including the suffering of children, professionally. After she became pregnant someone asked her if she would continue her crazy life:

"Oh, yes, and I'm looking for bulletproof Snuglies for the baby too!" I was determined to prove a professional woman can actually do it all. . . . I am able to dash off virtually at a moment's notice because I am lucky enough to have live-in help. My husband and I also agree to avoid traveling at the same time.[37]

But life and her perspective have changed:

Until you have your own child you never really understand the power of a parent's love and concern. . . . In the past decade, I have witnessed the effect of war on children from Africa to Afghanistan, Bosnia to Kosovo, and now in the Middle East. Too often, they are victims of their parents' wars. My reporting always has been affected by the sight of children who have been hurt or killed. But now, as any mother reading this will understand, it is sheer torture to enter a ward of moaning, wounded children. I am so much more aware that this kind of trauma suffered by children, wherever they are, could sow the seeds of sadness and strife for at least another generation.[38]

This war correspondent imagines the day her son will be old enough to look her in the face and ask, "Mummy, why do you go to those dangerous places? What will happen to me if you get killed." Echoing a theme of this book, she considers her reply: "Because I have to. Because if the storytellers quit, the bad people will win."[39]

An ancient Hebrew psalmist once wrote, "Out of the mouths of babes and infants, you have founded a bulwark"

---

[37] Ziv Cohen and Corbis Sygma, "Internal Strive," *USA Weekend,* 15–17 December 2000, 7.

[38] Ibid.

[39] Ibid.

(Ps 8:2a NRSV). Centuries later Jesus, quoting the psalm, affirmed the wisdom and courage of children:

> the children [were] crying out in the temple . . . [the chief priests and scribes] became angry and said to him, "Do you not hear what these [children] are saying?" Jesus said to them, "Yes; have you never read, 'Out of the mouths of infants and nursing babies you have prepared praise for yourself'?" (Matt 21:15–16 NRSV)

Another time Jesus thanked God for hiding crucial things from "the wise and intelligent" and "reveal[ing] them to infants" (Matt 11:25 NRSV).

Communities and societies are weakened when they ignore their children. It is not easy to listen seriously to children, but the path of hope for our times lies in serving the vulnerable, hearing their stories, and empowering them for action.

We must not only listen to and learn from children. We must offer them alternative models of athletics without angry aggression, games without excessive competitive pressures, adventure without evil violence, success without putting down others. We look for creative ways to model strong, peacemaking leadership.

This chapter describes deep resilience in children. It is also a story of grace: common grace outside the Christian community and the faith of believers. When God's people do not respond to human need, others will step forward to model divine intentions. We are deeply indebted to those Christians who have brought the grace of our Lord Jesus Christ into troubled situations. Where children are traumatized, we hope for an intersection of resilience and grace.

Questions for Reflection and Discussion

1. What three words would you use to describe the main ideas of this chapter?
2. What three-point outline would you give this chapter?

Questions, cont'd.

3. What struck you most forcefully as you read this chapter?

4. Can deep hurts be healed? How?

5. How do you understand resiliency, grace, and healing?

6. What in this chapter did you not understand, and how could you get more insight into that issue?

7. With what here did you disagree? Would it make for profitable discussion?

8. Why is reconciliation so difficult?

9. What part might children play in reconciliation?

10. What leadership and service can we expect from children and young people?

11. What is the role of adults in children and youth initiatives?

12. What concern and what hope do you take from this chapter?

Book Resources

Linda B. Hunter. *Images of Resiliency.* Palm Beach, Fla.: Behavioral Communications Institute, 1998. 🏃 Called Sandplay Therapy, this "impressive and deeply touching" book will show you how severely troubled children can be reached through sandplay and stories.

Douglas Wead. *The Compassionate Touch.* Minneapolis, Minn.: Bethany Fellowship, 1977. 🏃 The amazing ministry of Mark and Hulda Buntain brought God's grace to poor children of the streets trapped in prostitution, begging, and drugs. The book is honest enough to admit "failures" as well as "successes."

Internet Resources

www.bbc.co.uk/worldservice/people/features/childrensrights/
   childrenofconflict/wounded.shtml ⚐ The BBC World
   Service is an important site of statistics, general information, resources, and ways to help: "6 million children
   have been wounded in armed conflicts in the past 10
   years. . . . Mental health experts estimate that over the
   past decade some 10 million children have been psychologically traumatized by war. . . . An estimated 10 million
   land mines have been laid in Afghanistan and most
   of those killed or injured by land mines are children."
   p. 1, 2.

www.kidspeace.org ⚐ The goal of this site is to develop and
   propagate resources and services designed to cultivate
   resiliency in all kids.

www.savethechildren.org ⚐ National bases in several countries target help especially to children suffering with
   HIV/AIDS or from the ravages of war and land mines.

www.unicef.org ⚐ The United Nations Children's Fund (for-
   merly United Nations International Children's Emergency
   Fund, thus the acronym) exists to provide information
   about and aid to these children: "Every year 11 million
   children world-wide die from preventable causes." See
   "Voices of Youth."

9 | Suburban Shootings

You have killed them in a rage that has reached up
to heaven. — 2 Chron 28:9b, NRSV

A rush of analysis and attempted explanation followed school shootings that shocked the U.S. and the world during the 1990s. William Romanowski, a Calvin College scholar, quotes a British journalist who watched U.S. response to the 1999 Columbine tragedy:

> The religious right blames what happened on the federal ban on prayer in the schools. The Internet, where one of the suspects had a web site, was severely criticized, as were violent movies, television shows and video games. Child psychologists were happy to talk about how we don't encourage our boys to share their feelings. . . . The antigun lobby used the shootings to rail against the easy access to guns. But the progun lobby, incredibly, blamed the shooting deaths of the 15 people on the fact that we don't have *enough* guns. . . . The perennial white racist politician David Duke could not resist labeling the massacre a product of "diversity."[1]

How are we to understand and deal with such violence against classmates? Suburban school violence seemed to be under control by the end of the 1990s, but a spate of shootings and copycat threats occurred across the country in the spring of 2001. The debate regarding causes became more heated, and the second anniversary of Columbine brought bitter criticisms about the handling of that crisis.

Human response to violent tragedies range from numbness to hysteria, denial to blame, defensiveness to guilt, and

---

[1] Quoted by William D. Romanowski, *Eyes Wide Open* (Grand Rapids, Mich.: Brazos, 2001), 46–47.

apathy to impulsive interventions. My intention is to strike a balance: to care and examine, to understand and respond. We should not be dismayed by what is still a mystery, nor should we be dogmatic about what we think we comprehend. Can we approach God's perspective? Can we come to greater understanding and compassion in order to respond more effectively?[2]

Our society too often notices trouble in affluent, white suburbia while ignoring pain in cities, in rural areas, and on Native American reservations. According to the U.S. Department of Justice, for instance, Native Americans are twice as likely to be victims of crime as are blacks, whites, or Asians. The 1990s showed an overall decline in violent crimes against blacks (thirty-eight percent), whites (twenty-nine percent) and Hispanics (forty-five percent). Violence against Native Americans was about the same in 1998 as it was in 1993. Native American women are twice as likely to be abused by their partners as are black women. Native American violence is also considered more underreported than in other groups. James Alan Fox, a criminal justice professor at Northeastern University, assessed these findings: "The staggeringly high rates of violence, especially domestic violence, reflect the impact of severe poverty, alcoholism, and lack of access to social and legal support systems and education."[3]

Suburban whites have come to see urban shootings and the blight of drugs as urban realities, but when youthful suburban crises arise, they become national issues. To its discredit, America accepted the drug epidemic of the early 1960s until it hit white suburbs later in the decade. Inner-city drive-by killings were and remain casual news items, but middle-class school shootings in the 1990s brought national concern from media, politicians, and the public. Racism and class prejudice explain the difference.

---

[2] The godly wisdom of Prov 3:5–7 is important. We do our best to understand but do not rely on our insights or become wise in our eyes. Acknowledging God's moral order, we seek a balance between judgment and mercy.

[3] Karen Gullo, "Indians Likeliest Violence Victims," *Boston Globe,* 19 March 2001, A3.

Distress among urban, rural, and suburban young people ought to concern us and motivate us to make their lives fairer while ameliorating as many negative pressures as possible. The setting of this chapter is suburban violence, but its principles are of broader value.

This is a disconnected generation, in which too many young people feel rejected. Because much disconnection begins in the home, we will consider in the next chapter attachment and conduct disorders. Since so much of the rage in school shootings comes from teasing, taunting, and bullying, we must also consider rejection from peers. Finally, in a general way, many youth feel isolated from society.

Voices of Pain: Victims and Victimizers

Outsiders to school shootings ought to be careful in approaching a subject around which there is so much lingering pain. Individual experiences of pain should serve as reference points as we try to understand the larger picture of violence. In two school years, 1992 to 1994, ninety-nine students were killed in ninety-seven incidents. Here are just a few examples:

March 24, 1998. Mitchell Johnson, thirteen, and Andrew Golden, eleven, pull a fire alarm, retreat to higher ground, and open fire on classmates and teachers as they exit Westside Middle School in Jonesboro, Arkansas. Four girls and a teacher are killed and eleven students are wounded.

The boys are tried in juvenile court. This means that, while they are charged with five counts of capital murder and ten counts of battery, they cannot be convicted of murder and cannot receive a life sentence or the death penalty. Johnson pleads guilty. Golden pleads not guilty due to mental incompetence. Both boys are found guilty of juvenile delinquency and are sentenced to the custody of the Arkansas Division of Youth Services, which can hold the boys until they are twenty-one years old.

April 26, 1998. Fourteen-year-old Andrew Wurst shoots and kills a teacher, wounding two students, at a high school dance near Edinboro, Pennsylvania. Apprehended behind the school with marijuana and a hand gun, the boy is shown laughing as he is driven away.

May 19, 1998. High school senior Jacob Davis, eighteen, shoots and kills a fellow student, Nick Creson, eighteen, as they argue over a girl's affection in the Lincoln County High School parking lot in Fayetteville, Tennessee. This takes place just three days before they were to graduate. After shooting his classmate, Davis drops his gun, sits down, and puts his head in his hands. A passing friend stopped to say, "Man, you just flushed your life down the toilet." Davis responded, "Yes, but it's been fun."[4] He is now serving a life sentence.

May 21, 1998. In Springfield, Oregon, Kip Kinkel, fifteen, is expelled from Thurston High School for gun possession. The next day, after killing his parents at home, Kinkel arrives at school and opens fire in the school cafeteria. Twenty-six students are shot, two of them fatally. In police custody, Kip is hysterically disconsolate over killing his "good parents." Tried as an adult, he pleads guilty to four counts of murder and twenty-six counts of attempted murder. His sentence: 111 years in prison.

Craig Scott was in the midst of the shooting at Columbine High School on April 20, 1999. He was in the library with friends wounded and dying around him. He relates how he rounded up several students and escaped through a back exit, only to learn that his sister was one of the first people killed. He tells about feeling God's presence. Still, such trauma and loss don't heal quickly. It's been a long process for Craig, and it isn't finished yet. His parents see a serious side to Craig and a tendency to blame himself. He needs to keep things ordered and under control, and psychologists told his parents that such persons have a more difficult time rebounding from trauma. But Craig assured his mom he was all right.

---

[4] Timothy Roche, "Voices from the Cell," *Time*, 28 May 2001, 36.

The summer after the Columbine tragedy, Craig traveled with his father to speak to large audiences night after night. His parents thought it would be a good way of working things out and serving others, but speaking left Craig deeply exhausted and he felt a surging grief. Recurring flashbacks made him struggle with the notion of forgiveness and keeping himself sane. It became difficult for him to concentrate and focus on the questions put to him. Relying on a strong, personal faith, he struggled through the terrible grief process that such trauma and loss requires.

In March 2001 the country was aghast at the news of another school shooting. Charles Andrew Williams, fifteen, was seen, with a smile on his face, shooting and reloading in the corridor of Santee, California's Santana High School. He killed two and injured thirteen with a small-caliber pistol. The same day an eighth-grader became the first girl added to the list of school shooters when she allegedly shot thirteen-year-old Kimberly Marchese in the shoulder; this girl was planning to shoot herself until she was talked out of it.

In the two days after television and papers carried news of the California shooting, the Associated Press counted at least a dozen reported acts of school violence or serious threats.[5] ABC News reported that from the Columbine tragedy (20 April 1999) to April 2001, there were five thousand threats of school violence in the U.S., costing communities on average $50,000 each.[6]

A sad and instructive story lies behind Charles Andrew Williams's shooting spree. His parents divorced when he was about five. His older brother went with his mother and settled in North Augusta, South Carolina. Charles stayed with his father, first in Frederick, Maryland, and then, from November 1999, in the San Diego area. His brother remembers Charles being picked on from his early youth: "He has big

---

[5] Bryan Robinson, "Unflattering Imitation: Experts Explain Alleged Copycat Incidents after Santana Shooting." Online: abcnews.com, 8 March 2001.

[6] A report on the two-year anniversary of Columbine. Online: abcnews.com, April 2001.

ears and he's real skinny. People pick on him. It was like that as long as I could remember."[7]

According to sophomore classmate Scott Wilke, sixteen, "Even the people who got picked on picked on him. He would never defend himself at all. You could take the money out of his wallet, you could take the shirt off his back and throw it in the gutter and he would just walk away. He always told me he was going to get people back, but I never thought he would shoot people."[8] Twice his skateboard was stolen. Kids even took away his shoes.

> No matter how much he tried, and try he did, nothing about Williams seemed cool. Nice but dorky, as one friend says, a skateboarder who couldn't do tricks. A mediocre bass player. He talked a good game, acquaintances say, but was really just a poser, covering festering resentment.[9]

A final humiliation may have been his breakup with a twelve-year-old girlfriend. Kids spread rumors that he had tried to get her drunk. Fellow skateboarder Tony Friends, fourteen, watched Williams get jumped, pounded, and punched four times in the face. The next week he and two neighbors filled squirt guns with urine and shot folks in their apartment complex hallways.[10] Days later it was bullets.

Sunday, before the shooting, Katie Hutter, twelve, told Williams, "You don't have the guts to do it. . . . Next thing I heard, he shot at my sister. And that is just not cool."[11] Obviously, the full story goes far beyond the headlines.

Charles Andrew Williams was saving a bullet for himself, but the police cornered him in the boys' room before he took his life. Some of the teasers, and those with whom Charles shared his plans, wonder about their part in the tragedy.

---

[7] Quoted from an Atlanta paper by CBS News. Online: www.channel2000.com, 7 March 2001.

[8] Nancy Wride and Nora Zamichow, "Suspect Described as Troubled, Puny, and Picked-On," *Los Angeles Times*. Online: latimes.com, March 6, 2001, archives.

[9] Ibid.

[10] Ibid.

[11] Ibid.

Less than three weeks later and just six miles away from Santee, another shooting took place. At Granite Hills High, Jason Hoffman cut morning classes and showed up at noontime with a 12-gauge Mossberg shotgun and a .22-caliber pistol. Aiming at Vice Principal Dan Barnes, he began firing. Three students and two teachers were injured. According to a law enforcement officer, Jason claimed the vice-principal "always wished me dead" and thought his attendance policies caused him to be rejected by the navy a few days earlier. He had been disqualified, recruiters said, for being twenty-five pounds overweight, because of a skin condition, and having a record of assault against a fellow student.

Unlike the puny, taunted Williams, Hoffman was eighteen, six feet tall, and 230 pounds. Fellow students described him as large and intimidating, a muscular loner who had few friends.[12] As strong as the bully factor is in many of these shootings, no single explanation fits all. If Hoffman was bullied, it seems it was by systems he couldn't satisfy and standards to which he couldn't conform.

The incredible pain of these events exists in the terrible deaths and injuries that have marred lives and families forever. Further pain has come from frictions and enmity among victims and observers of the aftermath. Yet the resilience of the human spirit and the grace of God can be seen in the way students and adults struggled to recover. Pride and courage took students back into those halls. Images come to us from Columbine of students reaching out to each other. Craig Scott with the father of his deceased friend, Isaiah Shoel, Craig and his father speaking to audiences across the country, the high school's principal wearing a T-shirt "WE ARE . . ."

Years after the shootings, some boys are unwilling or unable to show remorse. Andrew Wurst is delusional; his mother's request for special therapy has been denied. Luke Woodham is refused counseling or opportunity to study. Mississippi Commissioner of Corrections Robert Johnson says, "We don't make any pretense about trying to rehabilitate

---

[12] MSNBC and wire reports. Online: www. msnbc.com, 24 March 2001.

someone who is going to spend their natural life in prison. What's the use?"[13]

Yet Woodham has written to *Time:* "If there's any way that I can, I would like to help stop these shootings."[14]

Evan Ramsey says, "I sit there, and I wish, I wish, I wish, I wish I didn't do what I did. I wish I would have known the things that I know now."[15]

And he wishes the two friends who egged him on had instead turned him in.

Jacob Davis, who once said killing the boy who had had sex with his girlfriend was fun, is now a different person. Plagued by nightmares and insomnia, he says, "When you got someone else's blood on your hands, it's not an easy thing to deal with. I will suffer my own personal hell the rest of my life. There's nothing you can do to make it go away. I'm truly remorseful for what's happened. He's gone, and I can't bring him back."[16]

🐾 **Thomas French** (see "Book Resources" at the end of this chapter) and **Patricia Hersch** are two adult journalists who took a year of their lives to enter the high school subculture. At first treated indifferently, and even with a bit of hostility, they both edged their way into the respect and confidence of teens in their respective high schools. They were accepted and given an intimate look into the high school scene and the lives of its students because they seemed to care and listened carefully. The books written as a result of their experiences have helped many. What would it take for you as an outsider to get into the heart of a high school's life . . . and what could you do from such a vantage point?

---

[13] Roche, "Voices from the Cell," 38.
[14] Ibid., 36.
[15] Ibid., 35.
[16] Ibid., 36.

Who or What to Blame?

Differences of opinion over proper responses to these tragedies have brought animosity and hurt. Those who endured these slaughters and those watching from a distance may be at variance in perspective. Both, however, have a right—perhaps even the responsibility—to analyze and comment. For the sake of perpetrators, victims, and prevention, we must try to understand these killings. Strong cases make the immediate villains to be guns[17] and violent video games.[18] Around the world, critics point to U.S. society as a violent one,[19] although many more violent crimes are committed in Columbia and South Africa. Among the developed countries, Australia, the United Kingdom, Finland, France and Netherlands had higher percentages of victims of violent crimes in 1999.[20]

Some people point to our loss of religious faith and the general moral decline of U.S. society.[21] It is a culture without

---

[17] Deborah Prothrow-Stith, *Deadly Consequences: How Violence Is Destroying Our Teenage Population, and a Plan to Begin Solving the Problem* (New York: HarperCollins, 1991). This book was written about urban shootings, but its analysis of guns in U.S. society and suggestion of making such instruments of death a public health issue is powerful. John R. Lott Jr., *More Guns, Less Crime: Understanding Crime and Gun-Control Laws,* Studies in Law and Economics (Chicago: University of Chicago Press, 2000) gives a contrary view. The author's multiple regression analysis in a January 1997 issue of *Journal of Legal Studies* created a furor. This book is a fuller argument that concealed-weapons permits reduce the crime rate.

[18] Dave Grossman and Gloria Degaetano, *Stop Teaching Our Kids to Kill: A Call to Action Against TV, Movie, and Video Games* (New York: Random House, 1999). Retired Lt. Col. Grossman has been a principal spokesman on how video games desensitize people to violence and encourage them to kill. Studies are cited showing that children are not only conditioned to kill but also taught the skills to do so.

[19] Michael A. Bellesiles, ed., *Lethal Imagination: Violence and Brutality in American History* (New York: New York University Press, 1999). These essays examine the role of violence in America's development, institutions, and voluntary associations. A primary theme in entertainment is violence, and primary exports of the U.S. are violent movies, video games, and media.

[20] From the International Crime Victims Survey of 2000, as reported in *The Economist,* 24 February–2 March 2001, 58.

[21] William J. Bennett, *The Index of Leading Cultural Indicators: American Society at the End of the Twentieth Century* (rev. ed.; Colorado

civility, they say—people enjoying painful disclosure and fights on talk shows. Music and media objectify women and make them fitting targets of male lust and anger. After careful scrutiny and documentation of current studies, the Hatch committee concluded: "The effect of media violence on our children is no longer open to debate. Countless studies have shown that a steady diet of television, movie, music, video game, and Internet violence plays a significant role in the disheartening number of violent acts committed by America's youth."[22]

Still open to debate is how and why media influence children and youth differently and what a democratic society can do about it.

Blame has also been placed on gothic subculture and the way young people dress and distort their bodies. Others see the occult or satanism behind many bizarre acts of violence. One theory puts the blame on the side effects of drugs (Prozac and Ritalin) some of these boys were taking.[23] Neurologists have suggested early brain damage,[24] and a biologist looks at this violence in evolutionary terms.[25]

Parents are particularly blamed along with the absence of positive role models in our society. In terms of the terrifying

---

Springs, Colo.: Waterbrook Press, 2000); see author's introduction and chapter on youth pathologies; also, James Davison Hunter, *The Death of Character: Moral Education in an Age Without Good and Evil* (New York: Perseus, 2000).

[22] Senate Judiciary Committee Media Violence Report. Majority staff of Senate Committee on the Judiciary, Chairman Orrin G. Hatch (14 September 1999), "Children, Violence, and the Media: A Report for Parents and Policy Makers."

[23] Jon Rappoport, "School Shootings in America: Why Did They Do It?" The Truth Seeker Foundation (San Diego). Online: http:/truthseeker .com, type "school violence" in search field.

[24] Nicholas Regush, "What Goes On In the Minds of Kids Who Kill?" Abcnews.com, quoting Michael Gazzaniga, a brain scientist from Dartmouth, and Dorothy Lewis, a New York University psychiatrist who has been compiling evidence for ten years regarding early head injury and later violence.

[25] Lyall Watson, *Dark Nature: A Natural History of Evil* (New York: HarperCollins, 1995). Although the author explains aggressive evil as a product of natural selection (261), he believes children who kill and serial killers cannot be explained in terms of mental illness but by an evil that exists in them (229). This evil has come from inheritance and experience.

event at Columbine, questions were raised about police, who, exchanging shots initially and hearing the shooting inside, made no decisive move. One father whose son was murdered wondered why so many kids but no police were shot. (Strategic response to school shootings has been changed.)

> 🏂 Could you imagine a public high school as your "parish"? How could you intervene in a way that would have avoided most of the shootings in this chapter? With whom did the most troubled kids in this chapter have to talk? How might you have gotten their stories from them? What good might that have done?

Some police officers expressed guilt because they had been repeatedly tipped off regarding Eric Harris's deadly threats, yet the Jefferson County sheriff's office failed to request a warrant to search his house. His web page was known. His violent videos were edited in class. Teachers knew about his violent tendencies. The investigation and its public relations also came under criticism. It seems as if everyone in the country has become angry with someone over these incidents, even as the boys predicted. The killers promised to visit us with flashbacks and, returning as ghosts, to drive us insane.[26]

It was especially painful for me to read hate-laced web pages making heroes out of devious killers and mocking images of slain victims. Discussions among a small minority of young people, extremists on both sides of the cultural divide, descend to obscene vitriol. In all this we sadly review the sickness of a society, many of its observers, and the perpetrators.

There is some truth in the attempts to pin the blame for ghastly events on something or someone specific. Few of us are willing to understand the idea of a whole society derailed, but if we are to get to important key factors, we must

---

[26] Nancy Gibbs and Timothy Roche, "The Columbine Tapes," *Time*, 20 December 1999, 42.

be willing to see the whole picture and accept our particular responsibility in what is not just a suburban American but a global problem.

Observing Behaviors and Communication

The fact that the shooters were almost always boys shows a great deal about how differently we socialize boys and girls. In a workshop or classroom write the words "boys" on one board or newsprint and "girls" on another. Then ask participants to give words or phrases that describe or are important to each. For girls, you will hear words describing appearance, relationships, or feelings. For boys, you will hear words like "muscles, strength, sports, competition, skateboards, fighting, spitting." These are the ways our society looks at and expects boys and girls to be. Still, there are the questions about why some boys explode when others do not. There are profiles, but no profile fits all. A euphemism for "profile," a "threat assessment," emphasizes actions and behavior rather than looks or type.[27]

The two-year FBI study of the incidents emphasizes that their model is not a "profile of the school shooter or a checklist of danger signs pointing to the next adolescent who will bring lethal violence to a school. Those things do not exist."[28] The FBI has put together a careful study of fourteen school shootings of the 1990s and four other episodes in which violence was averted by police intervention. Its emphasis is not on identifying troubled youth per se, but it provides help in assessing the seriousness of threats based on objective behavior.

---

[27] Mary Ellen O'Toole, *The School Shooter: A Threat Assessment Perspective* (Quantico, Va.: FBI Academy, 2000), a thirty-six-page report listing twenty-eight traits. See also Byran Vossekuil, Marisa Reddy, and Robert Fein, *Safe School Initiative: An Interim Report on the Prevention of Targeted Violence in Schools,* U.S. Secret Service National Threat Assessment Center in collaboration with U.S. Department of Education, a nine-page report that categorizes six incident characteristics with eight findings and implications.

[28] O'Toole, *The School Shooter,* 1.

The study sets up criteria for judging the type and seriousness of a threat with a four-pronged assessment model for evaluating specific cases. The model looks at the "personality of the student, family dynamics, school dynamics and student's role in those dynamics, and [broader] social dynamics."[29]

The model identifies twenty-eight clues to a student's personality as observed in his behavior. Among them are:

1. Intentional or unintentional clues to feelings, thoughts, fantasies, or intentions signaling an impending violent act.

2. Is easily bruised, insulted, angered, and lacking tolerance for frustration.

3. Lack of resiliency, being unable to bounce back from failures, setbacks, or disappointments.

4. Feelings of rejection or humiliation over love lost or a broken relationship.

5. Resentment over real or perceived injustices with an inability to forget or forgive over time.

6. Signs of depression: lethargy, fatigue, or a morose outlook on life.

7. Is self-centered; blames others for disappointments and lacks empathy for others.

8. Behaves as though he feels different from others. More than a loner, feels isolated and estranged. Appears introverted and has acquaintances or associates rather than friends.

9. Dehumanizes others, being unable to see them as fellow human beings but rather as objects or inferior beings.

10. Senses himself as superior, smarter, more creative . . . even though he may have low self-esteem. Has an exaggerated sense of entitlement.

11. Poses an exaggerated or pathological need for attention.

---

[29] Ibid., 10.

12. Externalizes blame and refuses to take responsibility for his actions.

13. Displays an inappropriate sense of humor . . . which may be macabre, insulting, or mean.

14. Is untrusting and chronically suspicious of others while at the same time attempts to manipulate or con others into agreement with him.

15. Appears rigid, judgmental, and cynical, with strong opinions not backed by facts, logic, or reasoning.

16. Has an unusual fascination with violence and violent entertainment along with negative, inappropriate role models like Hitler or Satan.[30]

Threats should be taken more seriously when the following behavior can be observed in family dynamics:

1. Turbulent, with difficult relations between students and parents. May express contempt for parents.

2. Parents fail to react to behavior that most parents would find disturbing or abnormal. Parents tend to deny or overlook pathological behavior.

3. Family keeps guns, and student has access to weapons. Guns may not be adequately secured or may be left loaded.

4. Family is not close and seems to lack intimacy . . . may have moved frequently or recently.

5. Student seems to rule the roost. Boundaries, limits, and rules seemed to have been broken. Parents may seem intimidated or in denial.

6. Parents are not able to limit or monitor music, television, or Internet use. Computer may be off limits to parents or beyond their understanding.[31]

Difficult it may be, especially for a school, to assess the school dynamics, it is important to understand the following factors:

---

[30] Ibid., 16–21.
[31] Ibid., 21–22.

1. The degree to which a student is "detached from school, others in school, and school activities."

2. The ability of the school to control and punish disrespectful behavior and to control bullying. (The National Threat Assessment Center found attackers felt persecuted or threatened, attacked, or injured in more than two-thirds of thirty-seven school shootings.[32]

3. The degree to which there is perceived inequity in the disciplining of students . . . how fairly rules are enforced.

4. The inflexibility of the school in a changing society and its ability to meet the needs of newer staff and students who are different.

5. The degree to which administration esteems, or caters to certain types of students, treating some groups or cliques as elite.

6. The strength of students' "code of silence"; their willingness to report concerns about other students . . . the level of trust between students and staff.[33]

The fourth prong of this model considers social dynamics. It focuses attention on:

1. The student's unmonitored access to violent movies, television shows, computer games, and Internet sites.

2. The student's involvement with a group who share a fascination for violence and extremist beliefs.

3. The student's use of drugs and alcohol and attitude toward these substances.

4. The student's interests outside school.

5. The copycat effect among alienated youth. Threats increase after each publicized shooting incident.[34]

Intervention, this report concludes, should begin with a clear school philosophy; involvement of all students, staff, and parents; the appointment of a threat assessment coordi-

---

[32] Nadya Labi, "Let Bullies Beware," *Time*, 2 April 2001, 46.
[33] O'Toole, *The School Shooter*, 22–23.
[34] Ibid., 23–24.

nator; and a multidisciplinary team. "It is especially important that a school not deal with threats by simply kicking
the problem out the door. Expelling or suspending a student
for making a threat must not be a substitute for careful threat
assessment and a considered, consistent policy of intervention."[35] Most experts agree that zero tolerance is a counterproductive approach to youthful violence.

The U.S. Secret Service is used to studying terrorism and
assassination plots, but the school shootings of the 1990s led
to a special study between the Secret Service National Threat
Assessment Center and the U.S. Department of Education
with support from the National Institute of Justice. The
range of its style and methods has produced new perspectives and policies.

Few people realize that U.S. school shootings began in
1974, when a student came to school with guns and homemade bombs and began shooting at janitors and firemen who
responded to the alarm he set off. This study examined that
shooting and those since: thirty-seven school shooting incidents involving forty-one attackers. For an incident to be
included, "the attacker(s) must chose the school for a particular purpose (and not simply as a site of opportunity).
Shootings that were clearly related to gang or drug activity,
or to an interpersonal or relationship dispute that just happened to occur at the school were not included."[36]

These incidents took place in twenty-six states, and
were all committed by boys or young men. In more than
half of the incidents, school staff were targeted; in more
than two-thirds, more than one students or staff were
killed; handguns, rifles, and shotguns were the primary
weapons used. The incidents were almost always planned
at least days before hand. "In virtually all of the cases in this
study, the person told a peer—a friend, schoolmate, or sibling. In only two cases did such a peer notify an adult of the
idea or plan."[37]

---

[35] Ibid., 26.
[36] Vossekuil, Reddy, and Fein, *Safe School Initiative*, 2.
[37] Ibid., 3–4.

Of special interest is this report's denial of any "accurate or useful profile of the school shooter."[38]

1. The attacker ages ranged from 11 to 21.

2. They came from a variety of racial and ethnic backgrounds, but more than three-quarters of shooters were white.

3. They came from a variety of family situations, from intact families with numerous ties to the community to foster homes with histories of neglect.

4. Their academic performance ranged from excellent to failing. Some attackers were taking Advanced Placement exams at the time of the incident.

5. They had a range of friendship patterns, from socially isolated to popular.

6. Their behavioral histories varied, from having no observed behavioral problems to multiple behaviors warranting reprimand and/or discipline.

7. Few attackers showed any marked change in academic performance, friendship status, interest in school, or disciplinary problems at school prior to the attack.

8. Few of the attackers had been diagnosed with any mental disorder prior to the incident. Additionally, fewer than one-third of attackers had histories of drug or alcohol abuse.[39]

The report views dependence on profiles of shooters to be ineffective. It would substitute a "focus on a student's behaviors and communications. . . . The ultimate question [it continues] is whether a student is on a path toward a violent attack, and if so to determine how fast they are moving and where intervention may be possible."[40]

Taken together, the FBI and Secret Service reports are valuable. They have a specific mission: to help school systems prevent deadly violence. This is imperative, but our

_____

[38] Ibid., 5.
[39] Ibid.
[40] Ibid.

goals should be deeper than preventing school shootings. We want to reach youth's pain. Parents, teachers, youth workers, and therapists need such analysis. The next chapter will examine factors behind this litany of tragedies.

One Made a Difference

He wasn't a youth worker in the ordinary sense, nor a pastor or teacher, but he did make a difference. He was just Marty Pino, who worked a variety of jobs, and for a time ran Marty's Ice Cream Shop in East Boston—until it closed because he gave so much away to kids who didn't have money.

Besides his regular jobs, he coached T-ball and led kids at summer camps. For many years he would get up early to take some of his neighborhood's most lonely and hungry to breakfast on the way to taking them to school—making sure they wouldn't skip. He was a father figure for many and every Father's Day would receive cards: "Thank you, you were my real father. I didn't have a father," signed "The Breakfast Club."[41]

There are many unsung heroes like that saving thousands of lives across America and hundreds of thousands in the world. It makes us not want to quit and to know more.

Questions for Reflection and Discussion

1. Do you remember your initial response to reports of these shootings (or if you were young to reading about this now)? How has your reaction changed?

2. Do you see those who shoot down their classmates and teachers as more angry or crazy?

---

[41] Peter DeMarco, "Marty Pino, 50, counselor, coach, East Boston hero," *The Boston Globe* Obituaries, 7 March 2003: E11.

Questions, cont'd.

3. What reasons for these killings have been noted in this chapter? How would you arrange them according to importance?

4. As jury or judge, what punishment would you give to shooters who have killed classmates? Should the state pay to rehabilitate someone with a life sentence?

5. What strategy would you employ to avoid such violent attacks? What do you see as your role and the role of others?

6. What more do you want to know about this issue?

Article Resource

"Voices from the Cell." ⚑ In May 2001, *Time* magazine looked "at the harsh realities facing 12 teens who shot up their schools." Some were remorseful; others weren't. Some are shunned; others have visitors. An insightful follow-up. *Time,* 28 May 2001: 33–38.

Book Resources

Thomas French. *South of Heaven: Welcome to High School at the End of the Twentieth Century.* New York: Doubleday, 1993. ⚑ This investigative reporter spent a year in a nice high school in Largo, Florida. Behind the scenes he found many kinds of troubled youth ready to explode. Although this is not the purpose of this book, you can use it to show you how to get into the life of a high school and make a difference.

Donna Gaines. *Teenage Wasteland: Suburbia's Dead End Kids.* New York: HarperCollins, 1990. ⚑ A suicide pact among four teenagers of Bergenfield, New Jersey brought

Gaines to this task. But studying non-affluent suburbs around New York and New Jersey explained to her why teenagers sometimes yield to extreme solutions.

Daniel J. Monti. *Wannabe: Gangs in Suburbs and Schools.* Cambridge, Mass.: Blackwell Publishers, 1994. 🛹 Based on interviews with 400 young people between the ages of ten and twenty, the author finds how troubled young people are further hurt in and by suburban gangs.

Internet Resources

www.albany.edu/sourcebook 🛹 This is the sourcebook of Criminal Justice Statistics. PDF files and charts trace trends in criminal activity including high school and college students.

www.bangbangyouredead.com 🛹 How William Mastrosimone came to write this play is an interesting story in itself. It is free for your youth or school group to download and use. It is an part of a program to prevent violence in schools.

www.fbi.gov/ucr/ucr.htm 🛹 U.S. Federal Bureau of Investigation provides crime statistics including those for hate crimes.

www.ileadyouth.com 🛹 LINC (Living in Christ) is an ecumenical site helping youth connect faith and life. Look for the article topic "violence" to find an article, "Positive Solutions to School Violence."

www.ojp.usdoj.gov/bjs 🛹 U.S. Department of Justice provides statistics.

http://ojjdp.ncjrs.org/site.html 🛹 This site allows you to submit Email questions about juvenile justice and delinquency, resources, and funding.

10 More Insights into Youthful Violence

> *Can a woman forget her nursing child, or show no compassion for the child of her womb? Even these may forget, yet I will not forget you.*
> — Isa 49:15, NRSV

> *Even jackals offer their breasts to nurse their young, but my people have become heartless.*
> — Lam 4:3, NIV

> *Then he said to me, "Have you seen this, O mortal? Is it not bad enough that (they) commit . . . abominations . . . ? Must they fill the land with violence, and provoke my anger still further?"*
> — Ezekiel 8:17, NRSV

From the beginning God saw that it was not good for human-kind to be alone. Animals may be good companions but cannot be our primary community (Gen 2:18–21a). We further believe a person cannot become human without human contact. Touch and attention from the beginning of a life is critical. Along with the mother's initial relationship, other "shepherds" of the child aid in developing the trust, skills and initiative needed by the growing child. Anywhere along the line, rejection, neglect, or improper training begin to warp the human personality. Society at large, together with all those around a child, contribute to a healthy, productive life or produce by default someone filled with rage and rebellion.

Many, though not all, of the shooters discussed in the previous chapter came from troubled or broken homes, and most of the boys suffered some special kind of neglect and abuse. Some of them may have suffered brain damage from having been shaken, struck, or knocked against a wall. Many lacked supervision from a father and mother or other caring adults. Childhood depression, especially in boys, has been called a hidden and repressed depression. It often results from abandonment, such as young Andrew Golden experienced when he lost his father, and his mother left him to be reared by grandparents.

Michael Carneal, Kip Kinkel, Mitchell Johnson, Eric Harris, and Dylan Klebold all had received psychotherapy. Kinkel and Harris were on psychotropic medications (Ritalin or a drug similar to Prozac). Depression was part of the diagnosis in several cases. When someone cannot talk about hurt or anger, these feelings can project themselves on something or someone outside. Angry outbursts and uncontrollable tantrums were part of these boys' behavior, although many of them could also be sweet, helpful, and respectful. They developed patterns of name calling and abusive language. As a result many were referred for discipline and/or counseling.

External Causes of Violence

Beyond each boy's genetic makeup are the external causes. These must be seen as global: in each case no one factor explains; no one person or persons can be blamed. U.S. society is built on and glorifies violence. Movies and history have celebrated rather than lamented our European forebears' conquest and decimation of American Indians, along with our Revolutionary and Mexican wars. The kidnapping and enslavement of Africans has too often been treated as an understandable and necessary part of history. American appetite for violent entertainment is immense.

The prevalence of arms in our country is also a factor; there are guns in half of U.S. homes. The National Center for Health Statistics reported that 35% of U.S. homes with children had at least one firearm. Furthermore, 43% of homes with children and guns kept firearm(s) in an unlocked place and without a trigger lock.[1]

Gavin de Becker, a safety expert and author, has compiled compelling facts alerting us to the danger of our guns.[2] U.S. Senate statistics estimate there are sixty million handguns in the United States, with some two to three million new and used handguns being sold each year. This weaponry annually produces 34,000 deaths from gunshot wounds, with seventy-five children shot each day, fifteen of them fatally.[3] An adolescent is twice as likely to commit suicide if a gun is kept in the home. In 1994, every day, sixteen children age nineteen and under were killed with guns, and sixty-four were wounded.

Despite reduction of violent crimes in the U.S., teen shootings rose in the 1990s. According to the U.S. Department of Justice (1998), gun killings by young people eighteen to twenty-four increased during the years 1980 to 1997 from about 5,000 to more than 7,500. During that same period, gun killings by people twenty-five and older fell by almost half, to about 5,000. The National Institute of Justice (1998) says that twenty-nine percent of high school boys have at least one firearm, most intended for hunting and sporting purposes. Six percent say they carry a gun outside the home. Senator Herb Kohl, sponsor of the safety lock measure, points out that nearly 7,000 violent crimes are committed each year by juveniles using guns they found in their homes.

In 1998, the Children's Defense Fund reported:

> Youth homicides are increasingly gun-related, and as with the other youth violence data, this is a uniquely American trend. Researchers believe that guns have become more easily available to children, and with this access, youth homi-

---

[1] American Journal of Public Health, April, 2002. See Report at (www.rand.org/hot/Press/guns.3.30.html)

[2] Gavin de Becker, *Protecting the Gift: Keeping Children and Teenagers Safe* (New York: Dell, 2000), and idem, *The Gift of Fear* (New York: Dell, 1999). His facts have been compiled by "Ask Jeeves," an Internet service (www.askJeeves.com).

[3] National Center for Health and Statistics, 1996.

cides have increased. [Children] found guns easier to obtain. Not surprisingly, gun murders by children rose sharply (until recently). Data from Office of Juvenile Justice show that between 1985 and 1994 such killings quadrupled, from more than 500 to more than 2,000. Meanwhile, the number of murders by children without guns held steady at about 500 annually.[4]

Deborah Prothrow-Stith, one of the experts who has studied gun violence, points out that although countries like Israel and Switzerland have an abundance of guns, they have far fewer handgun deaths than does the U.S. However, their cultures have not developed with the same ideas of violence, nor are they as heterogeneous as ours. We can benefit by looking at these differences and learning what in our society contributes to so much violence.

Seattle and Vancouver are two similar cities in proximity, but gun violence is significantly less in the Canadian city.[5] The simple fact is that U.S. children and youth are killing themselves and others with guns much more often than those in other countries. Many people will not want to hear this, but many U.S. children would be alive today if they grew up in another country. In a typical year (1985) there were more than 8,000 handgun deaths in the U.S., compared with forty-six in Japan, thirty-one in Switzerland, eighteen in Israel, eight in Great Britain, and five in Australia.[6]

Still, elimination or severe restriction of guns in the U.S., even if that were possible, would not stop the violence. The complexity of youthful violence demands careful consideration of all factors and viewpoints.

Causes of youthful violence are interrelated. At the beginning of the 1990s Kurt Cobain became the symbol of a new kind of pain and rage that fed on family dysfunction and

---

[4] Children's Defense Fund, The State of America's Children: Yearbook 1998, 79.
[5] Seattle, Washington, and Vancouver, British Columbia are in two different countries but only 140 miles apart. Alike in income levels and unemployment, they have similar rates of non-gun homicides, but Vancouver's death by hand guns is proportionately much lower.
[6] Children's Defense Fund (1998), 15.

a sense of social hopelessness, as well as, perhaps, the narcissism of adults and kids. Images of explicit sex and violence became merged, particularly in slasher films, in the 1980s. Satiated audiences, especially the young, were attracted to increased levels of shock, and the envelope was pushed in all media. Violence became part of the cultural atmosphere children breathe. Video games go further and have the potential of training killers—or at least of powerfully desensitizing young people to interpersonal violence.[7]

Most children who are exposed to violent entertainment do not become killers. In some cases, however, a young person can find media inspiration and encouragement for homicide or suicide. A significant problem with the media is that they generally do not show consequences. The immediate gratification of lust through sex and the instant solution of problems by violence are dramatized, but the resulting hurt is not depicted. Many of our young people are caught by surprise when they confront the pain that can follow promiscuous sex and impulsive aggression. We can never determine to what extent a particular movie, song, or video game was responsible for a killing in real life. The greater question about excessive violence and sexuality in popular culture has to do with what kind of children and what kind of culture we want. Do we want young people with sensitivity and deep moral character? Do we want a society built on truth, beauty, and decency? These are critical issues, although this is a discussion that goes beyond the intentions of this book.

Some children have adequate support and/or inner resources to withstand today's socially toxic environment. They may find support in their families, communities, friends, and places of worship. But when a young person's parents or support systems do not have time or ability to feel his or her hidden hurt and then peers taunt that young person, other despairing friends must be found. The power and prevalence

---

[7] David Grossman and Gloria Degaetano, *Stop Teaching Our Kids to Kill: A Call to Action Against TV, Movie and Video Games Violence* (New York: Random House, 1999). See also Grossman's articles and reports to Congress.

of taunting in schools can hardly be overemphasized, nor can its consequences, as tortured teens find solace in dark corners of culture.

Groups that collect outcasts or misfits in the mainstream of teenage life may find their subcultural support from suggestive media, violent video games, music with dismal or brutal lyrics, and the dark side of the Internet. In many cases video games that leave us aghast may serve as virtual release for rage that might otherwise be killing real people. This is not to justify or excuse gory and degrading media violence, but boys need significant activity and someone who cares rather than mere prohibitions against games that serve as outlets for their rage.

Internal Factors

In chapter 1, we estimated twenty percent of U.S. youth to be at risk and five percent to be at extreme risk, that is, on the brink of causing serious injury to themselves and/or others. Let us now try to understand what goes into the making of young murderers.

Police and other observers often notice remorseless, psychopathic characteristics in some killers. Others exhibit more normal attitudes of regret or confusion. Family, friends, and neighbors say they worried about some killers all along; in other cases everyone is surprised that such a good, normal kid could suddenly kill. Some killers seem bred to be vicious predators. I think we must hold all killers responsible *and* try to understand factors that lead to grisly crimes, not only to arrive at sane punishments but also to enable effective rehabilitation.

"These boys," writes James Garbarino, who has interviewed many of them in depth, "fall victim to an unfortunate synchronicity between the demons inhabiting their own internal world and the corrupting influences of modern American life."[8] And there is often a triggering factor, which may be

---

[8]James Garbarino, *Lost Boys: Why Our Sons Turn Violent and How We Can Save Them* (New York: Free Press, 1999), 23.

nothing more than two friends discussing common griev-
ances and coming to an impulsive decision.

We come to understand troubled (and all) youth as we
consider their personal makeup and their life situation. We
all come into the world with unique biological traits. Even in
the womb, environmental features affect a person's basic
traits. Our dispositions and our unique interaction with family and surroundings produce a personality and behaviors
unique to us. This uniqueness separates even identical twins
and is the reason close siblings react differently to what appears to be the same environment.

We want to pursue the factors that lead a child down
the path to killing. We seek to understand how a lack of personal resiliency combines with certain early life situations to
produce deadly consequences (see chapters 4, 5, and 7).

Attachment Disorders

Only recently have psychologists and social workers
come to see possible links between attachment disorders in
young children, conduct disorders in older children and adolescents, and antisocial personality (psychopathic or socio-
pathic) disorders in young adults.

Traumatic experiences, neglect or abuse, separation
from or changes in a child's primary caregiver, and maternal
depression or addiction, are thought to be among the causes
of attachment difficulties in children. Garbarino refers to
British psychiatrist Michael Rutter, whose "research makes it
clear that for a boy to be separated from his mother in infancy and early childhood is a very significant risk factor for
future development."[9]

Infants express their needs in cries of rage. Mothers or
caregivers normally respond by meeting the need behind
the cry. Loving looks, touches, and tones create a bonding
and trust. If, however, a baby's cries and needs are met with
physical or vocal rebuffs, the child will learn to mistrust and
to fend for itself with contrived defense mechanisms. Instead of the bonding and trust in a healthy attachment

---

[9] Ibid., 47.

cycle, an abusive cycle of fear and aggressiveness will be produced.

Subject to an abusive cycle, a child learns to defend, manipulate, and abuse others instead of relating, trusting, and caring in a healthy way. Children with attachment disorders may be superficially engaging and charming—indiscriminately affectionate to strangers—and manipulative. Such children may target and pay back the primary caregiver, whether or not this caregiver was the initial abuser. Strange eating patterns, such as rejecting food or social eating, eating alone, or hoarding food, may make for domestic discord. Children with such disorders may bully weaker children of the family in extreme ways.

Poor peer relationships, fighting for control, stealing, and lying may characterize children with attachment disorders. They may appear hypervigilant or hyperactive and have little impulse control. Their imaginations may be obsessed with fire, gore, death, weapons of destruction, and evil forces. Although we lack proof for this conclusion, it seems that infants with attachment disorders can grow into children with conduct disorders and subsequently may become adults with antisocial personality disorders.

Garbarino suggests three lines of defense against lethal youth violence:

> The place to begin . . . is at the beginning, before a boy is even born. The goal is two-fold: to prevent boys from coming into the world at a biological disadvantage and to prevent them from being maltreated by their parents. . . . Our second line lies in programs that promote positive parenting practices, practices that stimulate healthy child development. . . . The third line of defense is early intervention programs that deal with the attachment-related problems. . . . As we have seen, many boys who get lost are disconnected or detached from the earliest months and years of life. . . . High-quality early childhood educations programs—such as well-run preschools, high-quality Head Start centers, enriching nursery schools, and developmentally oriented day-care centers—are the fourth line of defense.[10]

---

[10] Ibid., 182–87.

Conduct Disorders

As late as 1994, the American Psychiatric Association's *Diagnostic and Statistical Manual of Mental Disorders (DSM-IV)* had no diagnosis for attachment or conduct disorders, although the latter has since been added. Not all children with attachment disorders will progress to conduct disorders, but the probability is clear. *DSM-IV* regards conduct disorder this way:

> The essential feature of Conduct Disorder is a repetitive and persistent pattern of behavior in which the rights of others or major age-appropriate societal norms or rules are violated. These behaviors fall into four main groupings: aggressive conduct . . [causing or threatening] physical harm to other people or animals . . . nonaggressive conduct that causes property loss or damage . . . , deceitfulness or theft . . . and serious violations of rules. . . . Three (or more) characteristic behaviors must have been present during the past 12 months, with at least one behavior present in the past 6 months. The disturbance in behavior causes clinically significant impairment in social, academic, or occupational functioning.[11]

Younger children with this disorder will be a particular problem at home; as they get older this behavior will bring difficulties to their classrooms. It is generally classed as a disruptive disorder because of the way such behavior patterns affect the child, family, neighbors, and school. Oppositional or defiant disorders often precedes conduct behaviors; both are classed as disruptive disorders. Among children and adolescents, mental disorders such as depression, attention-deficit/hyperactivity disorder, anxiety, disruptive, and eating disorders affect one in five youth. As many as one in ten children and adolescents are said to have conduct disorder.

There can be a tension between social services and inner-city folks. African-Americans have often complained that psychiatrists or social workers don't understand them and try to squeeze them into their categorical boxes or slap

---

[11] American Psychiatric Association, *Diagnostic and Statistical Manual of Mental Disorders* (Washington, D.C.: American Psychiatric Association, 1994), 85.

diagnostic numbers on them. *DSM-IV* seems to take this (and criticisms by feminists) into consideration by drawing attention to "specific culture, age, and gender features":

> Concerns have been raised that the Conduct Disorder diagnosis may at times be misapplied to individuals in settings where patterns of undesirable behavior are sometimes viewed as protective (e.g., threatening, impoverished, high-crime).[12]

> Individuals with Conduct Disorder may have little empathy and little concern for the feelings, wishes, and well-being of others . . . frequently misperceive the intentions of others . . . may be callous and lack appropriate feelings of guilt or remorse. . . . Self-esteem is usually low, although this person may project an image of "toughness."

> Conduct Disorder is often associated with an early onset of sexual behavior, drinking, smoking, use of illegal substances, and reckless and risk-taking acts.[13]

Therapists are instructed to understand how certain antisocial behaviors may be normative on the streets or other situations. Survival may demand being bad; to stay alive one may need to threaten or act aggressively. In such cases, the issue becomes the degree to which the behavior is impairing the functioning of an individual within his or her context.

Garbarino lists several lines of defense against lethal youth violence in terms of early detachment disorders. The last four suggestions in this strategic response are worth noting:

> The fifth line of defense is early recognition of cases of Conduct Disorder and effective responses to redirect behavior and reshape the social maps of vulnerable children. . . . The sixth developmental line of defense is violence prevention and reduction programs at the elementary school level. There are growing numbers of such programs in communities all over the country. . . . The seventh line of defense is character education. . . . Modern character education programs involve the mobilization of schools and the rest of the community to endorse and promote a set of core values or "pillars of character." . . . The eighth line of defense is teaching mediation,

---

[12] Ibid., 88.
[13] Ibid., 87.

conflict resolution, and peer counseling in programs for kids in middle school and junior high. An important element in these programs is that kids keep track of other kids.[14]

Antisocial or Psychopathic Personality Disorder

The disruptive patterns we have described can turn into even more serious psychopathic or antisocial disorders. According to the APA, "a substantial proportion of those with Conduct Disorders in childhood and adolescence, show behaviors in adulthood that meet the criteria for Antisocial Personality Disorder."[15]

> The essential feature of Antisocial Personality Disorder is a pervasive pattern of disregard for, and violation of, the rights of others—beginning in childhood or early adolescence and continuing into adulthood. This pattern has also been referred to as psychopathy, sociopathy, or dyssocial personality disorder . . . deceit and manipulation are central features of Antisocial Personality Disorder.[16]

An Internet medical encyclopedia suggests these symptoms for antisocial personality disorder:

- lack of concern for society's expectations and laws

- unlawful behavior

- violation of the rights of others (property, physical, sexual, legal, emotional)

- physical aggression

- lack of stability in job and home life

- lack of remorse[17]

All this should help us understand more about youthful killers. Put weak attachments and mistrust together with difficult learning and social environments; add possible abuse from parents, siblings, or relatives; add learning dis-

---

[14] Garbarino, *Lost Boys,* 190–96.
[15] APA, *Diagnostic and Statistical Manual of Mental Disorders,* 89.
[16] Ibid., 645.
[17] Medline plus health information. Online: medlineplus.adam.com/ ency/article/000921sym.htm.

orders and other visible handicaps; then combine teasing and bullying in neighborhood and school with strong negative reinforcement from the media. This is a formula for disaster. This is not to excuse but to explain youthful offenses that stagger us.

The mystery of why some people with more reasons to lash out do not do so while others with less reason take their lives or the lives of others remains. It is the mystery of resilience and grace. Our task is not to predict who will or who will not kill but to relate to all who are at risk in a way that may prevent harm.

Teasing, Hazing, and Bullying

Just after the Columbine shooting, a young man took to the Internet congratulating Eric Harris and Dylan Klebold, telling how much he hated his classmates and how he would like to copy the Columbine massacre. Most disheartening and frightening about his confession were the thousands of hits his website received. Messages said they had experienced the same taunts, were just as angry, and wanted to do the same thing.[18]

In 1994 sociologist Robert Hale wrote "The Role of Humiliation and Embarrassment in Serial Murder."[19] After attachment disorders and child abuse, humiliation often ranks third in predicting remorseless violence.

Throughout the 1990s, bullying was the most overlooked cause of school shootings. Bullying begins as social pecking orders emerge among children (see ch. 1). Disrespect leads to teasing, teasing leads to taunting, and taunting can lead to physical aggression.

Bullying, indeed, is a global problem; it has long been an issue in the U.K. A Scottish study of 942 pupils showed fifty percent saying they had been bullied at least once, forty-four percent admitting they had bullied someone else,

---

[18] From a 1999 program on NPR as cited by Scott Larson, *Risk In Our Midst* (Loveland, Colo.: Group, 2000), 13.

[19] Robert Hale, "The Role of Humiliation and Embarrassment in Serial Murder," *Psychology* 31 (1994): 17–23.

twenty-five percent saying their bullying was "sometimes or often." Studies in Norway showed similar rates.[20] In Australia, Elisabeth Wynhausen writes, "Australia is top of the class when it comes to bullying."[21]

Jim was a student at Eastern Senior High in Voorhees, New Jersey, who had endured taunts from the time he was a child. His story was featured on *Dateline.* Interviews with his father, a computer engineer, showed little bonding between the two. Jim had been different all his life, according to his father, himself, and others. Never fitting in, he was teased and pummeled. Three students known as bullies at his high school admitted he was an easy mark. Asked what he was feeling with all this taunting, Jim replied, "It's anger to the next level . . . an unfocused hatred . . . a feeling that this is the only answer to just cause as much pain and suffering as you possibly can because that's what you've been through."[22]

Finally Jim felt he could take it no more. Knowing how other boys had responded, he obtained a map of the school, plotted a route through the boiler room into the cafeteria, and obtained a gun. At first he planned to shoot blanks and shout at his adversaries. But, he admitted, he might have ended up killing them. Before that happened, an administrator saw him lurking by a pay phone and somehow felt an intervention was needed. "Well, Jim, what do you think of what happened at Columbine?" she asked.

When he replied, "I feel the same way—like doing the same thing," she took him into her office to talk. There he unloaded what he was feeling and what he intended to do. The administrator immediately sent Jim to a psychiatric center, where he was evaluated and treatment begun. With help, Jim learned how to handle bullies and relate to more of his classmates. Another tragedy was averted because one person was a careful observer and took time to intervene.

---

[20] The Scottish Council for Research in Education (1990). Online: www.scre.ac.uk.

[21] Elisabeth Wynhausen, "Hectored and Unprotected," *The Australian,* 21 February 2001. Online: http://ink.news.com.au.

[22] NBC's Dateline, "A Boy on the Brink," 9 February 2000.

Powerful cliques form and teasing begins in the early grades, as the Adlers have shown.[23] Giannetti and Sagarese devote a chapter to "Disarming Your Bully," which gives practical advice for dealing with malicious taunting in grade school.[24]
One study of bullying found

- Eighty percent of adolescents reported being bullied during their school years.

- Ninety percent of fourth through eighth graders report being victims.

- Ten to fifteen percent of all students practice bullying.

- Bullying begins in elementary school, peaks in middle school, and diminishes but does not disappear in high school.

- Students reported that seventy percent of the teachers or other adults in the classroom ignored bullying incidents. In only four percent of school bullying incidents do teachers intervene, according to those bullied, and in only eleven percent of instances do peers step in to help.

- Both boys and girls bully, usually same-sex classmates, with female bullying often taking indirect, manipulative forms.[25]

- Bullying can have devastating long-term effects on its victims.[26]

---

[23] Patricia A. Adler and Peter Adler, *Peer Power: Preadolescent Culture and Identity* (New Brunswick, N.J.: Rutgers University Press, 1998). Note references in their index for Teasing.

[24] Charlene C. Giannetti and Margaret Sagarese, *Cliques: Eight Steps to Help Your Child Survive the Social Jungle* (New York: Broadway, 2001).

[25] Rachel Simmons, *Odd Girl Out: The Hidden Culture of Aggression in Girls* (New York: Harcourt Brace, 2002). See also interview with Rachel Simmons, "Fighting with Friendship," *Dateline NBC,* 9 April 2002 (www.msnbc.com/news/735674.asp).

[26] Chuck Saufler and Cyndi Gagne, "A Survey of Bullying Behavior . . . ," Maine Project Against Bullying (2000). Online: http://lincoln.midcoast.com/~wps/against/execsummary.html; "Fighting with Friendship," http://www.msnbc.com/news/735674.asp. See also the extensive study of bullying in the *Journal of the American Medical Association* 285 (2001): 2094–2100.

Boys will fight and tend to get over it, but the under-the-radar maliciousness of girls can produce hate and hurt lasting for years.

Because peers are the mirror in which teenagers craft their self-image, the pain of rejection and taunting is critical. From a German perspective, Beate Schuster writes, "One of the most devastating experiences is to be the object of aggression by members of one's own group." Schuster goes on to define and estimate the prevalence of bullying in the following way:

> Estimates of the prevalence of bullying and mobbing have varied considerably in the literature. . . . Some studies (e.g., Hoover) have suggested incidence rates of 90 percent. The rates are lower when the standard definition of bullying . . . is followed. This definition specifies a variety of parameters including (a) duration for at least 6 months, (b) repetition of at least once a week, (c) imbalance in the strength of those involved (target unable to defend self). When these criteria are met, about 5 percent of children are identified as victims of bullying.[27]

Time ran an online poll with TimeForKids asking its student readers, Has a bully ever picked on you in school? The results:

- Yes, I've been picked on: forty-one percent
- No, I haven't been picked on: thirty-two percent
- No, I usually do the bullying: twenty-seven percent[28]

The same article quotes psychologist Peter Fonagy, who, according to his definition of bullying, estimates bullies and those bullied to be somewhere between ten and twenty percent of a given student population. Fonagy has worked on antibullying programs in Topeka, Kansas, and has contrib-

---

[27] Beate Schuster, "Nice Guys or bad guys? Victims of mobbing/bullying and peer rejection in the prisoner's dilemma paradigm" (German) "Zu brav oder boese? Mobbing-Opfer und Abgelehnte im Prisoner's Dilemma-Paradigma," Zeitschrift Für Sozialpsychologie. Vol. 30(2-3) Jul 1999, 179-93. Assessed sociometric and victimization status of 443 male and female children (age 5-11 years) in Germany.

[28] Nadya Labi, "Let Bullies Beware," *Time,* 2 April 2001, 46.

uted an important understanding of bullying as teenage, real-life theater: "The whole drama is supported by the by-stander. The theater can't take place if there's no audience."[29]

> ⚐ Think of someone who comes from a strong, loving family and a good church but went through school with an undetected learning disability. Teachers and fellow students treated him as slow and dumb. It is not until somewhere in high school that an alert teacher informed the parents, and the student himself, that he had a learning disability. Now he understands everything including his deep-seated anger. Consider how deep and difficult treating his pain and anger may be. This person has turned to hard music to ease the pain. What do you suggest?
>
> Now think about a bright person with a severe learning disability, and maybe attention deficit problems thrown in, who has no caring family. Parents and siblings continually call him a dumb jerk and treat him as second class in his or her own family. The learning disability is never detected, is masked by behavior problems and self-medication, and the abuse of family is now augmented by taunts and bullying from peers.

Anti-bullying programs open up general discussion through skits identifying Bully, Victim, and Bystander. The bully, of course, is the perpetrator, the victim is the one suffering the bully's taunts or abuse, and bystanders are those who watch. Because bullies are trying to enhance their own threatened self-image, they will usually bully while others are watching. Bystanders keep silent or fail to intervene out of fear and because they are relieved that others are suffering rather than they themselves. Such terminology came out of the Holocaust. Survivors today often disclose greater anger toward those who watched and did nothing than their

---

[29] Ibid.

tormentors whose sadism explains their actions. It is in units on the Holocaust that many young bystanders have come to understand the hypocrisy of their acquiescence in teasing and bullying.

> 🛹 A Role Play is a useful exercise. You might use athletes to play "Jocks" and alternatives or goths to play "Loser" or "Loner." They may play themselves straight in talking about losers in general, or you might get the jocks to play the losers and the alternatives to play the jocks. There are three parts to this exercise: brainstorming and writing the script, acting it out, and discussing it afterwards.
>
> Another important drama is between a bully, victim, and bystanders. Let the group write the script and then act it out. This might even be developed for presentation to a junior high audience or those in fourth through sixth grades. Discussion should follow.

Hazing has also increased in the U.S. When the national survey, Initiation Rites in American High Schools,[30] was released in August 2000, it became national news and was featured in a report on ABC television. "Initiation Rites Affect nearly 2 Million Teens a Year."[31]

Articles describing the abuse and humiliation suffered by students appeared across the country describing how high school students were beaten even when joining church groups.

Almost half the high school responders to this survey said they were made to abuse alcohol or drugs, drink or eat disgusting things, or perform humiliating or even illegal acts.

---

[30] Nadine C. Hoover and Norman J. Pollard, "Initiation Rites in American High Schools: A National Survey," Alfred University, 2000. Online: www.alfred.edu/news/html/hazing_study.html.

[31] ABC News, "Hazing Hits High Schools." Online: ABCNews.com. Go to abcnews.com and type title in search field.

Some have died from alcohol poisoning; others bear scars of sexual abuse. Hazing and bullying, which hurt the most vulnerable students most, are part of the global picture we seek in determining the causes and a proper response to youthful violence. Making schools safer for young people involves addressing these issues.

Responding to Painful Stories

When we put together the diagnostic categories of the psychiatric profession with principles of development, the stories of children raised by animals, and information about trauma and resiliency, we can begin to understand general situations.

I am not a psychologist or licensed therapist. Although I have an advanced degree in counseling, have attended professional workshops, and counseled many young people, I do not consider myself expert in these matters. However, in facing a given child or teenager in a tough situation, I find experience and this knowledge to be of great help. It works, of course, when I face a young man or woman not as a problem or in a category but as a person I respect and whose story I want to hear.

Social support from a community needs to surround all troubled young people. They need a unified structure that comes from common values and standards.[32]

Although it may take residential treatment centers or intensive group work, hope can come to hopeless situations when we work together. Youth at risk need big brother/sister, mother/father, and grandparent figures. Motherless and fatherless boys can be reparented. At any age and with

---

[32] Francis Ianni, *The Search for Structure: A Report on American Youth Today* (New York: Free Press, 1989). See also William Damon, *The Youth Charter: How Communities Can Work Together to Raise Standards for All Our Children* (New York: Free Press, 1997), and Peter L. Benson, *All Kids Are Our Kids: What Communities Can Do to Raise Caring and Responsible Children and Adolescents* (San Francisco: Jossey-Bass, 1997). Peter Benson is head of Search Institute and its Healthy Kids Healthy Communities program.

almost any emotional handicaps, they can respond to attention and interest, love and discipline, encouragement and affirmation. Abusive and dysfunctional cycles can be replaced
by healthy cycles of growth and performance.

Parents, teachers, and youth leaders who care about
kids and are concerned about negative factors in the culture
can provide positive alternatives and models of excitement
without danger, adventure without damage, and fulfillment
without remorse. Communities can encourage and support
those who will look for and spend time with rebels who wander the streets.

Although Garbarino is not known as a religious writer,
he suggests three anchors needed by the young people discussed in this chapter: "The Power of Spiritual, Psychological, and Social Anchors."[33]

His experience with troubled boys has convinced him
that "spiritual anchors lead to a new sense of purpose, to
meaningfulness, and to future orientation, where there
might otherwise be purposelessness, meaninglessness, and
terminal thinking."[34]

Ultimately each battered heart needs contact with the
Creator, who alone can fill all empty corners of a life. I would
like to see, and I try to imagine, Jesus interacting with each
boy named in these chapters. How would he have interacted
with Kip Kinkel or Eric Harris? What would he have said to
Dylan Klebold? What kind of advocate would he have been
for Charles Andrew Williams? Somehow he would have gotten to each one's story. As his representatives on earth how
can we intervene more effectively?

We have seen how one school administrator stepped in
to talk with a lonely boy planning mayhem against those
who taunted him. As those who have been forgiven and as
wounded healers, we are needed on the frontlines. Christ
and Christ-like mentors can provide friendship, meaning,
healing, and liberation. Each boy has a story. At first, for so
many reasons, he may not be able to tell it. Sometimes that

---

[33] Garbarino, *Lost Boys,* 149.
[34] Ibid., 159.

story begins to come out in pictures, play, or activities with someone he finally trusts. When painful stories are finally uncovered, there is hope for recovery and positive growth.

Questions for Reflection and Discussion

1. With what did you most agree or disagree in this chapter?

2. Did this chapter shed light on the ultimately mysterious combination of internal and external factors that produces school shooters?

3. Did this chapter keep the balance between that which can be understood and all that goes beyond conclusive analysis?

4. Were you satisfied with the way the chapter treated individual (boy, family, bully) and systemic (media, guns) causes of violence? Explain.

5. Did this chapter help you understand growth patterns and possible cycles of health and growth versus cycles of abuse, dysfunction, rage, and violence? Explain.

6. Do you agree that most troubled boys can be helped and violence prevented by timely and holistic interventions? Explain.

7. What in this chapter needs further analysis or explanation?

8. How specifically has this chapter helped you understand or relate to youth at risk?

Book Resources

Scott Larson and Dan Mercer, eds. *A Way Out.* Westboro, Mass.: Straight Ahead Ministries,1999. 🏃 This hopeful and helpful book is readable by teenagers as well as parents and adult leaders. Four felons tell how they found Christ and a way out of deep troubles.

Ken Magid and Carole A. McKelvey. *High Risk Children Without a Conscience.* New York: Bantam Books, 1987. ✕ This little-known book is an important source book for those who would understand the contents of this chapter in fuller detail and offer help to parents and others who serve children and young people.

Deborah Prothrow-Stith. *Deadly Consequences: How Violence is Destroying our Teenage Population and a Plan to Begin Solving the Problem.* New York: HarperCollins,1991. ✕ This is another analysis of youthful violence with a special look at the threat of guns as it affects especially urban African Americans. What's important here is the way the author deals with youthful violence as a public health issue.

Internet Resources

www.antibullying.net ✕ The Anti-Bullying Network provides advice, information, and links for young people and others.

http://medlineplus.gov ✕ Medline Plus Health Information gives you a broad range of medical and psychiatric information. Type in the disorder or problem on which you would like to see information at the search window.

www.straightahead.org ✕ This national Christian mission to juvenile offenders offers books and other resources along with a network of Christian juvenile justice ministries.

11 Urban Violence

Thus says the LORD of hosts, the God of Israel . . . seek the welfare of the city . . . and pray to the LORD on its behalf, for in its welfare you will find your welfare.
—Jeremiah 29:4a, 7 NRSV

Many sources of division exist in the world, but one of the most difficult and entrenched is the gulf between haves and have-nots. In most urban areas, the world of the rich exists alongside the poor, except in the case of isolated shantytowns. In many American cities, most whites live in affluent suburbs and most blacks in inner-city neighborhoods. They represent different worlds but are worlds apart. In the latter, racism and poverty increase the struggles of many urban youth.

A *polis* or city has usually meant a meeting place of all classes. In the U.S. after World War II, highways and a desire to escape many features of urban blight drove money, brains, and churches out of the city to protected suburban havens. Commuters to the city expect municipal services such as water, police and fire protection, and much more. Their suburban communities are often able to use a much higher percentage of town budgets on educating their children. Spending per pupil is often much lower in urban municipal budgets, and schools in poorer districts of a city receive less than schools in more favored sections of town.

Businesses also leave the inner city, and these neighborhoods are sometimes left without supermarkets and banks. Some pawn shops and check cashers take advantage of their customers. Redlining (biased bank refusal to make loans for homes or small businesses in certain neighborhoods) hinders home ownership and development. In many urban areas you will look in vain for employment that provides adequate income to support a family. All this is part of the picture of disadvantage that can drive young people to risk and rebellion.

The suburban picture of the city is too often one of violence, crime, drugs, unwed and pregnant teenagers, and welfare. Such images are reinforced by newspeople looking for violent or sensational stories. Unfair myths and stereotypes exist among urban and suburban dwellers. This is understandable, since they live in two different worlds described by Jonathan Kozol in the following way:

> The Number 6 train from Manhattan to the South Bronx makes nine stops in the 18-minute drive between East 59th Street and Brook Avenue. When you enter the train, you are in the seventh richest congressional district in the nation. When you leave, you are in the poorest.
>
> The 600,000 people who live here and the 450,000 people who live in Washington Heights and Harlem, which are separated from the South Bronx by a narrow river, make up on the largest racially segregated concentrations of poor people in our nation.[1]

Underground trains or protected highways often bring into business districts of the city commuters who are unaware of the slums they are passing. A resident of the South Bronx took Kozol to an overpass of I-95 and pointed out a housing complex, which she described:

> [The people there have] few economic possibilities. There aren't many branches of major banks. The "banks" are loan sharks—or check-cashing places. If you want to open a small business, there's no banker that you've come to know that you can talk with to obtain a loan. No libraries open in the evening. Few recreational opportunities for children. Many abandoned houses and abandoned people and abandoned cars.[2]

Then she pointed out something striking; Kozol turned and "noticed pictures of flowers, window shades, curtains and interiors of pretty-looking rooms, that had been painted

---

[1] Jonathan Kozol, *Amazing Grace: The Lives of Children and the Conscience of a Nation* (New York: HarperCollins, 1995), 3.
[2] Ibid., 30.

on these buildings that face the highway . . . the pictures have been done so well that when you look the first time, you imagine that you're seeing into people's homes."[3]

Kozol is intrigued, and asks if the residents had painted the murals. "Nobody lives here [she replies]. Those buildings are all empty. The city had these murals painted on the walls . . . not for the people in the neighborhood—because they're facing the wrong way—but for tourists and commuters."[4]

Problems of the ghetto, portrayed powerfully in the best of rap music, will never be solved if those of us in the two cities—the two worlds—are not brought together. Urban youth tend to deal more realistically with their problems than outsiders can imagine. Problems such as drugs and violence cannot be solved until we deal realistically with the issue of poverty.

Listening to Those Who Know

Neither romantic myths of ghetto happiness nor grim generalities of ghetto degradation and despair are true. There is beauty in the rich cultural diversity of urban life, its face-to-face relationships, the dynamics of street life, and sometimes a deep sense of community. The struggle to survive under tough social and economic disadvantages, and the rough responses expressed by some youth and rappers, are part of the other side.

Inner cities vary greatly; Watts and Compton are far different from sections of Detroit, Chicago, and the South Bronx. Just as all suburbs are not the same, so neighborhoods in the same city provide different opportunities and challenges—and neighborhoods can change strikingly over time. Urban life is rich and full of complex realities.

Suburban folk and policy makers need to spend quality time in the city, not just a ride-by. They need to walk through it with some resident open to educating them. They need to

---

[3] Ibid., 31.
[4] Ibid.

go into the homes and talk with the people who live there or spend a day with a social worker in a Salvation Army office. There is no way to understand this misunderstood world other than to partake of it. White, affluent Americans do not often think of culture and class; there is an unconscious presumption that their culture and class are the norm. Only those who care about the urban culture should be helping to rear its children. Many cities have made concerted efforts to get those who police urban streets and teach inner-city children to live in the communities they serve.

To understand urban realities we must listen to urban residents. We who are suburbanites should allow urban sociologists to explain urban complexities and frustrations to us. In his sociological study of two Chicago boys, Useni Perkins calls inner-city slums "ghetcolonies."[5] His study of the systems that are supposed to serve or control urban neighborhoods reveals not only the breakdown of municipal delivery systems but also a general flow of resources from the slums out to the larger economic world. Money invested or brought into the city tends to bounce only once. Outsiders are enriched; inner-city residents are impoverished. It is easy to imagine how police can easily be seen as an occupation army when they are not personally in touch with the neighborhood.

We should not be surprised that inner-city residents look at community difficulties far differently than do most middle-class, suburban observers. They ask outsiders to understand the complexity of urban crime and the complicity of outside systems in creating urban problems. Too many middle-class critics rely on biased logical explanations of urban problems that lead them to suggest simple and unrealistic solutions. It is important to read writers from a variety of perspectives as they probe the difficult issues of a culture of poverty and family dynamics.

---

[5] Useni Eugene Perkins, *Home Is A Dirty Street: The Social Oppression of Black Children* (Chicago: Third World Press, 1975, 1993). See chapter 1, "North Lawndale: Anatomy of a Black Ghetcolony."

While writing an article for the *Wall Street Journal,* Alex Kotlowitz met two young boys. After spending three years with them in the realities of the Horner housing projects, he wrote *There Are No Children Here,* a title suggested by their mother in giving permission for the book to be written. Jay Macleod's *Ain't No Makin' It* compares two groups, one mostly white, one black, in an urban slum. Interestingly, those who gave up on life early on were the whites—they were without hope and aspirations. The black group thought they were going to get out of the ghetto and find success in a larger world. This longitudinal study, however, shows how circumstances shut off achievement for both groups, despite the higher aspirations of the blacks.[6]

Understanding Urban Culture

Like Perkins, Elijah Anderson looks at the city from the standpoint of a black street sociologist. In *Streetwise,* he describes two adjacent urban communities, one poor and black and one a mixed, middle-class neighborhood. Most poor, inner-city residents are good, decent, hard-working people. Almost every urban mother loves her children and wants a better life for them. Economic, racial, and class factors, however, restrict urban opportunity. Street culture is a natural reaction providing alternative ways of making it with drugs, crime, and violence. Where education has failed and jobs have disappeared, young men are unable to support a family. Anderson writes:

> Of all the problems besetting the poor inner-city black community, none is more pressing than that of interpersonal violence and aggression. It wreaks havoc daily with lives of community residents and increasingly spills over into downtown and residential middle-class areas. Muggings, burglaries, car-jackings, and drug-related shootings, all of which may leave their victims or innocent bystanders dead, are

---

[6] Jay Macleod, *Ain't No Makin It: Leveled Aspirations in a Low-Income Neighborhood* (Boulder, Colo.: Westview, 1987).

now common enough to concern all urban and many suburban residents.[7]

For ten years I lived on the lower east side of Manhattan. The early years were spent as a street worker with gang kids and those on drugs. For a year of that time I worked in Harlem. While on the streets, I watched boys and girls leaving school or at least giving up on serious school achievement. In his first book,[8] Kozol described what I also saw in the eyes of kids who had lost hope and interest in school by third grade. These young folk have scant or no recreational leagues and few role positive models, and they cannot expect evenhanded justice from the police. The streets offer excitement, attention, and belonging. Bad buddies and attention are much better than no friends or notice, a fact that is borne out by those who study youth and those who spend time with them. The streets can provide home and peer groups as well as substitute educational, economic, and social institutions. Gangs promise protection, adventure, status, and something more: when boys talk about gangs, they often speak of finding a larger purpose and deeper sense of significance. The search for meaning is a spiritual quest—an inner longing for dignity and transcendent heroism.

Searching for significance and honor is not easy. Survival and respect on the streets come at a cost. One must learn the law of the jungle where the strongest and fittest survive. Anderson puts this in context:

> The inclination to violence springs from the circumstances of life among the ghetto poor—the lack of jobs that pay a living wage, the stigma of race, the fallout from rampant drug use and drug trafficking, and the resulting alienation and lack of hope for the future. Simply living in such an environment places young people at special risk of hope for the future.[9]

---

[7] Elijah Anderson, "The Code of the Streets," *Atlantic Monthly* (May 1994), 81.

[8] Jonathan Kozol, *Death at an Early Age: The Destruction of the Hearts and Minds of Negro Children in the Boston Public School System* (New York: Penguin, 1985, reissue, 1990). First published in 1967.

[9] Elijah Anderson, op. cit. 88.

Such adversity and a long history of oppression, combined with resulting changes in the family (young women
rearing children without fathers), can produce what some
scholars have called a culture of poverty. Anderson prefers
describing this as an "oppositional culture." This street culture is in opposition not only to mainstream dominant culture but also to the middle-class values and norms of inner-
city decent families—and the strong urban church. These
two cultures or orientations (decent and street) exist in
tension. The code of decent folks represents the majority
of inner-city inhabitants, but the minority code of the
streets becomes dominant as it captures the imagination of
young people and takes control of the neighborhood's
thoroughfares.

Respect and Survival

Since all urban people have to pass through the streets,
young men from decent backgrounds must learn the code of
the streets for defensive reasons. Only with such knowledge
can they safely navigate the neighborhood or go to school.
By the time they become teenagers, most urban youth have
either internalized the street code or learned enough of it to
get along—that is, he has learned to look bad. One must send
a message to any who might pose a threat that he is capable
of violence and ready to act. Anderson explains what this
communication includes according to the situation: "The
communication . . . can include facial expressions, gait, and
verbal aggression. Physical appearance, including clothes,
jewelry, and grooming, also plays an important part in how a
person is viewed; to be respected, it is important to have the
right look."[10]

If a boy, for instance, does not wear an expensive
jacket or sneakers, he may be dissed (teased, ribbed,
busted, capped) or worse, attacked. The attacker in this
case would gain juice, or respect. To gain real juice, however, one must wear something that might be stolen and be
able to protect it. Getting such a token of respect away from

---

[10] Ibid.

another involves even more juice. Outsiders do not understand why someone would kill for sneakers or a jacket until they understand juice and the fight for survival that takes place in some urban neighborhoods.

> Seemingly ordinary objects can become trophies imbued with symbolic value that far exceeds their monetary worth. Possession of the trophy can symbolize the ability to violate somebody—to "get in his face," to take something of value from him, to "dis" him, and thus to enhance one's own worth by stealing someone's else's. . . . Sneakers, a pistol, even somebody else's girlfriend, can become a trophy.
>
> An important aspect of this often violent give-and-take is its zero-sum quality. That is, the extent to which one person can raise himself up depends on his ability to put another person down. This underscores the alienation that permeates the inner-city ghetto community. There is a generalized sense that very little respect is to be had and therefore everyone competes to get what affirmation he can of the little that is available.[11]

Understanding this volatility of the street code also makes some sense out of the games played at school and outside: dissing, jivin' (lame excuses or misinformation to deceive someone), signifying (making up stories to embarrass or get out of something), and the dozens (putting down another; insulting the other's mother). It also explains louding (loud talking) to enhance one's status or let others in on an insulting comment. Motor mouthing—talking quickly to avoid pauses and response—may be done to protect or extricate oneself from a bad situation. Hustling includes all manner of ploys and deceitful maneuvers to extort money. In the case of students, it may involve running a game on school staff that gets them out of class or an assignment.

Dealing with Oppositional Behavior

Teachers and police are forced to see through all this, to stand up against attitudes and behavior meant to dissolve the code approved by decent folk within the ghetto and the mainstream without. But these enforcers represent a sys-

---

[11] Ibid., 89.

tem that has limited opportunity and respect in the hood (neighborhood).

Outsiders think that most urban violence is caused by vicious drug and turf gang wars. In some places, however, many of the drive-by shootings and personal assassinations have to do with she-said-he-said. Sex and gossip threaten personal status and group pride; action must be taken, and it is often violent.

Drugs and crime are part of the picture and need to be understood in context—not to excuse but to provide some idea of solutions. When tough love, resolve and collaboration combine, effective programs emerge and neighborhoods can begin to change. Faith-based community organization is making a difference in city after city.[12] More attention needs to be given to these models of hope. In other places, however, neighborhoods have been left to decay, or the emphasis has been placed almost entirely on law enforcement.

U.S. society adopted stern responses to rising crime rates in the late 1980s and 1990s and placed an increasingly heavy responsibility on the police. It is easy to see how the style described above meets a typical police force. Some believe the best way to gain control of the hood is to get everyone on the streets into the system—book them for something, even if it's jaywalking; then you have their picture and prints.

Prisons and the Criminal Justice System

The U.S. has more of its citizens in prison than any other nation on earth, having passed the high Russian percentage in 2000. With two million Americans in prison, fourteen million others face the likelihood of incarceration during their lifetime. Zero tolerance and "three strikes and you're out" laws are part of the cause. Almost fifty percent of American inmates are black.[13] Profiling, targeting black neighborhoods, and the general prejudice against the poor are part of the reason. "We

---

[12] See examples of such programs under "Resources" at end of this chapter.
[13] *The World Almanac 2000* (Mahwah, N.J.: Primedia Company).

incarcerate poor kids for things that middle-class kids get counseling for," says Los Angeles civil-rights attorney Connie Rice. My work with young people has shown me poor kids sent to jail while rich kids—for similar or more serious offenses—were let go after sessions in police stations or lawyers' offices.

Many prisoners are nonviolent drug felons. Underage offenders are going to adult prisons instead of county jails or youth detention centers. In Texas, the prison population has grown five hundred percent in twenty-five years, and most prisoners are minority inmates. Between 1985 and 1997 the increase of white inmates went from about 0.6 percent to just over one percent of the U.S. population, but for black males it was a jump from 3.5 percent to seven percent.[14]

The cost of imprisonment is astronomical. We were paying thirteen billion dollars for our state prisons in 1985; we paid twenty-seven billion dollars in 1996.[15] Much more devastating is the effect on families and communities. Two out of every one hundred American babies have their moms or dads in prison. Questions are also being asked about the effect of widespread incarceration on communities.

Diana R. Rose, a sociologist at New York's John Jay College of Criminal Justice, is among those studying the the prisons. "Until recently, nobody has really thought about incarceration in the aggregate. Many people assume that incarceration reduces crime. But when incarceration gets to a certain density, that is when you see the effects change."[16]

🏃 How could you use this chapter for a discussion in a workshop on urban life or urban programs? What would be the goals of such a session? How might you use music or a movie/television clip in the workshop? What kind of role play might be helpful?

[14] Ellis Cose, "The Prison Paradox," *Newsweek,* 13 November 2000, 40; U.S. Department of Justice statistics.
[15] Ibid., 42.
[16] Michael A. Fletcher, "High Incarceration Rate May Fuel Community Crime," *Washington Post,* 12 July 1999, A1.

Although incarceration is necessary to eliminate threats to public safety, in most other cases it is usually counterproductive. Creative punishments that would serve the community and its offenders could be found. Breaking up families, taking some mothers away from children, making women the primary leaders of the neighborhood, creating a prison initiation rite—or even a university with a crime major—and disillusioning a community toward the criminal justice system are powerful negative factors.

There is even more to this phenomenon. We are making ex-convicts into heroes and role models. Prisons have become a source of youth culture, creating many of the styles young people follow. "Shaved heads, tattoos, baggy pants worn below the hips, and unlaced sneakers all owe their origin to prison, where heads are frequently shaved, belts and shoelaces confiscated to prevent suicides, and jailhouse tattoos readily acquired."[17]

Christians should demand prison reform; we should be dissatisfied with rehabilitation that is counterproductive.[18] The system could be improved, and there are opportunities to supply answers for questions asked in lonely cells. Muslims and then Christians discovered the amazing potential for prison ministries. Secularists are forced to see positive results from faith-based service to convicts, especially ministries that follow up felons after release, when they need it most. There must be a greater willingness to minister to those coming out of the criminal justice system with two or three strikes against them.[19]

---

[17] Richard Moran, "Home Sweet Home: Given a Choice Many Convicts Are Opting for Jail Instead of Probation," *Boston Globe,* 29 October 2000, E1.

[18] For a quick education on this matter, see Mother Jones' Special Report, "Debt to Society" at www.motherjones.com/prisons. Click on "Map" first for a quick briefing, then explore the various aspects of this issue.

[19] As of 2002, even died-in-the-wool, "lock-'em-up-and-throw-away-the-key" leaders are rethinking their position on this matter and acknowledging that we must get nonviolent offenders out of prison. A strong emphasis on education and training must follow.

Further Understanding Needed

Despite many good programs and valiant efforts, many hardened convicts come out of prison only to return to gang activity in a neighborhood. Considering what sometimes looks like a culture of crime, many readers will ask, But why? Why are inner-city communities like this? Why the drugs, the crime, the violence? Why can't urban youth see the folly of it all, how life as an unwed mother with too many children or as a drug pusher on the corner is nothing but a dead end?

The quick answer is that many inner-city communities are not drug- and crime-infested and that most urban youth are choosing a positive way despite steep barriers.[20] Still, such questions need to get much closer to the situation, as did Philippe Bourgeois, an anthropologist who moved into East Harlem, New York, with his wife and baby. Living there, he gained the friendship and trust of crack and drug dealers. He was welcomed into crack houses where he observed, photographed, and tape recorded daily routines. He went to East Harlem to explore the underground economy of an area judged to be extremely poor, and yet its inhabitants, with little to show by way of downtown employment and facing the high costs of city rents and food, were not "homeless, starving, and dressed in rags."[21]

Trying to understand the underground economy, which includes informal car repair, trade and barter, and so forth, he was drawn into one powerful aspect of the people's free market: the crack and drug business. Bourgeois's experience and analysis of his Puerto Rican neighborhood confirms our understanding of street culture:

---

[20] Those with urban experience agree with the studies of Anderson and others that a minority of ghetto inhabitants are troublemakers, but their values and style can take over the streets of a community. There is the general 20-60-20 makeup of a community: twenty percent leaders, sixty percent followers, and twenty percent troublemakers.

[21] Philippe Bourgeois, *In Search of Respect* (Cambridge: Cambridge University Press, 1995), 2.

Substance abuse in the inner city is merely a symptom—and a vivid symbol—of deeper dynamics of social marginalization and alienation. . . .

The anguish of growing up poor in the richest city in the world is compounded by the cultural assault that El Barrio youths often face when they venture out of their neighborhood. This has spawned what I call "inner-city street culture": a complex and conflictual web of beliefs, symbols, modes of interaction, values, and ideologies that have emerged in opposition to exclusion from mainstream society. Street culture offers an alternative forum for autonomous personal dignity. . . .

This "street culture of resistance" is not a coherent, conscious universe of political opposition, but, rather, a spontaneous set of rebellious practices that in the long term have emerged as an oppositional style. Ironically, mainstream society through fashion, music, film, and television eventually recuperates and commercializes many of these oppositional street styles, recycling them as pop culture.[22]

While Hollywood and Madison Avenue capitalize on urban styles, many ghettos are left in critical condition. David Simon, a teacher and writer, was joined by a retired police officer, Edward Burns, in writing *The Corner* and a six-hour documentary that was made in a Baltimore neighborhood. What they convey is not a hopeful picture:

[Cocaine created a] freelance market with twenty-year-old wholesalers supplying seventeen-year-old dealers. . . . On every corner, street dealers began using minors, first as lookouts and runners, then as street-level slingers. . . .

The trend only accelerated as more young mothers went to the corner chasing coke, and single-parent families already under pressure began to implode. More than heroin ever did, cocaine battered at what had for generations been the rock-hard foundation for the urban black family.

. . . there was now raw anarchy in many homes. . . . Now there loomed the specter of children who were, in reality, parentless. Unattended and undisciplined, these children were raising themselves in the streets, free to begin their inexorable drift, drawn not only by quick money, but by the

---

[22]Ibid., 2, 8.

fame of it. . . . The corner became the funhouse, offering camaraderie and standing and adventure. . . . Slinging drugs was a rite of passage.[23]

Years of experience and the intensive year spent in their research convinced these two men that "we can't stop it. . . . The corner is rooted in human desire—crude and certain and immediate. And the hard truth is that all the law enforcement in the world can't mess with desire."[24] But they didn't quit. Their conclusion asks us "to shed our misconceptions and see [this world] fresh, from the inside."[25]

> We need to start over, to admit that somehow the forces of history and racism, economic theory and human weakness have conspired to create a new and peculiar universe in our largest cities. Our rules and imperatives don't work down here. We've got to leave behind the useless baggage of a society and culture that still maintains the luxury of reasonable judgments. Against all the sanction we can muster, this new world is surviving, expanding, consuming everything in its path. To insist that it should be otherwise on the merits of some external morality is to provoke a futile debate. In West Baltimore or East New York, in North Philly or South Chicago, they're not listening anymore, so how can our best arguments matter?[26]

The Soul and Paradox of Hip-Hop

The bleak outlook of such life and its inner rage is expressed in rap music. Our listening to those who know involves analysis of rap in particular and hip-hop in general. Hip-hop[27] is huge, and it is changing in the endless transfigurations of pop culture. Its popularity extends from the city, to the suburbs, in rural areas, and in many interesting config-

---

[23] David Simon and Edward Burns, *The Corner: A Year in the Life of an Inner-City Neighborhood* (New York: Broadway, 1997), 63–64.

[24] Ibid., 57.

[25] Ibid., 60.

[26] Ibid.

[27] "Hip-hop" is the larger term describing urban street culture. It originally included the pop urban arts: graffiti, rap music, and break dancing. The music and subculture of scratch is a different form of hip-hop than hard-core rap. The term "hip-hop" is broadening and its meaning and products have been widely commercialized.

urations, around the world. Devotees and creative local adaptations can be found in Paris, Tokyo, Jakarta, Cape Town, and in almost every culture. There are reasons for its popularity, and its influence is positive and negative. Rap music illustrates how the ghetto is both a victim of larger society and a perpetrator against itself and its own.

There are all kinds of rap. Urban voices from many countries and in the U.S., from the East Coast to the West Coast, have their own style and messages. It is perhaps poetic justice that rap is a way for marginalized urban youth to tell their stories and to find dignity along with plenty of money. As with all countercultural music, hip-hop as it goes mainstream is invited into capitalistic culture. The final irony is how hip-hop style and gangsta rap's nasty rhymes become popular with thirteen-year-old suburban white girls and boys. Some parents feel forced to pay rappers to offend their middle-class values and sensibilities.

From the street level, inner-city inhabitants feel not only marginalized and undermined by the power systems but also betrayed or at least neglected by their own who make it. Too often success stories from the hood—whether they be business and professional people, athletes, or musicians—move out and give little in return.

Hip-hop in general, and rap in particular, has not only sold out but also promoted itself at the expense of young ghetto listeners.[28] For years, because of white critics from without, it seemed a taboo to complain about rap from within. But excesses in style and substance have gradually become too much.

---

[28] For a different and more radical view of rap see Chuck D, *Fight the Power: Rap, Race, and Reality* (New York: Delta Trade Publications of Dell Publishers, 1998) and Hashim A. Shomari, *From the Underground: Hip Hop Culture as an Agent of Change* (Fanwood, N.J.: X-Factor Publications, 1999). Further background and balance can be found in Tricia Rose, *Black Noise: Rap Music and Black Culture in Contemporary America* (Middletown, Conn.: Wesleyan University Press, 1994) and William Eric Perkins, ed., *Droppin' Science: Critical Essays on Rap Music and Hip Hop Culture* (Philadelphia: Temple University Press, 1995).

Spike Lee's *Bamboozled* attacks the history of racist minstrel shows, satirizes the exploitation of African Americans by
the entertainment industries, but also suggests that African
Americans are carrying on their own play against themselves
in our time. For example, Martin Lawrence's *Big Momma's
House,* Eddie Murphy's *The Nutty Professor I* and *II,* and
Keenan Ivory Wayans's *Scary Movie* can be seen as examples of
old-fashioned minstrel shows in a new style. Sensationalizing
sex and violence and bling-bling culture (a mouth full of plati-
num, expensive rings, an extraordinary watch, and gold around
the neck) uses images and messages that derail the struggle of
young people on urban streets. In Spike Lee's words, "The sad
part is they [black actors and rappers] don't know it. One
could make the argument that certain parts of rap, you might
say gangsta rap, those videos could be construed as a contemporary minstrel act."[29] When *Newsweek* asked Lee if his movie
was not only harsh on the white media but tough on blacks as
well, he responded, "My people have to wake up and realize
what's going on and our responsibility in it. I mean, back in
[those times] we didn't have a choice. Hattie McDaniel and
Bojangles didn't have a choice. Nowadays we don't have to do
this stuff. So anything you do is on your own."[30]

Dr. Dre's (cofounder of the rap group N.W.A. and a creator of gangsta rap) promotion of Eminem, his boasts of
harder-core CDs to come, and the duo of Elton John and
Eminem illustrate how much the rap business is money-
driven. Meanwhile, criticism of rap's extremes grows within
the hip-hop nation. Chuck D, leader of Public Enemy, com-
plains about the dumbing down of rap on his website. Singer
Eve asserts that if Biggie and Tupac were alive, we wouldn't
be hearing the stuff we do now. Moss Deff, who has gone
gold besides many other ventures, provides a clear critique
of current trends: "In terms of what media outlets show you,
it's very one-dimensional. It's not just hip-hop music—TV

[29] Renée Graham, "*Bamboozled* Is a Daring Satire," *Boston Globe,*
24 October 2000, D1, D8.
    [30] Allison Samuels, Interview, "Spike's Minstrel Show," *Newsweek,* 2
October 2000, 75.

and movies in general are very narrow. Sex, violence, the underbelly, with junkies, prostitutes, alcoholics, gamblers. The new trend today is depravity."[31] Perhaps most significant is a conclusion of Reginald C. Dennis, thirty-four, a former editor of *The Source* and observer of hip-hop over many years: "Everything people hoped for came true, and everyone's miserable about it. It was a hollow dream."[32]

Graffiti, break dancing, and rap music were great expressions of street culture in the late 1970s and early 1980s. Something went wrong, however, as the reflection of urban realities turned to excess and manipulation. Drug pushing and the music business are sad extremes of American capitalism, an analysis with which some rappers agree. "The endless strip-club videos and the sexist views toward women aren't what hip-hop should be. Our women are the queens of the universe," says Common from Chicago.[33] But Dr. Dre's attempt at a more positive direction with "Dr. Dre Presents" (1997) fell flat, and he realized he had to get back to raw gangsta. Ice-T, long a defender of rap's excesses, recognizes the acceleration of its extremes: "they runnin' faster than you used to run. . . . I listen to some of them rap now—I mean, come on, that . . . is warp-factor-seven hip-hop. Hip-hop is like rock and roll. It's about wild men, scantily clad women and fast living. This is the food of human beings."[34]

But it is, many critics would contend, junk food—enjoyable and filling for the moment but dangerous to one's health and the welfare of the community. A professor of African-American studies at DePaul University, Michael Eric Dyson, sums it up: "There's a war going on for the soul of hip-hop."[35] It is a serious battle because those who tell the stories and write the songs control a culture. Hip-hop illustrates how the ghetto, as a victim of larger society, has become a perpetrator of additional ills against itself and its

---

[31] Allison Samuels, N'Gai Croal, and David Gates, "Battle for the Soul of Hip-Hop," *Newsweek,* 9 October 2000, 58–70.
[32] Ibid., 60.
[33] Ibid., 61.
[34] Ibid.
[35] Ibid.

own. Its stories need to be heard, but not uncritically. More important is listening to real voices of those who are striking out because they feel they have been struck down.

Listening to Urban Youth

How would a sixteen-year-old African-American from Chicago's Ida B. Wells housing project describe his hood, where fourteen-story highrises are daily witnesses to shootings and mayhem?

> Our neighborhood is a fun neighborhood if you know what you're doing. If you act like a little kid in this neighborhood, you're not gonna last too long. 'Cause if you play childish games in the ghetto, you're gonna find a childish bullet in your childish brain. If you live in the ghetto, when you're ten you know everything you're not supposed to know. When I was ten I knew where drugs came from. I knew about every different kind of gun. I knew about sex, I was a kid in age but my mind had the reality of a grown-up, 'cause I seen these things every day!
>
> Like when I was eight years old, my cousin Willy had a friend named Baby Tony and another friend, little Cecil. They used to hang out—watch TV, go to the park and hoop, sell drugs. They all went to jail. When Baby Tony came out he was walking through the park when a boy lit him up and blew his face off. His face was *entirely* blown off. And then a couple of days later Little Cecil sold somebody a dummy bag of plaster from off the walls, so the man who was using it came back and asked him for his money back. Little Cecil took off running and the man shot him. And Cecil was dead. That was both my cousin's friends that died in one week! And I hear about this when I was *eight!* I had just seen Baby Tony the day before he died.
>
> It's like Vietnam. I remember one time I was over my auntie's house spending the night. We were playing Super Nintendo and I heard this lady say, "I heard you been looking for me, nigger!" Then she just—Boom! Boom! Boom! Boom! She let off about eight shots. Then I heard the other gun fire off. We were just still there playing like nothing happened.[36]

---

[36] LeAlan Jones and Lloyd Newman with David Isay, *Our America: Life and Death on the South Side of Chicago* (New York: Washington Square Press, 1997), 33, 36.

This young writer, LeAlan Jones, was thirteen when he and his friend, Lloyd Newman, were found and chosen by David Isay to do a public radio narration about life in their neighborhood.[37] They proved to be unusually insightful observers and commentators on life in their hood. When they were fifteen, they investigated the terrible death of five-year-old Eric Morse. Derrick, eight, was Eric's older brother. Johnny, ten, and Tyrone, eleven, had tried to get Eric to steal candy from a local Jewel Supermarket (a frequent pastime of neighborhood shorties). Eric refused, and Derrick told his mother, who complained to the mothers of Johnny and Tyrone.

In retaliation, Johnny and Tyrone lured Derrick and Eric to a secret clubhouse. Once they got in this abandoned apartment, 1405 of 3833 South Langley, on the fourteenth floor, Johnny and Tyrone grabbed Eric and held him out the window. Derrick managed to pull his brother back inside. After punching Derrick, Johnny and Tyrone got Eric outside the window again. Derrick desperately fought for his brother but let go when he was bitten. The boys then dropped Eric to his death. Derrick rushed down the stairs in an attempt to catch his brother. He refused to leave the scene until his brother would "wake up." For weeks after, Derrick would be teased at school for not saving his brother.

🏃 How do you respond to the following words of LeAlan Jones? "We live in two different Americas. . . . We must somehow find a way to help one another. We must come together—no matter what you believe in— and find some concrete solutions for the problems of the ghetto." How might this be used in a class or group session?

---

[37] "Ghetto Life 101." Later they were to write "Remorse: The Fourteen Stories of Eric Morse." With David Isay, who used their hundreds of hours of recorded interviews and their comments, they have done this poignant and important book.

LeAlan and Lloyd were able to interview project police, juvenile justice officials, school teachers, and administration, but even more remarkable is the way they broke the code of silence and persuaded relatives of these boys and residents of the building to talk. These three authors have given us a significant story, not only the terrible tragedy of one little boy's death but also of life in the projects. LeAlan, now sixteen, has spoken across the country:

> I want to leave you with some final words about our America.

> We live in two different Americas. In the ghetto, our laws are totally different, our language is totally different, and our lives are totally different. I've never felt American, I've only felt African-American. An American is supposed to have life, liberty, prosperity, and happiness. But an African-American is due pain, poverty, stress, and anxiety. . . . I don't have it as bad as most—there are millions of young men and women living the struggle even harder than me. As children, they have to make day-to-day decisions about whether to go to school or whether to go on the corner and sell drugs. As children, they know there may not be a tomorrow. . . . Why must they look down the road to a future they might never see? What have my people done to this country to deserve this? . . .

> This is our neighborhood, this is our city, and this is our America. And we must find a way to help one another. We must come together—no matter what you believe in, no matter how you look—and find some concrete solutions to the problems of the ghetto. Right now we are at the point of no return. We've got to make a change. . . . Somehow, some way, I believe in my heart that we can make this happen. Not me by myself. Not you by yourself. I'm talking about all of us as one, living together in our America.

> This is LeAlan Jones on November 19, 1996. I hope I survive. I hope I survive. I hope I survive. Signing off. Peace.[38]

The wise and courageous voice of one teenager is joined by a growing number, a host of young people, who refuse to give up hope. They all realize this cannot be done by one

---

[38] LeAlan Jones and Lloyd Newman, with David Isay, *Our America* (New York: Washington Square Press, 1997), 199–200.

individual or organization in isolation. What they see as necessary is broad cooperation and a determined national will.
Many of these young urban voices insist also upon spiritual
motivation. The importance of church and faith, especially
in the inner city, has been demonstrated by experts. Support
for faith-based enterprises is a critical part of broad collaboration. If we are willing to listen to the stories of these
young people and their search for significance, if we are
willing to pay the price of personal and national resolve,
LeAlan and others can be right: with God's help we will find
peace and hope.

Questions for Reflection and Discussion

1. In which of the two worlds described in the beginning of the chapter do you live?

2. Do all urban people live in the same kind of
   community?

3. Can urban dwellers be unaware of all that goes on
   in the ghetto and on the streets?

4. How willing are the human race, your country,
   and you to deal with the radical divide between
   the haves and have-nots? With racism and ethnic
   divisions?

5. What has been added to your understanding of
   street culture, juice, and the need for respect?

6. Do you see killings from any different perspective
   than you did before?

7. How would you deal with such violence?

8. What was the saddest part of this chapter for you?

9. Did you find any hope in this chapter? How so?

10. Where do you think we should go from here?

Book Resources

Geoffrey Canada. *Fist, Stick, Knife, Gun: A Personal History of Violence in America.* Boston: Beacon Press, 1995. 🛹 Geoffrey Canada grew up in New York City and runs a program for urban youth in Harlem. He has studied and lived in Boston. Acknowledging the deep roots of violence in the codes of the streets, Canada shows how these can be overcome. He appreciates the power of stories and is a fine story teller himself.

Scott Larson, ed. *City Lights.* Loveland, Colo.: Group Publishing, 2002. 🛹 One of the few books on urban youth ministry currently available.

Richard M. Lerner, Carl S. Taylor, Alexander von Eye, eds. *Pathways to Positive Development among Diverse Youth.* San Francisco: Jossey-Bass, 2002. 🛹 Part of a series, "New Directions for Youth Development," this positive approach focuses on "the incredible potential of adolescents to maintain healthy trajectories and develop resilience, even in the face of myriad negative influences." It includes articles entitled "Identity Processes and the Positive Development of African Americans," "Adolescent Risk: The Costs of Affluence," and "Adolescent Development in Social and Community Context."

Deborah Prothrow-Stith. *Deadly Consequences: How Violence is Destroying Our Teenage Population and a Plan to Begin Solving the Problem.* New York: HarperCollins, 1991. 🛹 This is one of the best handbooks on violence in general and urban violence in particular. The author was director of Massachusetts Department of Health and a professor at Harvard School of Public Health. She has developed a further workbook for use of this material with school children and has led many workshops on the subject.

Amos N. Wilson. *Understanding Black Adolescent Male Violence: Its Remediation and Prevention.* New York: Afrikan World Infosystems, 1992. 🛹 This author first provides evidence that American society creates and sustains Black-on-Black youthful violence before giving a holistic, socio-economic remedies.

Internet Resources

There are vast resources on the Web. Use Google.com or Yahoo.com to search for the words "African American" or "Hispanic" or "Latino," etc. and find answers to your questions or informational resources. You may do the same with urban programs or urban ministry.

To mention just a few: The Council of Leadership Foundations (www.clf.okc.org/interlead.html) facilitates the development of many significant urban (including youth) programs in some 30 cities. On an even larger scale, Communities in Schools (www.cisnet.org) is holding down the drop-out rate and enabling many urban youth to get to college (note their Partners, www.cisnet.org/partners/partners.asp). Straight Ahead Ministries to felons and youth at risk (www.straightahead.org) and its Network of Juvenile Justice Ministries (http://njjm.org). Exciting programs have been developed in Memphis, TN. The Memphis Leadership Foundation website (www.mlfonline.org) unfortunately doesn't give you much information. Call 901-729-2931 to inquire about the youth programs they've helped start. Streets, MARRS, Eikon, urban Young Life, and the Emmanuel Episcopal Center are some programs you should check out in Memphis. Other programs include Project Equip, which aids urban youth ministers especially through its annual conference; World Vision (Vision Youth), Compassion USA (sponsoring Kingdomworks Conference); and World Impact.

Here are more sites:

www.aecf.org/kidscount/census 🛹 This site supplies the Annie E. Casey Foundation's easy to use census data for USA and individual states.

www.childrensdefense.org 🛹 The Children's Defense Fund acts as advocate for children at risk and children with disabilities. You will find up to date, startling statistics

on the state of poor black children in this society and
much more.

www.newbeginningschurch.com/devos.html 🛐 The DeVos
Family Foundation's Urban Leadership Initiative has provided excellent, professional training for urban youth
leaders.

www.uywi.org 🛐 Larry Acosta's Urban Youth Workers Institute (Azusa Pacific Univ., L.A., California) runs a fine
annual training conference for urban youth workers.

12 Children Who Are Killers

Human beings are born to trouble just as sparks
fly upward. — Job 5:7 NRSV

For the inclination of the human heart is evil
from youth. — Gen 8:21 NRSV

It would be better for you if a millstone were hung
around your neck and you were thrown into the sea
than for you to cause one of these little ones
to stumble. — Luke 17:2 NRSV

Let the little children come to me, and do not
stop them. — Matt 19:14a NRSV

Sin has been called the only empirically verifiable doctrine of
the Christian faith. Who can deny the prevalence of evil,
that, in a beautiful world of almost unlimited potential, so
much has gone wrong? Without some transcendent sense of
morality and some revealed principles of right and wrong,
society is bound to experience confusion regarding clear criteria of good and bad. According to Scripture, sin came with
the fall and is described as grasping more than is our ap-
pointed lot under God.[1] It results in such things as sibling
rivalry and murder.[2] This is not the place to argue about doctrines of original sin, but our experience demonstrates that
"human beings are born to trouble as the sparks fly upward,"

---

[1] "You will not die . . . you will be like God . . ." (Gen 3:4b,5b, NRSV)
[2] The Lord favored Abel's offering but not Cain's. So Cain was very
angry and killed Abel. (Paraphrase of Gen 4:4b, 5a, 8b).

and most honest human beings are aware of a dark side in
their nature.

The Bible explains evil as self-centered pride and rebellion against God (Isa 14:12–17). This restless and rebellious
nature or flesh (Rom 7:15–24; Eph 4:22), the world (2 Cor
4:4; Gal 1:4; Eph 4:12; Jas 1:27), and finally the Devil (1 Pet
5:8; 1 John 3:8) explain why human beings sin even when
they try not to. Regarding the human disposition to sin,
Christians generally agree that such sin does not destroy the
nature of God in all; human beings therefore possess some
divine light and are redeemable. We can summarize with
these teachings from Scripture:

> God created humankind in his image, in the image of God he
> created them; male and female he created them . . . and
> indeed, it was very good. . . . In the beginning was the Word,
> and the Word was with God, and the Word was God. All
> things came into being through him. . . . What has come into
> being in him was life, and the life was the light of all people
> . . . the true light . . . enlightens everyone. . . . What can be
> known about God is plain to [everyone], because God has
> shown it to them. Ever since the creation of the world his
> eternal power and divine nature, invisible though they are,
> have been understood and seen through the things he has
> made. . . . Though your sins are as scarlet, they shall be as
> snow; though they are red like crimson, they shall become
> like wool. . . . [Jesus said] I have come to call not the righ-
> teous but sinners (TEV: not respectable people, but the out-
> casts]. (Gen 1:27, 31b; John 1:1, 3, 4, 9b; Rom 1:19–20a; Isa
> 1:18b; Matt 9:13 NRSV)

How are we to understand an early age of innocence? At
what age can a child do evil? How are we to hold children accountable and punish them? Obviously there will be differences of opinion on these questions, and some readers may
feel that this book has neglected the matter of culpability—
that it is weak on sin and judgment. My purpose has not been
to develop a theology of punishment or a theory of juvenile
criminal justice but rather to seek wisdom from scientific insights and biblical principles so that we may become better
listeners to stories, advocates for those in crisis, and encour-
agers of recovery.

Children Killing Children

An Internet editorial from the *Indianapolis Star* begins:

It has been a difficult week for schools in Indiana and else-where as parents and administrators confront the threat of violence. Each of these stories made headlines in recent days:

- Three first-graders in Lake Station, IN, plotted to kill a classmate either by shooting, hanging, or stabbing. (They even drew up a crude map as to where the killing would take place.)

- Three girls in Hebron, IN, planned to poison a 13-year-old boy in their middle school cafeteria.

- In North Lauderdale, FL, two seventh-grade girls smuggled knives and razor blades (along with a bag of batteries to bludgeon the victims and then push down their throats so they couldn't cry out while their necks were being slashed) in a plot to cut the throats of three other students.

- In New York City, two 12-year-old boys are accused of raping a 9-year-old girl in a public school hallway. It is the third sex-ual assault committed by students at the school this year.[3]

All this took place on the eve of one-year-anniversary ceremonies at Columbine High School. Anger toward adoles-cent killers seems justified, but what about child killers? Grieving the innocent victims of those killed by children evokes deep questions about the motivations of a child who murders. Is it possible to understand the motivation of these killers? What stories do these immature killers have to tell? These questions are not merely academic; they inform our thinking and response to evil. They are needed if we are to know what to do with a child killer.

Studying child killers strips us of the notion that youthful violence is a recent phenomenon. A survey by British journalist David James Smith begins with the conviction of ten-year-old William York for stabbing a four-year-old girl to death in 1748.[4]

---

[3] *Indianapolis Star,* 15 April 2000 (www.starnews.com).

[4] Harold Schechter, *Fiend: The Shocking True Story of America's Youngest Serial Killer* (New York: Simon & Schuster, Pocket Books, 2000), 3.

In 1871, twelve-year-old Jesse Pomeroy of Boston began torturing little boys; coming out of reform school in 1874, he killed a little girl and boy and became known as Boston's boy-fiend or America's youngest serial killer. Between 1968 and 1993 there were six murders of children by children in Britain. More than that number were tried for murder in the U.S. during each decade of the twentieth century.[5]

Can a child ever be described as evil or culpable for serious crimes? At what age should we punish a child for murder—and to what extent? The six-year-old boy who killed his first-grade schoolmate in Flint, Michigan, in late February 2000 was back in another private school seven weeks later, all expenses being covered by the state. His pleased mother said, "He wants to be a lawyer and get his father out of jail." Meanwhile, parents of the little girl he killed continued mourning. [Before the tragedy, the boy's mother had been pushed away from child care to a welfare-to-work program. This much touted program forced her to commute eighty miles and work double shifts. Still she and her children were evicted from her house. They were staying in the home of a relative when the boy found the loaded gun. Who is to blame? What kind of punishment and rectifying actions should be enacted?]

🏃 When a child is doing poorly in school it is often our first clue that something is wrong. What questions should be asked and what steps can be taken when teachers and administration spot poor work? When this student is also unpopular with classmates, isolated, and perhaps taunted, this is a second red flag. At this point, appropriate questions should be raised about the home situation. Has the Department of Social Services been involved, or do they need to be? There are many fine

---

[5]Gita Sereny picks up on these statistics in *Cries Unheard, When Children Kill: The Story of Mary Bell* (New York: Henry Holt, 1998), xviii, 369.

programs aiding school and government in cases that need special attention. The Wall Street Journal (21 Apr 00, W15) noted "A church-based mentoring program helps students inside public schools." KidsHope USA is a volunteer program for children at risk (K-5). It has demonstrated remarkable results with children headed for serious trouble.

A twelve-year-old boy gets carried away in "play WWF-style wrestling" with a little girl and kills her—an accident, he tearfully explains. He receives a life sentence without parole. His mother, herself a police officer, and even the prosecuting attorney and mother of the slain girl consider the sentence too extreme. The U.S. stands almost alone in trying those as young as seven (in New York State) as adults.

How are we to think about the so-called age of innocence and accountability? Many Christian churches consider seven to be the age when a child reaches the age of reason and is able to receive communion. In Judaism and Islam children are liable for their actions at age thirteen for boys and twelve for girls. Are sixteen-year-olds as criminally culpable as adults? What then of children who are fourteen, twelve, ten—and younger?

Gita Sereny, described as an authority on matters of crimes, conscience, and guilt, struggled with this matter when she attended the trial of two girls accused of murder. The younger, Mary Bell, eleven, especially attracted Sereny's attention. She was, as Sereny remembers, small for her age, "exceptionally pretty, with short, dark hair and intensely blue eyes," [6] bright, and strikingly devoid of emotions.

Bell was convicted of killing two young boys: Martin Brown (four years and two months of age) in May, and Brian Howe (three years and four months of age) in July 1968. At first it was thought Martin died of some unlikely accident. But Brian's death was clearly, from bodily evidence, a

---

[6] Sereny, *Cries Unheard*, 9.

murder. The investigation turned to two girls, Mary and her older friend, Norma. Neither girl admitted to being present when Martin died. Both said they witnessed Brian's death, and each blamed the other. Because Mary was linked with several other cases of recent violence and because she seemed much more hardened during the trial, she was convicted while Norma was entirely acquitted and all attention focused on the younger initiator. Mary was called a monster, an evil child, and labeled by the court a psychopath.

What troubled Sereny was that the court knew nothing of Mary's background and seemed uninterested in her family and upbringing. There was no investigation of or reference to her home and family. All that shaped this girl into a killer was deemed irrelevant, yet Mary did not know her father, and her mother was a prostitute who would often go to Dublin for weeks at a time. Mary was made to witness scenes between her mother and johns. She was even brought into some of their games and sexually molested. "Between the ages of four and eight, her mother, then a prostitute, had involved her in one of the worst cases of child sexual abuse I have ever encountered."[7] Mary's mother had tried several times to give baby Mary away and even to murder her before using Mary with clients. The state ignored all these facts before and after the trial.

Besides her study of child killings, Sereny had studied the depths of evil as it played out in the Holocaust. Her relationships and interviews with Albert Speer[8] and Franz Stangl[9] had brought these Nazis to admissions of guilt. Just hours before his death, the ruthless Stangl finally admitted to Sereny his responsibility in the murder of 900,000 at his camp. Having looked into such adult darkness, Sereny was unable to see such evil in children. She takes exception to the attitude in Great Britain toward Mary Bell and to the two eleven-year-old killers of three-year-old Jamie Bulger in 1993. Sereny maintains

[7] Ibid., 12.

[8] Gita Sereny, *Albert Speer: His Battle with Truth* (New York: Vintage, 1996).

[9] Gita Sereny, *Into That Darkness: An Examination of Conscience* (New York: Vintage, 1983).

there is no such thing as an evil child, believing that their evil deeds clearly reflect evil that has been put in them by adults. "I think 14 is a fair age to make a child morally responsible," she says, "because there's been a moral growth. Children at 10, nine and eight are not morally grown. Why should they be, any more than intellectually or physically?"[10]

Studies do show that fourteen-year-olds have a clearer concept of law and consequences than those younger, but do averages in such studies constitute an absolute base line? Should we not rather think in terms of degree of responsibility?

The story of Jamie Bulger's murder contains some parallels to Mary Bell's killings of Martin Brown and Bryan Howe. Just as Mary apparently led Norma into the second murder, Robert Thompson (11) seems to have influenced Jon Venables (11) in their terrible abduction and torture of Jamie. Although there is no question as to their guilt in the murder, neither boy could give any reason for the deed. Rather than showing remorse, they were described as exchanging "cold, evil smiles" with one another in the courtroom.

As with Mary, these boys were labeled evil monsters. And like Mary, they came from poor, broken, and dysfunctional families in which they had been abused. Just as Mary would hurt others because "I like to hurt," these boys had tortured and killed cats. (The torture of animals often foreshadows violence toward the victims of a psychopath.) Careful consideration of child killers suggests some middle position. Neither seeing these child killers as monsters, nor as innocents, seem viable and satisfactory conclusions.

The crimes of twelve-year-old Jesse Pomeroy (Boston, Massachusetts) in the 1870s were especially sadistic. He would strip and beat his victims, which apparently brought him into a sexual frenzy; he later admitted he would masturbate during and after such sessions. Five boys testified against Jesse, and he was sent to the House of Reformation in Westborough, Massachusetts. Jesse was smart enough to realize that good behavior could shorten his incarceration, so he behaved well

---

[10]Sarah Lyall, "Close Enough to Evil to Look Beyond It," *New York Times,* 15 Aug 1998, B7.

and succeeded in his studies. This led to his promotion to dormitory monitor; the authority and power of this situation
suited him well. Some observers noticed warning signs during
his incarceration. Jesse was unusually interested in the disciplinary beatings that took place. Considering the stories and
details of these floggings would help him climax in his cot at
night. He was similarly attracted to the sight of blood. Once a
teacher asked his help in ridding her garden of a snake. Upon
finding the snake, he began to beat it until there seemed to be
little left. The teacher had to shake him to make him stop, and
his eyes and demeanor seemed distant and blank. Still, he impressed his supervisors enough to be released well before
completing the years of his sentence.

Only weeks after his release, Jesse lured a young girl into
a cellar and murdered her. Her body remained undetected for
weeks, although it was below her family's store. In the mean-
time Jesse led a young boy to the marshes and killed him. Both
bodies were terribly beaten and sexually mutilated. Again Jesse
denied, confessed, but then publicly denied the murders.

In many ways, Jesse Pomeroy may be seen as an exceptionally young and precocious serial killer. Harold Schechter
describes such killers:

> At the core of most serial killers is a bottomless well of self-
> loathing. Their crimes are a way, not only of striking back at
> the world, but of boosting their egos. Torturing helpless vic-
> tims becomes their perverse means of achieving a sense of
> power. The notoriety they receive provides them with a
> twisted feeling of significance, affirming that they are people
> to be reckoned with.[11]

But, we wonder, what could produce such a young
psychopath?

1. Jesse came from a family plagued by alcoholism, wife
   abuse, and child abuse. As a result, there were two
   divorces in two generations, an unusual circumstance in
   the nineteenth century. Jesse remembered and described
   how his father twice stripped and beat him, a pattern
   that seems to have inspired some of his atrocities.

---

[11] Schechter, *Fiend,* 238.

2. The domestic violence made his mother separate from her husband when Jesse was very young. Jesse never enjoyed a close bond with his mother, who seemed cold, strong, and preoccupied by hard work. Without nurturing, he had to fend for himself. There is evidence of what we call attachment and character disorders.

3. Jesse was conscious of his appearance and how it disgusted others, even his father. He was taunted and humiliated by other kids because his head and jaw were enlarged and one of his eyes was white with a cataract, and. According to Robert Hale, psychopathic killers are "releasing a smoldering rage that is rooted in early embarrassment."[12]

4. Jesse seems to have been different and difficult even as a child. There is the question of genetics; did he come into the world with some psychological disadvantages? According to his mother and defender, severe childhood diseases were responsible for some of his difficulties. Perhaps an unfortunate genetic disposition combined with negative consequences of early illness also pushed Pomeroy toward an antisocial personality.

5. With at least average intelligence, Jesse loved to read, and much of his reading was dime store novels. He is remembered as liking to talk about violence and torture in such things as the Indian wars (often the subject of such stories). From a young age, he would choose the role of the bad guys in neighborhood games.

Jesse's experience in the nineteenth century provides clues in understanding antisocial and psychopathic behavior today.[13]

Culpability, Punishment, and Rehabilitation

In response to a child's vicious killing of another, I would favor immediate punishment no matter what the age. Unfortunately our criminal justice system often has an all-or-nothing approach: adult or juvenile, death or walk free. Months in age may separate killers who serve a year or so until they are eigh-

---

[12] Ibid.
[13] See the discussion of thwarted growth in chapter 5.

teen and those who must serve life. But punishment should
not be our primary consideration, or we will resort to a vengeance philosophy and lose ourselves in endless cycles of violence. Punishment should be humane and age-appropriate. It
should be secondary to understanding what went wrong.
When a child kills, adults, community, and society carry a
greater weight of blame than does the child. Assessment of
culpability ought to be part of the sentencing process.

> 🏃 Young children are most likely to tell their stories
> through action, play, and art. Anyone in a caring
> relationship with children is responsible for detecting the
> hurts in children. In all cases, children with serious
> problems should be referred to experts. A Sunday School
> teacher might even pick up on something no one else
> has noticed. Remember, especially with young children,
> appropriate consultation and proper referral are critical.

It is better for a society to learn and prevent than to
sensationalize and punish, but when a child kills, media and
prosecutors fight over disclosure of evidence. The motive of
the media is primarily profit; for the prosecutors, success. It is
easy for schools, police, parents, and others to be concerned
with protecting their own interests, while the young perpetrator bears all the legal consequences. Instead there should be a
sharing of blame and an opportunity for all to see what went
wrong and how social dysfunction can be corrected. We must
learn more about restorative justice. Meanwhile, no child
capable of rehabilitation should be executed or put away for
life; nor should the child receive a trifling sentence.

According to an Internet tutorial, restorative justice "is
a process whereby parties with a stake in a specific offence
resolve collectively how to deal with the aftermath of the offence and its implications for the future."

Restorative justice is different from contemporary criminal justice in (the following ways):

- Viewing criminal acts more comprehensively . . . recognizing that offenders harm victims, communities, and even themselves.

- Involving more parties in responding to crime . . . including victims and communities as well.

- Measuring success differently . . . i.e. how many harms are repaired and prevented.[14]

Restorative justice is particularly appropriate and beneficial in dealing with young offenders. The possibility of extreme sentences, the unevenness of sentences given, the injustice of choosing a scapegoat when several youth are involved and some needed as witnesses, the oversight of culpable adults, and the counter-productivity of youthful confinement argue for a system of restorative justice. Further studies should be done to verify the effectiveness of such responses to juvenile crime.

A crime committed by a child may be heinous, but the younger the child, the more sure we are that adults and social systems should stand guilty with the juvenile perpetrator. Such cases must be a part of Jesus saying angrily, "It would be better for you if a millstone were hung around your neck and you were thrown into the sea than for you to cause one of these little ones to stumble." (Luke 17:2 NRSV)

On the other hand, how Jesus must love those who spot little ones starting to trip or slide.

Questions for Reflection and Discussion

1. When you learn about a child killing a child, what is your reaction?

2. How do you think you would respond if your child were killed by a classmate? Given time to contemplate the situation, might your response be different?

---

[14] Online: www.restorativejustice.org/rj3/intro_default.htm.

Questions, cont'd.

3. There have been many stories in this book about children killing children. How have these incidents affected you?

4. Do you agree that culpability and responsibility must be shared in the case of a very young killer? What does this mean?

5. How do you process the ideas of evil, punishment, restoration, forgiveness, healing, and reconciliation in regard to these stories?

6. Are you an advocate of restorative justice? How do you understand it?

7. What have you learned in this chapter—and how can this be used?

8. Are there points in this chapter with which you disagree? How would you change them or state them differently?

9. With what questions does this chapter leave you? How might they be resolved?

Book Resources

Dorothy W. Baruch. *One Little Boy: An Extraordinary Book that Explores the Mind of a Troubled Child.* New York: Dell Publishing, 1956 (reissued 1983). ✿ Few books get into a child's mind the way this does.

Paul Cavadino, ed. *Children Who Kill.* Winchester, England: Waterside Press,1996. ✿ Going beyond the Mary Bell and Bulger cases, this book examines world-wide cases of children committing homicide with important data and insights.

Ken Magid and Carole A. McKelvey. *High Risk: Children Without Conscience.* New York: Bantam Books, 1987. ✿ This book devotes one chapter to children who kill, but there is much more here: a broad range of childhood pathology and a whole spectrum of anti-social behavior are analyzed.

Harold Schechter. *Fiend: The Shocking True Story of America's Youngest Serial Killer.* New York: Pocket Books, 2000. ⚑ This is the story of young Jesse Pomeroy of Boston in the 1870s.

Gitta Sereny. *Cries Unheard: Why Children Kill: The Story of Mary Bell.* New York: Henry Holt & Company, 1998. ⚑ This is the full story of Mary Bell from a renowned European journalist with strong psycho-social interest.

Internet Resources

See previous resource listings. On your favorite search engine, type in "children at risk" and "childhood pathologies" for data and programs.

www.childrensaidsociety.org ⚑ The Children's Aid Society has bases in several countries. Its mission is to ensure the physical and emotional well-being of children and families.

www.gospelcom.net/ia/links/khop.htm ⚑ The Kids Hope USA Ministry is a program of International Aid Inc. mentioned in a side-bar of this chapter. It is a church-based volunteer mentoring program for children at risk K–5 and has achieved impressive results.

www.kidshope.com ⚑ This is a program directed by Gary Sprague focused on families and children in a single-parent situation, or having experienced divorce or death. This program offers books, videos, audio tapes and seminars.

13 Suicide: Violence Turned Within

> *Why did I not die at birth . . . why was I not buried*
> *like a stillborn child . . . Why is light given to one*
> *in misery, and life to the bitter in soul, who long*
> *for death?* —Job 3:11a, 16a, 20-21a NRSV

Parents who have watched a child suffer a slow, lingering
death about which they can do nothing say their pain is ex-
quisitely unique. Those whose teenage child dies in an accident cannot get over the lingering emptiness. And when a
son or daughter is taken by a senseless murder, loss is mixed
with anger. But parents have told me that losing a teenager
by suicide seems worse than other kinds of death and loss,
for it seems inexplicable and mixes guilt with anger and
grief. People resolve other tragedies in terms of fate or the
will of God, but when a young person takes his or her own
life, explanations fail and questions haunt.

Reviewing the Facts

An increasing number of young people are taking what
has been called a permanent solution to temporary problems. Although it is difficult to cite exact global statistics, we
know that suicide rates have been rising steeply since 1980.
A United Nations Report on Global Situation of Youth as-
sesses the situation:

In all regions, depression is an emerging problem for young
people. Adolescents undergo a very rapid process of physical,

emotional, psychological, social and spiritual development, more than in any other phase of life.

Studies have found that while young women from western nations have special problems such as eating disorders, young women from developing countries are at higher risk for suicide. A 49-nation study—based on data from the World Health Organization—found that in developing countries, the female suicide rate is 75 percent greater than the male rate for ages 5 to 24 years.

Nordic countries have had suicide prevention and education programmes for years, and initiatives are being considered in conjunction with the World Health Organization to explore the global implications of these projects.[1]

In the early 1990s, UNICEF's Youth Suicide League found suicide rates to be highest in Lithuania, the Russian Federation, New Zealand, Slovenia, Latvia, Finland, Estonia, Norway, and Australia, generally in that order.[2] Rates in Switzerland, Canada, Belarus, the U.S., Ireland, and Sweden were also high.

According to the U.S. Surgeon General

- One in five high school students have contemplated suicide—and most of these have drawn up some plan for doing so.

- One young person in the country commits suicide every two hours.

- Adolescents commit suicide at a rate higher than average of all ages.

- The rate of adolescent suicide in the U.S. tripled between 1960 and 1980.

- Suicide is the second leading cause of adolescent death after accidents. Many deaths due to extremely reckless behavior, especially single-car accidents, are thought by many to be suicides—though not counted as such.

---

[1] "United Nations Report on Global Situation of Youth Shows Changing Trends" to the World Conference of Ministers Responsible for Youth, Lisbon, Portugal. 8–12 August, 1998. Online: www.un.org/events/youth98/backinfo/yreport.htm.

[2] Online: www.unicef.org/pon96/insuicid.htm.

• Suicide claims more adolescent lives than any disease or natural cause.

Although more boys than girls, and more whites than youth of color, commit suicide,

• Suicide rates for adolescent females have increased between two- and three-fold in the past three decades.

• Young African American males are committing suicide at an increasingly higher rate. Some urban men and youth have pointed toy guns at police officers in order to be killed. Such deaths are not counted as suicides.

• Youthful Native Indian American suicides, always high, are still rising.

There is a noticeable increase in suicide in children under 14.[3]

A Department of Public Health study of four thousand students from fifty-eight Massachusetts high schools alarmed officials: ten percent of the students had attempted suicide in the past year, with four percent requiring medical attention. At Lawrence High School 753 of 1,500 students surveyed said they tried to kill themselves in the past year.[4]

At highest risk of suicide as a group are gay teens. "Based on community studies, reported suicide attempts among lesbian and gay youth range from 20–42%, compared with estimated rates of 8–13% among high school students in general."[5]

In the U.S., girls/women are two or three times more likely to attempt suicide than are men. Boys/men, however, are four times as likely to kill themselves in the attempts than women.

One striking but little known statistic is that for every adolescent suicide there are nearly four hundred suicide at-

---

[3] Carol Watkins, "Suicide in Youth," from "Suicide and the School: Recognition and Intervention for Suicidal Students in the School Setting." Online: www.ncpamd.com/Suicide.htm.

[4] Patrick Healy, "Data on Suicides Sets off Alarm: Suicide Attempts by Teens on Rise, Study Says," *Boston Globe,* 1 March 2001, B1.

[5] Caitland Ryan and Donna Futterman, "Experiences, Vulnerabilities, and Risks of Lesbian and Gay Students," *The Prevention Researcher* 8, no. 1 (February 2001): 8.

tempts.[6] Somewhat mitigating the severity of this fact is the opinion of experts that *"there is a fundamental distinction between suicide attempts and suicide completions.* While successful suicide is usually the result of a strongly held intent to end one's life, most suicide attempts are probably not. Instead, many suicide attempts can best be seen as a strategic action on the part of youths to resolve conflicts within oneself, with parents and with others."[7]

Behind these facts there is much pain. The mind tries to find reasons for suicide, but understanding will never satisfy the heart. In simplest terms, suicide may be brought on by three factors. If it is not caused by extreme depression, suicide often results from a sudden, dramatic loss or despair over a long-suffered frustration. Second, there seems to be no remedy or solution and no one seems to understand. Finally, suicide is a suggested remedy that may come from friends or from cultural or social encouragement.

Popular music, which reflects and influences young people, cannot be a scapegoat. Some hurting teenagers seem to find relief or work out their homicidal or suicidal feelings vicariously by listening to pounding music rather than by taking drastic actions. But some vulnerable teens have taken their lives under the influence of, or while playing, suicidal music.[8]

Still, it is important to realize that many teenagers, facing similar external and internal pressures have never thought seriously about ending their lives. Together, with those who have contemplated such a step but decided against it, they form the majority who have not attempted suicide.

---

[6] David M. Cutler, Edward L. Glaeser, and Karen E. Norberg, "Explaining the Rise in Youth Suicide," Boston University and NBER, May 2000, ii. Online: www.nber.org/papers/w7713.

[7] Ibid., 5.

[8] John McCollum, nineteen, took his life while listening to Ozzy Osbourne's "Suicide Solution" containing the line "Suicide is the only way out." In one teen magazine of the 1980s Ozzy posed with a gun to his head. Suicidal lyrics can be found in the work of older groups: Pink Floyd's "Goodbye Cruel World," AC/DC's "Shoot to Thrill," Black Sabbath's "Killing Yourself to Live," and Blue Oyster Cult's "Don't Fear the Reaper." One group's name is Suicidal Tendencies. Newer songs include Blink 182's "Adam's Song," REM's "Everybody Hurts," and Type O Negative, "Everything Dies."

Classifications of Suicide

Understanding is no great comfort to those who grieve loss through suicide, so our goal is to gain insight and therefore to contribute to preventing suicide. For all the study of this issue, mysteries and paradoxes remain. Each individual commits suicide for a different set of reasons or feelings. Whether we are discussing suicide with young people or their parents, whether to prevent such action or supporting those left in its wake, we need as many insights as we can get.

Emile Durkheim's *Suicide* (1897) is a classic early study of the subject. His sociological analysis led him to classify suicides as egoistic, altruistic, and anomic. Durkheim saw the roots of egoistic suicide in excessive individualism and loss of community, social sense, and meaning. Its mood is melancholic. Altruistic suicide lies at the other end of the spectrum, a result of placing too high a value on family or community; its mood is calm or serene. Anomic suicide, Durkheim continued, comes about in times of social crisis; the word denotes social deregulation or loss of structure. Motives for such suicides may also come from the breakdown of family or domestic anomie. Its mood is anger or disappointment.

> 🎿 "Suicide is not chosen; it happens when pain exceeds resources for coping with pain." Whether we fully agree with this statement or not, it helpfully reminds us we are not trying to talk someone out of their pain . . . or worse, denying the extent of the pain. We may suggest that others have gotten through their dark nights, and we can talk (or read) about how they did it.

From a more psychological standpoint, Keith Olson lists the following reasons for suicide: escape from pain or an intolerable situation, physical illness, death, or loss of parents, friend, or lover, desire to reunite with deceased loved one, avoiding a burden or shame, revenge, guilt, attention, manipulation, impulse or whim, delusions, mastery over fate (desperate attempt for control or power), or an expression of love.[9]

In somewhat similar fashion I have categorized youthful suicides as romantic, ideological or political, crisis or impulse, no-way-out or prison, cluster or copycat, psychotic, depressive, angry—or a final type—communication or a bid for attention.[10]

Obviously these categories overlap, and no classification fits all cases.

Romantic Suicides

In 1995 Christian Davila, fourteen, and Maryling Flores, thirteen, jumped into the Tamiami Canal in West Dade, Florida. Forbidden to date by their parents (because of their youth), the two slipped off without money or extra clothing and made their way to the canal. Neither could swim. Both left suicide notes.

Maryling wrote to her parents, "You'll never be able to understand the love between me and Christian. I feel that without him I can't live. You don't let me see him in this world, so we're going to another place. . . . Please don't cry for me, this is what I want." A note to a friend said simply, "I love him more than anyone here on this Earth. I'll never be happy without him."

Christian's thoughts were just as passionate and poignant: "I can't go on living. I've lost Maryling. I'm taking my life because without Maryling, I have no life. I've lost Maryling. That's something that hurts me very deep inside of my heart. I've put my best into these 14 years I've been on this hellhole called Earth. . . . I'm escaping into the darkness of the unknown. And as the immortal Beethoven once said: 'Applaud, friends, the comedy is over.' "[11] (We can excuse Christian's misquote.)

---

[9] G. Keith Olson, *Counseling Teenagers* (Loveland, Colo.: Group, 1984), 371–72.

[10] See "Suicide," topic discussion, *Encyclopedia of Youth Studies.* Online: www.centerforyouth.org.

[11] Gail Epstein and Frances Robles, "Teens Found In Canal," *Miami Herald,* 9 November 1995, 1A.

Christian had come to the United States from Mexico at
the age of five; Maryling from Nicarargua at the age of six.
They met in their ninth-grade pre-algebra class. Neither had
missed a day of school. About these young lovers, columnist
Ana Veciana-Suarez wrote:

> The only thing harder than being a 13-year-old is being the
> parent of one. . . . Two of my five children are teenagers now.
> . . . Try telling your hormone-crazed child—and I use those
> words emphatically—that she cannot see the love of her life,
> a love that likely will be as passing as an unseasonable frost.
> She will hate you and defy you and not believe you because
> she knows everything, and without the perspective of expe-
> rience, nothing can prove her wrong. I feel sorry for Mary-
> ling and Christian, for the lives they refused to continue, the
> love they chose not to wait for, the promise they gave up.
> Yet, I see them not as star-crossed lovers, but as foolish ones
> who, if they had only been able to bide their time, might have
> known a deeper, abiding happiness when they were older.
> True love resists the test of time. But that, of course, is an
> idea beyond the ken of most 13-year-olds.[12]

Although there is a tone of adult condescension, this
commentary provides adult perspectives and insights into
the dilemmas of parents. Teenage perspectives are different:
Their passion is unique and overwhelming, the crisis so final
and absolute, and the line between fantasy and reality vague.
Young people see their world as distinct and separate from
the world of adults.

One of the detectives investigating the case remarked,
"This is as sad a case as you can find. It's a Romeo and
Juliet story." Attention to romantic youthful suicide was
established by Shakespeare's play, which has been adapted
into new times and different cultures, as in *West Side Story*
and *Barefoot Youth*.

Ideological or Political Suicides

In some cultures self-immolation is an extreme but accepted form of social or political protest; in others suicide
bombing is an entrance to paradise and heroism. Adoles-

[12] Ana Veciana-Suarez, "Ending Lives Before They Began," *Miami Herald*, 12 November 1995, 1J.

cence is characterized by high ideals, strong mood swings, and impulsive decisions. Along with their idealism, youth are often highly critical of adults, adult institutions and enemies of their people. "With respect to adult society, young people center their attention upon the hypocrisy and deceitfulness of some adults, particularly those in public life."[13]

In some instances, sacrificing oneself for a cause may be similar to romantic suicides. All else has failed; now the supreme sacrifice will ennoble me. Such a suicide may be decided upon quickly or be the result of careful planning. It may or may not be combined with other emotional difficulties.

Crisis or Impulse Suicides

Todd's senior essay was filled with youthful optimism. He had just received the car of his dreams and likened his life to driving off into a "bright and productive future." He saw himself supported by caring family and friends who encouraged his growth to independent maturity. Yet, just two weeks after writing this essay, Todd drove his Camaro to the parking lot of an ice cream shop and golf driving range where he worked. Sitting in the front seat of his car, Todd detonated a homemade bomb that took his life. He had not yet reached his eighteenth birthday.

> 🏃 Many young lives have been saved through caring intervention. Though we can never be sure whether or not someone will take his or her life, we should know the clues that may signal suicide. Despairing statements, giving away special gifts, a sudden lifting of spirits out of previous gloom, anything that signifies final arrangements can be warning signs.

Although some suicides are planned after months of consideration and dropping of clues, adolescents more often than adults may decide to take their lives within minutes. Reasons for suicide may lie in the pain within, but seeds of

---

[13] David Elkind, *All Grown Up and No Place to Go* (Reading, Mass.: Addison-Wesley, 1997).

the act may be planted by friends or favorite songs. Individuals or friends have made the final decision while spending their last minutes listening over and over to a particular song of self-extinction. Fantasy and reality become blurred. Suicide is seen as an episode rather than a finality.

No-Way-Out and Prison Suicides

Spies and those who operate behind enemy lines often carry a lethal, fast-acting poison capsule to use if they are captured. Their instructions are to end their lives rather than endure torture that might reveal critical information. Ethics and morality of war are difficult issues, but the logic of such a situation is clear: someone takes his life in service to his country. Taking one's life in a painful and terminal illness is also understandable, and its ethical justification debated. Some people are overwhelmed by guilt or take their lives to relieve their families of shame or financial obligations. These suicides are committed by those who feel trapped.

Impulsivity can combine with feelings of entrapment in teenage life. Brian Head, of Woodstock, Georgia, was an overweight junior high student with glasses when he began to be teased. The taunting continued into high school, and one day it became intolerable for the fifteen-year-old. While a teacher on hall duty watched, classmates teased Brian and finally one slapped him. Quickly Brian pulled out a gun, shouted to the teacher, "I can't take it anymore," and shot himself in the head.[14]

Remember the power of cliques and the teasing that solidifies the power and prestige of higher social groups in schools (see chapter 1). Feelings of humiliation and being trapped can lead to youthful suicides. Even more understandable is the desperation felt by someone being repeatedly raped or brutalized in prison.

Jack Carpenter knows about kids taking their lives in hopeless situations. For fifty years he has worked with young people, as area and regional director for Young Life, and as the founder and director of Youth Forum Maine. He may be

---

[14] Nadya Labi, "Let Bullies Beware," *Time*, 2 April 2001, 46.

found trekking through the woods or paddling a kayak with kids who call themselves the Trekkers. Or he may be looking up someone in trouble at a local school or at home. Sometimes he drives a hundred miles to visit young friends at Maine's correctional institution or Youth Center. One of those friends was James Thomas.

James was in prison for something he said he did not do, but there was a list of things he had done illegally. At times he seemed unable to control his anger. James had a prison friend, Kenneth Moore, and they were able to converse through a ventilation vent. They became very close, and James told Kenneth he was all messed up and going to hurt himself. He shared with Kenneth the pain of his childhood and his sense that he could never change. Then one night, he told Kenneth he couldn't take it and was going to end his life. According to Kenneth:

> He says, "How do I do it?" Now I'm in a predicament. Here's my best friend. Now if he's serious about doing it and he messes up, what happens? I told him to bend down the sprinkler and wedge a sheet behind it and put it around his neck and jump off. The kid had me crying, and I never cry. This place is killing me. The last thing he ever said in this world was that he loved me. . . . I told him I loved him too.[15]

James had asked Kenneth to stand by the grate and listen: "He told me, 'I don't want to feel alone.' . . . I heard the noose tighten. I heard him choking."[16] Having made his confession and affirmed his love, James took his final step. Kenneth was true to the prison code: Always help a buddy and never snitch.

Most of James's young life had been spent in institutions, and he was sexually abused in the process. Correctional officers later gave up on this violent criminal, but Jack Carpenter became his friend and heard his story. On weekend leaves in Jack's home, James found a dog to love and seemed to be a sweet kid. With Jack he fished, read the Bible,

---

[15] Mary Lou Wendell, "Cruel and Unusual: Does the Supermax Mistreat the Mentally Ill?" *Maine Times* 33 no. 14 (10–16 August 2000), 407
[16] Ibid.

and prayed. It was Jack who carried James's message to his dying mother, "I love you, Mom, and I'm sorry for screwin' up like I have."

Jack was devastated over not being able to say goodbye and missing the memorial service. To his colleagues and friends Jack commemorated this aborted life:

> This is the story of James. It needs to be told.
>
> What a life . . . sentence. Abused from the get-go, even sexually molested by a staff workers at AMHI [mental hospital], father in prison, etc., etc. A childhood filled with horrible atrocities.
>
> His life sentence is done, his tortured life over, and he's at peace with the One whose heart was constantly breaking over what happened to Jimmy, the One who made him and always loved him. Jimmy caught glimpses of that Love, even experienced that Love, in spite of tragic and unjust treatment he had received as a child. . . . I want to—need to—share his story.[17]

We need to hear these stories because they represent people we should not ignore. Many more kids are taking the places of those now gone. Similar fates face too many younger children.

Copycat Suicides

Sociologist and suicide expert David Phillips studied suicide rates in Los Angeles and Detroit after the papers in those cities reported a suicide. He found such reports resulted in jumps in the suicide rate. In the same way he found a national increase when a suicide was reported in the national media. If the suicide victim was a celebrity, the jump was more significant. Young people are particularly susceptible to such suggestions.

In 1982 six teenagers took their lives in Clear Lake, Texas. The next year, between March 1983 and March 1984, seven students at Plano Public High School, in the wealthy Dallas suburb of Plano, committed suicide. It began with a drag race reenacting a scene from *Rebel Without a Cause*.

---

[17] Jack Carpenter, "Youth Forum Maine Update," winter 2001.

Friends Bill and Bruce organized the race; sideswiped by one of the racers, Bill was killed. The next day Bruce took his life in a closed car in the family garage. Police said the car's tape recorder was blaring. On the cassette was Pink Floyd's "Goodbye Cruel World." That began a series of suicides in town and elsewhere.

Startling instances and statistics can be ticked off, but the pain in families or in groups of friends huddled around the new gravesite and refusing to leave is unimaginable.

In the mid-1980s, a dramatic and extensively publicized example of copycat suicides began in Bergenfield, New Jersey, a suburban town of greater New York. Drinking heavily one night, a young high school dropout, Joseph Major, fell or jumped off a cliff to his death.[18] Opinion as to what happened was divided in town and among his friends. Four of these friends (Thomas Olton, Thomas Rizzo, Cheryl Burress, and her sister, Lisa) became deeply absorbed in Joseph's death and spent time weeping and talking at his grave. Finally they agreed to join him in death. Driving into an empty garage at an apartment complex, they closed the doors and asphyxiated themselves. The four bodies were found the next day.

News of these suicides traveled across the country. In Alsip, Illinois, Karen Logan and her best friend decided this was the way to end their problems. They killed themselves in a similar manner.

By contrast on April 24, 1997, a positive demonstration took place in response to a negative situation. One hundred teenagers with some adult friends marched to Boston's City Hall to highlight the youth crisis of their community—in particular, a series of suicides. Fifteen months before, a fifteen-year-old boy had died of an overdose in South Boston. Southie, as this community is affectionately known, saw itself as declining in substance and spirit. Its ethnic identity, its heroes—athletic, political, and criminal—its employment rate, its education, social, and recreation services

---

[18] The 1988 movie *Permanent Record* was criticized for having David Sinclair jump off a cliff to his death.

> ✺ While trying to prevent particular suicides, there is work to be done on the environment in which young people are growing up—in families, school, prisons, communities, and even in the media. Our objectives are open communication, life and hope rather than dysfunction, despair and death. We have referred to the Search Institute and their emphasis on healthy kids in healthy communities. Many others are working in the same direction producing local success stories. We should think of suicide (along with homicide) as a public health issue; what is now toxic in our societies must be changed for the welfare of all.

were all diminishing. At least, these were the strong perceptions. And hard drugs were coming into the community. The reason the movie *Good Will Hunting* was so positively received in Southie was expressed by seventeen-year-old Megan Greene: "We're not all racist, we're not all suicidal, and we're not all on drugs. The movie made it look like a smart kid came out of Southie. . . . The movie is a good thing for Southie."

The movie and the protest march were needed boosts for the community. The wake and funeral of the fifteen-year-old, who had become popular for stabbing the man accused of raping his sister, was attended by a thousand mourners. Young people of the community emblazoned his name on project walls, and some even tattooed his name on their bodies, but near the first anniversary of his death, the first suicide took place.

1. Kevin Geary, seventeen, lived with his mother in a housing project, wanted to be a state trooper, was issued an $85 traffic ticket for running a blinking red light, and hanged himself on December 30, 1996.

2. Duane Liotti, twenty-one, who lived with his mother in the same development, hanged himself in February 1997.

3. Tommy Mullen, fifteen, an especially popular young man, got drunk with a friend (also fifteen) the night before St. Patrick's Day, and they decided to hang themselves. The friend changed his mind just in time, but Tommy went through with it on March 16, 1997.

4. Jonathan Curtis, sixteen, hanged himself after a close friend died from a heroin overdose in April 1997.

5. Tommy Deckert, fifteen, was a former altar boy taken to the hospital after attempted suicide; he never regained consciousness and died June 13, 1997.

6. Kevin Cunningham, seventeen, hanged himself from the porch of his home on July 22, 1997. He left no note.

It hurts to create such a list, but the lingering pain experienced by those left behind is unspeakable.

Cluster Suicides

Similar to copy-cat suicides are cluster suicides. Youthful suicides have something to do with the fact that others have done it. It is important to consider the importance of social imitation and peer influence in these tragedies. The prestigious Massachusetts Institute of Technology (MIT) suffered three suicides in the first five months of 1999 and eleven suicides in eleven years between 1990 and early 2001. Some students even speak of a culture of suicide. Before taking her own life, Lucy Crespo Da Silva mentioned to her mother how some MIT students seemed to view suicide as an answer to pain and how several had jumped off tall buildings on the campus. That is what Lucy did on November 19, 2000, a month before she was to graduate.[19]

In many different ways, peer influences have something to do with adolescent suicide. In "Explaining the Rise in Youth Suicide," Cutler, Glaeser, and Norberg tell the stories of teen suicides as examples peer influence.

---

[19] Tovia Smith (NPR, 29 Aug 01) reported that MIT was taking steps to reduce these suicides by expanding clinic hours, providing extended coverage for off-campus therapy, and putting four new staff in student dormitories.

We find strong evidence that *social interactions are impor-tant in teen suicide.* Teenagers are much more likely to attempt suicide when they know someone else who has attempted suicide, and suicides are "clumped" across areas in a way suggesting local spillovers. Spillovers may occur in sev-eral ways: attempts by one person may be more credible if it follows attempts by others . . . youths may provoke other youths to attempt suicide. . . . The presence of social interac-tions means that small differences in aggregate fundamentals can trigger large shifts in the number of youth suicides.[20]

We continue to remind ourselves that no one ever knows why another person has taken her life. Still, we must learn more about the social and psychological factors contributing to such untimely ends.

Psychotic Suicides

Suicide experts note that most suicide attempts are not made by psychotic persons. People generally commit suicide not because they are severely mentally ill but because they are upset; it is the pain that kills. Still, a percentage of young people take their lives as a result of delusions and disordered thinking.

Schizophrenia may appear in childhood, but it is more likely to appear in adolescence and young adulthood. The Schizophrenia Research Branch of the National Institute of Mental Health explains schizophrenia as a complicated and puzzling disease, "the most chronic and disabling of the major mental illnesses."[21] Schizophrenia may cover a single or several disorders but is characterized by a sudden psy-chotic episode. Being psychotic means being unable to sepa-rate real from imagined experiences.

According to the National Mental Health Association, "one third of people with schizophrenia attempt suicide, and 5 to 10 percent eventually do so. The majority of these are

---

[20] David M. Cutler, Edward Glaeser, and Karen Norberg, "Explaining the Rise in Youth Suicide," Working Paper for National Bureau of Econ-omic Research, Working Paper W7713, 5–6 www.nber.org/papers/W7713, May 2000).

[21] Schizophrenia Research Branch of the National Institute of Mental Health, "Schizophrenia: Questions and Answers." Online: www.mentalhealth.com/book/p40-sc04.html.

young, unemployed males with no families. They are usually isolated and may also have substance abuse problems."[22]

In her suicide note, one woman described her psychosis:

> Everyone has been so good to me—tried so hard. . . . But there's some core-level spark of life that just isn't there. Despite what's been said about my having "gotten better" lately—the voice in my head that's driving me crazy is louder than ever. It's way beyond being reached by anyone or anything, it seems. I can't bear it any more. I think there's something psychologically-twisted—reversed that has taken over, that I can't fight any more. I wish that I could disappear without hurting anyone. I'm sorry.[23]

Psychotic suicides make up a very small percentage of adolescent suicides. But to them we must add those who experience psychotic episodes as a result of bad reactions from hallucinogenic drugs and have thrown themselves into traffic or fire, off buildings, or into the path of a train. For those who get proper treatment, effective antipsychotic drugs are available. The combination of professional care and newly developed medications have helped reduce the potential destruction of suicides in this category.

Depressive Suicides

Our last three categories of youthful suicides clearly overlap earlier types. Of all suicides, the most difficult to prevent may be those who seek to end the despair of depression. Those who suffer the deepest depression speak of inexplicable, unrelenting pain—the absence of joy or comfort. Those of us not lost in this dark pit must never underemphasize its terror.

Kay Redfield Jamison has suffered and studied the pain of depression. At twenty-eight she attempted suicide, and upon recovering, she studied suicide.[24]

---

[22] National Mental Health Association, "Suicide: General Information." Online: Go to www.nmha.org/infoctr. Click Fact Sheets; click Suicide; click General Information.

[23] Kay Redfield Jamison, *Night Falls Fast: Understanding Suicide* (New York: Alfred A. Knopf, 1999).

[24] Ibid.

Jamison brings us into a conversation with a close friend and fellow sufferer. Over the course of the discussion, they work out a covenant promising that if ever they are tempted to commit suicide, they will call the other. The details of their commitment were carefully laid out. Then came the chilling conclusion of the story:

> Many years later—Jack had long since married and I had moved to Washington—I received a telephone call from California: Jack had put a gun to his head, said a member of the family. Jack had killed himself. . . .

> Although shaken by Jack's suicide, I was not surprised by it. Nor was I surprised that he had not called me. I, after all, had been dangerously suicidal myself on several occasions since our compact and certainly had not called him. Nor had I even thought of calling. Suicide is not beholden to an evening's promises, nor does it always hearken to plans drawn up in lucid moments and banked in good intentions.[25]

Over the years my wife (a clinical therapist) and I have asked those whose attitudes and actions suggest suicidal tendencies to call us before taking any action. I will continue to do so—even though I recognize it is no guarantee—and know how counselors fight guilt and incriminating questions when a client is suddenly gone.

Jamison describes a young man graduating from the Air Force Academy. When his name, Drew Sopirak, is read, "a roar of appreciation goes up from his classmates" showing his "immense popularity; indeed, a fellow cadet described him as the most respected senior at the Academy, and his squadron given him its outstanding leadership award."[26]

Still, he was never commissioned, nor did he receive his pilot's wings. Society had been able to give this young man skills to conquer any combatant, but "manic depression proved to be an enemy out of range and beyond the usual rules of engagement."

---

[25] Ibid., 4–5.
[26] Ibid., 53.

Drew was to mention later that he had experienced occasional problems with racing thoughts and periods of depression prior to his first manic episode (graduation evening). But these he kept to himself. He was the last person any of his friends would have expected to become psychotic or to have to be confined in a psychiatric hospital. The very unexpectedness and the seeming incongruity, however, were themselves not a complete surprise, given the nature of the illness that was to kill Drew. Manic-depressive illness usually strikes the young, not uncommonly during their college years, and not uncommonly in the apparently invincible—the outgoing, the energetic, the academically successful.[27]

From postgraduation celebrations, Drew was taken to the base hospital. Not long after, despite professional treatment and family support, he realized that his long-held dreams were lost and his future bleak. It seemed too disappointing to bear. He purchased a .38 revolver. When it misfired on the first attempt, he killed himself with a second effort.

Even severe bipolar illness and severe depression can usually be treated and controlled. But those who have experienced the deep hole of depression speak of pain and hopelessness that others cannot comprehend. Stories of Blaise Pascal and Abraham Lincoln, who suffered bouts of deep emotional darkness, are needed to encourage others who feel no hope.

Angry Suicides

Lovers who have been betrayed, a parent who has lost custody, children who have been abused, and employees who feel used and rejected may sometimes lash out homicidally, commit suicide, or both. School shooters, sometimes taunted for years, may kill and commit suicide. A suicide note was left unsigned by a young man who hanged himself. It read, "F___ you."

When a man's wife fell in love with his brother, he asphyxiated himself and left her this note: "I used to love you, but I die hating you and my brother, too."[28]

---

[27] Ibid., 55.
[28] Ibid., 78.

Repressed anger may lead to depression. Such depression can produce a mechanical life, a bitter life, or an eruption of rage in destruction of others or self. We are only beginning to deal effectively with the growing phenomenon of anger among young people. Discussions of anger and training in anger management are desperately needed. We also need to deal with anger, as with all other problems, spiritually as well as on the emotional level. Scriptures are rich with practical principles as well as illustrations of anger controlled and misdirected.

Bid-for-Attention Suicides

Not to be noticed is to feel less than human. Sensitive teachers, youth leaders, and counselors know how vital it is for a young person to receive attention. Elkind describes teenagers as feeling they are on a stage, the center of a drama, and that all others are or should be engrossed with what preoccupies their consciousness—"namely themselves."[29]

If young people do not receive attention from preferred sources, they will accept it from anywhere; any attention is better than none. But what happens where there is none?

Suicide attempts are often a bid for attention. If they are undetected, such attempts can turn deadly. Some suicide notes have hinted at an unfulfilled need for attention. The manner and place of suicides around school grounds may also suggest lonely anger in which someone is saying, "You never noticed me; now you will." Jamison tells of a young boy who pinned a suicide note to his shirt and hanged himself behind the Christmas tree. The note said, "Merry Christmas."[30] He knew this would get his family's attention. Mixed into the emotions behind such a note may have been jealousy and anger. We—and his family—will never know for sure.

---

[29] Elkind, *All Grown Up*, 40.
[30] Jamison, *Night Falls Fast*, 73.

A Pastoral Theology of Suicide

Unfinished business may forever haunt the families and loved ones of those who take their lives. The almost universal cry of the bereaved is "We loved them"; "we tried to help"; "if we had only known"; "we have a hole in our souls nothing can ever fill." The grief process for a lost family member or loved one can last months or years or forever. If the process is not accepted, grief can harden as bitterness. In a unique way, loss by suicide may leave a hole that never goes away. Still, with the passage of years, there is a difference between a holy emptiness and a hole that roils with bitterness or self-incrimination.

Some Christians insist that suicide is the unpardonable sin; however, our interpretation of Christ's reference to the unforgivable sin, or blasphemy against the Holy Spirit (Matt 12:31–32; Mark 3:28–29; Luke 12:10), is best left in mystery. We can say what it is not, but attempts at a literal explanation are at best suggestions. I would guard my heart against any form of blasphemy against God the Father, God the Son, and God the Holy Spirit. But exactly how blasphemy against the Holy Spirit is different from or more serious than blasphemy against almighty God or Jesus Christ, I do not claim to know—I can only conjecture. What we do know is that the Bible does not describe suicide as the unpardonable sin.

Suicide is a desperate act, and it may be the act of someone who has no clarity of mind. I have tried to explain how some people reach that terrible point. In doing so I have not tried to justify suicide, which violates the sanctity of life. In societies increasingly undermining the value of human dignity and in which young people are losing respect for life, we must stand firm for life over death.

Depressed young people are often helped when they can talk about how they're feeling, get some exercise or give themselves a special treat. They can further help themselves as they develop a discipline of keeping up social routines, putting the past and sad thoughts out of mind, concentrating on the here and now, and taking any positive steps against unhappiness they can think of. It is important for them to consider that anyone should see a doctor and/or counselor when they can't figure out their depression, find their sleeping or eating hindered, or begin to have suicidal thoughts.[31]

Parents are wise to consider how family communication (parents and siblings) must go to deeper depths, often with outside help. More than ever before conversations need to focus on feelings. Parents should pay attention to what may seem trivial issues and work with a counselor in assessing the severity of depression, frustration or anger. Be appropriately direct and specific in discussing suicide, develop a plan and contact, remove or guard all lethal means of suicide, and be ready to hospitalize even for a brief time if necessary.

As friends of troubled young people we many times feel as if their lives mean more to us than they do to them. Through radical respect for them and their lives, we try to prevent suicide—as we do with homicide. We attempt this by powerful listening to individual stories, by sharing our sufferings and respect for life, by pointing them to the One who gives peace and hope beyond understanding, and by recommending treatments, including therapy and medication.

Furthermore, we realize that listening to stories is contagious and builds community. Such communities should be caring, nonjudgmental, and sensitive as the body of Christ, a life-gaining source of hope and attentive relationships. Young people are the best means for preventing the suicide of friends. We can help them to become even greater helpers.

The Bible does not teach explicitly about suicide. It does not tell us what happens to those who take their lives. To argue, as some have, that those who commit suicide cannot go to heaven, based on the death of Judas Iscariot, is woeful interpretation of God's Word.

For some teenagers, suicide is a five-minute, foolish decision. If someone we love has made suicide her final earthly

---

[31] Elizabeth Fenwick and Dr. Tony Smith, *Adolescence: The Survival Guide for Parents and Teenagers* (London and New York: DK Publishing, 1996), 251.

act, we commit her soul into the hands of God, whose character, above all, is revealed to us as merciful.

> God so loved the world that he gave his only Son . . . not . . . to condemn the world, but . . . that the world might be saved through him. (John 3:16–17 NRSV)

Questions for Reflection and Discussion

1. What experience with suicide do you bring to this chapter?

2. What most impressed you here?

3. What helped you most?

4. With what questions does this chapter leave you?

5. What criticisms or suggestions would you make?

6. This chapter offers an initial explanation of suicide. It is not meant as a prevention or treatment manual. Do you find here some explanation or useful categories to use in your life and work?

7. Where can you go for further resources? The Yellow Pages and the Center for Youth Studies' website can help you (www.centerforyouth.org). See what it offers you in regard to the topic of suicide.

8. How would you deal with a friend in whom you see some suicidal tendencies?

9. What do you have to offer those who are suffering from the loss of a friend or family member to suicide?

10. Is your pastoral theology of suicide similar to the brief suggestions found here? How does it differ? How would you develop it more fully?

Book Resources

Melody Beattie, ed. *A Reason to Live.* Wheaton, Ill.: Tyndale House, 1991. 🐧 Many of all ages have been helped by this and other books from this fine writer. This book offers Christian hope.

Trudy Carlson. *Depression in the Young: What We Can Do to Help Them.* Duluth, Minn.: Benline Press, 1998. 🐧 Written for parents, teachers, medical personnel, youth workers, and everyone who should be interested in this topic. Based on research, this book is written out of personal grief of the author over a family suicide.

Jerry Kreitzer and David Levine. *The Peer Partners Handbook: Helping Your Friends Live Free from Violence, Drug Use, Teen Pregnancy & Suicide: A Guide for Students in Leadership Programs.* Barrytown, N.Y.: Station Hill Press, 1995. 🐧 This is a handbook for peer counseling and helping teenage friends, not only regarding suicide but other problematic behaviors as well.

Hayley R. Mitchell. *Teen Suicide.* San Diego, Calif.: Lucent Books, 2000.

James M. Murphy. *Coping with Teen Suicide.* New York: Rosen Publishing Group, 1999.

Richard O'Connor. *Undoing Depression: What Therapy Doesn't Teach You and Medication Can't Give You.* Boston: Little & Brown, 1997. 🐧 The Spotlight Review on Amazon.com is worth reading in itself. This is one of the best books on depression in general and is *not* mean to be a substitute for therapy and medication. Its emphasis is on replacing depressive patterns of thinking with positive thinking, relating, and behavior.

Tamara L. Roleff, ed. *Teen Suicide: At Issue.* Ann Arbor, Mich.: Greenhaven Press, 2000. 🐧 This book looks at *both sides* of the issues involved in suicide.

Internet Resources

You will find good information on any search engine, but here are a couple of good ones.

www.metanoia.org/suicide 🐧 This Christian site is developed by Martha Ainsworth: "If you are thinking about suicide, read this first . . ." (what follows is good). And, "What can I do to help someone who may be suicidal?" (www.metanoia.org/suicide/whattodo.htm). This is a helpful guide of warning signals and more.

http://suicidehotlines.com 🐧 This beautifully designed website is sponsored by DepressionBooks.com and Amazon.com. You easily pick your state and scroll down to select a hotline near you or for your particular age and situation. Or, you can call 1-800-784-2433 (1-800-suicide).

14 Theology of Violence

*The LORD saw that the wickedness of humankind
was great in the earth ... and ... the thoughts of their
hearts were ... evil continually ... and the earth was
filled with violence. — Genesis 6:5, 11b, NRSV*

Part 3 of this book has considered various kinds of violence and responses. As Part 2 concluded with a theological consideration of the problem of suffering, these varieties of violence to others and self calls, at the end of Part 3, for a theology of violence—the most difficult chapter of this book. Experience with troubled youth demands serious reflection about where violence comes from, how it is to be tolerated, and how it may finally be resolved. In some ways, this task takes us away for troubled young people, but the issue is a persistent question that will not go away. Ultimately, don't we need a philosophy and theology of violence in dealing with violent youth? You may want to skim or skip this chapter, but at least note its conclusion.

Introduction

The continuously repeated image seared its way into the American soul and shocked the world. Violence had come to America in a new way. "Nothing will ever be the same!" stammered some shocked observers. A society inured by sensationalized media violence, fictional and real, still felt stunned by the four-fold terror of that September 11th morning, when the Twin Towers in New York City crumbled to the ground. Many around the world, even those who had suffered staggering violence themselves, found a special sympathy for those Americans and citizens of the world who met a sudden, random death so deviously planned and executed—and for the loved ones left behind.

Americans and the world were suddenly forced into three responses. First, rescue efforts had to be made. Second, steps had to be taken to provide protection from further attack. And finally, security called for ferreting out the source of this terror. This third challenge, of course, would be the most difficult one.

Immediate reaction to the blast and image of collapsing towers was shock, numbness and disbelief—along with overwhelming sadness and grief. Anger would follow for most, an anger often overpowering and demanding. Only the promise of revenge seemed adequate to quell the rage. A few were able to think of forgiveness.

Clearly emotion could not rule our global response to this twenty-first century violence. There were lessons to be learned from the excessive bombing of civilians in the past century. No bomb, no weapon could eradicate these terrorists; they were all over the world—amongst us everywhere. Limited, tactical force was needed.

Some voices lamented the expressions of patriotism and the government's military plans. They appeared as unrealistic sentimentalists to many. A total commitment to pacifism was being tested.

Most agreed the terrorists must be found, rooted out, and brought to justice, even if it involved necessary violence. Others warned that *any* violent response would produce a cycle of even more insidious violence.

Theological discussions of war were difficult in the immediate aftermath of the attack. The depth of personal and corporate trauma, along with the complexity of strategic responses, help explain why many Christians drew back from theological reflection on the nature and use of violence. It's not easy to think about God's perspective on such disasters. It is difficult to turn to God's Word to determine proper responses to such terrorism. What would Jesus be saying to firefighters, police, and soldiers? The terrorists' aberration of Islam, or at least its radical militant extreme, made Christians reluctant to be caught up in anything that sounded like a "crusade" mentality.

The difficulty and intensity of the discussion did not become easier with time. In fact the issue of wars in the Middle East and elsewhere became more complex, challenging and divisive.

This book has considered pain and violence among young people. Everyone admits the prevalence of such feelings and actions. But few youth conferences, few discussions and papers, really consider a theology of violence. This hard chapter is a necessary discipline for those who would think theologically about what we are teaching young people. Although this discussion will take us into passionate disagreements regarding the nature and proper use of violence, it is a necessary theological endeavor. We may need to agree to disagree, and still find some consensus in our teaching.

Three Responses to World Violence

It may be helpful, though perhaps simplistic, to divide opinions about violence after September 11th into three categories. A minority cried out, "Blast them!" "Nuke 'em." "We have the power; the only thing this kind of enemy understands is violence. If God doesn't will it, at least God understands." Such thinking tends to use the biblical fact of violence to validate and vindicate any kind of action against an evil enemy. It does not pause to understand theologically or politically the character of the enemy nor the action to be taken. Crucial to such thinking is seeing one side (ours) as right and the other as evil. This is a crusade mentality.

A second position argues that reasonable violence, as a means to a just end, is theologically and morally acceptable. Violence, from this perspective, is a terrible scourge on earth, but it is not inherently evil. There is a proper time and place for restrained and conscionable force. The cosmos should not be understood in terms of a dichotomy between violence and loving forgiveness. Violence is part of the way things are and must be judged in terms of higher realities: the

nature of God, the nature of human beings, the nature of society and redemption. The challenge is to distinguish violence attempting to ameliorate evils that violate human
nature and just society from random or self-serving violence.
Deciding the relative justness of specific actions involves difficult discussions regarding complex issues of personal motivation, criminal justice and just war.

A third perspective begs unconditional forgiveness. "Forgive them. And never return evil for evil." Any justification of
force begins a descent into a pit of darkness. Violence is understood to be evil by its very nature. To respond with any
kind of violence is to become what we hate and to perpetu-
ate a deadly spiral of revenge leading to utter chaos. This terror has come upon us because we haven't lived up to the
Golden Rule. We were not the loving community doing
good, even to our enemies. Had we loved and helped these
people, this might not have come upon us. For this we must
repent. But even if we are innocent victims, we must forgive.
Martin Luther King Jr. used to say, "The problem with a policy of 'an eye for an eye' is that it will leave everybody blind."
King did not mean his followers to be defenseless; pacifism
is not suggesting passive acceptance of violence against a
group. It rather advocates the use of aggressive nonviolent
resistance to power and violence. As a strategy for change, it
worked against the British in India and against white segrega-
tionists in the U.S. Can it work against ruthless terrorists?
Pacifists respond that complete nonviolence may seem to be
an inadequate strategy in the short run. But for them, it is the
only practical way for civilization to survive the long run.

Many easily reject the first position. But some of us find
ourselves stuck between the second and third perspectives.
Most sincere Christians, believers in other religions and humanists seek peace and justice. Achieving peace with justice,
we understand, involves love and forgiveness. It also entails a
resistance against all evil powers. We want this resistance
nonviolent—and some of us cautiously add, *if possible*. We
would *like* to agree fully with Martin Luther King Jr.'s pacifism. During his theological studies, Martin was intrigued by
Reinhold Niebuhr's political realism which allowed for just

war, but ultimately was more persuaded by the idealism (and
practical power) of Mohatma Gandhi's nonviolent resistance.

> Gandhi was probably the first person in history to lift the
> love ethic of Jesus above mere interaction between individu-
> als to a powerful and effective social force on a large scale.
> Love, for Gandhi, was a potent instrument for social and col-
> lective transformation. . . . Gandhi was able to mobilize and
> galvanize more people in his lifetime than any other person
> in the history of the world. And just with a little love and
> understanding, goodwill and a refusal to cooperate with an
> evil law, he was able to break the backbone of the British
> empire. This, I think, was one of the most significant things
> that ever happened in the history of the world. More than 390
> million people achieved their freedom, and they achieved it
> nonviolently. . . . It was in the Gandhian emphasis on love
> and nonviolence that I discovered the method for social
> reform that I had been seeking.[1]

It is a powerful Christian idea: following Jesus in transforming "an eye for an eye" into "turn the other cheek." It
challenges us, as disciples of Christ, to apply dynamic love
and forgiveness into our social and national strategy today. It
suggests that we must begin living out this ethic as a practical
personal and global strategy.

Most agree that nonviolence against oppression and tyr-
anny should be used wherever possible. The examples of
Gandhi and Martin Luther King, Jr. are powerful. But then,
questions about the real world and terrible exigencies come
to mind. There are times when unprincipled fanatics, rather
than conventional and orderly British, threaten relative justice and peace in the world. For many deeply committed
Christians, some circumstances in human affairs make violent means necessary. As evil distorts human goodness and
corrupts the structures of human society, tough love with
forceful expression, individually and nationally, occasionally
seems necessary. Should you take your family on a plane trip

---

[1] Clayborne Carson, ed., *The Autobiography of Martin Luther
King, Jr.* (New York: Warner Books, 1998), 26, 129. (Note that students in
F.O.R. and C.O.R.E. came to the same conclusion in the early 1940s during
WWII—as did Clarence Jordan at Koinonia Farms in Americus, Georgia.)

and notice a passenger trying to light a fuse from his shoe, *ought* you, with the strongest of your plane mates, attack and subdue him before he can ignite the bomb? Were those who violently brought down United Flight 93 in Pennsylvania on Sept 11th doing the right thing? Can we give armies credit for ending the Holocaust? Armed intervention by African, Europe, and America would have saved thousands, if not hundreds of thousands of human lives in the 1994 massacres in Rwanda.

Feelings among us, as well as misunderstandings, run terribly deep as we discuss this issue. Clearly, our discussion of violence involves dealing with demons in our own psyches, as well as global identities and principalities. One misunderstanding arises from different definitions of violence. We may define it broadly in terms of all aggressive actions, or we can consider it more narrowly as malicious force that injures another. General usage and dictionary definitions tend to the latter, although the dictionary does not suggest that all violent thoughts, expressions, and actions are evil. For purposes of this psycho-social and theological discussion, I am suggesting the need for a broad definition.

Thinking of violence more broadly suggests the need to delineate kinds and degrees of aggression. In broad terms there is a whole spectrum of violence in the world today which needs careful consideration. It moves from a baby's grasping and playfulness, to loving parental, nonabusive discipline, through the aggressive play of children, to sports, fishing, hunting, on through positive police action, and finally to just wars—if there can be such. I suggest we consider this wide spectrum of aggressiveness and broad definition of violence in considering how aggressive force ought to be used.

A theology of violence considers the nature of the universe. From its sub-atomic particles, the cosmos functions with violence. Our bodies defend themselves within by force. Violence is built into nature's struggle to survive.

Some theologians see violence in strictly negative terms and coming only after the fall with the homicides of Cain and Lamech's in the fourth chapter of Genesis. For them, God's first suggestion of violence are the words to Noah:

Whoever sheds the blood of a human,
By a human shall that person's blood be shed;
For in His own image God made humankind, (Gen 9:6)

Such interpretation sees this covenant with Noah, not as God's will, but as a capitulation on the part of God, or a human idea, in response to the reality of the times. God's will is seen as a continual moving away from violence to the Cross as the final triumph of forgiveness over revenge and sacrifice. Violence in the Old Testament, for such thinkers, does not express the true nature of God.

Another view sees violence in the very creation of the world, in the act of eating, in the dominion of human beings over animals and in God's shedding animal blood to provide clothing of animal skins for shamed Adam and Eve. Human beings, from the beginning, are given the power of dominion and force—and held accountable for how they use their power. Those holding this view accept the biblical descriptions of God's violence from Genesis to Revelation. They are not able to explain all passages of God's wrath and final judgment as metaphor or in terms of progressive revelation.

Difficulties of interpretation combine with deep feelings to hinder our discussion. But our times call for such difficult debate. We must explain punishment and war to young people today. If we deny all force, we seem weak and unrealistic to them. If we try to explain the difference between "just sentencing" and "just wars" in the adult world while denying schoolyard or gang fights, we may sound like hypocrites. Let's look further at what is being written about the subject.

Five Theories of Violence

A theology of violence needs to collect relevant facts, principles and theories. In much of what is being written about the subject, a theory to explain the actual *why* and *how* of violence is often missed. It is important to consider those who have attempted to explain the complexities of aggression. I will describe four theories. Each attempts to understand violence in our world. Noting weaknesses in these, I will suggest a fifth approach. Important implications for parenting, teaching, youth work, criminal justice, and national defense arise from these theories.

Violence, according to our first theory, is seen as a necessary ingredient in the evolutionary process. Many secular thinkers hold some variation of this position. In its "raw form" it assumes that natural selection involves violence to accomplish survival of the fittest. This is often referred to as the law of the jungle. Cynically this theory could conclude that destructive violence is inevitable. During the twentieth century and in two world wars, Germans used ideas of Nietzsche and Social Darwinism to justify their aggressive actions and genocide of Jews. Evolutionists generally look at such notions as aberrations and consider evolution to be moving from the violent law of the jungle to more sophisticated and peaceful forms of survival mechanisms. Many biological studies seek to understand aggression in terms of genetics, brain, endocrine, and nerve functions, as well as through comparisons among animal species.

Robin Fox, an anthropologist and evolutionist, says violence is as natural as copulation or eating.

> The assumption that violence is a disease is to make it the analog of diarrhea. But, what if it is in fact an analog of digestion, or of some subprocess like metabolization, ingestion, or excretion?. . . It is just what the organism does as part of its routine of living. . . . Whether we like violence or not is not the question here. We are not concerned with evaluating it but with explaining or understanding it.[2]

> The real "causal" question here then is not why so many young males act so violently. This is digestion; it just happens as long as the appropriate stimuli (the analogs of food) are fed in (females, other males, resources). The real causal question is how so many cultures manage through initiation, intimidation, sublimation, bribery, education, work, and superstition to stop them and divert their energy elsewhere.[3]

---

[2] Robin Fox, "The Human Nature of Violence," part 2, p. 1 (Social Issues Research Centre, Oxford, England) www.sirc.org/publik/foxviolence2.html. See also, Robin Fox, *The Search for Society: Quest for a Biosocial Science and Morality* (New Brunswick, N.J.: Rutgers University Press, 1989).

[3] Ibid., part 5, p. 1.

Psychoanalytic theory took the study of human aggression from evolutionary theory to another level. Freud thought of violence as an instinct and as such, inevitable. Since all human instincts move toward a reduction of tension and eventual elimination, aggressive tendencies are only resolved in death. Criticism of Freud's belief in the inevitability of violence from within the psychoanalytic movement have taken issue with the scientific basis of the notion of instinct. While agreeing with Freud that frustration is part of being human and that all frustration leads to aggression, psychoanalysts from a learning perspective think anger can be displaced, repressed, reinforced (as through the media), but also modified and reduced. Elements from all these studies are helpful to our inquiry.

Alice Miller[4] represents a second theory of violence. Violence is an inevitable result of coercive child rearing. Miller, and she has a strong following, believes that everything from child abuse to spanking and all forms of authoritarian child rearing, not only stunt the growth of children, but create trauma and cycles of violence in our world. Violence comes from homes where children are deprived of their natural rights and taught the necessity of aggression by the modeling of dominant parents over weaker children.

> When we spank children, we teach them exactly what we don't want to teach them: violence, ignorance, and hypocrisy. They learn quickly to do the same as we once did: first submit to the more powerful person, to obey out of fear, and to hide the pain of being humiliated. Then about 20 years later, they cover their own weakness with violence, are unable to act peacefully, and maintain that smacking their children is the right thing to do.[5]

Miller uses Adolph Hitler as a prime example of the potential consequences of German child-rearing. For it shows how violence in one home can have national and worldwide effects.

---

[4] Alice Miller is a psychoanalyst, renowned author, and an international leader of a natural childhood movement.

[5] "A Letter from Alice Miller" (2000) (www.noogenesis.com/malama/abuse/miller/letter.html) See also Alice Miller, *For Your Own Good: Hidden Cruelty in Child-Rearing and the Roots of Violence,* Noonday, 1990.

Like every other child, Hitler was born innocent, only to be raised, as were many children at the time, in a destructive fashion by his parents and later to make himself into a monster. He was the survivor of a machinery of annihilation that in turn-of-the-century Germany was called "child-rearing" and that *I* call "the concentration camp of childhood," which is never allowed to be recognized for what it is. . . . The Führer once told his secretary that during one of the regular beatings given him by his father he was able to stop crying, to feel nothing, and even to count the thirty-two blows he received. In this way, by totally denying his pain, his feelings of powerlessness, and his despair—in other words, by denying the truth—Hitler made himself into a master of violence and of contempt for human beings, . . . incapable of empathy for other people.[6]

People of good will and sound mind differ regarding the proper use of moderate spanking. Culture and theology have something to do with such opinions. Western European countries have generally moved away from any corporal punishment of children. Over many years I have seen children raised well with brief and moderate spankings or with non-corporal, sophisticated punishments. Whatever our position on this matter, Alice Miller's interpretation of childhood abuse is important. She joins many experts who see childhood abuse responsible for cycles of abuse over generations. She goes further to make this notion a basis for a theory about all human violence. Explaining global violence on child rearing alone seems inadequate to many.

A third theory of violence, James Gilligan's,[7] is developed within both an evolutionary and psychoanalytic framework. His zeal for this subject rises from three factors. First, as a boy he watched his father beating two older brothers. Secondly, he heard the "family story." One of their great grandparents was an Irish immigrant who ended up marrying an Indian "half-breed" on the Western plains. His physical abuse, especially of her beloved five-year-old son, despite her

---

[6] Alice Miller, www.naturalchild.com/alice_miller/adolf_hitler.html, 1998, pp. 1-2).

[7] James Gilligan is a psychoanalyst and forensic psychologist who was the director of the Center for the Study of Violence at the Harvard Medical School.

stern protests and final ultimatum, led to the child's dying from poison in a pie she baked—whether to put the boy out of his misery or to poison the abusive husband was never determined, for she disappeared at the same time. This background made Gilligan an especially sympathetic listener to the stories of condemned criminals. In their stories he heard constant reference to respect or honor, to rejection and shame, to twisted but understandable reasons for their misdeeds. These themes served as clues that pointed Gilligan to the elements of all great myths in a way that could be interpreted psychoanalytically.

For Gilligan, the origin of violence is in the shame of individuals, families, and societies. Shame finally makes even death preferable to a life tortured by rejection and dishonor. Anyone who has spent time on the streets or in prisons knows the power of dis-respect. Human search for significance is tied into our need for respect. Where such a human resource is lacking, men especially grow violent. Those inside the prison system know how power and honor drive the prison culture—in terms of relationships among prisoners as well as between administration/guards and inmates. As Gilligan listened to prisoners' stories, he heard this theme continually as men reported horrible acts without feeling or remorse.

Gilligan's theory sees violence as dramatic tragedy. He comes to the meaning of violence through the great stories of the past. True tragedy is neither melodrama (governed by moral considerations) nor pathos (interpreting violence as determined or fated). In his sessions with killers, the author was drawn to universal explanations found in myths:

> I have *seen* Oedipus—a man who killed his father and then blinded himself. . . in real life. I have seen Medea—a woman who killed her children in response to her husband's abandoning her for another woman. I have seen Othello—a man who murdered his wife and then took his own life. . . .

> These experiences in prison have led me to think that the classical myths and tragedies may have originated not so much as products of fantasy, the symbolic, "conscious" representation of the unconscious fantasies of healthy people, but as attempts to describe and represent, to cope with and

make sense of—indeed to survive, emotionally and mentally—the actual crimes and atrocities that people have inflicted on one another for as far back into history as our collective memories extend. . . . The blinding of Samson, Tiresias, and the Cyclops, the blinding of Gloucester in *King Lear,* are not so much mythic "fictions" as depictions of real acts that real people commit in real life.[8]

America's terrible complicity with violence throughout its history is compounded, in Gilligan's view, by its attempt to treat crime puritanical and punitively. The conviction of Ahab in Melville's *Moby Dick* is that he was right and the whale was evil; this led to his obsession with destroying the whale, a triumph that would make things right. For Gilligan, Melville's great novel illustrates the central flaw in American character: "the illusion that 'we' have a monopoly on the knowledge of good and evil . . . that we know that 'we' are 'good' and 'they' are 'evil.'" [9] Gilligan would not excuse violent crime, but asks that we understand its principles, listening intelligently to the condemned. Only then will healing come to individuals and families. And only in this way can societies find healing and become whole. Shame must be supplanted by mutual respect.

Still, the conclusion of Gilligan's book on this subject seems incomplete. Gilligan's final paragraph offers hope for civilization if it is willing to forsake patriarchy. Since little about the nature of patriarchy and its relationship to violence has been explained, we find it rather inconclusive. A more central argument of the book, that our society must reduce poverty if we are to reduce violence seems a more substantiated strategy. But it still leaves us seeking a full explanation of the origin of, and proper response to, violence.

The Girardians

A fourth and important theory of violence is that of René Girard. Girard writes from the perspective of a scientific and

---

[8] James Gilligan, *Violence: Reflections on a National Epidemic* (New York: Vintage Books, 1996), 58.
[9] Ibid., 246

humanistic anthropologist and literary critic. His far-reaching
ideas about the violence at the heart of human nature and its
key to the origin of religion and society have attracted many
Christian theologians.[10] He and his followers consider his
ideas to rival those of Marx and Freud as an interpretation of
human nature and our cultural and religious origins.

Some Christian theologians have used the ideas of Girard
to give us a significant, Christian theory of violence. For
these Girardians, violence explains the origins both of human civilization and religion. An understanding of original
violence and ancient myth is supposed to hold the secret for
freeing our culture from its violent cycles today. It was the
threat of chaotic violence, Girard and the Girardians believe,
that led to sacrifice and the establishment of primitive religion. Religious myth describes the original cohesion of dangerously rival factions in ancient societies. Ancient cultures
were brought together religiously and socially as they attempted to control the threat of internal violence through
the sacrifice of the scapegoat.

Because of its growing popularity, Girardian theology of
violence demands further consideration. Its psychological
and historical insights beg analysis and its prophetic message
regarding contemporary institutional violence calls for critical examination.

Girardians see violence, according to the biblical narrative, as coming after the fall—but not immediately. First,
there was rivalry. René Girard and his followers[11] point out

---

[10] René Girard, born 1923, is a professor of French language, literature, and civilization at Stanford University. See René Girard, *Violence
and the Sacred* (*Le Violence et le sacré*) (Johns Hopkins University
Press, 1977).

[11] Particularly James G. Williams, *The Bible, Violence & the Sa-
cred: Liberation from the Myth of Sanctioned Violence* (San Francisco:
HarperCollins, 1991) and Gil Bailie, *Violence Unveiled: Humanity at
the Crossroads* (New York: Crossroad Publishing Co., 1995). To a
somewhat lesser extent I include among the Girardians: Walter Wink,
*Engaging the Powers: Discernment and Resistance in a World of
Domination* (Minneapolis, Minn.: Fortress Press, 1992) and David
Augsburger, *Helping People Forgive* (Louisville, Ky.: Westminster John
Knox Press, 1996).

that mimetic[12] desire (coveting something treasured by another) produces rivalry, and this rivalry leads to violence. For
the Girardians, primal societies were able to limit anarchic
violence by accepting a common sacrifice. Powerful offenders and less powerful bystanders, including victims, were
caught up in the drama of an innocent scapegoat sacrificed
for all. If the guilty (the perpetrators) were sacrificed, the
cycle of revenge would only continue. This is why the drama
must present *an innocent victim.* Ancient myths are not figments of story-tellers. Nor are ancient rituals mere priestly
inventions. These point to the reality of human life as it was
experienced in ancient times. Universal myth and ritual
point to the reality of violence and chaos averted by religious
sacrifice.

As ancient cultures ameliorated profane and chaotic violence through the religious violence of sacrifice, Girardians
see the need of moving beyond sacred violence to nonviolence. The wrath of sacrificial systems must be replaced by
the peace of unconditional forgiveness.

> Aggression is elemental to human community. Violence is
> endemic. Religion has served to limit it by sacralizing the pro-
> cess of selecting a scapegoat to bear the community's collec-
> tive wrath. But the ritual is a lie. Its solution is brief, its
> ultimate impact destructive.
>
> The scapegoat mechanism, and with it the myth of redemp-
> tive violence, promises the resolution of a community's rage
> and the cessation of hostilities, but it is powerless to effect
> such a result. We need the interjection of the new element
> called forgiveness.[13]

A bit more must be said about the nature of the sacrificial scapegoat mechanism. The Girardians see most of our
mores and institutions built upon it. As David Augsburger
puts it: ". . . sacrifice . . . lies at the core of cultural myths . . .

---

[12] "Mimesis" and "mimetic" are important terms for Girardians. If
you want to substitute simply the word "covet," you will be catching the
primary idea but missing its full meaning and special use.

[13] David W. Augsburger, *Helping People Forgive,* 167.

and reenacts, reinterprets, and ritualizes" primal violence.[14]
Girard broadened Freud's Oedipal Complex into a social
rivalry needing a larger solution than personal psychotherapy. Girard and the Girardians call this the scapegoat
mechanism.

When Giradians speak of the scapegoat mechanism
they are thinking of a cluster or sequence of ideas. Human
beings learn what is desirable from imitating others. Once
we value what someone else values, mimetic rivalry ensues;
we covet as we imitate. This dynamic is at work in both the
personal and collective selves leading to a chaos which
threatens social order. Here is a social situation containing
dangerous double messages: "Be like me, value what I value,
but don't you dare be like me in touching what is mine." Such
a state can obviously lead to an escalation of rivalries and social disaster. To save itself from chaos, social groups tend to
look for someone safe to blame. A scapegoat must be found
on whom to lay the guilt. If the scapegoat is neither perpetrator nor victim, the group's violence can be averted or at least
diminished in the violent drama of a sacrifice. A successful
scapegoat mechanism becomes ritualized and dramatized in
society's stories and songs.[15]

Here then is a bold attempt to explain the origin of
violence and social control. It also warns of a modern dilemma. With modern rejection of religious sacrificial systems, human beings are now free to choose their own
scapegoats. The Enlightenment undermined belief in the
sacralized victim and religious rituals. Scapegoat myths and
rituals no longer restrain violence in the modern world.
Without such religious sacrifice and symbols, the modern
world's hubris and smoldering animosities must find other
scapegoats to appease anger and violence.

No one can deny residues of religious sensibilities in
contemporary society, a lingering of moral and religious concerns from the past. That partly explains the sudden concern
for victims, their needs and their rights in secular society.

---

[14] Ibid., 128.
[15] Ibid., 130–31.

Still, we flounder toward a precipice of violent disaster. We find ourselves unable to control the force of violence in the media and in global strife. The Girardians warn:

> Our world is now convulsing with disorder and violence, vivid scenes of which are beamed into our living rooms and burned into our sensibilities every day. . . . The epidemic of crime, drugs, and violence we are now experiencing is just the most conspicuous manifestation of a broader and deeper disintegration.

> Unless we better understand what is happening to us, we will continue to be buffeted by wave after wave of this disintegration, reluctant to recognize its scope, unable to appreciate its spiritual meaning, and unprepared to meet its historical challenges.[16]

Post-Enlightenment culture stands at an important juncture, Girardians believe. They see society moving deeper into dysfunctional anger and headed for apocalyptic violence. Two alternatives remain. We can choose to channel apocalyptic violence toward victims or scapegoats, lashing out at evil enemies, or we can renounce violence and choose a way of radical forgiveness. For Christian Giradians this is the clear challenge to followers of Christ as a counter-cultural force in a desperate world. They see this latter alternative as the message of the Bible. The biblical story, for Girardians, culminates in the radical forgiveness of the Cross.[17] It is good news for church and society.

Critique of Girardian Theology

The prophetic concern of the Girardians for violent principalities and powers is extremely helpful. Their ideas provide a key to power politics, crime, and urban "juice." For all its brilliance, however, some will raise questions about Girard's conception of violence.

---

[16] Gil Bailie, *Violence Unveiled,* 4–5.
[17] Ibid., 7, 25, 129.

In the first place, in substituting violence as the single explanation of human behavior, is Girard over-simplifying? Is he replacing Freud's view of sex or Marx's notion of class warfare with violence as the driving social issue? Can we go as far as to say that *all* worldly ills stem from violence? Girard seems also to impose a restrictive interpretation on the study of ancient myths and cultures.

Second, some may question its practicality. The Girardians are clearly pressing for an ideal—perhaps never to be perfected—of cultures ruled by the rule of love and forgiveness. A culture free of violence because it is ruled by love and forgiveness may await the end time and coming of the Lord. Is their hope too utopian and difficult to apply to real politics in the present? Are the Girardians hoping for Christians to take up this ideal as a counter-cultural witness to a violent world? Wink responds rather effectively explaining the process of forgiveness and reconciliation. Wink sees believers as a powerful intercessory force in prayer. Few of the Girardians make much of a distinction between life in the church and worldly realities.

Third, there is a question about the Girardian interpretation of Scripture. To make the Bible support a clear movement from sacred violence to a rejection of violence in forgiveness may undermine the authority of the biblical canon. For Girard the Bible is significant because it goes beyond all other myths in working out the scapegoat mechanism and our necessary identification with victims of violence. But for him and some of his followers it does not go far enough.

> In the Jewish and Christian Bible, we can see the gradual emergence of scapegoating in the modern and critical sense. It is there and there only that a genuine *theme* or *motif* of the scapegoat can make its appearance and, simultaneously with it, a growing realization that we will not become fully human unless we confront and restrain this unconscious activity of ours by all possible means.[18]

---

[18] René Girard, "Foreword," in James G. Williams' *The Bible, Violence, and the Sacred: Liberation from the Myth of Sanctioned Violence* (San Francisco: HarperSanFrancisco, 1991).

But although the Bible contains the supreme scapegoat myth[19] as a great story, biblical violence poses a real difficulty for these thinkers. With the Girardians, Augsburger sees "the violent stories of both Hebrew and Christian scriptures (as) troubling . . . (and) serving a transformative function."[20]

They function, that is, to expose the lie of sacrificial or punitive beliefs and move us toward a full forgiveness ethic. While the biblical stories do teach the need for forgiveness rather than violence, they still fall into the trap of sacrificial thinking: "their saving schemes are false." In other words, Augsburger and others cannot accept any kind of violence, even if found in Scripture, as part of God's redemptive will.[21]

In short, the Girardians seem to reject a single, unchanging God of all Scripture. David Augsburger quotes Walter Wink approvingly:

> the God of infinite mercy was metamorphosed by the church into the image of a wrathful God whose demand for blood atonement leads to God's requiring of his own Son a death on behalf of us all. The nonviolent God of Jesus comes to be depicted as a God of unequaled violence, since God . . . demands the blood of the victim who is closest and most precious to him. . . . Against such an image of God the revolt of atheism is an act of pure religion.[22]

Two radically different images of God exist in the Scripture for these thinkers: "the false God changes suffering into violence; the true God changes violence into suffering."[23] An archaic deity demands sacrifice before true divinity finds full satisfaction and resolution in forgiveness.

A fourth difficulty involves what some of us would see as a weakening of the full meaning of the Cross. A sacrificial

---

[19] Myth is popular used as a story contrary to fact. But its more classic sense is of a crucial story that attempts to explain origins or religious rites not completely explicable.

[20] Augsburger, op. cit., 134.

[21] Ibid., 134. Please note that our critique of Augsburger is only of one small section in his book, a book we highly respect and recommend.

[22] Ibid., 134. Wink, op. cit., 148.

[23] George A. Panichas, ed., *The Simone Weil Reader* (New York: David McKay Co., 1977), 334. This statement is quoted approvingly by both Wink and Augsburger.

atonement asks us to praise a God who demands and accepts a violent sacrifice. Girardians clearly reject a God who would ask Abraham to sacrifice his son—and worse, a God who could pour out wrath on his only beloved Son. Girardians avoid sacrificial and substitutionary aspects of the Atonement, as found in Paul's writings, because such an idea undermines their theology of unconditional love. To speak of Christ becoming sin for us and bearing the punishment of our sins seems to them a violation of God's love and forgiveness.

John Stott, on the other hand, is clear about the substitutionary atonement and sees the Cross as the place where justice and mercy, love and wrath dramatically met.

> in order to save us in such a way as to satisfy himself, God through Christ substituted himself for us. Divine love triumphed over divine wrath by divine self-sacrifice. The cross was an act simultaneously of punishment and amnesty, severity and grace, justice and mercy. Seen thus, the objections to a substitutionary atonement evaporate.[24]

God was *in* Christ reconciling the world to himself,[25] and yet, in the mystery of the atonement, God made Christ to be sin for us, and this Christ cried out, "My God, my God, why have you forsaken me."[26] We accept, though we cannot comprehend, the full drama of those words. All evil violence is overcome by the violence of the Cross.

Should we not accept all Scripture teaches and implies about the work of Christ on the Cross? Doing so would entail embracing most of the atonement theories advanced through church history. The mystery of that redemptive act seems to include the biblical idea of sacrifice; the early church's emphasis on Christ's ransom or victory over sin, death, and the devil; Anselm's satisfaction theory; the Reformer's stress on penal substitution; Grotius' governmental theory; and the liberal moral influence theory. There are, of

---

[24] John Stott, *The Cross of Christ* (Downers Grove, Ill.: InterVarsity Press, 1986), 159.
[25] 2 Corinthians 5:19.
[26] Matthew 27:46 and Mark 15:34.

course, even further expressions of the meaning of Christ's death. We can find hints of all these historic theories in the Bible as partial explanations of an atonement that passes our comprehension. Compassion and judgment, evil and wrath, hell and justification, justice and mercy were played out to the full at Calvary.

Girardians see in Jesus a radical break from revengeful and sacrificial thinking. They contend that the ideas of Jesus could not be preserved among the first Christians. Early Christians, Augsburger continues, were not able to maintain the radical "forgiveness only" teaching of Jesus. Instead, they retained some of the old scapegoat or sacrificial notions as they wrote the Gospels (rewrote the stories of Jesus) and instructed churches in the Epistles.

> The apostles vacillate; the vision becomes confused. Instead of maintaining the revelation that God has entered and ended the scapegoat mechanism, they return to the mechanism. God sends the son to be the scapegoat; God intends that Jesus be the final scapegoat; God requires an expiatory scapegoat to resolve the tension between God's own wrath and God's love.[27]

Such statements seem to threaten the Canon. Is it safe to reject dominant themes of the Old Testament, dismiss some of Paul's teaching regarding the Atonement, and overlook Jesus' whipping the traders out of the Temple—or damning the religious leaders?[28]

Many of us shrink back from describing some Gospel and Epistle materials as later insertions of confused apostles.

In some ways the denial of divine violence and punishment is a comfortable intellectual position. But such an intellectually pleasing synthesis seems to rob Scripture and the early church of some of their authority. This kind of pacifism may be questioned, not only for practical reasons, but for offering too little rectification for all the world's evil. It may also slight God's promise, "Vengeance is mine; I will

---

[27] Ibid., 133.
[28] See Thomas H. Troeger's "Holy Anger" (at www.pulpit.org/articles/holy_anger.asp).

repay. . . ." Of course some Christian pacifists accept the idea of *God* violently overthrowing all evil.

There is an emphasis about the nonviolence of Jesus[29] without focusing much attention on the second coming of Christ. The Bible describes the first mission of Christ in terms of suffering; the second is described more in terms of conquest. It is difficult to conceive of a nonviolent Christ turning today's world to justice and peace without force. How will violence finally be resolved? Can it be without violence?

Finally, Girardianism can lead to Carl Jung's extreme position. Jung's synthesis, and this is the position of many intellectuals today, sees all tensions between good and evil brought together *in* God. God must finally be reconciled to Lucifer and all that is fallen. Christ dies for the sins of an Old Testament God in order to bring about final unity between God and the Devil.[30]

I am concerned about any separation between the God of the Old and New Testaments, between the God of judgment and sacrifice and the God of forgiveness, between justice and mercy. Such thinking can lead to this extreme. This position does not distinguish between a transcendent God and creation and fails to see God as radically and ultimately separate from all evil.

More About the Fall

If we are not satisfied with the theories presented, what possible perspective remains? What alternative theology of violence is possible? Thinking this through involves a reconsideration of what theologians call the human fall.

---

[29] Ethicist Stephen Mott recognizes that "most Christian ethicists . . . assume that the Gospels present Jesus as teaching nonviolence, although they may differ on how his teachings relate to contemporary society" but stresses that Jesus was teaching about defending oneself bilaterally and not dealing with multilateral situations in which we are called upon to defend others. Implied here is the idea that Jesus did nothing to defend himself in his first coming, but will use mighty force to defend others bringing justice and peace in the second coming. See Stephen Mott, *Biblical Ethics and Social Change* (New York: Oxford University Press, 1982), 171–82.

[30] Carl Jung, *Answer to Job* (Princeton University Press, 1973).

God *has* made us creatures of desire. As Tournier[31] and others have pointed out, human beings are followers of the pleasure principle. In general, God intends that we avoid pain and follow the pleasurable or good.[32]

The pleasure-pain principle is meant to operate in a healthy way. When pleasure seeking takes place apart from the will of God, when we seek more than is right, it can become short-sighted, addictive, and destructive. Seeking pleasure according to God's will (Psalm 37:4) leads to ultimate good. True good gives the deepest and longest lasting pleasure. To seek real pleasure and the good is ultimately to seek God.

There is mystery aplenty in the Genesis accounts of creation and fall. Clearly the fall is a story of desire run amok. Inordinate desire, desire that seeks more than God has allotted and breaks out of God's will is the beginning of human downfall. Mimetic desire (to use the Girardian phrase) begins to seek what others prize and own. Eve is pictured as satisfied until the Serpent says she can have more. The fruit is there to be coveted, to be seized, and finally to make her more than she was meant to be. When being a perfect woman is not enough, why not be like God! She then begins to desire what the Serpent prizes, then Adam covets what Eve desires—and all of us have fallen in line. Mimetic desire—as its definition implies—leads to rivalry. Such rivalry speaks to the origin of violence in society. This far we are agreeing with the Girardians.

The fall moved us from theocentric individuals and community to the predicament of egocentricity and anthrocentricity. When we as individuals seek to be the center of things, when any human community wants to be the hub of the world, trouble ensues. Fundamentally, this shift away

---

[31] Paul Tournier (1977) *The Violence Within: How the Same Powerful Emotion Can be a Force for Good rather than Evil* (San Francisco: Harper & Row, 1982).

[32] This is not to deny God's desire for sacrificial acceptance of pain for a higher good and Christ's call to pick up our cross and follow Him. In other words, the basic pleasure-pain principle that keeps us alive, avoiding flame and desiring food can, and ought to be transcended, for altruistic and spiritual reasons.

from the center of our universe separates us from the whole and brings us into chaos. When each of us and every nation wants to go one better and be something more (as Adam and Eve did), there can be neither justice nor peace.

The first biblical story outside the Garden is found in Genesis 4. Rivalry and jealousy are the beginning of that story. Cain wants divine approval and sees Abel as the triumphant rival. Hurt from perceived rejection increases anger and fuels his rage until it erupts in a murderous act. Lamech goes him one better. This chapter contains two instances of the word "anger," five of "kill," and two mentions of blood along with three other expressions of aggression. Two separate murders are included in chapter four's description of the world's first civilization. These are the beginnings—but not the end—of violence in the Old Testament.

Having critiqued other theories of violence, I must admit tensions in my own psychology and theology of violence. I find myself incapable of drawing exact lines between healthy competition/achievement and the abuse of power or unjustified violence. There is no final proof of a just war or justified revolution. Certainly I do not read Old Testament violence with ease. Many of us admit difficulty—though we may have explanations—with Abraham's attempted sacrifice of Isaac and the imprecatory Psalms. Aware of Raymond Schwager's *Must There Be Scapegoats?* [33] we may find Old Testament violence going beyond our comfort zone.

Not only must *you* decide what to do with a Bible that contains so much violence. You must also be prepared to answer the questions of young inquiring minds and offended sensibilities. You may be called upon to do so within a secular framework (in schools or general youth clubs) as well as in churches and youth groups.

---

[33] Raymond Schwager, *Must There Be Scapegoats?* (San Francisco: Harper & Row, 1987), where he counts six hundred passages of explicit violence in the Old Testament, one thousand verses in which God's violent actions are described, one hundred passages in which God commands someone to kill people and stories where God kills or tries to kill for no apparent reason (e.g., Exodus 4:24–26).

We seek a practical theology realistic about existing evils, the difficulties in distinguishing necessary from wrongful aggression, and ultimate understanding of the mysteries of God. At the same time we need an ethic that will work in secular *and* faith communities. We accept the Church's early understanding of John 3:16, Romans 3:5, 5:9, and 2 Corinthians 5:21, but admit we do not fully comprehend the mystery of the atonement. We are not sure about the ultimate meaning of God's anger or vengeance when, for instance, God says: "Vengeance is mine!" We admire, though we may not fully understand, the paradox between Christ's whip in the temple and the towel with which he wiped his disciples' feet.

The Lingering Dilemma

How then are we to think about anger, aggression, and violence? Can there be justifiable anger and vengeance in the divine nature? Is a certain amount of aggression proper in our lives?

Let's consider a contact sport like football. Isn't there is a significant difference, although not beyond contesting, between a "good hit" and a "dirty hit?" That's what rules are for. Referees are there to make the calls based on the distinction between good violence (or aggressive contact if you please) and bad violence. All who have participated in hard sports recognize the difference between solid contact and trying to injure, between controlled aggression and losing one's temper.

I believe Christians should also be able to support the police and soldiers going off to war. We must, of course, speak out against police brutality and the misuse of power. Admitting the many excesses of war, in fact that war is a hellish experience, we recognize a strong tradition of Christian soldiers who have killed without rage and with a willingness to forgive their enemies.

Our goal today should be to move beyond the seeming impasse of "pacifism vs. just war" arguments and to wage peace aggressively. Our military academies should be matched with peace academies.

Hans Küng's writings[34] and the World Conference on Religion and Peace should be known more widely. The scholars who met together and wrote *Just Peacemaking* have shown us a way beyond the traditional deadlock. Pacifism does not deal with genocide very well, but we should all emulate its passion for aggressive peace-making. Just War theorists sense the occasional need for war but may fail to work out the implications of "just intentions" and "last resort." Glen Stassen and associates demonstrate ten steps or practices in waging peace. This report acknowledges the necessity of forceful interventions (especially in collaboration with UN and regional powers), while promoting nonviolent principles.[35]

How can we reconcile our peaceful intentions with a realization that some restrained and responsible force is appropriate? I believe there is another psychological and theological view of violence. It draws upon all preceding theories. It is not neat and does not solve all the problems involved. In fact, it leaves a tension and, lacking full clarity, begs acceptance of the matter's ultimate mystery. Such an approach certainly demands humility.

The Psychology of Sex and Violence

Any attempt at an alternative theology of violence must seek insight from psychological and social theory as well as biblical principles. To begin with, we must consider the basic drives from which aggression proceeds. Evil violence and sexual deviance make up most of our world's trouble. From where do these twin nemeses arise?

God has obviously created human beings as creatures of desire—*and* as imitative creatures. Two basic instincts—to grasp and to suck—drive our behavior. The newborn

---

[34] Hans Küng, *Global Responsibility: In Search of a New World Ethic* (London: SCM Press, 1991).

[35] Glen Stassen, ed., *Just Peacemaking: Ten Practices for Abolishing War* (Cleveland, Ohio: Pilgrim Press, 1998).

grasps and sucks the breast. These aggressive and "unitive" (union and nurturing) drives describe the way our energies are directed. Paul Tournier refers to love and violence as the primary pair of instinctive forces.[36] Freud's system did not hang on sex alone; he saw two basic human needs as love *and* work.

Our assumption here (disputed by many theologians of violence) is that human forcefulness and achievement (even when involving necessary aggression or violence) are *good*—if appropriately used. We are meant to grasp, to strive, to achieve; this is one side of our nature. The other includes our human sexuality and creativity—the drive toward union with another, the community, and with God. Aggressive aspects of our nature and our sexuality turn dangerous when they go beyond God's will, when they are no longer centered in the Creator. Then, sex and violence begin to express our tendency to lord it over others—to gain for ourselves at someone else's expense.

Children need tender nurturing *and* some aggressive activity in their play. Adolescents experiment with new-found sexuality and their increased ability to compete and achieve. We shouldn't try to repress all sexuality or to restrict all aggressiveness. Aggression is really akin to power. The word power has negative connotations to many—especially young people. Basically, power is the ability to act—and to enable others to act; it is the capacity to get something done. Tournier attacks the problem of destructive violence in terms of abuse of power and admits how easy it is for this abuse to be rationalized.[37]

---

[36] Paul Tournier, *The Violence Within: How the Same Powerful Emotion Can Be a Force for Good Rather Than Evil* (New York: Harper & Row Publishers, 1982), 77. Tournier follows Girard to some extent but relies on the sovereignty of God and the efficacy of divine grace to solve the problem of violence—as his title conveys. He speaks of godly violence. The frightful cacophony of human violence and disorder can become "heavenly music! And to get this music the organist does not have to spoil the instrument, to dislocate its mechanisms, but rather to press all its resources into service" (77).

[37] Ibid. See the opening chapters of his important book on this subject.

A Realistic Biblical Theology of Violence

Theologically, there is a difference between defining sin as violence and seeing destructive violence as a manifestation of sin. We are creatures of intense desire that we might seek God, and the grace and gifts bestowed by the blessed Trinity. We are natural imitators that we might model ourselves after godly shepherds and ultimately the divine nature. We are creatures with free will that we might make good choices. And finally, we have tremendous potential to do good or evil—achievements that demand power. All we are and all we do can be for right or wrong. The exercise of our power can be a force for good or evil. This is what Tournier was expressing in his subtitle: *How the Same Powerful Emotion Can Be a Force for Good Rather Than Evil.*[38]

We seek, then, a psychology and theology of violence that will translate into personal health, open relationships, and world order. In some writings we find, not only the questioning of Scriptural authority, but a lack of practical solutions for the real world. We look for a moral compass in all Scripture to help us navigate a violent world. If our theology is not biblical, it cannot be realistic; it will not work in the real world.

Redemptive Violence

Augsburger says "God refuses all redemptive violence."[39] Walter Wink's third book (of a trilogy to which we have been referring) is based on exploring and attacking the myth of redemptive violence—in ancient myths, in popular culture, and matters of national security. He sees this myth originating in the evil dominination systems that control our world. From the cartoons kids read to the action movies they watch, redemptive figures fight the "good fight" against evil forces—overcoming them with "good" violence. The Golden Rule of such media is, as Dick Tracy expressed it: "Violence is golden

---

[38] Ibid.
[39] Augsburger, op. cit. 144.

when it's used to put evil down." After looking at Superman, Batman, the police chief in "Jaws," James Bond, and others, Wink concludes:

> In a period when Christian Sunday schools are dwindling, the myth of redemptive violence has won children's voluntary acquiescence to a regimen of religious indoctrination more exhaustive and effective than any in the history of religions. . . . No other religious system has ever remotely rivaled the myth of redemptive violence in its ability to catechize its young so totally. [40]

Wink is making a very important point. Dominions of violence (and perverted sexuality) are driving much of popular culture. The question is whether we should attack the very nature of the stories *or* their excesses. If young children don't get any violence in their stories, they will invent some. In contrast to the Girardians, I believe that violence is part of God's story and all cultural stories. Admitting the excesses and dangers of popular culture, we still find in human stories reflections (often very pale or dark) of the conflict between good (guys) and bad (guys) and the great story of God's redemption. Biblical redemption includes violence leading to everlasting justice and peace. This will come about not by human efforts—though we are partners in the task—but through divine and supernatural intervention.

Girardian Contributions

What would a dialogue between pacifists and just war advocates look like? How can Girardians and non-Girardians learn from one another? This chapter has attempted both a critique *and* acknowledgement of our debt to the Girardians whose contributions merit further summary. The following list highlights how Girardian ideas can help us discuss and respond to violence.

- These thinkers have initiated a theology of violence and filled an important void in theological reflection.

---

[40] Wink, op. cit. 23.

- Collectively the Girardians have helped us understand mimetic desire. As creatures of desire and as imitators, we prize what those we admire and hold important. Such desire is the basis of human rivalry and a violence that threatens anarchy and mass destruction.

- Girardians see the danger of unrestrained violence as the primal impetus for sacrifice and human community. If we do not accept this as the only factor behind human religion, culture, and mythology, it at least helps us understand the near universality of the scapegoating theme and how this tendency of human societies has wreaked havoc throughout human history.

- Walter Wink prods us from individualistic theology and piety to consideration of principalities and powers. We need to see violence as coming from systemic evils. We may not be able to follow his critique of popular culture all the way, as we have noted. The concluding chapters to his trilogy of books are even more important. There he challenges us to love our enemies, to monitor our inner violence, and to engage in spiritual warfare and prayer against the powers of violence and evil.[41] Wink emphasizes a much broader and deeper spiritual warfare than the psychological references found in much popular spirituality. In the same vein, Jacques Ellul challenges Christians to break with dominant culture. His encouragement to identify with victims should be taken very seriously.

- David Augsburger's *Helping People Forgive* is a unique masterpiece despite the cautions we have mentioned. (Our critique is directed toward only a section of one chapter.) Perhaps nowhere else can we find such a penetrating psychology and theology of forgiveness. If we are to move beyond violence and conflicts today—and we must—his book must be understood and applied. Gregory Jones' book on forgiveness offers a powerful compliment to Augsburger's teaching.[42]

---

[41] Wink, op. cit. ch. 14, "The Acid Test: Loving Enemies," ch. 15, "Monitoring Our Inner Violence," and ch. 16, "Prayer and the Powers."

[42] L. Gregory Jones, *Embodying Forgiveness: A Theological Analysis* (Grand Rapids, Mich.: Eerdmans, 1995). Jones is part of the pacifist tradition denying that "forgiveness in general and love of enemies in particular can (only) temper the demands of the political world (without) challenging the (forceful) means by which (political) power is exercised" (268). Thus, there should not have been violent response to the terrorist bombing or to the Holocaust.

- A longer book than Augsburger's, it spends more time with historic examples such as Bonhoeffer, literary examples, and developing a theology of forgiveness.

- Non-violence is the best way to solve most conflicts in the world today. It is time for Christians and humanists to review both the rationale and techniques of nonviolence as found in the works quoted here.

Across deep and emotional differences, we must continue our consideration of violence and how its destructive effects can be curbed. Pacifists and non-pacifists need to continue their discussion. We need insights from both.

Conclusion

Those of us who very cautiously espouse the idea of just wars, understand that war is never a good thing, it is always the lesser of evils. Furthermore, no war is ever entirely successful; it can at best seem necessary.

Alongside the terrorist attack and the violent response against Al Qaeda and the Taliban, described at the beginning of this chapter, should be placed the many global situations where waging peace has worked. It may be that violence must be countered by both nonviolent and aggressive means in our complex world.

We are left, I believe, with the mystery of violence in our world. We must understand and eliminate as much of its excesses as we can. We should not set our expectations of demystifying and solving the mystery so high that the task is undermined. We acknowledge Christ's ultimate victory over evil, violence and suffering. We follow his way of forgiveness to the extent that we are able.

Both clear principles and the possibility for different interpretations and applications come from the important section of Romans (12:14-21). As Christians we are meant to bless, not curse, our enemies—to live harmoniously with one another—never returning wrong for wrongs. Is Paul primarily speaking individually or corporately at this point, to believers or to all society? The question is further compounded by the language of the next verse: "If it is possible, *as far as you can,* live peaceably with all men" (Wm. Barclay, emphasis mine). Finally, the overriding principle, "Do not be overcome with evil, but overcome evil with good." (Rom 12:21, NRSV)

To work this out in all situations takes principles and skills of anger management, conflict resolutions, and reconciliation. We would replace brutal and counterproductive punishments with as much restorative justice and rehabilitation as possible. Those in power must always beware of defeating external enemies (or controlling criminals) without accepting the challenge to face the enemy within themselves, the seductiveness of so much power. Secondary violence (or response to violence) must never mimic primary or initiating violence.

How can we understand the legitimacy of secondary violence? It is violence that defends others rather than ourselves. Physicists and astronomers see violence of the universe. Naturalists have long accepted the basic savagery of the jungle. Human physiology notes the violence of biology. Walter Wink (who seeks a way beyond the classic Just War and Pacifist positions) illustrates violence in our physical nature in this interesting way.

> It is amazing to see in the American Cancer Society's film *The Cell* how on bumping up or against a defective cell, a lymphocyte actually backs off, shapes itself into an arrow, and drives itself at the suspect cell until it penetrates its core, exploding the cell and giving its own life in the process.[43]

This image speaks to us as victims and peacemakers. Our goal is to be aggressively nonviolent, but some situations are violent by nature. Ultimately, the unfathomable presence of violence in the cosmos demands an appeal to higher mysteries: that of the Incarnation, the Cross, and final Judgment. In these mysteries we find a coming together of antitheses.

Human existence, from Genesis to the Apocalypse, continues to be driven by its two drives: creative/nurturing and the aggressive, by all that is involved in creative sexuality and

---

[43] Ibid., 289.

assertive achievement. Sex can be perverted and achievement turned malicious. Once the first and last of the Ten Commandments (which rabbis have held to be summary for all) are broken in personal and cultural lives, destructive violence, along with attending evils, becomes a fact of life. We must do our best to curb it, seek divine grace to change it, and hope for that day of supernatural intervention when all evil will finally be overthrown. Christ[44] and the Scriptures[45] describe even that denouement in violent terms.

Along with our theological reflections on violence we must, of course, devise strategies and interventions against all that hurts human life. James Garbarino,[46] Geoffrey Canada,[47] Deborah Prothrow-Stith,[48] Dan Kindlon & Michael Thompson,[49] Scott Larson[50] and others provide analyses and strategies for dealing with anger and violence. Showing young people how to avoid violence is critical for youth leaders and teachers these days—as is the healing of its victims.

The technique of violence prevention, then, *is* important. How we model its alternative of *shalom* and how we pray to overcome destructive violence, however, must be informed by our theology of violence. The purpose of this chapter has been to promote such reflection on violence. Hopefully, it also suggests how those in youth ministry

---

[44] Matt. 11:22–24; 25:31–46; Luke 10:12; 17:29–30.

[45] Isaiah 63:1–6; Ezekiel 39 (especially 17–24); Joel 2:1b–2; 2 Thess. 1:5–10; Rev. 19:17–21.

[46] Garbarino, op. cit.

[47] Geoffrey Canada, *Fist, Stick, Knife, Gun: A Personal History of Violence in America* (Boston: Beacon Press, 1995), and *Reaching Up for Manhood: Transforming the Lives of Boys in America* (Boston: Beacon Press, 1999).

[48] Deborah Prothrow-Stith, *Deadly Consequences: How Violence Is Destroying Our Teenage Population and a Plan to Begin Solving the Problem* (New York: HarperCollins, 1991). (See also her Workbook on Violence Prevention and Anger Management.)

[49] Dan Kindlon and Michael Thompson, *Raising Cain: Protecting the Emotional Life of Boys* (New York: Ballantine Books, 1999).

[50] Scott Larson and Larry Brendtro, *Reclaiming Our Prodigal Sons and Daughters: A Practical Approach for Connecting with Youth in Conflict* (Bloomington, Ind.: National Educational Service, 2000), and Scott Larson, *Risk In Our Midst: Empowering Teenagers to Love the Unlovable* (Loveland, Colo.: Group Publishing, 2000).

can contribute to the disciplines of practical and systematic theology and provide models of nonviolent engagement.

Application for Families, Schools, and Youth Ministry

Fortunately there are some fine resources for anger management and violence prevention. They will be listed at the end of this and our final chapter. What this chapter adds to these programs and curricula is a caution regarding attempts to stamp out anger or eliminate aggressive activity. Young people need to know that anger is a natural emotion, serves important functions, needs to be judiciously controlled and be channeled into helpful and healthy expressions.

How and Where Communities Can Begin to Address Youth Violence is a comprehensive resource manual listed at the end of this chapter. It is based on the following principles: that "collaboration among all social systems (family, neighborhood, school, peers) is essential, that efforts to reduce violence ought to boost protective factors proven to foster resiliency, that such asset building provides youth with skills, abilities, and confidences that stay with them forever." In addition societal factors contributing to youthful violence ought to be the focus of social change, i.e. that violence prevention must be "broadly focused." [51]

Young people will help us work through these difficult issues. They are looking for balance between extremes alluded to in this chapter. They are looking for tough love and aggressive peace. Together we will seek to understand the Jesus, who walked through a vicious crowd bent on killing him before his time, or whipped the money-changers out of the temple, who held a child tenderly in his arms, accepted the caresses of a woman of shame, submitted to humiliation and torture at the hands of Roman soldiers, who will come

---

[51] Laurel Dean & Judy Wallace, eds. (1995) *How and Where Communities Can Begin to Address Youth Violence,* University of California, 2–3.

again in triumph over all evil. This Jesus is certainly the key
to the mystery of violence.

Questions for Reflection and Discussion

1. How had you thought about the origin, nature,
   and theological relevance of violence before reading this chapter?

2. Has reading this chapter stretched your ideas
   about violence? How so?

3. Do you think this chapter was necessary for this
   book? How would you change it—or its location in
   the book?

4. Do you think the writer gives a fair presentation of
   the "Girardians"? How do you assess their important contributions?

5. Do you think the writer is fair in his assessment of
   the work of Walter Wink and of David Augsburger?
   Explain.

6. How do you interpret "Vengeance is mine, I will
   repay, says the Lord"?

7. How do you understand the work of Christ on the
   Cross in terms of violence and judgment for sins?

8. Do you agree that a theology of violence is important in the part of our teaching or ministry that
   deals with violence, victims, forgiveness, reconciliation, and prayer?

Book Resources

Robert G. Clouse, ed. *War: Four Christian Views.* Downers
Grove, Ill.: InterVarsity Press, 1991. 🗡 Four Christian leaders explain their positions: Myron Augsberger, that Christians cannot participate in military action in any way;
Herman Hoyt believing that biblical nonresistance allows

Christians to serve as medics and chaplains; Arthur Holmes describing the criteria for just war; and Harold O. J. Brown pushing these criteria to make room for preventive war.

Hans Küng. *Global Responsibility: In Search of a New World Ethic.* London: SCM Press, 1990.

Hans Küng, ed. *Yes to a Global Ethic.* London: SCM Press, 1996. ☧ In the first section, Küng lays out his call for the religions of the world to come together for global justice, peace and survival. This is not a call for a unitary religious synthesis, but for dialogue that will lead to common values agreed upon by major religions and the secular world. The second section brings affirmative response from leading theologians of Christian, Muslim, Jewish, and Eastern religion perspectives. This book deals with influence but not intervention in violent crises.

Stephen Charles Mott. *Biblical Ethics and Social Change.* New York: Oxford University Press, 1982. ☧ This is a brilliant biblical discussion of a key question of this chapter, "Is violence ever justified?" See especially Ch. 9 "After All Else—Then Arms?"

Glen Stassen, ed. *Just Peacemaking: Ten Practices for Abolishing War.* Cleveland, Ohio: Pilgrim Press, 1998. ☧ This is an excellent handbook for waging peace on many levels.

Manuals, Workbooks, and Curriculum

Laurel Dean and Judy Wallace, compilers. *How and Where Communities Can Begin to Address Youth Violence.* A Resource Manual, University of California, Davis. Cooperative Extension Service (510-642-2431), 1995. ☧ This is an unusually comprehensive collection of resources for prevention and intervention in youth violence.

Susan Klaw, Freada Klein, Wendy Sanford, and Adria Steinberg. *Preventing Family Violence: A Curriculum for Adolescents.* Resource Center for the Prevention of Family Violence and Sexual Assault, Massachusetts Department of Public Health (617-727-0941), 1984. ☧ This supplies discussions and activities for teenagers around the subjects of child abuse, sexual abuse, women abuse, date rape, domestic stress, and anger management.

Deborah Prothrow-Stith. *Violence Prevention: Curriculum for Adolescents.* Newton, Mass.: Education Development Center, 1987. 🏃 This acclaimed workbook is designed to help adolescents deal with anger in productive, nonviolent ways. It is adaptable for use in homes, schools, and youth groups.

Internet Resources

www.freethechildren.org/peace/kcftc/about.html 🏃 This is the site for Youth Ambassadors for Peace Project of Kids Can Free The Children, an organization that came out of one boy's concern for child labor on the Indian subcontinent. No matter our perspective on war, many of us believe children and youth can make a difference in breaking through political stalemates.

www.fullerseminary.net/sot/faculty/stassen/cp_content/homepage/homepage.htm 🏃 This site will explain to you the Ten Practices referred to in the text. These are effective ways for working toward world peace.

www.gsinstitute.org/rsp/view_appeal/10_3appeal.html 🏃 An Appeal for Responsible Security advocates for responsible disarmament. President Jimmy Carter has signed this appeal.

www.mtholyoke.edu/acad/intrel/pol116/justwar.htm 🏃 Here you will find the classic principles of Just War spelled out, as well as links to further information.

www.wagingpeace.org/peacelinks.html 🏃 This site will put you on to scores of peace links.

www.wcrp.org 🏃 This is the site for the World Conference on Religion and Peace referred to in this chapter. Its address is 777 United Nations Plaza, NY, NY 10017 (212-687-2163).

Part 4

Addictions, Healing, and Reconciliation

15 Smoking, Drinking, and Drugs

> *Wine is a mocker, strong drink a brawler, and whoever is led astray by it is not wise.*
> — Prov 20:1 NRSV

> *Hear, my child, and be wise.... Do not be among winebibbers, or among gluttonous eaters ...; for the drunkard and the glutton will come to poverty.*
> — Prov 23:19–21 NRSV

These ancient proverbs provide good advice for all, though contemporary parents might say, "I'm concerned for your safety. Don't go out drinking or using drugs . . . so many deadly accidents and unwise sexual decisions happen that way."

The conservative words of the wisdom literature need further biblical balance. Psalm 104 is a hymn of praise to God as Creator and Provider that blesses the Lord for setting the earth on its foundations, making springs to gush forth in valleys giving drink to every wild animal, and providing "wine to gladden the human heart" (Ps 104:15 NRSV). Paul warns Christians not to "get drunk with wine, for that is debauchery; but be filled with the Holy Spirit." Jesus, however, was called a "winebibber" probably because he was partying with a drinking crowd at Matthew's (Luke 5:27–32) and Zacchaeus's houses (Luke 19:5–7). The wine he took at the Last Supper was part of social custom and not to be condemned.

There are various opinions as to the drinking of alcohol by adults and young people. In East Africa, for most Christians to drink any alcoholic drink is a serious sin; many

European Christians drink socially and in moderation. Consuming alcoholic drinks needs to be put within the framework of culture as well as one's personal experience, but our purpose is to deal with the danger of excessive drinking and how it contributes to violence.

This book has stressed the systemic aspects of all youthful problems. Before kids thought smoking was cool, adult society made it so. Youthful misuse of alcohol and drugs reflects sustained examples of reckless consumption depicted by the media and is influenced by continuous suggestions from advertising. Teen addicts not only follow in the steps of adult addicts but also socialized in cultures of addiction. Adolescent curiosity, pain, risk taking, rebellion, and peer influence also may be involved.

A Global Problem

Over the past few decades teenagers, and increasingly children, the world over have been abusing drugs as never before. Youthful smoking is all too prevalent. Street kids with their cans of glue, ravers[1] popping pills, and binge drinking are all too common. The progression tends to be from smoking, to drinking, and then soft and hard drugs. Some people object correctly that this is not the pattern for all; however, it is a significant pattern for those who fall into drug use, and those who work with addicts understand how it works. Most addicts began by smoking, then proceeded to excessive drinking, smoking pot, and using the hard stuff.

Stephen Gaghan has written for *The Simpsons* and *NYPD Blue* while he was strung out on heroin and crack. In his concluding article for *Newsweek's* series on the drug war, he tells how he followed his grandfather's tendency for drinking:

> I started drinking young and hard in Louisville, KY., a town known for its bourbon, cigarettes, and horse racing. . . . I wasn't much different from my peers, except where they

---

[1] Those who attend rave dances, where drugs are often sold.

could stop drinking after three or six or 10 drinks, I couldn't
stop and wouldn't stop until I had progressed through marijuana, cocaine, heroin and finally, crack and freebase—which
seem for many people to be the last stop on the elevator.[2]

From the *South China Morning Post* we learn

It's after one in the morning . . . [in] *Lip Kei Mun* or The
Gate of Exotic Hunting, one of the most popular discos in
Shenzhen (in southern China). Bathed in gaudy red neon
glow and decorated with a painting of mystical animals, the
entrance looks like a big, bloody mouth. . . .

Vivid scarlet light drenches (these students') green and red
uniforms, giving the place a sinister air. Inside, techno music
is blaring. Only one glance at the glazed expressions on most
of the faces of the teenagers inside, some as young as 14,
reveals they are heavily under the influence of drugs.

These are not mainland kids. They come from Hong Kong.
. . . In a corner, a cluster of young men and women unwrap
Ecstasy tablets bound in white tissue and pop their pills,
which cost them 100 *yuan* (U.S. $12) each.

Once swamped by older Hong Kong men visiting mainland
prostitutes, Shenzhen is now flooded by a new breed of
weekenders: the SAR (Hong Kong Special Administrative
Region) teens. The fresh arrivals travel to the border city not
only to party and take drugs. Some also buy drugs in bulk to
bring home and peddle in Hong Kong, where they can
expect to make a ten-fold profit. . . . [3]

In country after country throughout Asia, meth use skyrock-
eted during the '90s. And with the crash of the region's high-
flying economies, the drug's use has surged again. The base
drug—ephedrine—was actually first synthesized in Asia: a
team of Japanese scientists derived if from the Chinese *mao*
herb in 1892. Unlike ecstasy, which requires sophisticated
chemical and pharmaceutical knowledge to manufacture, or
heroin, whose base product, the poppy plant, is a vulnerable
crop, ephedrine can be refined fairly easily into meth. This
makes meth labs an attractive family business for industrious

---

[2] Stephen Gaghan, "The Enemy Is Us," *Newsweek,* 12 February
2001, 55.
[3] "Disco Drug Dealers: Easy Ecstasy for Hong Kong Teens," *World
Press Review,* April 2001, 12.

Asians, who set them up in converted bathrooms, farm-
houses or even on the family hearth.[4]

Further reports describe the devastation drugs have
brought even to remote parts of Thailand. At 50 *baht* ($1.20),
meth has replaced heroin among the lower classes. So pervasive is substance abuse that we need to stop and examine the
way human beings are attracted to and become addicted to
chemical stimuli.

The Nature of Addiction

Human behavior works from needs and the meeting of
needs. Our needs are physical, emotional, intellectual, social, and spiritual. There is also the Maslovian hierarchy of
needs from instinctive survival needs (breathing, drinking,
eating, and excreting) to more complex needs (getting the
education and jobs to obtain food, clothing, and shelter), to
belonging and love, and finally spiritual fulfillment.

Within this framework, we spend our days sensing a
need for sleep, for food and drink, for activity, for relationships, for a desire to serve and help others—and so it goes.
Throughout any week, we find fulfillment in many ways. Personal and family chores, work or study, down time or recreation, partying or worship all have a place in meeting various
needs. But no matter how we fulfill a need, we find relief and
satisfaction to be always temporary, and we move on to the
demands of new needs.

Water is good for thirst, and our need for water can be
met in many ways, some of which are more pleasurable and
some more healthful than others. If we get tired of plain
water and drink only coffee, the coffee meets two different
needs with two different types of consequences. We are
tending not only the body's need for water but also experiencing a jolt for our nervous system.

---

[4] Karl Taro Greenfeld, "Speed Demons: Methamphetamines are rip-
ping across Asia, seducing the young with a promise of a fast, clean high,
Time, 2 April 2001, 36–37.

We might list chemicals that give some kind of physical or emotional reward:

- sugar

- chocolate

- caffeine in coffee, tea, or sodas

- alcohol in wine, beer, and harder liquors

- nicotine in cigarettes, cigars, and smokeless forms

- marijuana

- inhalants (household cleaners and petroleum products)

- depressants (or downers, yellow jacket, phennie, red devil)

- stimulants (or uppers, speed, meth, bennies)

- narcotics (heroin from opium or cocaine and crack from coca)

- hallucinogens (LSD or acid, PCP or angel dust, Ecstasy, e, or MDMA)

To this list we should add steroids, both anabolic (building) and androgenic (masculinizing) products, which include the male hormone testosterone and artificial derivatives. Short-term health hazards have been documented and long-term psychiatric effects are suspected when these substances are abused. Extreme pressure on younger children to compete and excel athletically has led to boys and girls as young as ten to take illegal steroids; a University of Massachusetts survey found 2.7 percent of middle school students using anabolic steroids.[5]

Many of us have mild or more severe addictions to sugar and caffeine. Deprived of caffeine for several days, we may suffer headaches or other symptoms. In general, societies must decide on the legal or illegal uses of these chemicals, and individuals need to determine their use and tolerances. The milder chemicals on this list may be socially enjoyed.

---

[5] Associated Press, "Children's Steroid Use Rising, Study Says," *Boston Globe,* 5 May 1998, A3.

Stronger drugs are prescribed by physicians for pain or other maladies. When someone's use of one of these chemicals is obsessive and over time causes dysfunction or damages interpersonal relationships, we consider the person to have a damaging addiction.

Understanding addiction from a behavioral perspective comes quite close to the classical Greek concept of harmony and imbalance or the Hebrew-Christian concept of sin as *hamartia,* a missing of the intended mark. In other words, the psychological sense of dysfunction approaches the theological concept of transgression or sin.

Human needs, then, may and should be fulfilled in normal and healthy ways. This is what children ought to be taught. When drugs are used as shortcuts or for euphoria, however, they have unintended consequences that include a gradual deadening of normal pleasures and an increasing dependence on the continual fix. When the drug is no longer a means to an end but an end in itself, it becomes an idol or god that must be served. Others, even loved ones and family, finally become merely means to that end.

Since the late 1990s especially, neuroscientists have been using MRIs and PET scans to study what happens in the brain of a drug abuser.[6] "Imaging and other techniques are driving home what we learned from decades of animal experiments. Drugs of abuse change the brain, hijack its motivational systems, and even change how its genes function."[7]

These researchers have documented neurobiological changes taking place through drug abuse—dramatically in the case of hard drugs, but also in the persistent and heavy use of softer drugs such as alcohol and nicotine. They observe how addictive drugs alter the brain's pleasure or reward circuits. The normal enjoyments of life activate this circuit in the chemical language of dopamine, the brain's chemical compound that transmits pleasurable nerve im-

---

[6] For instance, see the 1998 study of Dr. Scott Lukas of McLean Hospital in Belmont, Massachusetts.

[7] Dr. Alan Leshner, as interviewed by Sharon Begley, "How It All Starts Inside Your Brain," *Newsweek,* 12 February 2001, 40.

pulses and is involved in the formation of epinephrine. Dopamine affects other neurons in ways resulting in happiness, such as our enjoyment of a favorite food or drink, athletic victory, or sex.

In similar but distinct ways, addictive drugs take over the dopamine function with a mighty and pleasurable rush but also destroy dopamine receptors in a way that makes ordinary pleasures impotent and gradually reduces even the rush from the drug (what we have known as drug tolerance). For the addict, withdrawal and abstinence may mean not only the loss of habitual chemical highs and pleasures but also the onset of physical illness, anxiety, and depression.

> That is why addiction is a brain disease. It may start with the voluntary act of taking drugs, but once you've got it, you can't tell the addict, "Stop," any more than you can tell the smoker "Don't have emphysema." Starting may be volitional. Stopping isn't [explains Dr. Alan Leshner, director of NIDA, the National Institute of Drug and Alcohol].[8]

In a similar manner, hallucinogenic drugs like LSD and MDMA or Ecstasy disrupt the functioning of another neurotransmitter, serotonin. Serotonin causes a restriction of blood vessels around an injury and may affect mood swings. Its long, threadlike neurons reach distant parts of the brain and may allow us to feel bliss or empathy. No matter what advocates for these drugs contend, there is evidence that they produce long-term changes in serotonin, and therefore behavioral functioning. Ecstasy stimulates nerve cells to release all stored serotonin at once—causing a rush and heightening the senses, overwhelming serotonin receptors, and probably doing damage to axon endings.

These dramatic findings of neuroscientists must be supplemented by psychological and spiritual insights if we are to understand addiction more fully. Brain specialists, for example, can explain relapse (why those who are clean and whose dopamine receptors are restored will turn back to old, addictive ways) merely in terms of memory. But working

---

[8] Ibid., 42.

with addicts reveals more. There seems to be some genetic dispositions to addiction. There are also deep longings for nurturing missed in infancy and other developmental issues. True recovery includes spiritual and emotional maturity, the ability to self-discipline oneself in terms of delaying physical gratification we all need. Recovery establishes daily pleasure in accomplishing short- and long-term goals. It needs and derives pleasure from the affirmation of supporting friends and community.

Smoking

Do you remember the first time you saw a Joe Camel ad? I do. Why would they rent a whole billboard to portray a cartoon camel, I asked myself. Maybe it will be like the Volkswagen Beetle, I thought. You look at it enough and it becomes cute, especially if it's yours. But it was much more than that. As I watched the ads spread to *Rolling Stone* and magazines read by younger kids, I realized that marketers had detected a critical kind of cool that would attract many subcultures and ages down to the very young. Walk through an urban neighborhood and notice the Newport ads, which promote another kind of cool: fashion, sex, and athletes. And then there was the Marlboro man, with his powerful appeal to young guys and gals.

Lloyd D. Johnston and his staff at the University of Michigan's Monitoring the Future Study found smoking rates among teens rising to their highest levels in two decades during the 1990s and beginning at a younger level. Significantly, teenagers (eighty-eight percent of twelfth graders) were smoking primarily three cigarette brands:

- Philip Morris's Marlboro is the favorite brand of most young white and Hispanic smokers, males and females (sixty-five percent of twelfth graders).

- Lorillard's mentholated Newport is second (thirteen percent of all twelfth graders but seventy-five percent of black twelfth graders).

- R. J. Reynolds/Nabisco's Camel ranks third (ten percent of twelfth graders).[9]

Marlboro apparently gained the lion's share of the youthful market with the icon of the rugged, handsome, Western cowboy. They also made effective use of Formula One racing and other sports. Newport plastered urban streets with billboards associating their cigarette with popular sports and music celebrities. Camel's cool icon attracted broad attention, but not to the extent of Marlboro.

No other brand of cigarette is smoked by even two percent of U.S. teenagers. The impact of advertising is clear, the authors of this study conclude:

> In sum, the segment of the teen-age market which R. J. Reynolds has penetrated most completely with their Joe Camel theme is white males from well-educated families. Newport, made by Lorillard, accounts for most of the black segment of the underage market. But Philip Morris, the maker of Marlboro, clearly dominates the white and Hispanic underage market, and therefore the youth market as a whole.[10]

Tobacco companies spend $5 billion every year targeted at children and young people. Incriminating internal memos document their strategy: If they do not ensnare young, brand-loyal users, they have no future. As U.S. restrictions against the blatant targeting of children increase, the focus of tobacco companies moves overseas. Think of how many children, goaded by clever commercials, begin smoking every day (three thousand in the U.S.; maybe a hundred thousand worldwide). Soon they are hooked. Nearly nine of ten U.S. smokers started their habit before the age of nineteen.[11]

Some young people can quit smoking, but many cannot. Surveys show sixty percent of teenagers who are heavy smokers say they have tried to stop—and failed.

---

[9] University of Michigan, "Cigarette Brands Smoked by American Teens," April 14, 1999. Online: http://monitoringthefuture.org/pressreleases/cigbrandpr.html.

[10] Ibid., 2.

[11] Paula Lantz, Peter Jacobson, and Kenneth Warner, "Youthful Smoking Prevention: What Works?" *The Prevention Researcher,* 8, no. 2 (April 2001): 1.

🛹 Joey is 14 and you suspect he's begun to smoke. How concerned would you and should you be?

Leslie is 15 and you think she is drinking with friends though she denies it. What steps might you take?

Terry, 16, smokes and drinks moderately, away from home. He argues strongly that smoking pot is not as bad as drinking heavily but will not admit to doing it. You've seen the progression in the last couple of years . . . starting to smoke, then drinking with friends, and you are worried he is already using marijuana. What might come after that? You sense that most interventions can be counterproductive with Terry. What can you do?

What resources are available for you as a parent, teacher, and youth worker in the above cases?

Why Children Smoke

Kids do not generally admit to the influence that advertising has upon them. They will, however, admit to following the fads of friends, and they know that advertising has an influence over their peer group. When I ask them why they smoke, I get these answers:

- It's cool.
- It's sexy.
- It's fun to smoke with friends.
- It relaxes or picks me up.
- (For the very poor) It helps me forget my hunger.
- (Gradually and sadly) Because I can't stop.

The force of advertising added to frequent models of movie stars (coolness and sexiness) plus use by friends makes for powerful inducement. Smoking can be a symbol of adulthood and of rebellion against adults at the same time. It addicts by cool motions and use of hands, by smell and taste, by association with food or breaks, as well as by the addictive power of nicotine. Researchers have found smoking to be as difficult an addiction to break as heroin.

Close to fifty million Americans smoke, and one in five teenagers. There are four thousand chemicals in a cigarette, two hundred of them known poisons. Nearly 450,000 Americans die every year as a result of smoking. Almost one in five high school boys use smokeless (chewing or spit) tobacco and make themselves vulnerable to oral cancers and other diseases. Adolescent smokers are one hundred times more likely to smoke marijuana and are more likely to use other illegal drugs in their future. "Each day more than 3,000 people under the age of 18 become regular smokers. That's more than 1 million teens per year. Roughly one third of them will eventually die from a tobacco-related disease." [12]

Preventing Tobacco Use in Youth

The late 1990s and turn of the twenty-first century have seen a slight decline in smoking among teenagers in the U.S. This may to a lesser extent be true of smokeless tobacco use, although research on this dangerous practice, especially among baseball players, is inadequate. Several factors may contribute to this decline:

- Several types of school-based interventions, including peer education

- Community and family interventions

- Public education through mass media

- Tobacco advertising restrictions

- Youth access restrictions

- Tobacco excise taxes

Drinking

From Australia, Toby Hemming writes, "More than 70% of 15–17-year-olds drank alcohol in the past year—and most of

---

[12] Elks Drug Awareness Resource Center, "Tips for Teens: The Truth About Tobacco" (www.elks.org/drugs/dap200.cfm).

them drank to get drunk."[13] The Alcohol Advisory Council (Alac) of New Zealand reported that some teens are taking advantage of relaxed liquor laws: "just under half of all 14 to 18-year-olds reported . . . having five or more drinks on their last drinking occasion."[14] And *The Times* of London notes a rise in violent young drinkers and puts the blame on parents.[15]

Why Youth Drink to Excess

Teenage smoking may be in decline, but not drinking. Consider the reasons for youthful drinking. Positive suggestions and reinforcement come from parents and adults, media, peers, and internal desires. As individuals, adolescents are eager to test their limits, explore exciting and pleasurable highs and lows, reduce stress and anxiety, lessen shyness or personal inhibitions, fit in with others, have power over others, and escape boring, painful, or overwhelming reality.

As a group, young people are searching out replacements for vanishing markers[16] on their road to maturity. Losing one's virginity or getting blasted are touted by media and assumed by friends as ways to prove one's adulthood. If this is the subculture's rite of passage, then there will be pressure to conform. Most youthful groups, however, are still respectful of those who abstain as long as they are cool and nonjudgmental about it.

I hear many reasons for drinking:

- That's what we do at parties. You just grab a drink to fit in.

- Without a drink I'm shy. I become funnier and friendlier when I'm a little drunk.

---

[13] Toby Hemming, *The Age* (Melbourne), 20 February 2000, 1, citing a National Alcohol Campaign to be launched that day.

[14] *The New Zealand Herald Online,* 14 March 2001, 1.

[15] Stewart Tendler, "Parents Blamed for Teen Drunks," *London Times,* 19 January 2001, 2.

[16] David Elkind, *All Grown Up and No Place to Go* (rev. ed.; Reading, Mass.: Addison-Wesley, 1998). Chapter 5, "Vanishing Markers" misses the power of traditional rites of passage but shows how the loss of rites in contemporary society has left youth with no publicly affirmed external signs of their advancement toward maturity.

- I need to relax and take the edge off even before I go into a party.

- It makes sex easier for me when I've had a few drinks.

- I like the taste.

- Keg parties are the greatest; there's a lot more fun when we're drinking.

- By the weekend I need to escape a whole lot of things.

The Dangers of Drinking

Studies show that under the influence of alcohol, suicides and outbursts of violence are twenty to sixty times more likely to be committed. That obviously does not mean that drinking necessarily causes homicides or suicides. It does mean that if someone is on the brink of taking his or her own or someone else's life, alcohol or drugs can make it easier. In fact, most crimes and accidents take place under the influence of alcohol.

Even more insidiously, most date rapes take place under the influence of alcohol or the new rape drugs. The date rape drug Rohypnol was popular for a while at an Alamo, Texas, high school. A teen named Zenaida used roaches, as the Rohypnol pills were called, during her four years there but gave them up after one terrible night. At a party, three guys slyly dropped a handful of roaches into her drink. In minutes she was out, and the three men raped and beat her. When she awoke the next morning, she found herself in a bloody pool of vomit with hickeys and bruises covering her body. "I don't remember anything," she says. That's when she quit, but it's been harder getting other girls to do so. "I tell all my friends to stop taking them because of what happened to me, but nobody listens."[17]

Resistance to Intervention

"Nobody listens," Zenaida said. You would think her friends would listen to a peer who had gone through such a terrifying experience, but the rush of highs and the pressure of peers and situations often prevail. The same reasons that

---

[17] Jenifer Joseph, "The Young Women's Drug." Online: ABCNEWS .com, 6 May 2001.

lead young people into rebellious and reckless abuse of chemicals makes them unwilling to stop. They give many reasons, including

- Sure you can get raped, and you can get killed drinking and driving. You can overdose, for that matter. It can happen to anyone, anytime. But it's not going to happen to me.

- Nobody is going to tell me what to do or not do.

- It isn't anybody else's business.

- I know what I can take and can get out of this any time I want.

Rebellious Children

For a wife and family to suffer an alcoholic and abusive husband and father can be a horrible experience. A woman's alcoholism can also tear apart a family and her husband's heart. But especially intense are the frustration and pain of parents as they watch a child slip into addiction. Gradually, effective communication is cut off.

Young people need some freedom to fail, but there is a point at which parents must exert tough love—for the sake of the household and ultimately their addicted child's future. Addicts sometimes have to hit bottom before, they come to themselves, like the prodigal son. Some studies, however, have shown that the recovery rate of those who are forced into recovery programs through the intervention of family, friends, or law enforcement officials is similar to those who have hit bottom and desperately sought help.

Martha Dudman remembers when she first smelled cigarette smoke on her eleven-year-old daughter's clothes. Later Martha began to suspect she was smoking pot, but her daughter denied any of it. In a couple of years there was not only drinking and smoking pot but also lying and stealing. By the time she was in senior high school, Augusta (not her real name) was stealing cars and dealing drugs. She would stay out most of the night and often ran away from home. She defiantly told her mother she hated her, cursed her, and threatened to stab her. Meanwhile she was bingeing, then refusing to eat, cutting herself, and threatening suicide.[18]

> My kids were driving me nuts. This happened all the time now, ever since they started edging toward adolescence. They were angry at me. They were scornful. My daughter was furious. My son (2 years younger) was bored. I couldn't even remember how it had been anymore; our sweet little household. The candlelit dinners. The fires. The books. The stories and the special treats and the rituals of family I had tended. . . . Whenever it got to be too much for me I would go out. . . . Just get out and start walking.[19]

Exhausted as a single parent and executive director of three radio stations, chasing down her daughter through long nights, and isolated from extended family and community, Dudman found herself losing the battle:

> These are the definitions she has set for herself: she always goes barefoot, she's not good at school, she loves drugs, she smokes, she doesn't like rich people, she's against war, she wears only thrift-store clothes, she doesn't comb her hair.
>
> One by one I release my own rules for my daughter. Rules about when she comes in. Rules about what she wears. Rules about school. Rules about what constitutes sickness (for getting out of school). Rules about what constitutes sanity. And each edge she pushes.[20]

Augusta and her mother seem to agree on one thing: they are alike. "You should understand. You were like me," Augusta says.[21] And Dudman is frank about her own teenage rebellion, drug use, and sexual activities. She is now more conscious of her self-reproach.

> There's too much self-reproach in seeing her stoned, lying, dirty, lost. The kind of girl you never meant to have. And it seems as if she is the daughter you most deserve. . . . You don't want to see what you've done wrong.[22]

---

[18] Martha Tod Dudman, *Augusta Gone: A True Story* (New York: Simon & Schuster, 2001).

[19] Ibid., 17.

[20] Ibid., 21.

[21] Ibid., 61.

[22] Ibid., 73.

After rejecting the notion of tough love a long time, Dudman finally sends her daughter off to Wilderness Camp and then a school for troubled youth. Augusta hates both, and she runs away from the school twice. It may be her days on the streets of San Francisco—eating garbage out of a dumpster—that finally brings Augusta to some sense of limits and what she does not want to be. Slowly she is making her way without drugs.

Dudman wrote this story to work out her struggles and remorse and published it with her daughter's permission. When she was interviewed by a reporter, Augusta would say only:

> I'm glad I did what I did. It was hard and it was scary, but I have a story to tell now. [Asked if she has remorse for all she put her mother through, she says] I ask my mom, "Would you rather have a dull daughter, one that just went through the motions, or would you rather have me?"[23]

Mother's reply seems remarkably in line with her daughter's rebellious spirit:

> You know there's a part of me that's proud of her for resisting, for sticking up for herself no matter how wrong she was. . . . I think the children who are the most creative, bright, and interesting have the worst time being teens.[24]

🏃 How can you help teens who are drifting toward trouble? In the first place, it is important that you care and are willing to stick with this young person. You need to stay calm and do much more listening than talking—though some teenagers will not open up at first. Prayer is the all important starting point. Then, you also need good counsel and feedback on your approach from an objective, wise party.

---

[23] Bella English, "Darling to Delinquent: A Mother Recounts Her Teen Daughter's Descent into Hell and Struggle Back," *Boston Globe,* 12 April 2001, D7.

[24] Ibid.

Try a three-part strategy. First list the troubling behaviors, from minor to what you consider most serious. Then list the resources available for dealing with the issue. Your first list may include extreme mood swings, refusal to keep rules or to communicate, truancy and failing grades, hurting an animal or picking on younger siblings, abusing alcohol or drugs, running away.

Next, try to get inside the skin of this young person. List particular stresses in his or her life. What causes special anxiety or what are they especially trying to avoid? This may be quite difficult, but listen to siblings or friends, and your own sensibilities. This list may slowly grow. Any kind of learning disability or childhood abuse are crucial clues. Or there may be more subtle difficulties. What this person needs, what all of us need, are love, understanding, encouragement, and practical guidelines.

Then write up all the resources available. There may be someone in your extended family, or a church or neighborhood friend, who could be a special friend and help. School visits are extremely important. Some teacher, counselor, or coach might have an important perspective or ability to help. In some cases, a sensitive police officer might go out of his or her way to have a talk with the young person. Are there any groups that might help this young person? Counseling, special programs, summer camps, alternative schools are all possibilities that will need to be considered somewhere along the line of unhealthy behaviors that lead to addiction.

The story of single mother Vicki Robinson and her daughter Valessa is similar but with a much more tragic ending. According to her older sister, Valessa took the divorce of her parents when she was eleven very hard. She essentially lost her father, who moved out of state looking for work. Her mother was a successful real estate agent and active in her church, so Valessa did not receive much attention from her. Her mother also had an active social life.

By the time she was twelve, Valessa was on her own and was allowed to join a rock band made up of twenty-year-old men. This is when she began skipping school and doing drugs. "Acid was the main thing that we did; we also did Ecstasy." Her sister remembers her staying out all night and says, "She was out of control, pretty much."[25]

When Valessa was fourteen, she refused to go on a vacation with her mother and her mother's boyfriend. Finally they left her, went away for two weeks, and never called home to check on Valessa. That fall, entering ninth grade, Valessa met eighteen-year-old Adam Davis. They became inseparable. Adam's mother had abandoned him when he was two, and his father was dead. Living on the streets, he got into drugs and drug dealing and dropped out of school. "He acted like he cared about me. I mean, that's why I started dating him in the first place. Looking back I realize that he had this overwhelming control over me."[26]

With Adam and his friend Jon Whispel in the house most of the time, things became difficult. Sensing things were out of hand, Vicki Robinson enrolled her rebellious daughter in a year-long program for troubled teenagers, Steppin' Stone Farm, without telling Valessa. But ten days before her daughter was to go into the program, Vicki was killed. She was allegedly mauled by Adam and Valessa. Adam was convicted of first-degree murder, Jon and Valessa as accomplices. In prison, Valessa first took responsibility for the crime and affirmed her love and loyalty for Adam. After a few months her story changed.

Valessa now responds to questions about what went wrong by saying she wished her mother had set limits and stuck to rules. She encourages parents of kids doing drugs and with a boyfriend like Adam to pay attention: "They need to be there for them, see that there's something wrong going on. Get them away from the crowd that they're

---

[25] CBS News, *48 Hours*, 23 April 2001.
[26] Ibid.

around."[27] Nothing will bring Vicki Robinson back, and Valessa will spend her life dealing with her complicity in the act.

Effective Intervention

Americans are losing the drug war just as clearly as we lost the war in Vietnam. We must reduce the demand for drugs, because as long as billions are to be made, we will never stop the supply. It does not make sense to give up on law enforcement; nor should American society capitulate and legalize the scourge. But the emphasis must be on prevention and treatment.

Addiction rarely appears as a singular problem in the life of an individual. Substance abuse is usually accompanied by and may cover up all sorts of fears, depressions, past hurts, and unfulfilled desires. In most cases, however, addiction to alcohol or drugs must be dealt with before working out deeper problems. Tough Love and wilderness/adventure programs for teenagers and Twelve-Step programs with group support/confrontation have proved effective in dealing with addictions. Professional therapy may be needed after a person is dry or clean.

There are programs that adapt the Twelve Steps to Christian settings and to young people. The Steps are meant to be discussed. The power of AA and related programs is that they allow alcoholics and addicts to hear people's stories. *Alcoholics Anonymous,* the *Big Book* is mostly stories and this is its power. The power of Twelve Step programs is two-fold: belief in God or a Higher Power and admission of one's own failure *and* strong support of a group of friends who share one's problem and determination to change. This is really the secret of powerful youth ministry. Twelve Step programs are adaptable to secular and Christian settings. Belief can be in a Higher Power, in a personal God, or even more specifically in Jesus Christ.

---

[27] Ibid.

How can you talk to someone who does not want to be talked to? Our only recourse may be to listen and set clear boundaries. This takes time. The person who does not want to hear your advice may not even want to talk with you. Effective conversation may happen because you care, you are aware, you are open and non-condemning, and you are prepared. We may not succeed unless we care about a young person more than he cares for himself. Our attitude and style must be nonjudgmental and accepting. We must also be aware of the issues and where this particular young person is. Finally, we must be prepared with skills of active listening and resources for referral. Above all we must be there today, and when he's ready—and prepared for many hours of follow-through.

With more resistant persons—after exhausting our personal resources—we may get them to talk with us and a friend or two. A more formal intervention sometimes works, although more often this helps older abusers. Sometimes a trip to a treatment center or a visit to a recovery group is in order, where we can talk on the way and traveling back. Seeds must be planted; growth and harvest may be delayed.

Sometimes nothing works with people we love. We must let them go. We refuse codependency, but our love and prayers need never fail.

Young people become addicts in an addictive culture. While ultimate cure is not on the horizon for societies or individuals, we must do our best and not lose heart. Humanist heroes and Christian saints are fighting these curses around the world. They are mostly unknown folks in under-funded programs. We are called to join them. Those who recover and find a life are reward enough.

Questions for Reflection and Discussion

1. What is, or might be, your addiction?
2. How might you be helped? What kind of intervention would you resist?
   3.
   What has been your experience in trying to help someone with an addiction?
4. What are the strongest influences that encourage substance abuse (smoking, drinking, drugs) in young people?
5. How can churches and youth groups best help youth with these problems? (Discuss last section of chapter and listed resources.)
6. With what resources are you familiar that can help youth recover from substance abuse? (Study resource list below and consider your own research starting with the Yellow Pages, getting good advice from those you trust, and checking out the Internet.)
7. What did you find most helpful in this chapter?
8. With what did you disagree or take exception?
9. What suggestions can you offer?

Book Resources

The resources after each chapter overlap, so you always need to look back at what has already been suggested. Here's one we've mentioned and a few more.

Adolescent Peer Pressure: Theory, Coorelates, and Program Implications for Drug Abuse Prevention. U.S. Department of Health and Human Services, Public Health Service, DHHS Publication No. (ADM) 86-1152, 1981, 1986. ♣ The first chapter discusses adolescent society, the second explores influences on adolescent problem behavior, the third describes types of peer program approaches, the fourth describes program planning, and the fifth offers resources.

Stephen Arterburn and Jim Burns. *Drug-Proof Your Kids: A Prevention Guide & An Intervention Plan.* Pomona, Calif.: Focus on the Family Publishing, 1989. ⚑ A director of a treatment center and a respected trainer of youth workers combine to help families in distress over their children's alcohol or drug abuse.

Kathleen Hamilton Eschner and Nancy G. Nelson. *Drugs, God & Me.* Loveland, Colo.: Group Publishing, 1988. ⚑. This is an alcohol and drug abuse prevention program for junior highers and their parents. This 8-session curriculum goes far beyond "Just say no," and includes retreat designs, curriculum, a bibliography, and a resource list.

Elizabeth Fenwick and Dr. Tony Smith. *Adolescence: The Survival Guide for Parents and Teenagers.* New York: DK Publishing, 1996. ⚑The secular, liberal perspective makes the recommendation of this book problematic here. You may disagree with its position on teenage sex, contraception, abortion, and homosexuality. But there is much of value here, from case histories, positive parent/teen dialogues, questionnaires to help parents and teens figure out their thoughts and feelings, to advice for parents and for teenagers on smoking, drinking, drugs, and a whole range of topics.

Ron Keller. *The Twelve Steps for Kids.* Burnsville, Minn.: Prince of Peace Publishing, 1989. ⚑ This book is a fine adaptation of the Twelve Steps for young people open to faith in Jesus Christ. It is written by a person with youth work and addiction treatment experience, and is a wonderful source, though long out of print.

Ron Keller. *Twelve Steps to a New Day.* Nashville: Thomas Nelson, 1993. ⚑ Unfortunately, this book is also out of print, but available through some used book services. It broadens the Twelve Steps to the spiritual journey of any teen.

Scott Larson. *When Teens Stray: Parenting for the Long Haul.* Ann Arbor: Servant Press, 2002. ⚑ A new book from a Christian perspective with practical help from a seasoned youth worker, who is the founder and director of Straight

Ahead Ministries. This is not just for parents; youth ministers will find important principles here.

Miriam Neff. *Helping Teens In Crisis.* Wheaton, Ill.: Tyndale House, 1993. 🛹 Mentioned before, this is a very helpful advice and practical suggestions from a Christian counselor. Ch. 10 deals with drugs and alcohol.

John Reaves and James B. Austin. *How to Find Help for a Troubled Kid: A Parent's Guide to Programs and Services for Adolescents.* New York: Henry Holt, 1990. 🛹 This book is slightly dated now, but is still a great source of help for parents who know their child needs help but don't know where to find it. After introductory chapters on troubled kids and troubled parents and evaluation, you will find suggestions for alternative schools, counseling, self-help groups, boarding schools, group homes and shelters, residential treatment centers, alcohol and drug treatment, hospitals, the juvenile justice system, and more. (Although out of print, there are still copies available on the Internet and in some libraries.)

The Twelve Steps for Christians: Based on Biblical Principles. RPI (revised edition) 1994. 🛹 This book is being used by many churches and has brought great help to many.

Phyllis York, David York, and Ted Wachtel. *ToughLove Solutions.* New York: Bantam Books, 1984. 🛹 The founders of the ToughLove movement explain their rationale and methods of dealing with teenage runaways, sex, suicide, drugs, alcohol, abuse, disrupted families, and community indifference.

Internet Resources

www.health.org/features/youth 🛹 National Clearing House for Alcohol and Drug Information (NCADI) provides links to resources for teens.

www.nick.com/all_nick/everything_nick/kaiser 🛹 Nickelodian and Talking With Kids helps parents and younger kids deal with issues of alcohol, tobacco, and drugs.

www.talkingwithkids.org 🐧 Sponsored by the Kaiser Family
Foundation, this site promotes talking with kids about
tough issues including alcohol and drugs.

www.tobaccofree.org 🐧 Patrick Reynolds and The Foundation for a Smoke Free America sponsors this site with information, short motivational speeches, and a message to
youth.

16 Sexual Issues

*Jesus said . . . "from the beginning of creation, God
made them male and female. For this reason a man
shall leave his father and mother and be joined to
his wife, and the two shall become one flesh. So they
are no longer two but one flesh. Therefore what God
has joined together, let no one separate."*
— *Mark 10:5-9* NRSV

*Drink water from your own cistern, running water
from your own well. Should your springs overflow in
the streets, your streams of water in public squares?
. . . May your fountain be blessed, and may you
rejoice in the wife of your youth. A loving doe, a
graceful deer—may her breasts satisfy you always,
may you ever be captivated by her love.*
— *Prov 5:15-19* NIV

If the pain of all sexual sins were heaped in one place, its enor-
mity would be incomprehensible. People suffer a lifetime of
anguish because of sexual abuse and rape. Remorse and
shame are carried by those who capitulated to impulses
somewhere in their past. Sex is one of earth's great pleasures; it is also a constant preoccupation, temptation, and
source of pain. A consideration of sex going wrong is a serious and important part of this book.

In the Sermon on the Mount Jesus describes sexual attraction as properly directed exclusively toward one's spouse
("everyone who looks at a woman with lust has already committed adultery with her in her heart" [Matt 5:28 NRSV]).
Jesus, as the quotation from Mark above expresses, sees the
bond between one man and one woman established as God's
original intent.

Throughout history, religions and traditional societies sought to bring order to sexual activities as, we have seen, they did with power and violence.[1]

From the beginning, as far as we know, there were also deviations. The rich and powerful were allowed special license; others were castigated. The ancient book of Proverbs recognizes two patterns of sexual activity: a right and good way and the wrong way. Most societies and religions have similar teachings.

Our society no longer thinks of sexual activity and moral codes in terms of right and wrong. It seems that almost anything goes, and we are asked to tolerate sexual deviations as private matters. USA Today posted a picture of teen idol Britney Spears with boyfriend Colin Farrell. The article quotes the Irish actor's interview in the March issue of "Playboy" in which Farrell brags about his love for porn, Ecstasy, and prostitutes. "I've always been a firm believer that casual sex is a [expletive] good thing. Sometimes . . . all I'm looking for is the simple act of sexual intimacy. It's like ordering a [expletive] pizza."[2]

Adults and teenagers seem confused about right ways and wrong ways when it comes to sex, as a young woman, seventeen, from Tennessee hints:

> My opinion about premarital sex is that no matter what anyone says, it's always going to happen. I really don't think people should do it. It's a sin. But also teenagers and grown-ups think that they should have sex with their boyfriends to hold on to them. . . .
>
> I asked my preacher if it was okay to have sex if you were planning to get married and he said that it was okay. . . . But as for my mother and other grownups like her, I don't think that what they do is right—having sex and even another child by a man she'd been going with

---

[1] We are continuing consideration of the twin human drives toward union and achievement or power. This chapter deals with misuse of our sexual energies, as chapter 14 dealt with abuse of our drive toward achievement (power and violence).

[2] Cesar G. Soriano, "Spears, Farrell officially an item?" *USA Today*, posted 29 January 2003.

and they don't have any intentions whatsoever to get married. That's not right. If they love each other, they would get married.[3]

More than 100,000 children in British schools received a sex course (called "A Pause") advocating sexual "stopping points" before intercourse. It encourages students under 16 to experiment with oral sex—in order to cut teen pregnancy rates. Robert Whelan, director of the Family Education Trust objects: "I don't think anyone believes teaching pupils about oral sex will stop them having full sex—it is more likely to make them want to try it, and it doesn't protect them from sexually transmitted diseases." A teacher from Doncaster who attended the course's training day said she was taught to deal with questions about oral and anal sex. "I was amazed. Are these really the sort of questions to which we as a profession ought to be responding?"[4]

Teen ambivalence about sex reflects society's confusion. Most teenagers have a conscious or subconscious need for order, for some sense of what is right or wrong in regards to their sexuality. A great deal of stress young people feel today comes from the lack of clear boundaries in our society and in their lives, as David Elkind[5] and Francis Ianni[6] have been saying about young people since the 1980s.

---

[3] *Teenagers Themselves,* compiled by Glenbard East *Echo,* advised by Howard Spanogle (New York: Adama Books, 1984).

[4] Glen Owen, "Government urges under-16s to experiment with oral sex," TIMESONLINE, 21 February 2003.

[5] David Elkind, *All Grown Up and No Place to Go.* Hurried children and abandoned teenagers, Elkind says, "have not had the adult guidance, direction, and support they need to make a healthy transition to adulthood" (xii). The result of this is stress.

[6] Francis Ianni, *The Search for Structure: A Report on American Youth Today* (New York: Free Press, 1989). The author carried out one of the most extensive and relational studies of adolescents of the 1980s. He found that youthful "conflict and confusion must occur when the home, the school, the workplace, and other social institutions present different standards of adulthood and different means of attaining it" (7).

The Global Picture

It is important that Americans and Europeans—in fact, all of us the world over—have a global perspective on problems affecting young people. Urbanization and globalization are changing economies, the structure of the family, and social values worldwide. Ubiquitous pop culture erodes traditional values and restraints. Sexual titillation is part of a child's socialization in Lagos, St. Petersburg, Tokyo, Beijing, Sidney, Liverpool, Spokane, or Rio. In small rural villages of Kenya, children watch WWF wrestling and suggestive sitcoms.

As the world experienced the transition from traditional to more urbanized and global cultures, mass media heightened its glamorization of licentious lifestyles.[7]

The U.S. and Great Britain share a great deal of responsibility—though they are not alone—for their exportation of sensationalized sex and pornography. This has certainly contributed to the anger of traditional societies and religious fundamentalists.

American youth hit all-time highs of teenage sexual activity in the 1980s. In Africa, premarital teenage sex seems to be on the rise. In Eastern Europe and Russia, the collapse of communism lowered restraints and led to an upsurge in sexual behaviors among teens.

The twenty-first century is seeing radical increases of sexual activity in Asia. Although mainland China does not allow the word "sex" in advertisements or product names, Shanghai radio has a sexologist, Chen Kai, who gives risqué, on-air advice. In Phnom Penh educators say fifty percent of high school boys are having sex with their girlfriends.

In Kyoto, Japan, a young woman tells Kate Drake about how she slipped into Internet sex and prostitution *(enjo kosai)*.

I started doing enjo kosai my second year of high school. . . .

---

[7] We must admit that this is at least *one* reason for radical Arab Islamic rage and one example of capitalism run amok.

I was going to school like usual but I was bored and had no money. My boyfriend, the guy I lost my virginity to, had just broken up with me. I wouldn't do enjo kosai if I had a boyfriend. Losing him was really tough. So I just posted a message about myself on a cyber message board and chose a sex partner from the guys who wrote back. It wasn't hard. Guys who want sex and dinner, guys who just want sex. Guys who just want dinner—they're all out there. They leave messages like, "Any girl who will have sex for 50,000 yen ($420) send a message here." . . . I just had to say I was a high school girl, you know? . . .

I don't even know if there's a law against enjo kosai. No one but me knew what I was doing so I thought it was O.K. My parents definitely don't know. . . . They'd think I'm shameless.

I stopped doing enjo kosai after a while. When I did it, all I was thinking was that it's only for today so it doesn't matter. Stuff like, "No problem, don't worry that it's not someone you like." At the same time I didn't think I was doing anything bad, but now I think it was bad.[8]

In the same series, Tim McGirk describes Chinese prostitution:

Little Jade is one of 200 million rural laborers (according to Beijing economists) streaming into cities to find work. Jobs for this mass of migrants are simply not available. Little Jade worked in a restaurant before she was fired for dropping dishes. Drifting into heroin addiction she was forced to prostitute.

Now she says she will sell herself (for $17) only until she has enough money to help her boyfriend get off drugs. Most of her customers refuse to use condoms. She refuses to be tested because she does not have proper work papers and could be detained. Little Jade will probably join the many dying of AIDS. That, and fear of what her customers or police might do to her, probably explains why she was shaking when she got into the taxi and began this interview.

Chinese health authorities estimated 200,000 HIV cases by the end of 1996. A year later the figure had doubled. According to O. C. Line, director of Hong Kong's AIDS

---

[8] Kate Drake, "Sex in Asia." *Time,* 19 March 2001: 38–39.

Foundation, "If China acts swiftly to contain the epidemic, it can slow the disease's spread to 1.5 million HIV-infected people by 2010. That's the best scenario. In the worst case (given the country's present under-funded health services) China could have 15 million HIV cases by 2010."[9]

A countervailing danger can be seen in a drastic return to traditional values where vigilante justice is taking many lives and putting women especially at risk. Among fundamentalist Muslims, for instance, honor killings are on the rise. The military ruler of Pakistan, General Pervez Musharraf, promised to curb honor killings of women by close relatives when he took office in spring of 2000. He told a national convention on human rights: "Killing in the name of honor is murder and will be treated as such." Yet, within a month of his taking office, one thousand honor killings were counted. A young man strangled his younger sister near Tek Singh because, he claimed, he found her in a compromising position with her lover (who escaped). In Multan city, Ismail killed his sister, Assia, alleging that she engaged in premarital sex.[10]

A Muslim court in northern Nigeria sentenced a woman to death for bearing a child out of rape—while the rapist was never charged. An appeal court overturned her sentence. A government investigation of maternal health in Nigeria revealed that almost thirty percent of teenage women had induced abortions and that such procedures were the main cause of death among unmarried women between fifteen and twenty-four.[11]

According to global studies of slavery there may be thirty million slaves in the world, more than at any other time in world history. They are imported immigrants in the U.S., rug weavers and house servants in the Asian subcontinent, young girls placed by the Russian mob in places like Israel.

---

[9] Tim McGirk, "Ticking Time Bomb," *Time*, 19 March 2001: 44.

[10] Reported in *The Tribune* (online edition), 2 June 2000, from Chandigarh, India.

[11] T. Odejide, "Offering an Alternative to Illegal Abortions in Nigeria," *New Era Nursing Image International* 2 (1986): 39–42.

They may be child slave prostitutes in eastern Asia from whom entrepreneurs profit.

Global politics surround the weakness of the UN and other organizations in condemning and pressing for an end to large-scale slave trading in Sudan. Not willing to confront the Arab bloc, world leaders have overlooked the selling of children for labor and sexual favors. The world's denial has led some organizations to buy Sudanese children, sending some to their homes and families but others, without a place to go, into foster homes abroad.

The search for the Nigerian ship *MV Etireno* off Benin in April 2001 highlighted the fact that, according to the UN's Nicholas Pron in Cotonou, "There are one, two, four or five child-trafficking ships in the Gulf of Guinea that are trafficking children at any one time." Some of these children end up as domestics or shop workers; many are sexually abused or become sexual slaves.

Laurie Nicole Robinson did extensive doctoral work on this subject and writes:

> Female child prostitution is an epidemic that touches every corner of the world. The female child (under 18) usually finds her way into prostitution by being bought, kidnapped, tricked, sold by her parents, or traded. Figures estimate that the child prostitution business employs approximately 1 million children in Asia, 1.5 to 2 million children in India, 100,000 children in the United States, and 500,000 children in Latin America. Statistics also estimate that in one year's time, a child prostitute will service over 2,000 men.[12]

Besides the psychological damage done to these girls, many will not live to see the age of thirty. Those who do live and somehow free themselves will struggle in poverty with terrible problems of self-esteem.

In the U.S. and other developed countries teenage girls may drift into prostitution because they have run away from abusive homes, older boyfriends, drugs, and street life. The future for most of them is also bleak.

---

[12] Laurie Nicole Robinson, 4 June 1998, *Indiana Journal of Global Legal Studies*, Vol. 5, No. 1.

The U. S. Picture

There is good news and bad news in the complicated story of teenage sex in America. The bad news includes the exploitation of sex in advertising and entertainment, riskier sex at lower ages, the striking increase in oral sex (under mistaken notions that this is not really sex and that it is safe), the increase both in the number of STDs and of venereal viruses—especially human papilloma virus (HPV)—the dramatic increase of infertility and death through cancers related to STDs, and the failure of "safe sex" thinking and programs.[13]

In the midst of sexual chaos, a growing number of U.S. teenagers are choosing abstinence. Fear of pregnancy or breaking religious codes against fornication have persuaded many adolescents into alternatives to vaginal intercourse. Some of these behaviors, however, put them at greater risk for sexually transmitted diseases. An Alan Guttmacher Institute study by Gary Gates and Freya Sonenstein explored heterosexual genital sexual activity among adolescent males from 1988 to 1995. "Between 1988 and 1995, the proportion of males who reported having ever been masturbated by a female increased significantly, from 40% to 53%. There were less sizable shifts in the proportions who received oral sex."[14] In 1995

- fifty-five percent of males (fifteen through nineteen) reported they had engaged in vaginal intercourse

- fifty-three percent said they had been masturbated by a female

- forty-nine percent said that they had received oral sex

- thirty-nine percent said that they had given oral sex

- eleven percent said that they had engaged in anal sex.

---

[13] Pediatrician Meg Meeker calls this situation an epidemic in her book: *Epidemic: How Teen Sex Is Killing Our Kids* (Washington, D.C.: Lifeline Press, 2002).

[14] Gary J. Gates and Freya L. Sonenstein, "Heterosexual Genital Activity Among Adolescent Males: 1988 and 1995," The Alan Guttmacher Institute, *Family Planning Perspectives* 32, no. 6 (November/December 2000): 1.

The U.S. Centers for Disease Control and Prevention reported a study of teen sexual activity from 1991 to 2001 by the Alan Guttmacher Institute which found more teens remaining virgins during that ten-year period, a 16% increase from 38% to 54%. Teen pregnancy rates also fell in those ten years.

Reporting on sexual activity among teens in the 1990s, Child Trends makes a distinction between sexual experience and sexual activity. A sexually experienced teen, according to this definition, has had sexual intercourse at least once in his or her lifetime; a sexually active teen has had sexual intercourse in the past three months. Sexual experience increases with age, with a higher percentage of males than females having had intercourse. About a quarter of all fifteen-year-olds reported they had sex at least once (twenty-seven percent of males and twenty-five percent of females). By age seventeen, more than half of males (fifty-nine percent) and females (fifty-two percent) reported having had sex. By age nineteen, eighty-five percent of males and seventy-seven percent of females reported that they had had sex.[15]

> While close to half of high school males and females were sexually experienced (had had sexual intercourse) in 1997, only 37 percent of females and 33 percent of males were sexually active (had sex in the last 3 months).
>
> The majority of sexually experienced teens had either 0 or 1 partners in the past year (54 percent of males and 70 percent of females). However, 20 percent of teen males and 13 percent of teen females had 3 or more partners in the past year.[16]

The Henry J. Kaiser Family Foundation also tracks studies on teen sexual activity and found[17]

- The median age at first intercourse (for both males and females—males just one-tenth of percentage younger) is sixteen and a half years.

---

[15] "Trends in Sexual Activity and Contraceptive Use Among Teens." Online: www.childtrends.org/PDF/teentrends.pdf.

[16] Ibid., 1–2.

[17] The Henry J. Kaiser Family Foundation, "Facts and Fact Sheet," August 2000, 1.

- The percentage of students who had initiated sexual intercourse before the age of thirteen has fluctuated . . . 9 percent in 1995; 7.2 percent in 1997; 8.3 percent in 1999.

- Reasons given by fifteen- to seventeen-year-olds for having
first sexual experience were "having met the right person"
(thirty-one percent), "the other person wanted to" (sixteen percent), or "just curious" (fifteen percent).

- Teen girls (fifteen through nineteen) described their first
sexual intercourse as "voluntary and wanted" (sixty-nine
percent), "voluntary but unwanted" (twenty-four percent), or "non-voluntary" (seven percent).

More than one in four (twenty-seven percent) of high
school students who had had sexual intercourse report to
being currently abstinent. Alcohol or drugs were used by
nineteen percent of females and thirty-one percent of males
in their most recent sexual experience.

> 🏃 A youth group is asking guidelines from leaders they
> respect as to "how far to go" physically in their dating
> and relationships. You sense they are asking you to put
> your beliefs and personal guidelines out in the open
> without taking whatever you have to say seriously in
> their own practices. In this particular area, they seem to
> believe you and they are living in two different worlds.
> How might you proceed?

In regard to sexual pressure and dating violence, almost
half (forty-eight percent) of twelve- to seventeen-year-olds
say teens feel "a lot" of pressure regarding sex; another
thirty-eight percent say, "some." More than a third (thirty-six
percent) of teens say they felt pressured to do something sexual they didn't feel ready to do. About nine percent of high
school students report they have been forced to have sexual
intercourse although they did not feel they were ready to.
Female adolescents with a history of abuse are at greater risk
for becoming pregnant than females who were not abused.

Summing up the picture of youthful pregnancy in the U.S., The National Campaign to Prevent Teen Pregnancy says:

> The United States has the highest rates of teen pregnancy and births in the western industrialized world. Teen pregnancy costs the United States at least $1 billion annually. Nearly four in 10 young women become pregnant at least once before they reach the age of 20—nearly one million a year. Eight in ten of these pregnancies are unintended and 79 percent are to unmarried teens.[18]

Three respected studies (The Alan Guttmacher Institute, The National Center for Health Statistics, and the Centers for Disease Control) show a significant decline in teen pregnancies since 1990.[19]

Abstinence and Decline of Sexual Activity
Studies show a rise in teen sexual activity in the 1980s followed by a decline in sexual activity during the 1990s and into the 2000s, although the decline is not dramatic. "Between 1988 and 1995, the percentage of male and female teens who were sexually experienced declined slightly. . . . The percentage of *all* high school students (9th–12th grades) who report ever having sexual intercourse has *declined* over the last decade."[20]

Teen pregnancy rates also declined in the late 1990s. Birth rates for U.S. 15–19-year-olds dropped 22%, from 62.1 births per 1000 in 1991 to 48.5 per 1000 in 2000.[21]

Abortion rates among teenagers is also decreasing.[22]

---

[18] Figures through February 2002. The National Council to Prevent Teen Pregnancy (www.teenpregnancy.org/resources/data/genlfact.asp), 1.

[19] Ibid.

[20] "Trends in Sexual Activity and Contraceptive Use Among Teens."

[21] U.S. Centers for Disease Control, "Teen Pregnancy Rate Reaches a Record Low in 1997: Trends in Pregnancy Rates for the United States, 1976–1997: An Update," *NVSR* 49: No. 4. Online: www.cdc.gov/nchs/releases/01news/trendpreg.htm.

[22] Alan Guttmacher Institute and the National Campaign to Prevent Teen Pregnancy report "teen abortion rates are down." 8 October 2002 (www.teenpregnancy.org/about/announcements/pr/2002/abortionrates10_08 .asp).

As you interpret this data, keep in mind the differing definitions of sex as well as the different methods of sexual activity.

What has driven this decline is a combination of factors: the fear of AIDS, prevention programs *and* the abstinence movement ("True Love Waits" and virginity pledges). These factors have *both* increased use of contraceptives and reduced the rates of teen sexual activity.

Regarding abstinence programs researchers Bearman and Bruechner found:

- About fifty percent of those who formally promise to avoid premarital sex remain virgins until about the age twenty.

- Fifty percent of nonpledgers are no longer virgins by the age seventeen.

- Pledging, in other words, delays sexual intercourse by about eighteen months.

- The data shows pledgers have a thirty-four percent lower likelihood of engaging in teenage sexual activity.

- Pledgers are significantly more religious than nonpledgers, and academic achievement and athletic participation, along with parents disapproving of premarital sex, (all of these) are strong delaying factors.[23]

At the same time, among teens who are sexually active, rates of contraceptive use, including condom use, have increased. Both factors help to account for the decrease in teen pregnancy rates.[24]

The good news about teen pregnancy is that despite a rising teen population, there is a drop in pregnancy (from about one million teenagers in 1987 to 863,000 in 1997).[25]

---

[23] Peter S. Bearman and Hannah Bruechner, "Virginity Pledges," *American Journal of Sociology,* # 106 (2001): 859-912.

[24] Henry J. Kaiser Family Foundation, "Facts and Fact Sheet," 1.

[25] U.S. Centers for Disease Control and Prevention, "National . . . Pregnancy Rates among Adolescents—US 1995-1997," *Morbidity and Mortality Weekly Report,* Atlanta: Centers for Disease Control and Prevention, 49 (27): 605-11.

The U.S. still continues to have one the highest teen pregnancy and abortion rates among the developed nations.

> 🦆 Some sophomores come to you asking about a Virginity Pledge, how it might be made into a rite of passage type thing which would strengthen their commitments without making others feel condemned. How could this be worked out?

Children and STDs

The main concern among U.S. experts is focused on early teen and preteen risky sexual activities. Despite general declines, there is a disturbing rise in the number of children having sex before they are fifteen. Girls who have sex at such a young age and with multiple partners have a high risk of becoming infertile or developing cervical cancer later in life.

Most sexually active teens (sixty-eight percent of fifteen- to seventeen-year-olds) do not consider themselves to be at much risk of contracting a sexually transmitted disease,[26] but about one in four do get a sexually transmitted disease (STD) every year.

The U.S. has one of the highest rates of chlamydia among its teenagers, and AIDS is listed as the sixth leading cause of death among fifteen- to twenty-four-year-olds here.

Why Teens Have Sex: The Story of Conyers

Homes in Conyers, Georgia, range from comfortable to luxurious with pools and tennis courts. With such a tax base, Conyers built three of the state's best high schools, and when it was chosen to host the equestrian events of the summer Olympics (1996), the town built a new horse park. The hardworking adults of Conyers were so excited about the Olympics and so absorbed in their own lives they missed what led

---

[26] Ibid., 2.

to two youth crises. Exactly one month after the killing at Columbine High School in Colorado, there was a school shooting in Conyers. But years before that, a sexual crisis was emerging—largely unnoticed by the press and public.

Wealthy, successful, and apparently bored, high school kids in Conyers began doing their own thing. Nicole was in a group of fifteen-year-old girls who hung out, dared each other to shoplift, and rode around town in cars with blaring music past the midnight curfew for anyone under sixteen.

> We'd ride around in Conyers at 3:00 in the morning in somebody's parents' car and never think about getting caught. We never thought about the consequences back then.

> There was *a lot* of sex then. . . . We would fight. There was about four of the guys that drove BMWs and had everything. . . . All the girls wanted to be with those guys, so we would all fight over them or do whatever. And then you'd have sex with them, so you'd be like, "Yeah, I had sex with your man last night, da, da, da, do." It was everybody having sex with everybody.[27]

One of the boys in the fast lane was D. J. At fourteen he was younger than most, but his looks, charm, strength, and bravado—and access to unlimited money—earned him popularity. He chose mostly older friends, rich and poor, black and white. He tells this revealing story:

> I never—I felt like I never had anybody. I've always been alone. I've never had a family that would be there for you . . . or friends that would be there for you. I always felt out in the cold. . . .

> [Interviewer: "Your parents?"] When they started, they were both—my father was a policeman. My mother was Miss Arkansas. . . . They were, you know, the ideal couple, and they were both very happy.

> [But D. J.'s father left for another woman when D. J. was 9.] And as things turned out, my father just—just everything started going for the worse. My father was the only thing my mother ever had, and her kids. And after he left, she didn't know how to deal with herself. I didn't even feel she was around. I couldn't deal with people my age who I didn't feel

---

[27] Rachel Dretzin Goodman, "The Lost Children of Rockdale County," *Frontline,* 19 October 1999. Online: Frontline:/pbsonline/ugbs, 3.

they could understand. And so I sort of—attached myself to people that were older than me.[28]

When D. J.'s mother fell apart, he was taken in by a friend, a wealthy man with a beautiful house and pool. "My father . . . my godfather . . . is a good businessman. He would buy me anything and just give me all the money I wanted, anytime I needed it. Whatever I wanted, he'd buy it for me."[29]

On weekends D. J. would have parties at his house. His friend Kevin describes these times: "He'd have a party of, like 200 people. Everybody'd get drunk, spend the night, swim in the pool. (And there was lots of sex.) His (surrogate) dad didn't care what he did."[30]

Asked about the pressure they must have put on many, many girls, D. J. replies: "I don't think it was a real pressure issue. I mean, it might have been for them. Subliminally, it might have been. Subconsciously, it might have been. But it really—I mean, there really wasn't any pressure to. It was more of—they just gave in, really."[31]

In contrast, Amy explains how the guys treated girls:

> They were mean to them a lot. They treated them like they were just—I don't know, not trash, but not very, like, respectable. And the girls didn't seem to care. I don't know why. I guess they just—I think most of it was the alcohol. They just—they knew that we would like it, and so—but they didn't treat us like we were anything real important. . . . I couldn't really do anything about it because they just—wouldn't care. They'd just tell you to go home or something.[32]

Amy came from a close family who encouraged and taught her right from wrong. Her dad was her coach and buddy until she began to draw back. By the time the children approached their teens, there were televisions in each room, and Amy's father admits that the family would be home without being together. Increasingly Amy would be out late. He worried but did not know quite what to do or how to talk with her.

---

[28] Ibid., 7.
[29] Ibid., 3.
[30] Ibid.
[31] Ibid., 6.
[32] Ibid.

> 🎿 You find out a group of senior girls have their eye on
> three or four boys who, the grapevine says, are holding
> out on sex. First, do you consider this a possible reality?
> And second, how might you intervene? Isn't this a place
> where consultation with sensitive school personnel,
> willing parents, and church could make a difference?
> Can you imagine a discussion that might break through
> this kind of connivance for the good of all?

Through middle school, Amy had a best friend, but
when that friend rejected her, Amy gravitated toward a group
ready to accept her. They were a rougher crowd and called
Amy when they needed a car—she had her driver's license
and access to a car. That led to hanging out with boys who
would offer Amy beer. Drinking changed her personality and
enabled her to be more outgoing and fun.

One night Amy was babysitting her three- or four-year-
old nephew with a friend when some boys called and asked
if they could come over. Nobody else was at home, and they
got drunk. Two of the guys asked the girls to come upstairs
with them. "We said, 'Okay.' You know, I didn't really know
what was going on. Everything was sort of—you know, well,
we were just wanting to do whatever they wanted us to do,
and so—it got kind of nasty in the room. We were doing
some—a few things. And I had forgotten about my cousin."[33]
Amy's young cousin wandered into the room and would later
tell his mother he thought the boys were trying to kill Amy.
In response, Amy's aunt said she didn't want Amy around her
son any more. Amy was crushed and remorseful.

In the spring of 1996, when Conyers was absorbed in
the coming Olympics, few people noticed a small news article about an outbreak of syphilis among young teenagers.
Complaints to a guidance counselor from girls who were beginning to feel trapped in risky sex, and the visit of a young
boy with the disease to a local clinic, caught the attention

---

[33] Ibid., 10.

of the staff members at the Georgia Division of Public Health. Cynthia Noel, a county public health nurse, Kathleen Toomey from Georgia's Division of Public Health, and a consulting professor, Claire Sterk, from Emory University became leaders in the investigation. The nature of syphilis made it possible to chart the sexual histories of each teen infected with the disease. The chart, with its crisscrossing lines and thicker and thicker connections, was astounding. According to Noel, "You don't expect to see a 14-year-old with 20, 30, 40, 50 or 100 sex partners. You expect that of someone who is more into the line of being a prostitute or something. And these girls were not homeless. They were not abused in any way. They were just normal, everyday, regular kids."[34]

Peggy Cooper was a school guidance counselor at the time, and her middle school kids—some as young as twelve—began talking to her about their parties.

> My students were talking to me about parties they were having on weekends, and there was one place in particular that had a lot of privacy. The parents were . . . gone. And they said they were watching the Playboy Channel in the girl's bedroom. There would be, like 10 or 12 of them up there.
>
> . . . one of the little guys says, "And we're getting pretty good at it, too." I said, "Good at what?" So he said, "Well, we—you have to do—the game is you have to imitate what the *Playboy* people are doing." . . . One of them said, "And sometimes it's all mixed up, too. You know, it's just like—there may be three or four of us at one time. And it doesn't matter if you're two girls or two guys or a girl and a guy. It doesn't matter. You just do what they're doing."[35]

With Sterk, the teens became exceptionally honest about their activities.

> One of the things interesting about this group was that there was not necessarily a clearly defined leader. There was nobody around who fulfilled that role. So nobody stepped in,

---

[34] Ibid., 4.
[35] Ibid., 5.

and the group kind of kept moving on without having any-body around who could put on the brakes.

In some ways, the "sandwich" was the point of escalation. It was the point when a number of them became really, really scared. What I understand "sandwich" to be is one girl having oral sex with one of the men, having vaginal sex with another man and having anal sex with a third man. So she literally is smushed in between three guys, and the only way that I've heard it described by some of the teens is a "sandwich."

[Interviewer: "Did any of the girls describe the sex as pleasur-able?"] Initially, they described the sex as pleasurable . . . physically . . . and also psychologically . . . like this was an initiation into the next step of their life. . . . Over time, how-ever, very few girls talked about sex in terms of it being plea-surable at all. It became something that was so painful, that in some cases they couldn't even remember what they did anymore. So it became very negative.

A lot of the adolescents had parents who worked, . . . parents who put in 40, 60, 80-hour work weeks and were doing that to ensure that all the resources that they wanted to give to their children were available. . . . [The kids] were at home alone.[36]

The official public health report found fifty young people involved in extreme sexual behavior, seventeen teenagers testing positive for syphilis, and more than two hundred exposed and treated.

Nicole's mother, Cindy, tells of going with her daughter when the two hundred were called in to be tested. Cindy ex-pected a sad, traumatic situation; instead she was surprised to see "these kids high-fiving each other, laughing." Nicole, fifteen at the time of the outbreak, explains the teenage mindset:

We thought it was funny, thought it was—"Oh, you got syphi-lis! Oh!" You know? . . . We all felt invincible. Nobody could do anything to us. We could do whatever we wanted to do. And we pretty much did everything we wanted to do.

[Interviewer: "You like breaking rules?"] Yeah. It was—it was, like—it wasn't really I liked breaking rules, it was just I didn't

---

[36] Ibid., 9, 5-6.

care. Your rules meant nothing to me. If they didn't benefit me, I had nothing to do with it. That's really how I felt then.[37]

Now, at nineteen, as she coolly blows smoke in the direction of the camera, nothing in Nicole's demeanor or explanation resembles remorse or a change of mind.

Seeking Moral Freedom

How can individuals and societies find their way? Can we return to a simpler age, to traditional morality, or to logically secure theologies and ethical systems? Or must we deal with new and difficult complexities with more laxity? The failed idealism of the 1960s, the empty narcissism of the 1970s, and what some critics described as social Darwinism in the 1980s have left Americans stranded among the possibilities of cynicism, reactionary nostalgia, and libertarianism.

Sociologist Alan Wolfe sees in American culture a quest for freedom: for economic freedom in the nineteenth century, political freedom in the twentieth century, and moral freedom in the late twentieth and twenty first century. He cautions about optimism regarding the benefits of freedom generally and moral freedom in particular:

> Economic freedom did not create a hoped-for society of independent yeomen but a regime of mass consumption. Political freedom did not result in active and enlightened civic participation but in voter apathy. In a similar way, moral freedom is highly unlikely to produce a nation of individuals exercising their autonomy with the serious and dispassionate judgment of Immanuel Kant.[38]

Wolfe does not see Americans becoming secularists: "They cling to their faith and religion . . . but want freedom of denominational choice and faith expression. Far from being secular humanists, Americans want faith and freedom

---

[37] Ibid., 4, 9.
[38] Alan Wolfe, "The Final Freedom," *New York Times Magazine,* 18 March 2001, 48.

simultaneously."[39] Nor does he think we can turn the back the religious clock: "Whatever emerges from the efforts on the parts of so many Americans to redefine their faith, it is unlikely to resemble Jonathan Edward's Northampton, the urban parishes of 1950's Catholicism, the revival meetings of Billy Sunday or synagogue life on the Lower East Side."[40]

If mere subjectivism that leads to moral chaos is untenable and rigid traditionalism that hides from contemporary complexities is unworkable in today's complex realities, where are we to turn? "Although critics of America's condition insist on the need to return to the morality of yesterday," Wolfe concludes, "it may be better, given its inevitability, to think of moral freedom as a challenge to be met rather than as a condition to be cured."[41]

In their sexual lives, teenagers reflect the quandaries of adult societies. The world wants what it wants now, and it wants higher meaning and some sense of order. So do young people, but they tend to operate on the edge of immediate desires. Walt Mueller quotes from a Teen Bill of Rights:[42]

- I have the right to think for myself.

- I have the right to decide whether to have sex and who to have it with.

- I have the right to use protection when I have sex.

- I have the right to buy and use condoms.

- I have the right to express myself.

On the other hand, I hear teenagers expressing their need for structure and autonomy (see the introductory comments in this chapter). Too often, however, freedom takes precedence over order. The challenge always is to balance independence and risky behaviors with structure and adult input.

---

[39] Ibid., 51.

[40] Ibid.

[41] Ibid. See also Alan Wolfe, *Moral Freedom: The Search for Virtue in a World of Choice* (New York: Norton, 2001).

[42] Walt Mueller, *Understanding Today's Youth Culture* (Wheaton, Ill.: Tyndale, 1999), 241.

In the context of sexual behaviors, it is one thing to stray from the way; it is another to have no way. Strictly speaking, none of us has kept the sexual ideal found in the Sermon on the Mount.[43] Many young people are no longer virgins, but they are trying to do the right thing. Others are lost in promiscuity—and sometimes violent sex. They are our particular concern.

Sex Education

Most of us would agree that sex education takes place most effectively at home and in the church. When children lack home instruction, responsibility is generally placed on schools. The reality, however, is that many children and teenagers are not being helped to become sexually mature and healthy by parents, church, or school curricula. Media can become insidiously counterproductive for wholesome socialization, and peer pressure can follow suit.

We do not want youthful sexual natures to be repressed and stunted. Nor should they be overstimulated and desensitized. To follow every sexual urge and seize any sexual provocation are obviously dangerous and abhorrent behaviors. We know how to teach two-year-olds about fireplaces and hot stoves; children learn about the dangers of traffic, poisons, and heights. In analogous ways, we must find ways to teach teens about premature and dangerous sex.

Any worthy sex education program, faith-based or secular, will strongly promote abstinence as the only safe sex. But we must recognize that many young people are having sex. Youth need adult role models who are honest about sex, who admit to being slightly confused by all that is going on, yet are confident that the place for sex is in marriage. It is an illusion to think that because young people have made a faith commitment and are going to church, they have not had or might not have sex. (And as the research by Bearman and

---

[43] "You have heard that it was said, 'You shall not commit adultery.' But I say to you that everyone who looks at a woman with lust has already committed adultery with her in his heart" (Matt 5:27–28 NRSV).

Breuchner indicates, many who pledge abstinence fail in their commitment.)

Sex education in America is polarized because we find it difficult to compromise and say, "It is best to save sex for marriage, but if you are going to have sex, protect yourself." That is a fairly simple statement, and sex education ought to be about demonstrating its veracity. People of faith and agnostics ought to see the sense in such a twofold curriculum. Secularists need to admit the possibility and desirability of postponing sex as religious folks must admit that many of *their* kids—and they ought to have concern for *all* kids—are having sex.

Some Christians find such a statement incompatible with biblical faith and common sense. If we are to be true to the biblical command of sexual fidelity in marriage they say, we undermine the ideal and social mores by giving this double message: "If you can't restrain yourselves, at least protect yourselves." Other Christians want to remain loyal to the ideal but also adapt realistically to the apparent needs of Christian and unchurched youth. They find in the Bible clear affirmation that sex ought to be saved for marriage as well as examples of sex outside of marriage. Old Testament saints were not always monogamous—or faithful even within the practice of polygamy (2 Sam 5:13). In New Testament times, St. Paul recognized that Christians would be dealing with fornicators and immoral people in secular society. If there were concessions in ancient cultures, some sorts of compromises or adaptations may be necessary in contemporary culture. Christians need to find some common ground with secular humanists regarding what should be taught in public schools. The fact is that young people *can accept* the ambiguity of a double message when it is adequately explained.

Experts who have studied the physical, emotional, and social consequences of teenage sex before marriage favor postponing sex. And in their study of "five rigorously evaluated adolescent pregnancy prevention programs," Frost and Forrest found that "all five incorporate an emphasis on abstinence or delay of sexual initiation, training in decision-making and negotiation skills, and education on sexuality and contraception. . . . Four of the five directly or indirectly provide access to contraceptive services."[44] The authors affirm that "the goal of [sex education] programs is to reduce the proportionate increase in the number of teenagers initiating sexual activity."[45]

The nature of sexual identity, the power of sexual fantasies, the seductive possibilities of virtual sex on the Internet, the matter of sexual addiction, peer pressure, sexual harassment, and issues of self-esteem and self-nurturing must all be openly discussed with young people. Skills of sensitivity, assertiveness, and negotiation must be taught. Kids need to understand how to say "No," *and* how to respect a No. The challenge of choice, self-discipline, and virtue can challenge young people everywhere in powerful ways. Above all, young people need good role models. Good role models often care more about young people than young people care about themselves. Such care should say, "I want the best for you. But I will be here for you if you choose less than the best. When you falter, we will together seek solutions."

Because God made it that way, sex is fun and powerful. Sex is also best enjoyed and serves its natural purpose when it is part of real love and genuine commitment. In the twentieth century, society spent a great deal of energy and creativity freeing sex from permanent commitment, but in the process it freed sex from love. When sex loses its partnership with love and commitment, it descends to a toilet function. That is how the girls in Conyers experienced it.

Sexual Deviation

The secular world does not quite know what to make of sexual deviation. It is popular to say that what goes on in private between consenting adults is their business, and in secular society this is to a certain extent true. But the saying,

[44]Jennifer J. Frost and Jacqueline Darroch Forrest, "Understanding the Impact of Effective Teenage Pregnancy Prevention Programs," *Family Planning Perspectives* 27 (1995): 188–95. Online: www.guttmacher.org/pubs/journals/2718895.html, 1 of printout.

[45]Ibid., 9 of Internet printout.

"When anyone is tortured, all suffer" implies that all behavior has broad consequences. Individuals and societies can easily wander off the path; we can miss the mark, as the literal meanings of biblical words for "sin" and "transgression" indicate. There seems to be a progression down the road of sexual deviation.

We are all reeling from the revelations and extent of pedophilia (especially but not at all exclusively) in the Catholic Church. Among priestly predators, one had contact with man-boy love societies. All Christians feel the shame of this. Beyond people of faith, secularists ought to see how this scandal challenges their subjective and permissive moral opinions. Not all that feels good is right; some things done in private, even with certain measures of consent, need to be condemned.

Infidelity to one's spouse or sexual ideal is a shortcut to sexual happiness and fulfillment but turns out to be a detour. Licentious images and seemingly harmless pornography encourage the traveler. All kinds of professional services offer substitutes for marital intimacy. Open marriages and spouse swapping can move toward group sex. Sex becomes mixed with power and violence in sadomasochistic sex (S&M). There is a descending moral spiral few have discussed.

Some rapes may begin with lust, but they are mixed with, and become a need to exert, power and control. For many rapists the act is primarily a power issue. Violence may titillate the rapist, and power replaces sexual intimacy. Eventually, in the outworking of this perversion, torturing brings sexual release. Finally a person may descend to cannibalism and necrophilia in the name of sex. Yet social scientists and therapists are strangely silent regarding this descent. These are terrible things to talk about, but they make an important point.

Peter Singer argues not only for animal rights but also for freedom in regard to human-animal coupling.[46] For this controversial philosopher, condemning bestiality is as irrational as condemning homosexual activity. All such arguments,

---

[46] Peter Singer, *Animal Liberation* (New York: Avon/Hearst Corporation, 1977).

according to Singer, are based upon "our desire to diffcrenti-
ate ourselves . . . from animals."[47] As mere members of the animal kingdom, Singer contends, we can hardly affirm moral
superiority to animals or deny animals moral autonomy.
Claiming special moral or spiritual status for human beings
amounts to a "speciesism" similar to racism.[48]

That such an argument presents logical difficulties is
one thing, but more remarkable is the fact that ideas such as
Singer's have remained relatively unchallenged. Justifications
of bestiality ought to illustrate degeneration of the sexual
ideal and of moral reasoning. The point is that human beings
are moral creatures, distinguished from animals by the Spirit
of God (Gen 2:7; 1:26). Moral standards for sexuality must
point to some kind of transcendence. Within secular societies, agreement for such an ideal ought to come from all religious constituencies and some humanists.

Rejection of the norm of heterosexual fidelity in marriage, I would argue, leads down a path of deviancy. Sexual
deviancy is made clear to believers in Scripture, but defining
sexual deviation in secular society is more difficult. Laws and
O'Donahue's *Sexual Deviance* (1997), a standard on this
topic, includes articles on

- Exhibitionism (displaying one's genitals to a stranger)

- Fetishism (need of an inanimate object for sexual arousal)

- Frotteurism (erotic rubbing against a stranger in crowds)

- Pedophilia (adult attraction to children as sex objects)

- Sexual sadism (the need to inflict pain on another for sexual arousal)

- Sexual masochism (the need to be humiliated or pained
  for arousal)

- Transvestic fetishism (the need to cross-dress)

- Voyeurism (spying on a sex act or on a naked or undress-
  ing person)

---

[47] Quoted by Cathy Young, "No Heavy Petting," *Boston Globe*, 11
April 2001, A19.
[48] Ibid.

• Rape (using force or drugs to have sex with an unwilling person)

The American Psychiatric Association's *DSM-IV* (1994, 1999), the standard manual of mental disorders that is used by therapists, deals with sexual deviation from a functional perspective. Using the term "paraphilia" to distinguish deviancies from sexual dysfunctions (e.g., desire and arousal disorders) and gender disorders, *DSM-IV* defines a mental disorder as impairing normal functioning and lasting six months. Deviancies described in *DSM-IV* are exhibitionism, fetishism, Frotteurism, pedophilia, sexual masochism, sexual sadism, transvestic fetishism, and voyeurism.

As important as these definitions and categories are, they lack a moral framework and spiritual ideal. A moral discussion of sex must deal with changing standards of society generally (e.g., social acceptance of homosexual unions) as well as with extreme groups such as those that justify pedophilia.

The arguments and research of man-boy advocates move toward a softening of the negative effects of child sex abuse, at least in the case of boys. The North American Man Boy Love Association (NAMBLA) states its case in the context of a worldview enamored by rights and weak on responsibility. Such a worldview lacks clear definitions of right and wrong. Pedophiles, according to this group, are in need of a civil rights movement. One extreme group, the Pedophile Liberation Front, posted The Slurp's open letter to children:

• You can say no, but you can also say yes.

• Why you shouldn't tell anyone, if you say yes.

• Somebody probably told you that "You can say no". Maybe they explained what it meant; if some adult asks you to do "things", you don't have to do them. . . . Well just remember one thing: if you can say no, you can also say yes. That means that if you feel like doing something, you have the right to do it. No matter what your teacher told you. Because it's right. You have the choice.[49]

---

[49] At the time, this was found at http://pedo-lib-front.home.ml.org.

Extreme examples and justifications for fulfilling sexual desires through predation, torture, vampirism, cannibalism, and bestiality should not relieve us from moral judgments on all sexual misconduct. Instead these extremes should reinforce for us the notion that all sexual discussions must begin with a moral ideal, should see sex holistically in the context of a person's whole life and relationships, and understand that private behavior ultimately influences the wholeness and health of a culture. Christians are held to a higher standard than are nonbelievers,[50] but they are meant to contribute moral help to all the world.[51]

I urge secular sex education to take the high moral road, and there is growing consensus for postponing sexual activity. At the same time we must realize that young people within faith communities are as pressured and confused as anyone else. In fact, some studies have shown rates of premarital sex as about the same in faith communities as elsewhere.

Our Social Responsibility to Athletes

Society seems to have given athletes the sense that sex as their prerogative. Sports magazines and other media document and commenteon excessive and illegal behaviors, but I'll use two stories that demonstrate two attitudes communities can have regarding the victimization of women.

Blaming the Victim
In the suburb of Glen Ridge, on a March afternoon in 1998, a group of boys—star football players and wrestlers—lured a retarded girl[52] they had known since kindergarten into the basement of a home and raped her. Although rumors of the ugly incident quickly circulated through the high school and town, it was weeks before any report reached the police.

---

[50] This is the implication of 1 Cor 5:1, for instance.
[51] This would seem clear from Jesus' teaching about Christians being salt and light in the world (Matt 5:13–14), Jer 29:7, and many other passages.
[52] Two separate assessments scored her IQ at 49. A score of 70 is usually taken to be the demarcation of retardation.

Several questions bothered the investigative reporter and most of us who read the story:

- How could these young leaders in their high school so brutalize a classmate they had known since childhood?

- How could so many of their parents and elders deny the rape and rally to support the perpetrators?

- How could a community so proud of its status refuse to examine itself and learn a lesson from such an event?

One answer was to be found in the prevailing attitudes. The passion of Glen Ridge was winning, and successful football and wrestling teams were symbols of that attitude. "To the sports-obsessed crowd of Glen Ridge, you were a jock or you were nothing."[53] "The tie between sex and football heroics was very strong in Glen Ridge."[54]

The heroes in this town's drama were males; females could achieve only in supportive roles. Talented athletes grew up encouraged by fathers and coaches. These boys would look up to upper-grade athletes and were followed by those younger. Their identities and status were pumped up by younger boys, girls who sought their favor, and older men who cheered them on.

> 🏂 How likely is it that a group of junior and senior athletes might plan to make as many sexual conquests as possible, especially among freshmen and sophomore girls? Should you, might you, be informed about something like this? How could a coach, youth leader, or pastor get to the heart of this clique's plans? Consider how this could be handled in both separate gender groups and a co-ed group.

The sexual pattern of this group was pornographic and voyeuristic. From porno videos to watching their buddies

---

[53] Bernard Lefkowitz, *Our Guys: The Glen Ridge Rape and the Secret Life of the Perfect Suburb* (New York: Vintage, 1998), 126.

[54] Ibid., 124.

perform, the boys became sexual spectators and predators rather than involved participants. Intimacy and vulnerability were neither part of their social scene or personal growth. Cheerleaders and girls their own age were friends, like submissive younger sisters. The athletes preyed upon younger girls for sexual gratification.

The mentally retarded girl desperately wanted to be a friend of the boys. She was set up: her rape was staged, and it was an especially ugly affair. The situation in the basement felt so ominous, six boys left—but seven remained. The girl was at least partially undressed, forced into oral sex, and then raped with a baseball bat. After they were done with her, the boys huddled up, and promised secrecy. The girl later testified hearing them say, "We're not going to tell anybody. This is our little secret. Hurry up. Go. Get out of here."[55]

Even after this shocking news came out, most people in town blamed the incident on "the flirtatious and promiscuous ways" of the victim rather than on the boys.

> Where were the grownups of Glen Ridge while this was going on? The most common explanation they gave for their passivity was that they didn't know. The Jocks, they said, were sustained by an impenetrable, subterranean youth culture whose members were bound by a code of secrecy.

> Adults heard the warning [signs] and saw the evidence, but they chose to ignore them. Partly, this was because they didn't want to taint the town they treasured—the place they considered "Valhalla," as one school official put it—with scandal. But there was another reason: self-protection. The Jocks didn't invent the idea of mistreating young women. The ruling clique of teenagers adhered to a code of behavior that mimicked, distorted, and exaggerated the values of the adult world around them. These values extolled "winners"— the rich businessmen, the esteemed professionals, the attractive, fashion-conscious wives, the high-achieving children. They denigrated the "losers"—the less affluent breadwinners, the decidedly dowdy wives, the inconspicuous, bashful, ungainly kids.[56]

---

[55] Ibid., 25.
[56] Ibid., 492–93.

Eight years after the rape, none of the young men had served time, and appeals of their convictions were pending. The sentence for those found guilty was so light that the boys "hugged each other and laughed as if they were celebrating a victory."[57] Their parents beamed and gave a thumbs-up. This chapter's stories of teen orgies and athletes taking advantage of their status are not exceptional; they have been duplicated in many places.

Standing on Principles

A contrasting story comes from the prestigious St. Paul's School for Boys in Baltimore. This school is noted for its lacrosse team, a sport popular in the mid-Atlantic states. And St. Paul's, with a sixty-year history of lacrosse excellence, is where many go who hope to play at the college level.

After a scrimmage game early on in the season, the athletes began discussing the movie *American Pie.* In it a boy secretly videotapes his sexual conquest and broadcasts it on the Internet. One sixteen-year-old St. Paul player took this as a personal challenge. He videotaped his sexual experience with a fifteen-year-old girl from another private school. He showed the tape to eight junior varsity players. The week that St. Paul's, ranked number one nationally, was to play unranked St. Mary's, this student showed his video to most of the varsity team. No one in the group protested or challenged the showing. The team lost to St. Mary's a day and a half later and dropped to number three in the national polls.

Word about the videotape got back to the lacrosse coach through staff from other schools. St. Paul's administrators huddled and then took action:

- The offending student was expelled from school.

- The eight junior varsity players would sit out the season.

- Thirty varsity players were suspended from school for three days.

- During the suspension, players would go through counseling from the school's psychologist and chaplain.

---

[57] Ibid., 487.

- The varsity lacrosse season was cancelled.

- The entire school (eight hundred students) was brought into discussions about the value of sports in general and the "jocks rule mentality" in particular.[58]

In a letter to parents, Headmaster Robert Hallett wrote, "In a real sense this will never be over or finished. The education they take away from this will last a lifetime. At a minimum we should expect each boy here will, in the future, have the courage to stand up for, to quote the Lower School prayer, 'The hard right against the easy wrong.'"[59]

Richard Lapchick, director of Northeastern University's Center for the Study of Sport in Society, knows about this case only through the media. But from what he has read he finds the school's actions appropriate. "Athletes have tended—if they are great athletes—to not have faced serious consequences. There is an expectation that they'll be able to get away with something because they see lots of cases where athletes get off lightly. The fact that this school has done something will be a wake-up call."[60]

This is a case where school, community, and families— many of them the elite of the area—stood up for principle against an unbridled sense of entitlement. It remains for all of us to confess or at least admit that we allow athletics to get out of hand, condone movies like *American Pie,* and then don't take time to discuss these things with them.

Finding the Way: A Moral Framework

The realities of sexual deviancy and dangers beg adequate response. Appeals to science and social consensus alone cannot settle matters of sexuality. Sexual mores demand a moral framework, and morality seeks transcendence.

---

[58] On the privilege and pressure we've put upon high school athletes, see H. G. Bissinger, *Friday Night Lights: A Town, a Team, and a Dream* (New York: HarperCollins, 1991).

[59] Andy Carpenter, "Maryland School Puts Athletics in Perspective," *Boston Globe,* 22 April 2001, A14.

[60] Ibid.

We are made in the image of God, and the divine image is the basis for the way things are and the way they rightly work.

We fail if we do not consider and teach sex holistically. Young people desperately need explicit discussions about sex. But more than that, they need opportunity to ponder the nature of relationships, the benefits of abstinence until marriage, and respect and self-discipline with caring mentors. Respect is based on human dignity. Even without a trust in God, children can be taught to respect others as they should respect themselves. To be able to respect oneself because one is respected by God allows children to respect others even more deeply.

For all of this, it is difficult to define sex. Sexual energy is a powerful fountain of human creativity, establishing a lifetime bond of intimacy, bringing eternal souls into the world, and affecting fundamental aspects of society. Sex drives us toward union and an ecstasy freeing us from bonds of individuation as two become one. Sexual energies are similar and run parallel to our spiritual drives. Sexual energies can be sublimated creatively in all kinds of healthy relationships and in union with God for those who are single or widowed.

Human spirituality is bent on union with God—a drive that is also a source of religious creativity. Human life includes the paradox of personal individuation and communion with others. Recent neurological studies point to a place in the top rear of the brain where self and the world are delineated.[61] Prayer and ecstasy have been shown to quiet that working boundary between self and other. Sex and prayer take us beyond the necessary boundaries of self. Not only must we refuse to separate sex from love and commitment; we need to realize the hopelessness of understanding sexuality apart from biblical metaphors linking it with spirituality.[62]

---

[61] The work of Drs. V. S. Ramachan, Andrew Newberg, and Eugene d'Aquili, as cited in Sharon Begley's "Searching for the God Within," *Newsweek*, 29 January 2001, 59. See also Andrew Newberg, Eugene d'Aquili, and Vince Rause, *Why God Won't Go Away* (New York: Ballantine, 2001).

[62] Notably Eph 5:23–33, but also continued references to God as lover and Israel as wife or adulterer (e.g., Hos 2) and especially the Song of Songs.

Scripture's high principles can bring sanity to sexual chaos, challenge disorder and sexual oppression, establish guidelines for sexual fulfillment, prevent sexual injury, and offer compassionate forgiveness and healing.

Many people will have difficulty with biblical norms. I hope they will find that relationships, not laws, are the real basis for sexual health in biblical perspective. The human soul is not ultimately called into subjection to law but to living relationships. Relationship with God through Christ in the power of the Spirit is the key to all other relationships and is the fulfilling of biblical standards. The hope of sex, the full enjoyment of sex, forgiveness for sexual transgressions, and healing for sexual injuries are all to be found in the compassionate Savior. Christ created sex for our fulfillment, Christ modeled full expression of human sexuality without marriage or intercourse, Christ forgave the sins of those who fell to lust and healed the hurts of those who had been abused.

The consequences of deviating from right norms of sexual behavior are enormous. The anguish of those whose innocence was ripped from them is hard to comprehend. The reminder of the painful consequences of permissive and perverted sex began this chapter. Realizing how Christ took the sexual sins of the world to the Cross for our healing and forgiveness, is an important part of our conclusion to this investigation of sexuality.

Young people are called to sexual freedom in Jesus Christ. Freedom was once defined as voluntary submission to legitimate authority. A young generation is giving us new models of exceptional behavior. Their examples can provide a basis for higher standards and healthier sexual mores among others. In that sense they will be light and salt in the world.

Questions for Reflection and Discussion

1. How comfortable are you with your sexuality?

2. Are you ready to discuss with young people the many issues of this chapter?

3. What steps might you take for your sexual healing or for a better understanding of this complex issue?

4. What most impressed or distressed you in this chapter? How would you like to see these discussed or addressed?

5. What criticisms or suggestions do you have regarding this chapter?

6. Do you agree that sex cannot be adequately discussed by itself—that sexuality must be placed in a much larger context?

7. Do you agree that sexual deviations tend to descend gradually into deeper perversions?

8. Do you think secular society needs a moral framework if it is to elevate the level of sexual imagery, thinking, and behavior? Explain.

9. Do you think the secular world can benefit from the implications of a Judeo-Christian ethic? What challenge does this give Christians and the church?

Book Resources

Jim Auer. *Sex and the Christian Teen.* Liguori, Mo.: Liguori Publications, 1994. ⚹ This is short, clear, cheap, and very readable. It provides common sense about abstinence in a positive, powerful message.

Mark DeVries, compiler. *True Love Waits.* Nashville, Tenn.: Broadman & Holman Publishers, 1997. ⚹ This book supplies short, pithy statements from the Inventor of Sex and others, along with stories and insights toward the goal of waiting for marriage.

Meg Meeker. *Epidemic: How Teen Sex Is Killing Our Kids.* Washington, D.C.: Lifeline Press, 2002. Clearly a polemic, this pediatrician's book is written out of her personal experience, study, and speaking engagements. It presents the crisis of youthful sexual promiscuity these days and the failure of "safe sex" thinking. Its statistics regarding new strains of viruses and resulting infertility and cancer deaths are frightening. It concludes with a clear challenge for parents and adults to get involved.

Dennis Rainey, Barbara Rainey, and Samuel Rainey. *So You Want To Be a Teenager: What Every Pre-Teen Must Know about Friends, Love, Sex, Dating, and Other Life Issues.* Nashville, Tenn.: Thomas Nelson, 2002. 🔥 Eleven years teaching a sixth grade Sunday School class and raising a family of six prepared this father with his wife and son to write this book.

Video Resources

"The Teen Files: The Truth about Sex," A Comprehensive Teachers' Lesson Plan, ATM AIMS Multimedia. DVD or Video and Instructional Guide, this secular resource motivates discussion and learning. 9710 DeSoto Ave., Chatsworth, CA 91311-4469. 800-367-2467. 🔥 Instruction in this is founded on Bloom's "Six Levels of Cognitive Complexity." This presents dramatic real-life experiences such as teens taken to a laboratory that determines STDs, a couple viewing a premature baby of a young teen mother who is incapacitated for life and teens spending time with two teenage single parents. Eye-opening scenes promote discussion.

"Teen Sex Challenges and Decisions," 1995. 🔥 American Portrait Films has produced this video in popular media style including clips from Dr. Stephen Genuis (author of *Risky Sex*), dramatic teen re-enactments, and an interview with a woman with HIV to encourage serious thought and discussion about sex.

Internet Resources

www.clubac.com and www.acgreen.com ⚡ These sites are
   by the great basketball player, A.C. Green, who is also a
   Life Athlete member. They provide encouragement, resources, statistics, and curriculum for middle school and
   senior high. One outstanding page presents 40 reasons
   for abstinence given by teenagers.

www.kff.org ⚡ This is the site for the Henry J. Kaiser Family
   Foundation. Click on Reproductive Sexual Health and
   HIV/AIDS for the latest statistics and archives of past fact
   sheets and studies. There are also links to many other important sources.

www.lifeathletes.org ⚡ Life Athletes present encouragement
   from outstanding athletes, statistics, and a four-point
   commitment to live by the rules. This program promotes
   abstinence with an open and forgiving spirit. Not explicitly religious in content, this site is nicely laid out for
   young people.

www.lifeway.com/tlw ⚡ The authentic site of True Love
   Waits, an abstinence program with a Southern Baptist
   background. www.lifeway.com/tlw/pdt_tools.asp will get
   you to their abstinence resources for teens and parents/
   youth leaders.

www.silverringthing.com ⚡ The Silver Ring Thing is a dynamic web site (for young people and adults) that provides a program and resources for promoting abstinence
   for teenagers. It encourages those who have had sex to
   start over and get a second chance at virginity. Their
   public school assemblies have been well received.

www.teenpregnancy.org ⚡ The National Campaign to Prevent Teen Pregnancy will provide you with quick, clear
   general facts and stats, bibliography, and many current
   studies of CDC, the National Center for Health Statistics,
   The Alan Guttmacher Institute, and more.

17 Theology of Personal Healing and Reconciliation

Leaves for healing. — Ezek 47:12b

The Miracle of Forgiveness

A healing river flowing from the throne of God is the beautiful image found in the apocalyptic literature of the Bible (Ezek 47:1, 8, 12; Joel 3:18; Zech 14:8 and Rev 22:1-7). Ezekiel describes this river as flowing from the altar in the temple, making salty, stagnant waters fresh and watering trees whose leaves are for healing (Ezek 47:1, 8-9, 12). There is, in nature and God's grace, a strong inclination moving from partial to ultimate healing of all hurts.

We invoke the image of this healing river to flow through all previous chapters of this book. Young people need healing—for things done to them and for things they have done to others. Many have been sexually abused; have abused others, have really abused themselves. Kids like Alice (in chapter 6) and Amy (in the last chapter) have longed to be clean—to be able to start out fresh all over again. We must give them that help.

The healing cycle, like the love cycle, begins with accepting God's forgiveness and healing, forgiving ourselves, and offering forgiveness to others. So much of this book has been about the "Hurt Cycle." Each of us has been hurt in many, and some particular, ways. In a strange way being hurt teaches or programs us ways in which to hurt ourselves.

Apart from counseling, this is very difficult to see. Still, and all, we do put ourselves down, deny ourselves little pleasures, don't really love ourselves—which hurts. As hurting people we hurt others, often without even knowing it. And all this hurts God. People of faith have understood the hurt cycle as the sin cycle. The Ten Commandments are really a loving God saying: "Don't hurt each other, and don't wallow in your hurt, because then you'll just go on hurting others, and that hurts me."

The healing cycle is really the beginning of the love cycle. We receive God's love in a way that allows us to love ourselves at a deeper level. Then, we are able to love our neighbors as ourselves, and in this way show love toward God. The healing cycle is also entwined in the forgiveness cycle. We cannot heal without being forgiven. We ask to be forgiven by God as we have forgiven others. It's easy to see how our whole book points toward this chapter and these ideas.

About this healing of human hurts and forgiveness, Archbishop Tutu has written:

> In the act of forgiveness we are declaring our faith in the future of a relationship and in the capacity of the wrongdoer to make a new beginning on a course that will be different from the one that caused us the wrong. We are saying there is a chance to make a new beginning.[1]

Remarkable stories tell of healing even in those who have suffered terrible hurt. After Laura Blumenfeld's father was shot by a Palestinian, she not only decided to seek revenge, but to study revenge. Her *Washington Post* reporting job took her to Bosnia, Sicily and Iran where she interviewed assassins as well as religious leaders in order to gain information regarding the skills and wisdom of revenge. Finally, she was able to enter the Arab home and listen to the story of the son who shot her father (wounding her father but failing to kill him). From the young man she

---

[1] Desmond Mpilo Tutu, *No Future Without Forgiveness* (New York: Doubleday, 2000), 273.

heard of several chilling murders. Blumenfeld's book tells of her correspondence with the shooter himself, still planning on revenge, the gradual change in her attitude, and her final and dramatic pleas for the young man in court. Revenge had given place to reconciliation, an eye-for-an-eye to forgiveness.

In Nigeria Chris Anyanwu was snatched away from her two young children and tortured for 1,251 days under the vicious regime of General Sani Abacha. Despite that terrible abuse, she remains loyal to her country and calls on the Nigerian state to "apologize for killing its children and causing damage to others, make reparations for the damage and destruction done by those in control of state power (and) take measures to ensure such abuse never recurs." More dramatically she seeks reconciliation, has brought herself to sorrow towards her torturers, and wants to give them a second chance.

> I have observed the terrorists and torturers from a special vantage point. I know they also cry. They are humans . . . on the inside they are crying out to be saved from themselves; from what they have become. . . . If we claim to be superior to the torturers and terrorists, then we must demonstrate it by the superiority of our responses and actions. . . . the torturers wanted to teach us a lesson we would never forget. Now, it is our turn to teach them.[2]

Out of her long experience with Criminal Justice, Marie Ragghianti collected stories of incredible forgiveness.[3] She writes of a twenty-nine-year-old policeman with a wife pregnant shot on the streets of New York City. Now a quadriplegic confined to a wheelchair and attached to a ventilator he travels the country describing how he found the strength to forgive. Ellen Halbert was attacked so viciously and degradingly she promised herself never to talk about it, but she learned to forgive and took up the cause of victims' rights. Azim Khamisa could have spent his life in

---

    [2] Chris Anyanwu, "Forgiven," *The Boston Globe,* 18 Feb 2001: D 1-2.
    [3] Marie Ragghianti, "Every Day I Have To Forgive Again," *Parade Magazine,* 23 April 2000: 6.

bitterness after his twenty-year-old son, Tariq, was shot and killed by fourteen-year-old Tony Hicks in San Diego. Instead Azim got together with the father of the shooter and began a program against gun violence.[4] Having read of so much violence in earlier chapters, we must find respite and hope in these stories.

Sometimes it is the perpetrator who moves toward forgiveness. Richard Luttrell was a puny eighteen-year-old soldier, as he describes himself, when on one of his first forays into the hot, wet jungle of Vietnam in 1967, he found himself facing a North Vietnamese soldier who was pointing an AK-47 directly at him. For some reason that soldier never pulled the trigger. But Luttrell did. As his buddies gathered around the dead body of the man, they pulled out a wallet and a small picture dropped out. Not really knowing why, Luttrell grabbed the photo and put it in his wallet. Details must be skipped in this long, interesting story, but that picture of the soldier and a small girl that must have been his daughter would take Luttrell on an arduous journey.

The sad expressions on both faces led to an obsession with the photo. Finally, Luttrell takes it to the Memorial Wall and leaves it there hoping for relief and closure. Years later a friend points out a story and the picture in a book called *Offerings at the Wall.* When Luttrell sees it, he breaks down and weeps. He knows closure has not come. He sends a copy of the photo to Vietnam's ambassador in Washington who sends it on to an editor in Hanoi. By a miracle a page of that paper is used to wrap a present headed to the very girl, now a grown woman, in a remote village. She recognizes it. Letters are exchanged. Richard Luttrell decides he must continue his odyssey all the way to Korea. Finally arriving with flowers and the original picture, he speaks a sentence in broken Korean he has memorized:

> "Today I return the photo of you and your father, which I have kept for 33 years. Please forgive me."

---

[4] See feature article *Parade Magazine,* 2 March 1997.

She hugs him and cries. She clutches Richard as if he were her father himself finally coming home from the war. Her brother tells us that both of them believe that their father's spirit lives on in Richard. They expect we'll think it's just superstition. And, perhaps, they say, it is. But for them, today is the day their father's spirit has come back to them.

"Tell her this is the photo I took from her father's wallet the day I shot and killed him and that I'm returning it," Richard says.

Lan and Richard hug and cry. It is clear now. She forgives him . . . Thirty-three years after he pulled the trigger in the jungle that hot confusing day, Richard forgives himself.[5]

In short, Richard made war and took a life. Through guilt, grief, and persistence, he gained a family and found peace. The horrors of war demand painful forgiveness. Without forgiveness there can never be reconciliation, only bitterness and guilt.

Individual Healing in the Midst of Hurting Systems

Having, throughout this book, faced and sought to understand problems of troubled youth with new eyes and open minds, we seek healing strategies in these concluding chapters. The emphasis of this chapter is upon personal healing; the matter of systemic healing and reconciliation is left for the final chapter. We begin with the healing of individuals because compassion begins with individuals and moves to systems. Without love for hurting individuals, our attempts to change systems will never be sustained. But personal compassion leads to frustration without attention to larger systems. Helping victims of systemic dysfunction will be frustrated if we do not see the larger context.

---

[5] This story was written for the *St. Louis Dispatch* and presented on NBC's *Dateline,* 19 December 2000. It was placed on dateline.msnbc .com's archives, "Lasting Impressions" part 5, 3.

> ✗ There is nobody in the world who doesn't need
> healing; we all need Jesus to heal us in some way. In fact,
> there is no one, even in deepest need, to whom you can't
> offer healing. You may offer healing time and a
> relationship, or perhaps a healing touch. Don't discount
> even a healing look. Jesus helps us understand the power
> of (mere) healing presence. In these ways Jesus can use
> you in the healing of any sufferer.

Preventing troubles and healing the hurts of wounded youth call for insights and commitment from many sources. Today's wounds require stories and studies of victims and perpetrators, of experts and practitioners. Students, youth leaders, social scientists, theologians, pastors, those who wound, and the wounded—all of us must bring our resources to the table.[6]

Only as nations and communities gather to solve the problems of violence and suffering will we see real progress toward peace and healing.

Combining Resources for Healing

The challenges presented in this book demand humility, a new spirit of collaboration, and reliance on God's healing and reconciling power. True healing of individuals demands positive change in the environment.

---

[6]The abuse of children by a small percentage but large number of Catholic priests presents a challenging case study in the interaction of personal and institutional wounding, need for rectification, and healing. First, we have those wounded for life by terrible misuse of power and prestige. Then, there are the predator pastors never brought to justice. Bishops and church hierarchy served, not only as bystander, but to cover up these terrible acts for their own protection. Obviously, the church needs corporate repentance while the lengthy process of individual healing goes on. Clearly, a whole community (secular and religious) has been deeply wounded by these hidden actions and perversion of justice. All churches and the whole society ought to be sorry about this abuse, praying "Lord have mercy on us." We all share guilt; we hope for renewal through repentance and reform. While we consider individual healing here, this situation anticipates the next chapter's discussion of systemic repentance and reconciliation.

My wife, Gail, and I taught a class in counseling at a seminary in Africa some years ago. Traditional African counseling often came from the wise women of the village, and therapy involved the family and town as much or more than the troubled person. In the West we have only slowly learned the importance of holistic, family systems therapy. The community is the healing context of troubled youth.

Young People as Resources

Studies and experts[7] suggest that youthful violence and other problems can be averted as we find ways for young people to become a primary community resource. Young people, possessing insights and strengths a community needs, want to be positively engaged in the life of this world.

Utopian visions of youthful participation will fail unless they begin with the way things are and proceed with sound strategy. It is not enough to repeat the cliché: Youth are not the future of the church (or society); they are today's church. Most young people do not want to endure clerical meetings or political bureaucracies. They do not like political controversies and compromises, and the adult world is not especially attractive to most teenagers. What most teenagers want is adult freedom within the youthful world of their friends. In that world, young people can serve successfully as peer counselors, and group sessions of young people deal effectively with many troubles. Such groups suggest the importance of adult facilitators.

Relationships Needed

Many young people are already too estranged or hurt to care, so they need to be reached before they can become

---

[7] See studies of Search Institute in Peter L. Benson, *All Kids Are Our Kids: What Communities Must Do to Raise Caring and Responsible Children and Adolescents* (San Francisco: Jossey-Bass, 1997). See also The Carnegie Council on Adolescent Development, *Fateful Choices: Healthy Youth for the Twenty-First Century* (The Carnegie Foundation of New York, 1992), and "Great Transitions: Preparing Adolescents for a New Century" (1995). Online: carnegie.org/sub/pubs/reports. Or obtainable for $10.00 from Carnegie Corporation of New York, P.O. Box 753, Waldorf, MD 20604 [800-998-2269].

involved. Every major study concludes that young people need deeper relationships with their parents and/or other interested adults.

Youthful truancy, children leaving school and homes, drug use, and crime have increased in Great Britain, where School Standards Minister Estelle Morris announced that four hundred fifty urban schools would be given eight hundred learning mentors. These part-time workers will not teach, although most are qualified to do so. Instead they are to help students with family and motivational problems.

Another new pilot scheme selects older students to mentor younger pupils in local schools. These mentors will develop relationships and then help with homework, organizing time, and personal problems. They will be there to hear the stories of their younger peers.[8] British experts found little or no correlation between success and the age or education of tutors. The key to helping is rather empathy— mentors who care, can listen, and respond.

All studies and specialists agree to this critical need for someone to care. The troubled youth described in this book need someone to listen. Many of them, however, are not at all ready to talk. It will take love, perseverance, and skill before they open up.

Healthy and Healing Communities

We have explained how societies and communities foster violence and risk among young people. Books by Francis Ianni, William Damon, and Peter Benson provide hope as to how negative communal influences can be turned in positive directions.[9] Search Institute, of which Benson is president,

---

[8] Evangelical Alliance Youth and Children's Unit electronic monthly bulletin, December 1999. Grahame_Knox@compuserve.com.

[9] Francis Ianni, *The Search for Structure: A Report on American Youth Today* (New York: Free Press, 1989); see especially "The Search for Structure and the Caring Community"; William Damon, *The Youth Charter: How Communities Can Work Together to Raise Standards for All Our Children* (New York: Free Press, 1997); Peter L. Benson, *All Kids Are*

has done research identifying forty assets young people need for healthy growth. The results of this study challenge the whole community: "families, neighbors, schools, religious congregations, youth organizations, local governments, employers, and residents—to reclaim their capacity and responsibility for raising healthy, successful, and caring" youth.[10] Slighted in this fine work are more intense interventions needed in pockets of poverty. Still, the conclusions of this work should be the goals of all communities.

From this work has come Search Institute's proposed community initiative that is working successfully in many places. Called Healthy Communities: Healthy Youth, it shows the forty assets broken down into eight types of assets a community can use to encourage healthy growth. Would you place such responsibility for children and youth on every community?

1. Support: Experiencing people and places that are accepting and loving.

2. Empowerment: Knowing they are valued and valuable.

3. Boundaries and Expectations: Understanding the limits and possibilities.

4. Constructive Use of Time: Being involved in enriching and structured activities.

5. Commitment to Learning: Believing that education is important and engaging.

6. Positive Values: Caring for others and holding high standards for self.

7. Social Competencies: Developing skills and relationships for life.

8. Positive Identity: Believing in their personal power, purpose and potential.[11]

Our Kids: What Communities Must Do to Raise Caring and Responsible Children and Adolescents (San Francisco: Jossey-Bass, 1997).

[10] Benson, *All Kids Are Our Kids,* book jacket.

[11] Search Institute, 700 S. 3rd Street, Suite 210, Minneapolis, MN 55415; online: www.search-institute.org.

No one would claim these principles are exclusive to Search Institute. They are found in communities that are reclaiming young people in urban and rural areas as well as in troubled suburbs. But they are well expressed here and have moved from careful research to practical programs that are being used and evaluated. They clearly articulate what it means to get ourselves together and take care of the business of rearing healthy youth. In these principles are hope and help for our previous considerations.

The Importance of Communication

A primary block in programs such as those mentioned is often found in faulty communication. A theme of this book has been listening to the stories and viewpoints of young people, and we had best not hasten to establish the best program imaginable if we have not come close enough to listen and hear what's going on in and among youth. A good start would be to re-institute a family dinner several times a week where everyone is heard. That obviously can't happen where critical family members are not present or don't know how to communicate.

We move from dysfunction to healthy relationships and communication by considering the relationship and communication within God. When we speak of God as triune, we acknowledge the idea that God is eternally a social being. God made human beings for communion with, and after the pattern of, the blessed Trinity—with the angels, and with other human beings. The nature of our sinfulness involves a broken communion with God, with our spouses, children, neighbors and enemies.

Communion involves communication. Faulty communication results from failures of union and community; it is a source of most conflict. It is important to reflect on the way in which self-centeredness leads to intended and unintended hurts, dysfunction in all our relationships, and faulty communication.

The following points are helpful in developing more effective communication.

- All our relationships are hindered by faulty communication.

- To reduce conflict and violence, we must undo faulty communication and establish more effective communication.

- Faulty communication begins within ourselves! Most of us don't understand this. We have hidden hurts and fears and unexpressed feelings. Parts of us in tension must get together. A neglected or a crying "child within" needs our attention. Many are still blaming their parents, or those around them, for not giving them the love and attention they need to give themselves. Good counseling helps one communicate with oneself. Good communication within allows us to love and communicate with others. "Love your neighbor *as* you love yourself."

- Parents often project their hurts and fears, or their sense of inadequacy, onto their children. We want our kids to avoid what hurt us or somehow make up for our failures. Some parents try to find or live out their lives through those of their kids. A family finds healing as it unravels snarled communications and hears what each is suffering and needs. Understanding our family habits helps us to better understand how we treat ourselves. I may not be able to nurture the child within me because I was never nurtured. I may be too critical of myself because I felt criticized by my parents growing up. Now it is time for me to take responsibility for all that I need.

- Teenage children are individuating away from their parents, that is, they are at the point of getting a life of their own. They do not understand everything going on in their parents' lives or much of their inner baggage and issues, so communication can easily break down.

- Few parents have been trained in parenting and communication skills. They have often learned ineffective patterns from their parents and friends.

- Preaching often emphasizes hierarchical notions and the headship of the father. Autocratic or even abusive headship may be rationalized in terms of traditional mores.

- Too often, churches provide little or no clear instruction about family dysfunction and communication skills.

- Churches may exhibit dysfunctional relationships and poor communication. The pastor, elders, leaders, adults, and youth all face different pressures and often develop hidden agendas that do not get communicated. The result is confusion, superficial spirituality, and clichés. Faithful and confused congregations can be challenged to repent when the issue is with the church's structure and communication patterns. Or there may be a drive to restructure dysfunctional church structures without critical change. Such restructuring fails to deal with real hurts, fears, and needs, so people withdraw into silence, indifference, or absence.

- Faulty communication and dysfunction can also be found in academia, businesses, and government bureaucracies.

- The world, especially businesses, pays large fees to bring in consultants to uncover dysfunction and establish effective communication. The church rarely does, but it could easily set up low-cost yet beneficial workshops and conferences.

Communication involves tough love—the willingness to hurt and be hurt for another's growth and welfare.[12] And it requires a willingness to take the time and endure the hard work that communication requires. There are signs that we are recognizing the importance of communication and moving toward an era of better understanding.

Let us consider the following essential aspects of clear communication:

- Clear communication is based on respect and desire for another's growth and welfare as well as the growth and welfare of the family, group, or church.

- Clear communication is based on listening first and then giving feedback. Such listening demands suspending your feelings and opinions and putting yourself in the speaker's shoes.

---

[12]The story of David and Nathan (2 Sam 11:26–12:10, 13–15) involves tough love on the part of God and Nathan. This confrontation was for David's growth and welfare.

- Clear communication demands feedback to what has been said. It is more "I" (am feeling or notice) than "you" (said or did such and such).

- Clear communication needs openness—being as transparent as possible to self and listeners. This is the main risk and barrier to real communication. We must be willing to be known as we are. Clear communication thus demands exposure.

- Clear communication is culturally and personally clear. It avoids static (personal or ideological irritants or hang-ups) and tries to make sure the speaker is honest and the listener receptive.

- Clear communication has respect for the context or situation; it tries to be appropriate and to avoid hurt.

- To communicate clearly requires respect for self, the other, and the larger context.

Types of Healing

Wounds and scars hinder open communication. Healing of deeply wounded or troubled young people comes in several ways. Healing attends to physical causes, to emotional and social factors, and also to spiritual symptoms. The medical profession, psychiatric and mental health organizations, paraprofessional organizations (youth work), and faith communities all play a part in preventing and healing destructive violence.

Medical doctors are increasingly being trained to see patients in terms of their whole being and the context of their lives. Many young people will respect an authority talking to them in terms of their physical well-being.

Prevention of violence enlists all social systems influencing young people in the task of reinforcing healthy behavior and healthy communities.[13] There must be concerted intervention and treatment of the victims and perpetrators of violence.

---

[13] We again note the importance of congruent messages from family, community, schools, media, and peers. See Ianni, *The Search for Structure*, 7, 262–66.

From the model of the physical and spiritual ministry of Jesus, both of which are need-based, Christian youth workers develop patterns of intervention and helping youth at risk. Primary human needs are food, clothing, shelter, safety, and security. Providing for people without these basics demands a genuine respect for their dignity. They and those who help must come to love and trust. As primary needs are provided, secondary needs—attention, belonging, identity, achievement, and mastery—become evident. Note the relationship among these five issues. A teenager can belong only if someone has paid attention to him. It is primarily in a peer group that teenagers clarify their identities. Similarly, recognition of achievements comes from peers, family, and society. As a person moves toward mastery, affirmation comes increasingly from within.

> 🏃 How will you use the hurt and love, the forgiveness and healing cycles with young people and families? Will you be able to explain the love and hurt cycles in simple language and illustrations? We hurt others (in so many little or subtle ways) because we have been or are hurting ourselves. And all of that hurts God. We receive God's love so we can love ourselves and our neighbor as we love ourselves. So it is with healing. As we receive healing from God, we work out our own healing, then we can be better healers of others through Christ. Does this make sense to you, and will it make sense to young people you know?

Those who have grown used to antisocial ways or self-destructive behavior must unlearn such patterns and relearn a healthy and socially approved lifestyle. By approved I mean a lifestyle that is affirmed by the person, by significant others, by the culture, and for believers, by God.

Intervention in the lives of deeply troubled young people works best in therapeutic communities that can redress dysfunction and wounds from the past. In a sense, therapy is about re-parenting and having another chance to grow up and put broken pieces together. Apart from live-in situations, weekly support groups are most effective. In both situations, some combination of behavior modification, encounter or confrontational method, psychotherapy (e.g., psychoanalytic, humanistic, eclectic), and twelve-step principles may be helpful.

Finally, there is the need for spiritual healing, a need often missed by advocates for youth.[14]

Admittedly, there are varying and sometimes conflicting styles of spiritual healing outside and within the Christian faith. Some approaches promote a primary emphasis on conversion; others, on spiritual deliverance. Critics of such approaches may encourage support in a faith community, while others may stress liturgical and sacramental healing. Resolution of such differences may come as we try to understand what each group has to offer and to place all possibilities within our spiritual context.

Pastoral Theology

Pastoral theology also offers forgiveness and healing. The *Book of Common Prayer* is rather widely seen as classic even outside Anglican circles, and its Pastoral Offices offer wide opportunities for spiritual healing.[15] The following outline of these pastoral services attempts to show their significance.

---

[14] The Carnegie Council on Adolescent Development, for all its marvelous studies and reports in the 1980s and 1990s, missed the spiritual needs of young people and the importance of faith-based organizations, especially among urban youth. *Fateful Choices* notes how the welfare of children and adolescents is "inextricably linked to the health of communities" but limits the "key actors for implementation" to "federal, state, and local governments, health providers; school officials; business and industry; foundations" (226). "Great Transitions" names five institutions influencing youth: "families, schools, the health sector, community organizations, and the media" (8, online report). The more recent secular work of James Garbarino and others, by contrast, clearly calls for "spiritual anchors" in terms of prevention and "amazing grace," even "divine intervention" as necessary for a healing process.

[15] This is my tradition, and in my teaching I have found it to be helpful to those from other traditions.

Confirmation. The pastor has a pastoral concern for the faith of the individual. If the person was baptized, how is this adolescent working out the faith of parents and faith community in her identity and view of life? Each young person's faith needs clarification and confirmation.

Marriage. Every young person deals with sexual issues; some are beginning to think of marriage. As young people clarify the place of sex, love, and marriage (these three pieces of the triangle must come together) in their lives, they take important steps toward maturity and wholeness. Instruction on marriage should always be balanced with teaching on singleness and wholeness.

Thanksgiving for the birth of a child. A significant percentage of young people are involved in the birth or abortion of a child. Both situations need pastoral attention. Here are creative pastoral possibilities for the healing and education of youthful parents as well as prevention of needless trouble and pain.

Reconciliation. Many celebrities work out their therapy in public, and young people flock to concerts and mosh pits[16] to find release for raging emotions. The church has not given youth a chance to lament or confess appropriately, even though youth feel a need, subconsciously perhaps, for public and private expression of despair and remorse. God's mercy needs to be celebrated by young people today! In loving contexts, they need to experience and celebrate God's forgiveness and healing.

Ministration to the sick. Sickness of body and soul needs special attention from pastors. The office for the sick is set up in three parts: ministry of God's Word, laying on of hands and anointing, and Holy Communion. Most churches require the service of ordained pastors to celebrate communion. This should not be a barrier; clergy should be invited to serve, sometimes in special youth services.

---

[16] Mosh pits are designated places at rock concerts for slam dancing. Some people need to slam or be slammed in order to feel or get out their aggressions. The section just in front of the stage has become a place of strong physical contact.

Ministration at the time of death and burial service. Lest anyone sigh and think this is going too far in a book about troubled youth, remember how concerned young people are about death. High schools and friendship groups usually feel most spiritual when one of their own has died.

We must address this obsession with death; if, however, youth seem careless about their death or anyone else's, we must live and teach a deep respect for life and death. Young people need to celebrate the death and life of their friends as well as their own life and impending death. Ash Wednesday is a very appropriate time to do this. The church has missed great opportunities here.

As with the other offices described, "The Litany and Vigil at the Time of Death" found in the Prayer Book is based on the gospel, the love of God, and the work of Christ for a troubled world. The opening words of the burial service rings out: "I am the resurrection and the life, says the Lord." Its great prayers for those who have entered eternity lets us know and celebrate how precious life is and what it is about. Isn't it remarkable that so few youth ministry books ever deal with the subject of death? May this remind us that we cannot fully live unless we are prepared to die and that young people need to grow in their respect for life and death.

Forgiveness

As much as we are "preaching" forgiveness in this chapter, it is very important to note there is a time not to forgive. It would be a terrible thing for Gail, my wife, to say to the women who come to her suffering from early sexual abuse, "Well, you know you need to forgive the perpetrator." They are already wracked with guilt. For twenty or thirty years they have been blaming themselves. No, first of all, they must find the strength to blame their abusers—to express hidden, repressed anger. Someone who has committed terrible crimes against someone's humanity and dignity should not ask for forgiveness. All they have the right to do is to express sorrow and remorse. Slowly, abused victims may

finally, after they have been able to accept and forgive themselves, come to forgive the other—in a healthy way. Neither
the counselor nor the arbitrator/reconciler has a right to ask
of those terribly offended to forgive. Rather, we who would
be peacemakers or reconcilers must ask for stories to be
told. Then, often with deep and painful struggles, victims
may find the grace and strength to forgive.

You will sense the difficulty of this process in the following story. In June 1983, Ron Carlson learned that his sister had
been brutally murdered during a clumsy break-in robbery.[17]

The axe that killed Deborah Carlson Thornton was
stuck to her rib cage. Ron's anger toward the murderers,
Danny Garret and Karla Faye Tucker, was fierce. Scars in his
life preceded this terrible event. By the time he was six, his
parents had divorced; his mother had remarried and then
died. At the time there was no one to mother the boy, so Ron
was reared by his older sister.

Deborah finally took Ron back to Texas to look for their
father. When they found Bill List, he was a four-hundred-
pound alcoholic, drinking a bottle of whiskey and fifteen
cups of coffee while smoking a half carton of cigarettes each
day. A godly doctor helped Bill get clean of his addictions and
gave him a Bible, although Bill wanted nothing to do with
faith. Nor could Bill relate to his long-lost children, Ron and
Deborah. Their efforts to connect with their father and frustration only strengthened the bond between Ron and his
older sister.

The terrible pictures displayed and testimony given during the trial of those who killed his sister fed a hatred that ate
away at Ron's heart. Although he sensed it was wrong, he
wanted to kill the two murderers. In anger and despair, his
abuse of alcohol and drugs deepened, and his relationship
with his father deteriorated.

Then, only a year and a half after his sister's death, a
teenager, Elbert Homan, shot and killed Ron's father! Going
through Bill List's house, a friend of the family and one-time

---

[17] As told by Marcy W. Bryan in "Love Your Enemies," *Light Magazine,* International Bible Society, Summer 1998, 6–10.

drug dealer found something he thought Ron ought to have. It was a Bible and some tapes given Bill by the doctor who had treated and helped him. Curious, Ron began reading his father's Bible; he could not put it down. It led him to pray: "Please take the pain away. Please take the hatred away. Replace it with love, joy, and compassion." Ron felt himself changed, but it was not easy: "When I read where Christ said to forgive seventy times seven, I cried out to Him, 'I can't do *that.*' Then, He seemed to say, 'You're right, you cannot. But with me, you can.'"

One can imagine the struggle to forgive those who had so ravaged Ron's life. There was the teenager who murdered his father. Dave Garret and Karla Faye Tucker had killed the older sister who had been a mother to him. Dave Garret died before Ron could meet him, but Ron knew he must reconcile with Elbert and Karla. It was Karla who was to make a great impression on Ron. He met her at the Harris County Jail. Sitting across the table, he asked, "Do you know who I am? I'm Ron Carlson, Deborah Thornton's brother." Karla's head drooped as she began to sob. Ron went on: "Whatever comes out of this, I just want you to know I don't hold anything against you. *I forgive you.*"

Going to that jail and forgiving was the hardest thing Ron had ever done. Karla told Ron how she had become a Christian, and the two began corresponding. There were other visits; Ron became an advocate for a stay of execution. But despite protests, Karla was the first woman put to death in Texas since the Civil War. Her appeals denied, she asked Ron to be present at her execution as a witness for her rather than the victim. In granting that request, Ron showed how costly forgiveness can be.

For me, David Augsburger is an expert on forgiveness. In the preface of one of his books, this fine counselor, who knows the cost and complexity of forgiving, writes:

> Forgiveness has always had its detractors. From the one side it is seen as too easy, too simple, too quick a fix for any significant injury. From the other, it is viewed as too difficult, too complex, too long and tortuous a road when revenge and retaliation would get to the point more economically. . . .

Helping people forgive is our calling, our vocation as persons, whether we are in the "helping professions" formally, or offering help informally in the daily brushes and abrasions. In each effort to "help another" we find help for ourselves, for the pain we have inflicted, for the pain we have suffered. And in this healing journey, we discover the trajectory of the soul.[18]

At the end of that book, Augsburger explains many things we've struggled with in this book:

Reconciliation begins with the victim, but the identification of the victim is not simple or easy. All participants are, to a surprising degree, victims of violence in general and victimized by the particular occurrence. We stand on more level ground than we know; we are all in need of being reconciled and forgiven.[19]

Such language brings us back to the perfect Victim, who said, "Father, forgive them" and who taught us to pray, "Forgive us . . . as we forgive those who have hurt us."

Punishment and litigation are not the full answers to crime. They may be necessary but are not our best hope. The stories told in this chapter hold out the promise for better understanding and greater hope. I hope you wonder with me where every young person mentioned in this book is today. As a society we should learn from every tragic crime, how might it have been prevented, how can we do better. We should work to bring every murderer to remorse and repentance. As long as they are alive, our goal should be their growth. Many youthful crimes should be treated in terms of restorative justice: how can we help the perpetrator learn and pay back to family and society? Of course, when there is no willingness, tough love must be our guide. Some criminals will never be redeemed. But we can learn even from them.

Youth leaders are peacemakers. We try to avert violence and damaging behaviors; we attempt to bring reconciliation and forgiveness. Ministering to troubled youth involves intervention and advocacy. We are often the only ones interested

---

[18] David W. Augsburger, *Helping People Forgive*, (Louisville, Ky.: Westminster John Knox, 1996), ix–x.
[19] Ibid., 164.

in all aspects of a young person's life, and free from being an authority figure. This can give us incredible opportunities for good. It gives us the chance to hear the whole story.

Questions for Reflection and Discussion

1. Do we need to work together to stop the dangers young people experience—and to heal their hurts? Explain.

2. Exactly who are the "we" who should collaborate, and how can this happen?

3. Is healing an individual often only a partial healing if we don't pay attention to groups and systems that also need to be healed? Explain.

4. What place do family and community play in rearing children and preventing youthful violence?

5. Do you believe that personal dysfunction usually stems from family or systemic dysfunction? What example would you give of this?

6. What hope do you have for the improvement of communication?

7. What hope do you have for mobilizing families and communities to care about kids?

8. Do you know anyone who cannot forgive? What do you say to such a person?

9. Can youth workers take the principles of this book and make a difference among troubled young people? How do you see this happening?

Book Resources

Jim B. Allender and Larry Crabb. *The Wounded Heart: Hope for Adult Victims of Childhood Sexual Abuse.* Colorado Springs, Colo.: Navpress, 1990. 🏃 The pain and shame of childhood abuse can be terrible. Two psychotherapists help bring healing and recovery to those who suffer this wound.

Melody Beattie. *Codependent No More* and *Beyond Codependency.* New York: HarperCollins, 1989. ♠ The title of an audio tape of this book is subtitled: How to Stop Controlling Others and Start Caring for Yourself. This book offers hope for all who grew up in alcoholic or dysfunctional families and became Adult Children or pleasers.

Henry Cloud and John Townsend. *Boundaries.* Grand Rapids, Mich.: Zondervan Publishing House, 1992. ♠ Psychologically sound and biblically based, this book helps those whose personal boundaries are too loose (can't say no) or too tight (sanctimonious and critical). This provides help for relationships and communication in families and church communities.

M. Scott Peck. *The Road Less Traveled: A New Psychology of Love.* 2d ed. New York: Simon & Schuster, 1998. ♠ This helps people grow up and become responsible for difficult lives in a difficult world. It has helped many. You may be interested in a second book of his, *People of the Lie: Hope for Healing Human Evil* (1997, 2d ed.)

Spencer Perkins and Chris Rice. *More than Equals: Racial Healing for the Sake of the Gospel.* Downers Grove, Ill.: InterVarsity Press, 1993. ♠ Certainly racial confession, forgiveness, and reconciliation are unresolved and nagging issues in our churches and society. Many have been helped by these authors' personal experiences and their threefold strategy: Admit, Submit, Commit.

Internet Resources

Many of the Internet Resources given already provide information and resources for specific types of problems and healing needs especially among young people. The following are two Christian ministry resources.

www.christianhealingmin.org ♠ This site describes the ministry and resources of Francis and Judith McNutt's healing ministry with links to other such websites.

www.orderofstluke.org ♠ The Order of St. Luke the Physician is an international healing order supporting those with a call to healing ministries.

18 Theology of Corporate Healing and Reconciliation

Your kingdom come. — Matt 6:10a NRSV

Approaching Change

The challenge of corporate healing and reconciliation is great. What do we know about corporate repentance and forgiveness? How can we bring about change in this world, and what does the Bible tell us about being agents of social change? Do we want, can we expect, this world to be a better place?

What are we praying when we ask day after day, "Thy kingdom come, thy will be done, *on earth* as it is in heaven"? Do we dare believe *we* can make a difference, make this world a better place for all? The previous chapter focused on personal healing, reconciliation, and wholeness. It is best to start with individual change and personal relationships, but we must also deal with our desperate need for collective justice and peace.

We have acknowledged that youth's troubles stem from causes within and without. We are more likely to hurt others when we have been hurt or find ourselves in a threatening world. Researchers note that abuse and conflict often appear in cycles; those who are hurt often go on to hurt others. Inner and outer conflicts interact. We have seen, in previous chapters, how many social systems today are programming young people to violence and dysfunction. We

must be committed, then to *change*—within *and* without.
This means we must change people *and* change systems.

Our study has seen negative effects of many systems
on young people. In our last chapter we looked at correcting the
dysfunction of families through better communication. Families and individuals are, however, also affected by larger systems: the community, media, economics, education, criminal
justice, and politics. Do we have the strength and courage, the
faith and hope it takes to look at possible change?

For too long parts of the Christian Church have been divided between those who say social improvement comes
only from change of heart and those who think new laws will
eliminate our problems. Good laws do not guarantee a beloved community, and godly people with seemingly changed
hearts can have terrible blind spots (allowing for slavery, for
instance). Evangelicals in the U.S. lost out on the Civil Rights
Movement, yet had to admit to the positive results civil rights
legislation made in the country. New hearts *and* good laws
can both bring about important change. Justice and peace
come as individuals of good will affect society *and* as social
change influences every person. To accomplish justice and
peace means collaboration across many lines.

Reid Carpenter, director of the national Council of Leadership Foundations, often comments that "people of faith"
often lack good will and "people of good will" may lack faith.
That is why, he says, they need to get together.

A story is told of a strong swimmer who jumped into
a river to save someone floating by. Soon another person
floated by, and then another. Suddenly, the swimmer came out
of the river and started running away. Those who watched
asked in amazement where he was going, "Upstream," he
cried, "I want to find out who's throwing them in!" While we
continue to treat individuals for some deadly disease, someone must be doing research to find its source and cure. The
source of the problem "upstream" may be an evil individual,
or more likely, an evil system using bad or weak people.

So we take up the challenge of changing systems. We will
first consider changing organizational systems, then reconciling
ethnic and racial systems, and finally changing the whole

world—at least working in some way toward world peace. Just because we can't change the world doesn't mean we ought not to be working at it. Tom Skinner, the evangelist who came out of Harlem and was radicalized in Chicago, once said:

> I'd rather be involved and fail at something that is eventually going to succeed than to be involved and succeed at something that is eventually going to fail.

We need youth workers relating to troubled kids. But they, and the rest of us, must also be advocates for systemic change. Such change needs to take place in families, neighborhoods and schools, the criminal justice system, and society at large. Change must come to unbridled capitalism and its media, which programs children in negative ways. Business may reap large profits while kids get hurt. We must be against systems that reward its leaders with obscene benefits for private success at terrible cost to the common good. Hierarchical systems and bungling bureaucracies need reform. Social cancers of racism, classism, sexism, consumerism, and materialism demand radical treatment in God's name, . . . or out of common sense, for the sake of the young and our future life together. Christian revolutionaries have this advantage over secular radicals: we have hope and a strong confidence that we are involved in a mission that must ultimately succeed. That is the hope of the resurrection and the apocalypse.

Tony Campolo has reminded us—to great audience applause—of the power of Black preaching in the midst of trouble: "Friday's here, but Easter's coming!" We may, even in this book, get bogged down in Good Friday depression, but our Eucharists continually celebrate Easter. We haven't reached our goal yet, but signs of justice and peace are breaking out among us. This may sound good, but someone asks, "What is the biblical basis for changing systems?"

A Biblical Theology of Social Change

The gospel of Isaiah begins with a call to corporate repentance. Its call is to social structures more than to individuals. God is asking the systems of ancient Israel (the nation, the city, princes, judges and rulers, citizens at large—study chapter 1) to ". . . come now and reason (or argue) together . . ." (Isa 1:18, paraphrase). God is still calling nations of this world and their social systems: "Come on, now, and let's reason together." I think God does want people talking things over and wanting things right.

"Your injustice and oppression of the weak are corporate sins, deep-dyed as scarlet," Isaiah says (v. 17, paraphrase). Institutional or corporate blessing depends on *institutional* repentance and change (1:19-20). Can this be? Are we to be prophets to that end? Shouldn't all the dysfunctional systems of this book be called to account . . . and asked to change?

We follow the gospel of Isaiah through the wonderful 26th chapter (which answers many of the cries in this book), the new hope of chapter 40, the severe challenge of chapter 58 and finally the reaffirmation of Jubilee (Lev 25) in chapter 61. The oppressed shall be released. The weak will be lifted up; the rich and arrogant laid low. Those who hurt will be healed, and ugly things will be made beautiful. Finally, we will do the right thing, which is justice, and justice will bring peace.

We are reminded of two definitions of the Gospel in the New Testament: that Christ died for our sins and rose again (1 Cor 15:3) *and* that the oppressed are to be freed (Luke 4:18-19). Jesus intentionally quotes Isaiah (ch. 61) in his first public address. Social reform is not just an implication of the Gospel; it is part of the Good News of God's Kingdom. Jesus did a lot of good to hurting people, and He also forgave sins. We are called to be Gospel people in all the world.

Some respond that nations today are not theocracies as was Israel, to whom Isaiah originally spoke. We remind them that Israel was meant to be a theocratic model for all nations of the earth. We also refer them to chapters in Isaiah spoken, not to a theocracy, but to pagan nations (e.g., Isaiah 14:5-19; 21; 24). God explains to the nations of Syria, Gaza, Tyre, Moab, and the Ammonites what is unjust in their societies in Amos 1 and 2. In fact, Jonah preached a gospel of repentance to the pagan Assyrian capital of Nineveh. Again and again, the Bible reminds us that God is a God of all nations!

It is not easy to determine how Christians should join others of good will to bring change to pluralistic and secular societies today. No clear methodology is laid out in the Bible. God leaves strategy and methods to be figured out by the faithful in each generation—with the help of biblical principles. This book has been written with the secular world in mind. The Incarnation encourages us to find ways in which God's justice can be worked out in public schools, secular clinics, criminal courts, and in diverse communities. It attempts to make sense of an ethic that can work for secularists and biblically-based Christians. While we cannot "force religion" on our neighbors in a pluralistic, secular society, we must—as Jesus put it—be salt and light (Matt 5:13–16).

Yes, America and other countries do need to repent, to humble themselves and seek help from above—however they understand that. We can preach that; in fact, we must. But judgment must begin in the House of God (1 Peter 4:17). Sadly, most churches are concerned, not about society and world situations, but only about their own business. So they can hardly model the kind of repentance needed today.

> ✦ How do you understand corporate repentance? How might your church or youth group address evils of our history and society? What biblical passages of corporate responsibility and repentance might you study? Is there relief in such confession? What part does confession have in the liturgy of your worship?

Changing Systems, Organizations, or Communities

Changing systems is a complex and awesome task. It's not just nations, but systems within nations, that need change. Speaking at a conference of Children Home Chaplains (associated with the National Consortium on Alternatives for Youth At Risk), I found that despite their heroic work, they faced a two-fold frustration. First, there was a concern regarding the great gulf between them and their young people. They struggled to understand the radically different world from which these boys and girls come. Secondly, they were dealing with the unresponsiveness, even dysfunction, of their organizations. Besides the tremendous energy it takes to deal with troubled youth, we must be prepared to deal with organizations that are uncooperative, or at least systems slow to respond. This is all part of what needs to be understood and changed.

To change the way things are is a daunting task. "Don't count on it" and "Don't give up" are probably the best encouragement we can give young agents of change. A biblical theology of social justice and reconciliation is based on prayer (the cry of the distressed, Exod 3:7 and Ps 107), the word of prophets (2 Chron 15:1-7), and the work of reformers (2 Chron 15:8-18). But how does this work?

Changing organizations or systems begins with prayer and a love for those who need to change. Martin Luther King, Jr. cautioned that we can only change those we love. We need to understand the relationship of spiritual renewal and organizational change. There should be an appreciation of the many parties needed: prayer warriors, prophets, activists, quiet supporters. Consultants with an outside perspective are very valuable. We should know why we— and why God—would want to see this change. We need to understand the timing of change and how the particular organization in question is interlocked with other institutions and systems. Social change begins with good systems thinking.

When it comes to changing things in a school or any organization, you will find three attitudes or categories of opinions—three responses to the changes you see as necessary. Hopefully there will be some Constructive Critics (who with you want to see and are willing to work for change). The majority, however, will fall into the category of Sluggish Moderates who are apathetic, unknowing, or uncaring. Finally, you will be saddened or stung by Strong Resisters who don't want change and will dig in their heels. In general the Constructive Critics tend to number about 20%; they must to be mobilized. Sluggish Moderates (about 60%) need to be motivated. And the Strong Resisters (20%) who are your critics need to be softened.

Institutional reform is complicated. To see things change demands a clear understanding of an organization's purpose, goals, functions, recruitment, training, and advancement policies. Roles, status, and rewards within the system must be determined along with communication patterns, both formal and informal. Sound institutional analysis demands a power analysis within the organization or community.

A clear plan of action is often a result of study on the part of a task force. Their report must include a clear aim and goals. Key implementers of change should meet regularly and informally. Initial success around some low-threat goals is important. Then, everyone must be prepared for more difficult challenges. Like a huge ship, it takes time and distance before an organization or social system can turn itself around.

Some of this must work itself out in pure "politics." However, it must be inspired by vision (Prov 29:18) and upheld with prayer. Some may be called to deeper and more constant prayer and understanding of spiritual warfare. Others are more natural activists. All must understand what is going on as corporate healing and reconciliation.

Underneath the need for change in many of our organizations and societies today—though many tend to deny its existence or force—is the need for racial and ethnic healing. Let's face this seemingly impossible challenge together.

Ethnic Reconciliation: Healing Deep Animosities in Complex Situations

A theme of this book has been the telling of stories. Personal healing demands the telling of stories to someone or group who understands and is able to respond. Corporate healing also demands the chance to tell a collective story— and sense relief from pain or shame in a healing response.

Within nations and beyond our social systems, ethnic and racial divisions need to be reconciled. Conflicts of the 21st century are fed by deep animosities. Many of them reflect culture against culture and religion against religion. Reconciliation between blacks and whites, Catholics and Protestants (in Northern Ireland), Israelis and Palestinians, Christians and Muslims may seem impossible. The Afghan and Iraqi wars leave terrible vacuums and bitterness.

It is particularly sad to see world leaders so caught up with politics they cannot see deeper social issues. Peace cannot come without justice, and true justice demands hearing stories that need to be set right. In the midst of world turmoil, it can be hard to remember that solutions have been found for seemingly impossible situations. Unknown heroes have shared the tension of hatreds that defied reconciliation. Let us take the time to hear stories of seemingly impossible forgiveness and reconciliation between groups.

Several years ago, a friend of mine traveled with a Ugandan bishop over dangerous roads to a village that had been ravaged by a rebel group. Teenaged rebel soldiers were about to rob and shoot them at one impromptu checkpoint. Calmly the bishop got out of their vehicle, shook the rebels' hands, gave them copies of the New Testament, and prayed for them. The young soldiers were very impressed and waved them on. When the bishop arrived at the village, it was less than a week after most of the men and boys had been killed; the women and girls raped. It seemed to my friend, they were driving into a completely bitter and hopeless situation.

Instead, the remaining villagers met their bishop with great rejoicing. Days after the decimation, they all prayed the Lord's Prayer in the context of the Eucharist. They experienced the kingdom and realized they were God's future people now. How they could pray "forgive us our sins as we forgive those who have sinned against us" goes beyond my comprehension. Certainly their loss and pain would endure a lifetime. But they did forgive and began to experience God's peace and hope. The Bishop had come, he had heard and responded in the name of the Lord.

Rwandan Reconciliation

Is there a method the Spirit of healing can use in seemingly impossible situations? The bitterness left by the massacre of almost a million Tutsi in one horrendous month in Rwanda continues to this day. But some healing has occurred from which we have much to learn. Welsh psychiatrist Rhiannon Lloyd is linked with the Reconciliation Networks of Our World. At the request of local Christian leaders in Rwanda, he has conducted several seminars on healing, forgiveness, and reconciliation. Principles followed in these seminars include:[1]

1. Recognizing the church as God's agent of healing and reconciliation. God is the God of hope (Rom 15:13), and he places his hope in his people (Eph 3:10). His strategy is to use the church (Col 1:27).

2. Finding the right sequence for the seminar. Listening must precede teaching; experiencing some healing and forgiveness must come before theory.

3. Overcoming cultural barriers in expressing emotion. Lloyd found that Liberians express their emotion easily, but in Rwandan culture there is little expression of emotion and no word for emotion in the language. Rwandans have a saying that a man's tears ought to flow into his stomach and not down his cheeks. They also believe that talking about traumatic experiences traumatizes people even more. Lloyd would sensitively begin to talk about Jesus as a transcultural model of perfect humanity who expressed emotion and from whom all cultures can learn.

4. Finding God in the midst of suffering. Here is Lloyd's description.

> I usually began my seminars by asking the questions that were agitating in most people's hearts. "Where was God in April '94? Did He send these troubles? Has God abandoned us?" I wanted to create a safe place where participants could own their doubts and voice their inner questions without fear of being

---

[1] The following is taken and adapted from the Boston Theological Institute newsletter, 8 November 2000.

condemned. Story telling is a well-received form of teaching in Rwanda. . . .

It is amazing how what was learned in the heart of Africa is similar to lessons learned among urban youth over many long years! We do need a safe place for the telling of stories leading to the great story.

5. Discovering Jesus as the Painbearer. We can risk coming to God when we are assured of God's intentions and feelings toward us. Jesus is not only our Sinbearer, Lloyd teaches; Jesus is also our Painbearer. To make the transfer of pain to Jesus more real, Lloyd used the symbolism of nailing their terrible stories to a large wooden cross carried around the country. Finally the cross was taken outside and the paper burned. People finally felt their pain to be left at the cross. Healing can occur dramatically, or gradually in personal counseling, as well as in group experiences.

6. The need to hear and be heard. Despite resistance, people from different ethnic groups and different denominations were put into small groups. Dividing walls were gradually demolished. The practice of listening to one's enemies enabled people to return to difficult situations still needing reconciliation.

7. Understanding real forgiveness. Many people would say, "I've forgiven—it's all past" as a means of avoiding the pain. Others had problems with a theology of forgiveness that seemed to diminish the offense or condone the wrong. Lloyd felt it important to stress the atoning sacrifice of the Lamb of God. Such teaching underlay the experience of nailing stories to the cross. "It was only on the third day, after bringing their pain to the cross, that we would begin to teach on forgiveness, only to discover that a miracle had already taken place in the hearts of many the previous afternoon."

8. Discovering Jesus as Redeemer. Another key was to discover Jesus as Redeemer, not only of our sins, but of all our lives' tragedies. He *can* "turn our trials into gold" as stated in a Keith Green song. John 1:5 tells us that "the light shines in the darkness but the darkness could not comprehend it." A better translation reads, "the darkness could not overpower it." And it never will! Jesus will always have the last word!

9. Exploring God's way of dealing with ethnic conflict. This is how Lloyd describes the process:

> We spent quite a lot of time looking at the roots of ethnic conflict, and where we learn our beliefs and prejudices. Because our ethnicity gives us a significant part of our identity, ethnic conflict is an attack on the core of our being. Here, I used my own testimony of growing up feeling like a second-class citizen because I was Welsh. We focused on two ways of coming to a place of reconciliation.
>
> First, we needed to discover our identity as citizens of God's community as with God's call to Abraham to leave his natural ethnic background. Second, I shared with them how God had disarmed my heart of resentment and prejudice against the English through the repentance of some English Christians on behalf of their forefathers.
>
> I have found that identificational repentance is a very powerful key to healing woundedness (i.e., taking on the priestly role of repenting on behalf of our nation, people-group, forefathers, men, women, fathers, mothers, doctors, etc., etc.) Each time I taught on this, God said to me, "You start!" And time after time, God gave me the gift of repentance as a white European in Africa.
>
> Though it was completely uncultural for them, both Hutu and Tutsi began to stand in the gap, asking forgiveness on behalf of their people group as well as confessing their own sinful attitudes. In seminar after seminar we saw them weeping in each other's arms as God did a deep reconciling work amongst us. God anointed a song by David Ruis, "We will break dividing walls," which someone translated into Kinyarwanda, as a further means of touching hearts deeply. They love singing, so music was often a powerful communicator.

Stories had been told, healing rituals had been found, reconciliation was possible. The application of these healing principles is universal. We can pray for godly facilitators of such sessions in the midst of all kind of violence and degradation. "Blessed are the peacemakers."

In my classes on racism, we find ourselves going through a similar healing process. Students, representing a cross-section of our society, approach the class with varying feelings of tiredness (it's such an old and nagging issue), frustration, anxiety, or fear. Among white students there is often traces of ignorance and denial. Some black students admit to lingering bitterness against whites in general. Slowly we begin to hear one another's stories; without those stories we would get nowhere. We face the negative impact of this psychological, social, and spiritual issue on all of us. The pathology has touched perpetrators, victims, and bystanders. Pain, sadness, and anger are expressed. Slowly, we begin to understand at deeper levels. Finally, there is the will for reconciliation; for a few it may be rather superficial; others will say it is life changing. It begins to give one hope for the world.

> 🏃 Your brother, sister, son or daughter was serving with the Peace Corp overseas when you received the terrible news that he or she has been shot by a wild gang of teenagers. What is your reaction, and what do you plan to do?
>
> Amy Biehl was valedictorian of her high school class in Santa Fe, New Mexico and an honor student at Stanford University. As a Fulbright Scholar, she was conducting research on women in the New South Africa in a township near Cape Town. One day a wild mob of youth stoned and stabbed Amy to death. The loss was a terrible blow to her parents and family.
>
> Instead of bitterness Linda and Peter Biehl tried to make sense of the tragedy. They set up a positive program against the poverty of that area. Today two of the murderers, Mr. Nofomela and Mr. Peni drive trucks for the Amy Biehl Foundation Trust delivering bread to the hungry.

Peacemaking in a Violent World

The twentieth century was a century of war. To whatever extent war is necessary, this book has also recognized society's willingness to celebrate and enjoy violence. It reminds us of Paul's words in his letter to the Romans as he talks about the guilt of humankind in the first chapter: Knowing God's attitude toward acts of "envy, murder, strife, deceit . . . they not only do them but even applaud others who practice them." Violence and sexual lust are casually used as hooks in much of our advertising and entertainment. The news desensitizes us to the violence of war and terrorism. Especially unfortunate is the fact that religions have contributed to a militant spirit and justification of religious wars.

In a violent world, there are also counter forces committed to peacemaking. Previous mention has been made of the eminent theologian Hans Küng who has written extensively and organized toward world peace. We need a reminder of his teaching and organization for world peace.

> No survival without a world ethic. No world peace without peace between religions. No peace between religions without dialogue between the religions. That is what this book [and his work] is about.[2]

It is my opinion that the world's religions must talk about four urgent challenges that concern youth and those who work with young people:

- Resist the tendency of the media to lower the moral standards of young people.

- Take responsible action regarding our stewardship of the environment. (Biblical creation accounts make us caretakers of this world, and young people sense that responsibility that greedy systems may ignore.)

- Provide justice for the disadvantaged peoples of the world.

---

[2] Hans Küng, *Global Responsibility: In Search of a New World Ethic* (London: SCM, 1990), xv.

- Work toward peace rather than war—establish a peace founded on justice.

I do not fool myself that such an enterprise will be fully realized before the coming Christ our King. But I am committed to praying and working on "thy kingdom come, thy will be done on earth."

Other initiatives to overcome violence and bring about peace are taking place.

> [In 1999] the Eighth Assembly of the World Council of Churches gathered together under an African cross, in Harare, Zimbabwe . . . [establishing] a Decade to Overcome Violence (DOV). The Assembly stated that the WCC must "work strategically with the churches on these issues of nonviolence and reconciliation to create a culture of nonviolence, linking and interacting with other international partners and organizations, and examining and developing appropriate approaches to conflict transformation and just peace-making in the new globalized context. . . . growing together with the world communion of people who are building cultures of nonviolence and peace.
>
> "Violence" is not only physical. "Violence" is also emotional, intellectual, structural.[3]

The document specifically explains itself as seeking response and prevention of various forms of violence:

- Overcoming violence between nations

- Overcoming violence within nations

- Overcoming violence in local communities

- Overcoming violence within home and family

- Overcoming violence in the church

- Overcoming sexual violence

- Overcoming socioeconomic violence

---

[3] "A Basic Framework for the Decade to Overcome Violence: Working Document adopted by the Central Committee of the World Council of Churches, 26 August–3 September 1999." Online: Search on Google for the article title up to the colon.

- Overcoming violence among youth (and five other categories).[4]

Finally, there is another organization of conservative and moderate theologians who are responsible for *Just Peacemaking*,[5] previously mentioned. The specific ways of achieving peace suggested by these writers, hardly notes the work of Küng and others. But their work should be noticed, lauded and applied to foreign policy. Hopefully, extremes of hawkish diplomacy can be softened by these principles.

Just Peacemaking seeks to avoid the stalemate between pacifism and just war theory. It sees our times (*kairos* or divine time) as critical for such an endeavor. The book is scholarly and practical. Its first four chapters suggest peacemaking initiatives: support nonviolent direct action, take independent initiatives to reduce threat, use cooperative conflict resolution, and acknowledge responsibility for conflict and injustice. The second section examines justice issues always basic to real peace: advance democracy and human rights; foster just and sustainable economic development.

Part three of the book has to do with important concepts and principles of love and community: work with emerging cooperative forces, strengthen the United Nations and international efforts for cooperation and human rights, reduce offensive weapons and weapons trade, and encourage grassroots peacemaking groups and voluntary associations.

This "vision is grounded in three theological convictions" (underlying the three parts of the book):

Initiatives: A biblically informed concept of discipleship and peacemaking initiatives grounded in the life, teachings, death, and resurrection of Jesus Christ.

Justice: A church committed to seek the peace of the city where its people dwell (Jer 29:7); to further God's reign, not only by withdrawal or quietism or by uncritical support of or reliance on the government, but by engaging the issues of

---

[4] Ibid.
[5] Glen Stassen, ed., *Just Peacemaking: Ten Practices for Abolishing War* (Cleveland, Ohio: Pilgrim Press, 1998).

peace; and justice—especially justice—actively within the brokenness of the world.

Love and community: The church community as the eschatological sign of God's love and reign in the world, embodied in a concrete gathering of persons who seek to discern together what just peacemaking means and to model peacemaking practices in our corporate and individual lives.[6]

These three examples of contemporary peacemaking efforts are critically important in a world of armed might. Hopefully the U.S. might add to its fine military academies an outstanding peace academy to study and apply the principles above. Global diplomacy should proceed on several tracks.

Peace and Justice from a Worshiping Community

Peacekeeping, social change, and all that's been discussed in this book needs to be offered up at the altar of our worship. Only there can our limited efforts and weaknesses find eternal strength.

Throughout this book Jesus Christ is seen as the "authoritative model for our ethical practice."[7] We have assumed that those outside such faith can accept the basic human social values that flow out of our doctrines of creation and justice; our hope is that they can even commit to the means and ends suggested here. As we work with those of other faiths and ideologies, it is important to keep ourselves strong in our identities, values, and center. It is easy to become overwhelmed by the needs of this world. Only in community can we find necessary strength, and the grace of Christian community is found especially in its worship.

When we gather together in public worship,

- we hear God's Word,

- we profess our common and historic faith,

- we confess our sins and the sins of the world,

---

[6] Ibid., 6.
[7] Ibid.

- and, we offer up our intentions for healing and reconciliation, justice and peace.

Worship joins together saints suffering, saints struggling, and saints rewarded in eternal rest. It directs and prepares us for service in the world. Worship surveys God's mighty works of creation, judgment, and redemption. In worship we re-enact the life, death, and resurrection of Jesus Christ looking forward to the hope of His coming again, to final justice and peace. Such worship makes Christians observant of suffering—yet positive about outcomes. Such worship guarantees that our efforts to realize God's kingdom will not fail.

The evangelist John seems to use the sixth chapter of his Gospel as a Eucharistic reflection[8] (it is the only Gospel not to repeat the institution of the Lord's Body and Blood). Jesus says to us, as he did to his disciples in this story, "Feed the world." And like them, we hesitate, and stutter that it is impossible, for so many reasons. But as strong leaders do, Christ forcefully looks at us and says, "Feed them." We try to explain, but His look remains the same. Finally, we deal with the only available resource—so pathetic in terms of the need. Whatever trifling ability or gift we have Christ *takes* and *when* He has *given thanks,* He *breaks* the bread and *distributes* to the whole crowd. These four motions of Holy Communion were well known throughout history. John, when he wrote this story, had been "breaking bread" like that for 60 years, his first readers all their lives. But the main point here is our need to present our seemingly pathetic gifts and offerings at the altar continually. Any good intentions from reading this book, any prayers or commitments, need to be brought to God. In this celebration at the Lord's table,

---

[8] See Oscar Cullmann, *Early Christian Worship* (London: SCM Press, 1953) 93–102. ". . . it must at all events be presupposed that the evangelist saw, as he was writing down this story, a reference in this miracle to the Eucharist, that he had the Eucharist in mind therefore without actually saying so." (p. 94) Bette Midler's "From a Distance" and Joan Osborne's "One of Us" have gotten young people discussing the importance of God's transcendence and immanence.

the community of faith finds strength and hope to carry on, they become God's future people now!

Whatever your efforts to realize God's kingdom, no matter how discouraged you may be as to results, they become significant and somehow effective as they are offered up at the Table of our Lord. Whatever you have gotten from this book must get to the altar where, in worship, you will find renewed faith, strength, courage.

A Theology of Healing in the Lord's Prayer

With all that has been pondered and suggested here, prayer must be central. The simplicity of prayer can bring relief to the complexity of social problems. The difficult issues of this book have often driven me back to the Lord's Prayer, and I remember many dark and painful situations when a group of us have prayed these words.

Our Father brings Almighty God down to a fatherless generation providing parental comfort and support in the direst times.

In heaven assures us that this imminent God is above all. Feeling mired in human pain and violence or lost in swirling controversies, we seek the certainty and relief that is above all the losses and changes of life.

Your Kingdom come is the prayer and hope of all the faithful. It should be our prayer over the evening news. As God's kingdom people, God's future people now, we find strength to carry on as perpetual revolutionaries.

On earth as it is in heaven is our motto. God's kingdom cannot wait. It *will* come, but also it is breaking in on us right *now.* This is our daily prayer: we work with God to make it so.

Give us today our daily bread. Christianity is the most materialistic of all religions, it has often been said. The Incarnation brought God into our material world. God wants to fulfill the physical needs of all people. The heavenly food of our communion, without which there is no life, begins with earthly bread. So, Lord, feed us all today.

And forgive us our sins. "Lord, have mercy!" We are sorry. For all that's going on, for all that's in this book, Good God, we are sorry. This is the starting point for all healing and reconciliation.

As we forgive those who have hurt us. The hurting triangle (having been hurt and feeling hurt, I hurt others, which hurts God) must give way to the forgiving triangle (accepting God's forgiveness, I begin to forgive myself so I can really forgive others—and receive forgiveness from others). Only then can we enter the dynamic love triangle (being loved by God, I can love myself and learn to love others as I love myself). What seems impossible from a human perspective, is possible with God.

And lead us not into temptation. It is dangerous to think we have passed beyond temptation. No matter how much we've learned, we are still stupidly seduced by pleasure, possessions, or power. We also ask to be delivered from earth's great trials and persecutions: "Lord, protect us."

But deliver us from evil. Beyond all psychological maladies and social ills, great spiritual warfare surrounds us. From all of these, from principalities and powers and the Accuser himself, "Good Lord, deliver us."

And finally, trusting the sovereignty of God and realizing the initiative of divine grace, we praise God in the added doxology: *For yours is the kingdom, and the power, and the glory forever. Amen.*

Questions for Reflection and Discussion

1. Do you end this book feeling hopeless, despairing, numb, discouraged, and apathetic—or with real determination to make a difference?

2. Has this chapter convinced you that our challenge against violence and oppression is worldwide— and that in prayer and attitude, as well as perhaps symbolic actions, we can accomplish something?

Questions, cont'd.

3. Do you have a sense that in the midst of powerful forces and complicated factors, there are resources for your future instruction?

4. Do you think that as you soak up the principles of this book and the important resources to which it has pointed, you can begin to intervene helpfully in your corner of life and the world?

5. What is the one thing in this last chapter that helped or encouraged you most?

6. What do you think you will take away from this book as a whole?

7. How do you think the principles in this book will come back to you in the future?

Book Resources

Kim Bobo, Jackie Kenoall, Steve Max, Kimberly Bobo. *Organizing for Social Change: Manual for Activists.* 3d ed. Santa Ana, Calif.: Seven Locks Press, 2001. 🐧 Written from a progressive, liberal standpoint particularly for the labor union movement, this book is considered a classic for social activists. Its four parts include Direct Action Organizing, Organizing Skills, Support for Organization, and Selected Resources.

Gary Haugen. *Good News About Injustice: A Witness of Courage in a Hurting World,* Downers Grove, Ill.: InterVarsity Press, 1999. 🐧 A Wheaton College professor of Business and Economics looks at injustice in the world and challenges response in terms of holistic Christian mission and development work. Missing some complexities of sanctions and indebtedness, he does provide a challenging case for world reform through transformed Christian change agents.

David Hutchens. *Shadows of the Neanderthal: Illuminating the Beliefs that Limit Our Organizations,* Waltham, Mass.:

Pegasus Communications, 1999. ⚷ A simple, humorous parable points to mental models we need but which at the same time can divide us. Exposition following the story shows our need for flexibility and openness to systems thinking. This is an important discussion starter on reconciliation and organizational change.

Lyle Schaller. *Interventionist* and *Discontinuity and Hope.* Nashville, Tenn.: Abingdon Press, 1997, 1999. ⚷ Schaller analyzes and gives advice concerning difficult change in the church. His older and out-of-print books (*The Change Agent* and *Strategies for Change*) deal with bringing about social change generally.

John Stott. *The Contemporary Christian: Applying God's Word to Today's World.* Downers Grove, Ill.: InterVarsity Press, 1992. ⚷ This is an Evangelical perspective on holistic mission of the Church in today's world. See especially ch. 20, "Holistic Mission," and the Conclusion. Besides, there is much here on how one actually lives out discipleship in a relevant way.

John Stott. *Issues Facing Christians Today: New Perspectives on Social and Moral Dilemmas.* London: Marshall Pickering, 1984. ⚷ Besides general social issues such as industrial relations, racism, sexism poverty and wealth, Stott discusses war and the nuclear threat, the environment, North-South economic inequality, and human rights.

Desmond Mpilo Tutu. *No Future Without Forgiveness.* New York: Doubleday, 2000. ⚷ Out of his experience as Chair of the South African Truth and Reconciliation Commission, the Archbishop writes with humor and profundity. Emerging from apartheid, some South Africans sought revenge; many wished the past to be forgotten. Tutu speaks for a "third way" through the telling of stories with perpetrators of atrocities and their victims face to face.

Workbooks and Curriculum

Kathy Bickmore, Prill Goldthwait, and John Looney. *Alternatives to Violence: A Manual for Teaching Peacemaking to*

Youth and Adults. Akron, Ohio: Peace Grows, 1984. 🌂
This is a resource manual and introductory course in creative conflict resolution. It presents an interactive and ex-
periential learning method in dealing with violence from
personal lives to international levels.

Jim Handcock and the International Justice Mission. *The
Justice Mission Curriculum.* Grand Rapids, Mich.: Youth
Specialties, 2002. This is a video-enhanced curriculum re-
flecting on the heart of God for the oppressed of the world.

Salim J. Munayer, ed. *Ministry of Reconciliation: In the Foot-
steps of our Father Abraham.* Jerusalem: Yanetz Ltd., 1993.
🌂 This curriculum uses the reconciliation of Jacob and
Esau as a model for a vision of reconciling Arabs and Jews,
working first with teenagers in wilderness programs (following the travels of Abraham) that moves toward telling
their stories and finding reconciliation.

Internet Resources

*See resources listed at the end of other chapters such as the
one on Violence.*

www.cpjustice.org 🌂 This is an important site of a Christian
independent civic and policy research organization. Here
you will find moderate and balanced (though you may
not always agree with them) evaluations of current
issues. The Center for Public Justice is dedicated to serve
God, advance justice, and transform public life.

www.doj.gov.za/trc/index.html 🌂 The South African Truth
and Reconciliation Commission is well known for its
commitment to confront the past crimes of apartheid. It
continues to confront injustice and crimes against
human rights in order to promote national unity and
reconciliation. It offers hope and practical methods to
other societies.

www.freethechildren.org 🌂 Free The Children is a unique
international youth organization started by a kid for kids.
It has had great success in its campaigns against child

labor, child poverty, wars that injure kids, and more. See
its Youth Ambassadors for Peace.

www.ifor.org 🏃 The International Fellowship of Reconciliation is an non-violent, anti-war organization (started by a
Quaker and a German Lutheran) welcoming those who
would work for peace through protests and positive development projects. Its U.S. website is (www.forusa.org).

www.oriononline.org 🏃 Orion OnLine deals with issues of
the environment, technological and industrial injustice,
and global peace. See especially the articles by Wendell
Berry.

A Personal Conclusion

Whether you are reading this in the Northern or Southern Hemisphere, on an island or in a teeming city, in a rural or suburban setting, some young person near you needs to tell her story. She needs to be affirmed and helped to ask the deep questions of life, which can ultimately lead to truth and to the Way.

You may be a student overloaded with work, a teacher, chaplain, or social worker in a discouraging situation. You could be working across cultural, class, or ethnic lines. It is so hard when you try, year after year, to make a difference and feel that little or nothing is accomplished. Young people can tell their stories—consider their past and future dream—only in their world. We often fail when we try to drag them into our world, teach them our values, and share our faith in our cultural way. It is we who must make a radical jump across class or culture to enter another world. There we can share stories in a new way. Those we would help are able to set realistic goals only from their perspective.

I worry that the emphasis of this book on problems, the intensity of the stories, and the enormity of the challenges may have exhausted or discouraged you. Remember that most young people are doing well, and some are actually way ahead of many adults. But because others are in imminent danger of seriously hurting themselves or others, this book is needed.

Besides those in *critical* trouble, other young people around you are feeling stress and pain. They tell us so in conversations, in surveys, and on the Internet. May your passion and joy in life encourage the telling of stories, the healing of lives, and promotion of growth.

Rays of Hope

One weekend I watched a group of kids at a birthday celebration. Two of them had lost their mother three years before, but they have a wonderful father and supportive relatives. The father's new girlfriend has two children, their father (her husband) has drifted off. Another boy whose life was torn apart by a difficult divorce spends a great deal of time with this emerging, blended family.

My five-year-old grandson joined the group that day, making a group of kids from age fourteen (the birthday boy) to a four-year-old girl (the rest were all boys). I was pleased and amazed by the way they played with each other. The older ones looked out for the younger ones, taking punches and kicks from them, cautioning them when needed. Sometimes, I thought, the younger ones got a little annoying, but an amazing patience prevailed.

During breakfast we saw volunteer firemen at work across the parking lot. Joined by two nine-year-olds, I walked across the lot, and as we walked, one of the boys said to his friend of me, "It's nice to have a grown-up along." Then they stood there, listening to the older men as if they were part of the gang. Simple scenes, but hopeful ones. So many young people around the world are looking for a "grown-up" like you to go alongside them.

David Pelzer has written about his mother, Catherine Roerva. To outsiders she seemed to be a devoted Cub Scout denmother and a fine mother to her children. But inside the family things were different. To the dismay of her weak and alcoholic husband, she despised David more and more and gradually made him the family scapegoat.[1]

Under clothed and malnourished, he was forced to sleep on a cot in the garage. In crazy, alcoholic fits she beat and stabbed him, played manipulative games with him, smashed his face into mirrors, burned his hand over a gas stove, and forced him to eat feces from a sibling's diaper.

---

[1] David J. Pelzer, *A Child Called 'It': One Child's Courage to Survive* (Deerfield Beach, Fla.: Health Communications, 1995).

Finally, delivered from this domestic hell, David bounced around the foster care and juvenile facilities. A few adult heroes helped him survive.[2]

Although many people had given up on him as a child who would have to be institutionalized the rest of his life, David somehow got past acting out behaviors, finally achieving academic success. Three U.S. presidents have honored Pelzer for his inspirational speeches and writings about resiliency, recovery, and responsibility. Pelzer is the only American ever to have received The Outstanding Young Persons of the World award. You may have seen him carrying the Centennial Olympic Torch. At the end of a book like this, he gives us hope.

Suffering with Christ for Troubled Youth

I am wrapping up this difficult book during Holy Week. All religions teach compassion at some level or other; higher religions teach compassion for those outside their faith or ethnic community. But Jesus goes further. Find the most despicable person, he says, and love him. Consider the person who has hurt you or yours the worst and forgive him. In fact, Jesus does more. If someone cannot be loved or forgiven, die for him.

The main drama in Gethsemane is Christ's trembling before the full cost of compassionate forgiveness. He was about to take on the evil of the world's sins. The secondary drama involves Christ's trying to teach his disciples to pray for compassion and compassionate forgiveness. They were, after all, the ones who had declared themselves ready to drink the cup before which Christ now struggled (Matt 20:22; Mark 10:38; Matt 26:39). At the critical hour Jesus felt the failure of his primary human support system.

The resurrection of Jesus Christ and the gift of the Holy Spirit at Pentecost transformed those faltering disciples into

---

[2] David Pelzer, *The Lost Boy: A Foster Child's Search for the Love of a Family* (Deerfield Beach, Fla.: Health Communications, 1997).

powerful apostles. Saul of Tarsus joined them later. Converted, he may have come closest to what Christ had in mind for the disciples in Gethsemane—and for us today. This is what Paul prayed and lived: "I want to know Christ and the power of his resurrection and the sharing of his sufferings by becoming like him in his death" (Phil 3:10 NRSV). Regarding the cup of compassion—where judgment and mercy meet— Paul goes still further, suggesting some sort of secondary partnership with our Lord in his atoning work: "I am now rejoicing in my sufferings for your sake, and in my flesh I am completing what is lacking in Christ's afflictions for the sake of his body, that is, the church" (Col 1:24 NRSV).

Although we may not understand Paul's full meaning, we sense that we, with Paul, are to bring all the suffering of the world into the redeeming presence of Christ. To do so, we need great empathy and spiritual resolve.

Practical Suggestions

The examples of Christ and Paul are not meant to give us a messiah complex. We cannot save the world, and we ought not to bleed ourselves dry of compassion. Emotionally we may want to heal all sufferers, but we must be realistic about the strength and gifts God gives us and perform, each day, our small part of God's redemptive endeavor. It is essential to keep our boundaries clear. We have human and professional limits, and these ought not to be violated.[3]

We are meant to enjoy life. Suffering and the valley of shadows point, not to fear and despondency, but to a future and a hope (Ps 23; Jer 29:11). If we cannot have fun, if we are unable to care for ourselves tenderly at the end of a day and each week, we are approaching burn-out. Take care of yourself.

---

[3] Again, Jesus is our example. Notice how he attended one person and turned his back on all others that day in Jerusalem's "hopeless ward." (John 5:2-13). We also must do "our thing" and be able to leave it at that trusting God's mercy.

Response to This Study

I trust, by God's grace, that you have found helpful illustrations, principles, and resources in this book. I hope this information is so practical you can take it into schoolyard trouble among a bully, victim, and bystanders. To be sure, this is not a manual—you have not found "just add water and stir" instructions. But we have faced horrendous wartime atrocities, insidious childhood abuse, random and remorseless teenage killings, rape and sexual degradation, and more. Although easy explanations or cures have not been found, we have struggled to understand and respond more compassionately and effectively.

Effective response needs great care and respect. Our hope is based on God's creative intent, the image of God in all, and the resilience of the human spirit. Our attitude is one of humility before profound mysteries. We strive to understand our identity, strengths, and weaknesses. Understanding proper boundaries, we learn to practice tough love. Above all, we follow the model of our Lord Jesus Christ and depend upon divine grace.

We long for a return of the family dinner hour—stemming from shared meals and stories extended families enjoyed throughout history. Sometimes we create such dinners for youth. We long for families who listen and support. We want to provide a safe place for those who are at risk, a place where they can hear others telling their stories until they get the courage to tell their story, receive affirmation, and finally hear the great story of God's love.

When stories are told, people find the attention, sense of belonging, clarification of identity, love, and power to achieve that they need. These stories may best be told in family circles, but they enrich all other human groups that care to listen. Our response to stories gives necessary significance to the tellers.

Nothing in this book should lead to conclusions of hopelessness. The pages of this book include stories of great individual exploits and positive accomplishments of programs dedicated to healing and empowerment.

As you listen to the cries, all kinds of youthful stories, may God give you the compassion to care and wisdom to respond. And may you be supported in a praying community of faith.

> Almighty God, whose most dear Son went not up to joy but first he suffered pain, and entered not into glory before he was crucified: Mercifully grant that we, walking in the way of the cross, may find it none other than the way of life and peace, through Jesus Christ your Son our Lord. Amen.[4]

---

[4] *The Book of Common Prayer* (New York: The Church Hymnal Society, 1979), 9.